French Leave

French Leave

Michael de Larrabeiti

ROBERT HALE · LONDON

ISBN 0 7090 7172 8

Robert Hale Limited
Clerkenwell House
Clerkenwell Green
London EC1R 0HT

A catalogue record for this book is available from the British Library

2 4 6 8 10 9 7 5 3 1

Typeset by
Derek Doyle and Associates, Liverpool.
Printed in Great Britain by
St Edmundsbury Press Limited, Bury St Edmunds, and
bound by Woolnough Bookbinding Limited, Irthlingborough

For Susan

'. . . for I love France so well that I will not part with a village of it; I will have it all mine . . .'

Henry V (Act V, scene II)

Contents

Prologue

I was twenty-two, hitch-hiking at night across central France, lost in the dark, close to despair and wet, hungry and exhausted. I was rescued at last by a farmer who overtook me on his bike; '*Je peux pas te laisser là comme ça*...' he'd said and taken me into his house, where he'd fed me a big bowl of soup and given me a truckle bed to sleep on.

In the dark before dawn I was woken by a grunting and squealing from the other end of the shed that was my shelter for the night – the farm sow was giving birth to a dozen piglets. The farmer and his wife came into the place, lit the lamps and made sure the sow did not roll onto her offspring.

'She's called Brigitte,' the farmer explained, 'after Bardot, and she always gives birth in the small hours . . . that's why I put you in here.' And he and his wife laughed and there was no more sleeping that night – only celebration and wine and a very early breakfast.

For me happenings of this special kind seemed only to occur in France, and over the years I have had scores of such moments, and so the English prejudices – and the jealousies – that had been handed down to me softened and gradually disappeared, leaving in their place an affection that gradually turned to love. And such moments too: the first taste of Rabelais' wine in Chinon; the heart-stopping vision of the Unicorn tapestries in the Musée de Cluny; raising the blind in my couchette and seeing Provence for the first time, all dreamlike and still under the pale light of an early morning.

11

Most of us have our own private French landscape. For some it will be Brittany or the Auvergne; for others it will be the mud or the dust of the grape harvest they did as a student. My own favourite road is the one that leaves Cogolin in the Var and heads directly north for the French Alps, 150 miles away. I walked it once with some shepherds, who took me under their wing with that strange mixture of detached irony and amusement which often characterizes the French way of dealing with the English, those they like at any rate.

The shepherds gave me the worst job, of course – leading the mule-cart and the provisions it carried, stumbling along behind the flock in a cloud of dust and horse-fly. Another lesson to learn.

But then, after the pain, the reward: those endless meals, under the deep shade of plane trees, overlooking green and hazy valleys full of vine and peach orchards. Meals where wisdom became simple and life was easy to cherish.

What follows is the history of my romance with the 'Divine Hexagon', how it began and never ended; and these chapters also concern those individuals who showed me their country and made sure that I fell in love with it for ever. This book is for them.

1

1949

Paris and the Green Chartreuse.

I cycled to Paris that first time. It was August, the summer holidays, and I was just fifteen, travelling on my own. The reason was simple: I disliked my French teacher and he was leading the school trip that summer, but there was another reason – cheap as the school trip was I couldn't afford it. My mother was a waitress earning £4 a week, and my father was an absentee. It would be less expensive if I cycled. I could stay in youth hostels.

I don't know how I talked my mother into letting me go without an accompanying adult. It was only four years after the war and there were still burnt-out tanks in the hedgerows. 'You'll be murdered,' said the kids in the street, 'they're all foreign over there.' Stabbed to death was what I'd be. I was frightened, very frightened. I'd never been further than Southend before, on a charabanc outing.

It took me all day to cycle the 60 miles from London to Newhaven but I got there in time for the night boat. My blood bubbled with the excitement of such an adventure. Up late on my own, the dark all around me, the smell of the sea, and the shouts of the dockers and the clanking of the cranes.

I had reserved a bunk but I couldn't sleep and stayed on deck to watch the coast of England disappear. I was on deck again as the ferry pulled into Dieppe, at 3.30 in the morning. The air smelt like buttered kippers, and the lamplight shone into a dark asphalt. In those days Dieppe was what a Channel port ought to be: a place where the sea went right into the town and where ferries and fishing boats tied up at the bottom of the High Street. Even now, fifty years later, it is romantic and picturesque, full of life. Dieppe, my first landfall in France, was the beginning of manhood – the love affair.

And, I could hardly believe it, in the middle of the night there were cafés open, the lights spilling out of their windows to gleam on the railway lines that ran down the middle of the street. And one by one the cars from England were lifted out of the ship's hold in a huge net, a net that was also used, so they said, to swing unconscious English drunks back on to the boat when their pockets were empty.

There was one other passenger on deck with me, and unlike England, no policeman guarded the gangway that led down into France. The man watched while his car was unloaded and then he and I went ashore, without permission, without passports. We went into the nearest café, the Brighton it was called, and the man ordered a coffee for himself and a lemonade for me. Lemonade at four in the morning – sin of a high order.

A fight broke out between two dockers as we sat there. I don't know what caused it. Perhaps they were disputing the favours of the blowsy woman who sat behind the till, *bien faisandée* she was – ripe as a hung pheasant, nursing her soft bosoms in folded arms where they rested on the zinc counter. The two men were drinking at the bar; their voices flared suddenly, and one of them threw a punch. There was a yell, a blow in the face, a table scraped across the floor. Both men struck out.

The woman hardly raised an eyebrow. The loser stormed out of the bar and disappeared onto the quayside, but not for long. In a second he reappeared, shouted something I couldn't understand, picked up one of the terrace chairs and slung it through the plate glass window, smashing it to smithereens. I was delighted. I had only been in France a minute or two. 'Ah,' said the 15-year-old me, 'this is life.'

As soon as my bike was ashore I cycled, lonely as hell, up that great hill that leads out of Dieppe: the Paris road. I went via Rouen, where I stayed a night in the youth hostel, and then on to Pontoise so that I could catch a train to the Gare du Nord, avoiding in that way the miles and miles of suburbs. At the terminus an English-speaking French couple, appalled that I was travelling on my own – although fifteen I looked about twelve – took me under their wing and installed me in a cheap hotel in the rue de St Quentin, and there I dwelt for three nights in a tiny attic under the roof, like a refugee.

Since that first visit I have been back to Paris on hundreds of occasions. I have lived there, studied there and worked there. I have had quarrels there, got drunk there and, of course, fallen in and out of love there. No matter, every time I walk through the portals of the Gare du Nord a frisson of dread and expectation runs through me, and for a second or two I am once again that scared teenager pushing his bike across the streams of traffic, looking right instead of left, and wishing to high heaven that he'd stayed at home and not been such a show-off.

I was so terrified during those three days that I ventured no more than a stone's throw from the hotel. I didn't see the Eiffel Tower or the Arc de Triomphe – something I did not admit to the kids in the street when I got home – I didn't even see the River Seine, and my first run-in with a bidet was a cloacinal disaster. I did, however, manage to order one meal – I knew what *une omelette au jambon* was. For the rest of it I lived off what I could point to in shop windows – baguettes, bars of chocolate and ice-creams.

Yet there was one thing I was determined to have, and no mountain of embarrassment was going to come between me and it. And 'it' was a huge, cool, emerald drink that sparkled like dreams and looked as fresh and as big as an iceberg. Every child in Paris seemed to be drinking one and envy rose within me.

I know now that the mixture was *un diabolo menthe* – peppermint cordial and lemonade clinking in a frosty glass – but how was I to order it? On the eve of my departure I sat on a café terrace and thumbed through the wine list until I came to the word *verte*. That must be it – green – *chartreuse verte*.

The waiter was one of those old men who had seen everything, slept with all the women and read all the books. '*Verte*,' I said, pointing, '*chartreuse verte . . .*'

The waiter raised an eyebrow that encompassed my beardless face, my khaki shorts and half the northern hemisphere.

He plodded away on his sore feet and, from the corner of a self-conscious eye, I saw him stop at the till and speak to Madame. Her face turned slowly towards me, heavy and world-weary, like a gun turret on a dreadnought. Then, without any change in expression, she shrugged. It was my first Gallic shrug and I have never forgotten it. It spoke volumes, it spoke the whole of the Bibliothèque Nationale: 'If that is what he wants, give it to him. Experience is a ruby . . . and should he ask for the *bordel*, make sure he gets there.'

The chartreuse was presented. It glinted, pale green and evil in the decadent bulge of a brandy glass. It was nothing like the vulgar tumbler of effervescence I had expected. The entire world held its breath, everyone was watching and waiting; I had no option but to drink it – a fiery liquor with an odour that rose like an enchantment through my nostrils and into my brain.

I felt ill quite quickly, my limbs were unstrung. In the hotel I fell onto the bed and the ceiling swooped and soared above me, and for a bilious hour I rode a mythical bird into an upside-down rainbow sky.

The next morning, when I awoke, I smiled through my nausea and blinked away the shooting stars that were exploding in my head – I had won my French spurs, and ever since that day, when I emerge from the Gare du Nord, I go directly to that same bar and drink a toast to the little boy who was there before me; not in chartreuse but in bright white wine, as dry as destiny. '*Quel courage*,' I say of him, '*quelle simplicité!*'

2

1950

The Loire Valley and the Two Lovers

A year later I went to France again, again cycling, this time along the Loire Valley. Somewhere south of Angers, my map said there was a youth hostel. I had cycled nearly 70 miles that day, on deserted roads. I was exhausted and longing for company. I was borne up by the hope that the hostel would be like the ones at Blois and Amboise – lively, with lots of English spoken at the table.

It wasn't like that at all. My small scale map wasn't much use but it got me to the hamlet where the hostel was meant to be. There were a few houses, a dusty road, and one of those ancient grocer's shops that don't exist any more. Inside the shop there was a silence brooding, a mausoleum silence, and there was a brown light the colour of strong tea hanging on the air, a murkiness made heavy by smells that were warm and soft, violent and astringent: fresh bread, cream, coffee, ham, methylated spirits, *eau de javel*, tobacco.

The owner, a woman, was large and leant her weight on straight arms that propped her against a counter of dark wood, its surface scarred deep, the scars black with grease. To one side was a door leading into the living room; it stood open revealing a circular table with an oilcloth on it, worn thin to the separate threads. I could see plates scattered, still covered with the debris of the midday meal: half a loaf and half a litre of red wine. To the left of the counter the shelves sloped and spilled goods out across the floor; boxes of matches, tins of pilchards, jars of sweets, newspapers and cartons of macaroni. There was hardly room to move, and the woman didn't.

She told me where the hostel was. '*C'est pas une auberge,*' she explained, '*c'est plutôt un relais.*' She looked at me with pity in her eyes but I was a proud sixteen and pretended not to notice – besides I didn't know what a *relais* was. I nodded wisely, bought what I thought was a tin of sardines, a loaf and a pot of jam, and set off down a dirt track that was dangerous with potholes. The track led me between high reeds which grew thicker and higher as I approached a river. The wind was up and the sounds that came from the rushes were not reassuring. The sky was five minutes away from being night.

When I reached the *relais* I realized why the woman had looked at me so strangely. It was an uninhabited ruin with creaking shutters and no glass in the windows; the doors hung askew on rusted hinges. I explored and found a kitchen with a calor gas stove, but that was of little use to me for I carried no matches – previous hostels had been provided with electric power, and had been full of people willing to share food and take me under their wing as the youngest person on the road. Beyond the kitchen was a long dormitory of bunk beds which were furnished with straw mattresses and rough blankets, blankets full of itch and dust. A smaller dormitory lay beyond that.

I was petrified. I ate nothing. The gloom in that hovel was deeper than anywhere else in the world; it clung to me and was evil. It crept into the building like a murderer, going for my throat and deadening my eyes.

Then it was dark, horribly dark, thick velvet. The river was full of noise, the wind rippling its black back, and the murmur in the rushes was a voice whispering. I wheeled my bike into the house and leant it against the kitchen door, the door to the outside; then

I shoved the table behind it, fixing it in position so that no one could get at me without making a commotion.

Once these defences were in order I climbed into an upper bunk, pulled a pile of blankets on top of me and prayed that I would still be alive in the morning. It was obvious that if there were a maniac in the village he would know exactly where I was and would come for me in the small hours.

It couldn't have been very late, say nine or ten o'clock, when I was woken by the sound of the table being scraped along the kitchen floor and the crash of my bike as it fell over. I sat bolt upright in my bunk, a scream ready in my throat, my heart leaping, bashing at my ribs like a wild bird suddenly caged. Was I to die so young, only just sixteen, sexually assaulted, stabbed to death? The scream I needed to scream came out only as a whimper.

I sat still, perched on my lonely bed. I heard voices . . . a man's, then a woman's, a girl's? I heard a match struck; a candle was lit and I saw a line of light at the door. A cupboard was opened, then an oil lamp blossomed. Whoever it was in the kitchen dragged the table back into the centre of the room.

'*Il y a un vélo,*' said someone, and the door to the dormitory was pushed open and I saw a young man standing on the threshold, a girl behind him. He held his lamp up and laughed when he saw me, my hair ruffled, my child's face pale with fright, rigid with terror.

I said nothing. I had been brought up in the streets of South London, brought up to trust no one.

'You look hungry,' said the man, 'I've seen more meat on a butcher's pencil.' He went back into the kitchen and eventually I followed. The woman lit more candles and then the gas stove and brought provisions from a bag. There was soup in a glass jar, *pain de campagne, pâté,* a cold roast of pork, butter, wine and a bottle of champagne. 'I'll cool it in the stream,' said the man.

I pushed my loaf forward, the tin of sardines and the pot of jam. The girl smiled. 'These are not sardines,' she said, 'they are *maquereaux au vin blanc,* much better,' and she was right. I had never tasted anything like it.

In no time the shack was transformed; the light in the kitchen was golden. The river noises disappeared – the ghosts were gone. The young couple made a superb meal, and kissed and touched while they were doing it. 'You will eat with us,' they said. And so they welcomed me when in all honesty they must have been disappointed to find a cuckoo in their love nest. For the truth was that they came to that deserted spot every weekend, enjoying the anonymity of it, for in those days it was not easy for the unmarried to take rooms in hotels, and who could afford a hotel anyway, certainly not them, they were far too young – *Amor vincit omnia*.

And there was love for me too, spilling over; they had enough of it between them to open their arms and take me in. It was a lesson in generosity – life was full of love. I sat at the table with them and they filled my plate with food, and plied me with good Loire wine: 'For a waif like you to cycle a hundred kilometres in a day is wonderful,' they said, 'but you will need to eat for tomorrow.'

When the meal was over they taught me a handful of new French words, and I have never forgotten them – *cornichon, escogriffe, libellule, papillon*. They sang too and taught me a song which they wrote on a lined page torn from the hostel's register.

> Étoile des neiges, mon coeur amoureux
> Est pris au piège de tes grands yeux
>
> For ever and ever, my heart will be true,
> Sweetheart for ever I'll wait for you . . .

And then they tucked me into my bunk, and gave me goodnight kisses to sleep with, and promised me that the next day would begin with a breakfast as good as the dinner had been. Then they went into the other room and the *relais* became dark again, but it was a different dark from the one that had threatened me before, a dark I could hold close. And, as I fell asleep, I could hear their voices as they talked and held each other in their arms.

And in the morning we did have breakfast together, outside in

21

the sun, while the river gurgled over rounded stones and the rushes swayed. The coffee smelt like a drug and my jar of jam, though crystallized, was perfect for the occasion. And then, pretending to be a man of the world who met such people often, I packed my pannier bags and strapped them onto the bike. How I hated leaving those lovers – for years they were the whole country of love in my mind; I wanted to hold them and that place in aspic, wanted to lounge through another day with them, and the night and the next day, as I knew they were bound to do. So I left, too proud to ask for their address, and I never saw them again. But I brought good things away with me from that *relais*. In one night I had matured many years; France had altered me once more and I was never to be the same again.

3

1954

Corbigny and the Devil of a Grocer

I left school at sixteen and worked for a year at the public library in Magdalen Road in Earlsfield, providing westerns and romances to the pensioners who asked for them. 'I wish I'd gone to university,' the branch-librarian used to say from time to time, and I suppose that's where the idea came from. I signed on at what was called the University Entrance Department of Regent Street Polytechnic and supported myself by working in Joe Lyons teashops, clearing tables and pouring cups of tea for the workers of Bond Street.

The Polytechnic was a university for me. The Department was not in the main building but in a tall house in Balderton Street opposite the front entrance of Selfridges, and it was full of oddballs who hadn't passed their examinations when they should have done: they'd not worked hard enough, they'd been expelled from their schools or they were Army children with no education at all.

I loved it; I loved it so much that I hardly opened a book. I talked a lot in pubs with Mike and Max, Bill and Charlie. I fell in love with Rosie Dineen, and went to the theatre at least twice a week, queuing up for the cheap seats in the 'gods' – *Joan of Arc, Porgy and Bess, Two Gentlemen of Verona* and *Look Back in Anger*. I stayed at Balderton Street for a year or more and failed my French exams regularly. I was getting nowhere.

One of my chums at the Polytechnic was a girl called Anne-Marie Cahouet. Her father was the chief chef of the Hyde Park Hotel and, every Sunday, drove a big Wolseley saloon into Surrey or Sussex and ate lunch in the biggest hotel he could find, and never bothered to look at the bill. He lived in a spacious house in Fulham, and had another for the summers in his home village in central France. The first time I went to Fulham for dinner Monsieur Cahouet opened a bottle of Chambertin 1945 as casually as if it had been sweet cider, and watched me closely as I tasted it. Such a wine. I knew then that I had to go to France, really go to France.

It was difficult in those days: no European Union, no freedom of movement for those who wanted to work. Girls could look after children abroad and be called an *au pair*. For young men it was almost impossible to get a work permit, but Monsieur Cahouet was a close friend of the mayor of his village: a job was found and a *permis de séjour* was wangled. The *permis de travail* was no problem; I was never asked for one.

I left the Joe Lyons teashop in Clifford Street, kissed Rosie Dineen goodbye, and went to work for Henri Foulet, a wholesale grocer in the town of Corbigny, in the department of the Nièvre, on the edge of an area known as the Morvan.

Corbigny, a town with a population of some 2,000, slept – and indeed still sleeps – quietly at the end of a single-track railway line, and I got there in a Micheline – a couple of carriages painted yellow and red that looked and sounded like a tram. The station was just one building with one outside light, a clock and a level crossing.

It was dusk when I climbed from the train. A man was leaning against a wall smoking a *Gitane maïs*. He was dressed in blue overalls and beside him was a wooden trolley made of an old crate and bicycle wheels. I was the only person to appear on the platform so he knew who I was. He threw my case into the handcart and we set off along the main street, down the hill and into a square which was really a triangle. This man was Robert Foulet, Henri's son, glad to see me because I was taking his place; that meant he could leave Corbigny and the heavy tyranny of his father. He wanted to see the world.

Henri Foulet was a grocer of such evil temper and vicious energy that no one could work for him – not son nor daughter. I did, for eight months, unpaid, from seven to seven, five days a week and half a day on Saturdays. I unloaded lorries. I humped sacks of salt on my back until my shirt was stiff with it and my shoulder was raw. I weighed sugar into kilo bags, washed bottles and barrels and filled them with vinegar.

Day after day Henri Foulet harried me from side to side and from end to end of the large dusty courtyard that lay behind his eighteenth-century house. It was a yard piled high with crates of bottled bleach, cartons of wooden taps, deck scrubbers, tins of old nails he made me straighten with a hammer, and tangles of string he made me unravel when there was nothing else for me to do. Henri Foulet was a devil, always in movement, striding across his domain, weaving in and out between the stacked crates, his long brown dust-coat floating behind him, held in the air by the speed of his movement, hunting me to work – *Chaque chose a sa place, Michel, et chaque place a sa chose . . . mais non, mon pauvre . . . mais non, c'est pas comme ça qu'il faut faire, c'est pas comme ça!'*

But, once or twice a week, I was sent out on deliveries with André the lorry driver, carting orders into the most remote of the Morvan's grocery shops, shops that were half-cave, half-café, smelling of *saucisson sec* and cheese, of paraffin and nutmeg. By the end of my stay there wasn't a grocer's in the hills I hadn't drunk wine in, raising cheap glasses high at the end of each delivery, and swigging down the rough red, rough as sandpaper; grinning at André with coated teeth and 'purple-stainèd mouth'.

And every one of those shebeens existed in the fourth dimension, places where Einstein's theories were utterly disproved. He had been mistaken about time; it had wandered into the Morvan and then vanished. The hours did not exist in those backwaters, they were not even a memory.

So it was that sometime during that long, slow Corbigny summer, in a hamlet on the banks of the River Cure, André and I delivered a cargo of goods to a grocer's shop where the back room was also a bar, and I waited there while he went off in our lorry to visit a cousin. It was a café that dated from the turn of the century – that is to say 1900. The *patronne* stood behind the zinc counter, mutton dressed as lamb – long black cardigan, a tight skirt and high heels. She wore an expression of world-weariness that was several lifetimes beyond surprise.

Four men played *belote* in the gloom of a corner, complaining in loud voices that their wives never did anything in the garden. They wore double-breasted jackets inherited from the suits of deceased friends, and baggy trousers that gleamed with usage. The oldest of them spoke with teeth so loose that they made his words sound like someone stirring blancmange. The tables had cast-iron legs stolen from sewing machines, and the tiles on the floor, which had long ago lost their patterns, were worn into shallow troughs along certain routes; from the door to the bar and from the bar to the shop. Against the wall stood a wooden fridge as big as a small room; the hinges and clasps on it were made of brass and when its doors slammed they made a noise as final as death.

The embossed wallpaper that had once been cream was now a yellow that thought it was brown, impregnated with generations of moist, nicotine-laden breath. There was no noise from outside; it was too hot and the air too exhausted to move.

A clock ticked to no end. I wondered about it.

'Oh, I don't know how old it is,' the *patronne* sighed, answering my question. She raised her all-knowing eyes to glance at the pendulum and sighed again. 'It has always been here.'

One of the men at the table nodded and then shuffled the cards.

He was a hard man, Henri Foulet, and he allowed me little rest, but I learnt French in his house and a lot of other things besides. He had a cellar full of the finest Burgundies and he wasn't mean with them. His wife, Marie-Louise, was an exquisite cook and her *tomates farcies* and her *gnocchi* are legends even now. After work I could sit and talk to her, quiet in the garden, the gentlest of women, always dressed in a faded wrap-round blue overall and that frayed wide-brimmed straw hat of hers. She was much put upon, Marie-Louise, but when Henri Foulet's temper erupted she would say little or nothing, only smile and tilt her hat upwards so that I might see her face as she raised her eyes to heaven.

And on those blessed days when her husband disappeared in his old 'Rosalie' Citroen to collect orders, she and I and André could linger over lunch and spend an idle hour or two chatting about how they had survived the war, and how the Germans had burnt down the town of Montsauche – stolen hours that were made more sweet and precious by the knowledge that before long Henri Foulet would return from the dark forests of the Morvan, angry, like an avenging and jealous god, bent on destroying any vestige of pleasure that might still be lurking in his residence.

Yet out of working hours Henri Foulet could exude an irresistible charm if he chose to. Sometimes he would take me by the elbow and we would stroll to the Promenade in the company of his grand-daughter Yveline, a tiny 3-year-old, and there, for ten minutes or so, we would sit by the still, green waters of the river and watch as the child drew pictures in the dust with a stick. And, when we returned to the house, there would be lemonade for Yveline and an aperitif for everyone else.

And he took me to Vézelay and Autun, vast, cool churches with magnificent capitals, deserted spaces where the mind could romp, as Marie-Louise had it, like the mind of God. And there were picnics too that summer, with the Cahouets come from London for two months, bearing wines and delicacies. Three or four cars loaded with families and food would set off to some sunny field by a trout stream, the swallows skimming along beside us like dolphins alongside a ship at sea, past the old road signs, enamelled in white and blue, through hamlets where the old men sat against the warm walls, their skinny limbs still draped in the overalls of their working lives; gazing at their winter's wood, piled high and straight, wondering if there was enough for the cold months, or maybe thinking they'd cut too much for the time they had left. In due course we'd arrive at the chosen field, spread the white tablecloths on the grass, pour the wine, break the bread and laze and eat and talk.

It is little wonder then that I came to love Corbigny, and the whole of the Foulet family, even Henri. For a while I became one of them, went to their *fêtes* and birthdays, sat at their tables and shared their joys and sorrows. And the Morvan too: the woods and forests bent thick over the roads, and the shady rivers rippling where the *libellules* – the dragonflies – were greener than the sunlit leaves and more sapphire than the sky itself.

For many years Corbigny meant all of France to me; it was perfection of a sort, a perfection of that French provincial life which up until then I had only read about or glimpsed in paintings. Now it is with me forever. He was a hard man that Henri Foulet, but he chose a good place to live in.

4

1957

Paris Weekends: A Tale of Two Tapestries

I met Howard Jones in a Greek restaurant in St Giles' High Street a couple of years after my return from Corbigny. I was envious of Howard – in fact I hated him: his French was much better than mine and he had a job as a courier with FTS, the French Travel Service, taking train-loads of tourists to the south of France every Friday, and bringing back the previous week's contingent on Mondays. He seduced women effortlessly, yet he was no better looking than I was; he smoked *Gitanes* and smuggled watches. And he swam in the Mediterranean every weekend – in the 1950s that was no small achievement. And what was I doing meanwhile? I was working seven to four in the Accounts Department of the Savoy Hotel, where the dust lay thick on the filing cabinets and the desks were stand-up ones that Dickens would have recognized. I was paid £6 a week.

But then someone in FTS got the sack and Howard was promoted and everyone moved up a step. This left a vacancy at the bottom of the ladder. The weekend trips to Paris needed an *accompagnateur* – me.

Howard couldn't have been aware of my jealousy because it was he who put me in the way of the work, introducing me to the FTS office on the second floor of French Railways at 179 Piccadilly, across the road from Fortnum's, and there I met Joe Evans.

Joe Evans was something special. An accountant by training he had been a commando during the war, had been captured twice and escaped twice: the first time in North Africa, and secondly by crawling into a pile of dead bodies in a ditch in Hungary when the Germans were fleeing from the advancing Russians.

When I took a tour to Tunisia once he got out a large-scale map and pointed at a particular location north of Dougga. 'I want you to climb to the top of that hill,' he said, 'and if you find a pair of Zweiss binoculars, a Luger pistol and a pile of shit they're all mine . . . I had to leave them there when the Afrika Corps dropped some paratroops behind us one day. I've always meant to go back for them.'

Joe had a round pink face, a leprechaun's expression, the brightest of blue eyes and a smile that said he knew all the tricks and was up to them. He was wicked and careless with women and always got away with it. I took one look at him and wanted to join his club.

There was no interview. He didn't even ask me if I spoke French. 'This Friday night,' he explained, 'twenty-seven people, Newhaven –Dieppe, you'll be met at the Gare St Lazare by a chap called Colin Norris, wear this armband so people can see you. Bring 'em back alive Sunday night . . . Colin will show you the ropes.'

I was in heaven and left the Accounts Department of the Savoy for the last time with a spring in my step. Now it was me going into the big blue yonder, now it was me who would smoke *Gitanes* and smuggle watches and seduce train-loads of women.

It started off badly and I panicked. I only found two of my clients at the station, and, completely without experience, I lost my head. Between Victoria and Newhaven I ran up and down the train continually, searching for my charges, the arm with the armband stuck rigidly out before me. By the time we reached Newhaven I had found a mere six of my twenty-seven. I perspired, cold with fear; I'd be sacked before I'd started.

On the boat I found perhaps another ten, including a young

bride and groom taking a short and romantic honeymoon in the city of honeymoons. That still left ten unaccounted for; my arm with the armband became stiffer and stiffer. I was so busy searching that I ate nothing, though I did take several drinks. Then, at three in the morning, as we walked down the gangplank onto the quayside of Dieppe, the very one where I had landed as a 15-year-old, I found the last members of my group, or rather they found me. They weren't a bit anxious; they had worked themselves into a party mood, and duty-free bottles clinked in the pockets of their gabardine macs. On the train the party continued until most of them fell asleep, their mouths open, their minds empty.

In Paris, bedraggled and blinking, they staggered down the platform and into the waiting arms of Colin Norris. In theory I was then free of my clients until Sunday evening, but that weekend, and for most of the weekends that followed, I went with Colin everywhere . . . I had things to learn.

I never fully understood why, but Colin took my education, *sentimentale* and otherwise, very seriously.

'It's who you meet in life that forms you,' he used to say, 'as much as anything else – just the luck of it. If you travel as much as you can, then you'll meet the people who'll make you think just that little bit deeper, alter you. If you stay at home . . .' At this point he would shrug his shoulders.

Colin was a rangy man in his forties when I met him. He was bald, with a lean face and a bizarre, halting tic in his manner of speaking. He had been sent down from Cambridge and had fought the war as an artillery officer. At the beginning of the 1950s he was sleeping rough across Europe, and not a bit interested in returning to England. All he knew was how to drop a shell onto a target, so, begging his food on the way, he tramped to Marseille and joined the Foreign Legion. He did most of his service in Indo-China, was captured at Dien Bien Phu, and had written a book about his adventures. Now here he was taking tourists up the Eiffel Tower and into the Louvre to see the Mona Lisa.

This man taught me Paris. The restaurants in Les Halles, le

Marais, la place des Vosges and the tiny shops under the arcades in the gardens of the Palais Royal. And he made sure that I appreciated the beauty of the Sainte Chapelle, a building without walls held aloft by magic, the stained glass windows flamboyant with brilliant colour, so that when the sun shines through them the air tingles with light: reds and yellows, mauves and lavenders, full of fire.

And he sent me to see, for the very first time, the tapestries of the Lady and the Unicorn in the Cluny Museum. It is a peaceful place, even now, modest in size and rich in wonderful things, but the tapestries are the great treasure – sublime, they exert a strange power and they draw the onlooker into another world, another era; more magic of a high order.

There are six tapestries in all, ablaze with red, and in each an elegant lady stands on an island of dark blue, and over all these scenes bright flowers have been strewn, thousands of them – *mille-fleurs*. There are trees too with dark green leaves, holly burning with berries, pine, and oak with golden acorns, oranges and orange blossom together, and banners bearing crescent moons, unfurled but motionless in an embroidered, windless sky. There are animals everywhere: a lion, a goat, rabbits, dogs, foxes, birds and monkeys and above all the unicorn, white and serene and fantastical. This darkened gallery in the Cluny never fails to astound me and, no matter how often I go there, it is Colin's spirit that greets me.

Colin taught me generosity as well as Paris. I knew he was perpetually short of funds, that much was obvious, but he never hesitated to share his percentages with me – the money that came his way for taking his clients to the Moulin Rouge, Le Pied de Cochon, and the cafés in Les Halles. I was flattered.

At Les Invalides we often used to drink in a bar-cum-souvenir-shop while our clients visited Napoleon's tomb. After five or ten minutes' sightseeing they would catch up with us and buy trinkets, postcards and large glasses of beer, spending a great deal of money. As we left Colin would shake hands with the *patron* and pick up 20 or 30 francs. Outside, sitting at an easel, a woman painted views of Notre Dame in the hope of selling them to our trippers at outrageous prices. Colin introduced her to me one day: 'This is Alice,' he said, 'my wife.'

He didn't have to but Colin saw me off at the Gare St Lazare that first Sunday night. I was to take trips to Paris often that summer but he was always there; always sharing. All twenty-seven of my charges turned up on time, much the worse for wear – their Paris weekend had been sleepless and submerged in alcohol.

It was a rough crossing to Newhaven, a force 10 was blowing up the Channel, knocking our ferry from side to side, lifting it high then slamming it down into great treacherous troughs of water, hard as iron. Even the sailors were being seasick and plates were crashing to the floor in the restaurants and kitchens.

The young bridegroom began to throw up as soon as we left the protection of the harbour wall at Dieppe, and soon afterwards he lapsed into a deep coma, much to the joy of his bride, for the movement of the boat had a totally different effect on her – she became amorous, no doubt encouraged into concupiscence by two days and nights of honeymoon. She grabbed my hand and dragged me from the bar, up a staircase and out onto the deck. There, wedged between a lifeboat and a rail, we attacked each other with rough hands, squeezing our bodies close.

The weather was right for it, the wind fierce, the sea high, the waves all black with lines of white foam racing along their crests, appearing and disappearing, changing shape and hurling themselves in madness at the side of the ship. The waters poured onto the decks, drenching both the bride and me, and washing over the little bundle of cloth that was my trousers, soggy and pathetic at my ankles.

Back in Joe Evans' office on Tuesday morning I handed over some cigarettes and a couple of watches. I was wearing a clean pair of trousers; the others had a lace tracery of sea-salt on them. Joe read my report and then his blue eyes did the leprechaun thing.

'It went all right, then?'

'Yes,' I said.

'No complaints?'

'No, no complaints.'

'You look exhausted. It isn't easy, being a travel guide, is it?'

'No,' I said, 'it certainly isn't . . . .'

Some thirty years later I visited the chateau at Boussac where the Unicorn tapestries had been 'discovered' by George Sand.

She claimed to have seen eight of these masterpieces, though now only six remain. Nevertheless it is more than possible that there were others; several testimonies from the nineteenth century agree on this point. Prosper Mérimée, who at the time was the Inspector of Historic Monuments, also saw the tapestries in the 1840s, and reported that the local mayor had told him that many other panels had been cut up by one of the Comtes de Carbonnières, to cover his carts and to be used as rugs.

For decades the tapestries had sustained damage from the damp walls of the chateau. Nothing was done to protect them and they continued to deteriorate; in fact three panels, which had decorated a dining room, were rolled up and abandoned to become the haunt of a nest of rats. The tapestries were not bought by the State until 1882, when the six panels were placed in the Cluny Museum and put on exhibition a year later. Finally in June 1975, all six tapestries were cleaned by means of the most modern techniques, restoring to them the original brilliance of their colours.

In the Cloisters Museum in New York another series of Unicorn tapestries are exhibited; they depict the hunting of the unicorn, and they too have a *millefleurs* background, just as colourful as those at Cluny, and date from approximately the same period.

In 1728 these tapestries were recorded as hanging in the Château de la Rochefoucauld at Verteuil, about 250 miles south of Paris, where they remained until the Revolution, when village peasants ransacked the chateau and, it is said, stole the tapestries and used them 'to protect their potatoes from the frost'.

In the mid-1850s the damaged tapestries came to light once more and were repaired and restored – a peasant's wife had told the Comtesse Hippolyte de la Rochefoucauld about some 'old curtains' her husband used in his barn to cover vegetables.

In 1922 these 'old curtains' were sent to New York for an exhibition where John D. Rockefeller saw them.

'I merely lingered five minutes,' he said afterwards, 'to satisfy my eye with the beauty and richness of their colour and design and bought them forthwith.' What it is to be a millionaire.

On my first visit to New York, in 1993, I went directly from the airport to the Cloisters Museum in Tryon Park, to contemplate what I had come so far and so fast to see. There they were, that set of seven fifteenth-century tapestries hanging in the north of Manhattan – the tapestries of the hunting of the unicorn, each with its fabled *millefleurs* background, the colours breathtaking: blue and gold, scarlet and green.

In the embroidered orchards, crowded with huntsmen, the flowers and foliage of all four seasons blossomed miraculously together. On the small horizons were small castles, out of perspective, with large faces watching from casements, while closer at hand the hunting dogs were leaping forward and hard-faced grooms, muscular and stylized, thrust spears into their quarry; blood gushed from the unicorn's side. And in the very last of the tapestries the unicorn was captured, its face full of sadness, imprisoned behind a circular palisade.

A few yards from me a teacher of fine arts was explaining the tapestries to his students, serious on their folding chairs as they stared at pictures made at about the time Columbus sailed. When the students had gone the teacher and I talked and I led the conversation exactly where I wanted it to go.

'Oh, yes,' he said, 'you're right, there's another set of Unicorn tapestries in the Musée de Cluny, Paris, France . . . just as lovely as these.'

This was the moment I had been waiting for. 'I know,' I answered. 'I saw them this morning.'

His jaw dropped; he stared at me. 'What?' he said.

'Concorde,' I said, 'mach two.' I had left Paris at eleven-thirty and arrived in New York at nine the same morning.

'Oh, my God,' he said. 'Do you know you must be the only man in the world, ever, who has seen both collections in the same day. It's gotta be a first.'

'I sincerely hope so,' I said. 'It's my only claim to fame.'

5

1957

Night Train to the Riviera

Howard Jones was promoted again and, following in his wake, so was I. I was now number one assistant to Joe Evans, both of us in charge of a train that once a week left Victoria for Fréjus, carrying anything between 250 and 500 people to a kind of holiday camp on the Mediterranean coast at St Aygulf – les Auberges au Soleil. There the clients were accommodated in single-storey pavilions that were dotted about a dusty, sweet-smelling parkland shaded by pine trees, eucalyptus and mimosa. Each pavilion was made up of fourteen twin-bedded rooms, and the showers and lavatories were located at the end of each building. There was also a central clubhouse which contained, on two floors, a large restaurant, a bar, kitchens, a shop, an office and an open area for dancing.

The temptations that went with Howard's new position – Assistant Manager of the Auberges – were many and powerful, and in due course he succumbed, though he wasn't the only one. The Assistant Manager before him had run away with as much money as he could lay his hands on; the one before that had been excessively convivial at the bar and had drunk himself into a permanent stupor, while Howard himself found it difficult to resist the lures of carnality.

At the height of the season there were 500 clients at St Aygulf, with new ones arriving every week. At least 300 of those clients would be women; 150 of them would be nubile, and fifty of those would find the assistant manager, in his Italian-cut trousers and white gigolo shoes, irresistibly attractive. Howard was to disappear eventually under an avalanche of female flesh.

This was the very beginning of mass tourism – it was all very amateurish, and there were no wide-bodied jets to carry us down to Nice or Marseille. Joe Evans and I would stand at the gate of Platform 17, Victoria, our bright armbands showing, crossing people off our list as they came by, and directing them to their reserved coaches. We would round up the stragglers on the ferry and make sure they boarded our 'special' at Dieppe – the Blue Sky Express.

This was a train that travelled all afternoon and all night, looping round Paris with a two-hour stop at the Gare Montparnasse. Clutching hundreds of cards stamped with seat numbers, Joe and I would spend hours tramping from carriage to carriage, organizing the sittings for dinner and breakfast – all served in the restaurant car. We also sold, for as much as we could, empty couchette compartments to those couples who wanted to be alone through the hours of darkness. And we always kept a compartment each for ourselves, stocked with duty-free spirits, ready to entertain any young woman who was game enough to attend our impromptu parties.

Anything could happen on those journeys and it generally did. There were upset stomachs, spats of jealous rage, lost children; there was even a man who quarrelled with his wife, got off the train at Avignon in the middle of the night and was never seen again. There was a death from a heart attack and a couple of broken legs. It was varied work.

One carriage of the Blue Sky Express had been converted into a bar and dance floor where our holidaymakers could jive the night away and drink themselves into oblivion; sometimes there was trouble.

So it was that at about eleven-thirty one night, in the middle of the season, June or July, two SNCF *contrôleurs* knocked on the door of my compartment, dragged me from the arms of a young woman from Aylesbury, and insisted that I went with them – there was a fracas of some sort in the bar, and they couldn't handle it. I didn't even think of asking Joe Evans for help – he was busy in his own compartment, and besides I had dealt with similar situations before.

A snappy dresser in those days, I affected a lightweight mohair suit of pale blue as my south of France gear. I slipped into it and made my way along the train, through the heavy smell of sleep and whisky fumes.

I halted at the door of the bar, which the *contrôleurs* had locked, and peered through the glass. I saw nothing at first, then I noticed a man's body lying on the floor and, helping himself to drinks behind the counter, another man, a giant, say 6 feet 6 tall and almost as wide, with arms as broad as my thighs. At the time I weighed about 10 stone.

The *contrôleurs* explained: 'They're friends . . . They had a quarrel and the big one hit the small one on the head. Everyone else ran away, including the barman . . . We tried to get the little one out, but the big one couldn't understand us and threw bottles . . . You'll have to speak to him.'

For some reason I wasn't frightened. It was misplaced pride I suppose, the invulnerability of youth. I unlocked the door and went in. The little man was definitely unconscious, or stoned, but he was breathing. I began to talk to the big man who was swigging neat vodka. He was in shirt sleeves, and there was blood all over his hands and arms; he must have cut himself on a broken bottle. The cool voice of reason, I thought, was what was needed.

The big man was having none of that. He didn't hear a word I said. He grabbed me with a strength that brooked no resistance, both bloody hands on the lapels of my spotless mohair suit. Then he lifted me, weightless into the air, and my feet turned in a blur like a cartoon character trying to run away. The smell of blood and booze filled my nostrils. My suit was ruined and I was convinced I was going to die, even more so when the man bore me to an open window and began to shove my body out of it. The night roared by me; the rush of the wind was in my ears, and the rattle and sway of the train at high speed added to my terror. Even if I managed to cling on I knew that the first train to pass in the opposite direction would splatter my brains across half of France.

The two *contrôleurs* were as terrified as I was, but they rushed in nevertheless, like men with capes saving a matador from an enraged bull. The big man dropped me; I could hardly draw breath, I had been half-strangled. The man made for the two Frenchmen but they kicked him, together, hard, in the groin and in the head when he bent momentarily. They were brutal but I was glad they were brutal, surprised to be still alive. I beat a swift retreat out of the bar, the two *contrôleurs* close behind me. Once we were safe we slid the door across and locked it again. We were all shaking violently.

'We'd better get the police at Lyon,' I said.

But the big man had not finished. He began throwing bottles and glasses around the bar, full and empty. Then he went to the window and began to climb out of it. I was not brave enough to stop him; I watched, that was all.

The man got completely out of the carriage, clinging to the open window. Then, unbelievably, he swung along the outside of the train, from window to window, like Tarzan from tree to tree. Now there was no danger, the *contrôleurs* and I went back into the bar and tended to the casualty. We bathed his head in water for a while and his eyes flickered; he came round and we propped him up against the wall in a sitting position. He couldn't see very much.

At this stage we were able to watch the big man as he swung along the outside of the carriage. We could see the strain on his face, his bloody hands leaving marks on each window. At last he reached the end of the carriage and disappeared. I was positive he had fallen off the train to be mangled to ribbons under the wheels. But he hadn't; one of the *contrôleurs* leant out into the night to look. 'He's sitting on the buffer,' he said, 'riding it like a horse, holding on with his hands.' And the big man stayed there, drunk as he was, until we reached Lyon.

By the time the police got to us it was too late. The big man had climbed over a guard rail, hung on for a moment or two, and then allowed himself to drop to the road which ran under the station, about 30 or 40 feet below. I heard his head hit the pavement, like a coconut cracking; an ambulance was sent for and they took him away. Half an hour later the Blue Sky Express moved on, its clients still sleeping. When I returned to my couchette the girl from Aylesbury was fast asleep, and I was in no mood to wake her. On my next trip to St Aygulf Howard told me that the big man was still in hospital, and it was certain that he would spend the rest of his life in a wheelchair. As for the friend, he had enjoyed his holiday, caused no trouble at all and had drunk only a reasonable amount. He hadn't even bothered to enquire if his travelling companion was still alive.

6

1958

Les Auberges au Soleil

It was late spring and the temperature in Fréjus station was high, and even higher on top of the bus where I was stacking the luggage for the transfer to the Auberges. The clients carried their suitcases from the train, the coach drivers threw them up and Joe and I made them safe on the roof-rack. Someone shouted at me, ordering me to climb down. I was shoved into a car and driven to St Aygulf. It had happened. Howard had run away with a Jamaican girl and I was the Assistant Manager.

It was the deep end all right. I found that I was in charge of a staff of about thirty: barmen, cooks, waitresses, gardeners and an ever-changing population of casuals who had stopped off at St Aygulf to sunbathe, drink and make love; and they all lived in some kind of commune at the back of the hotel. Everyone was eating lotuses, except me – I was working, from six in the morning until two the next morning.

I supervised the restaurant, organized excursions to Monte Carlo and St Tropez, and was master of ceremonies for the soirées that were held on the terrace. There was no dance that I dared not tackle, no partner that I feared to approach. I could rhumba and I could cha-cha-cha, I could jive and I could tango. In my selection of suits and co-respondent shoes, I was the nattiest of fellows. I was no longer jealous of Howard Jones, now the women came to me like butterflies to buddleia – I fell in love, truly and passionately, every week.

My boss, the Manager of the hotel, was a podgy little ex-waiter with poisonous eyes and a thumb of a nose planted in the middle of a round and heavy face – a face mottled like the leaf of a Savoy cabbage. His thin black hair was smarmed in streaks across his skull, glued there by some perfumed and oily pomade. When he emerged into the open air I could smell his scalp frying in the sun.

His name was Garreau: he looked choleric and was. He disliked everybody, was obsessively jealous of others and resented every holiday romance I indulged in. He trusted no one and had married a woman with a face as narrow as a knife. We called her Queenie, after her dog.

But I remembered what Colin Norris had said in Paris: that the quality of life is decided in large part by the people you meet. Garreau was capable of spoiling life itself, but there was another man at the Auberges whom no evil could touch; he made the whole world shine and his smile could make everyone smile.

Jean Renoult had emigrated from Normandy in order to follow the sun, having decided that work of any serious kind was a waste of valuable time. He'd married a girl from Toulon – Licette – sailed a canoe along the Mediterranean, been a ski-soldier on the Italian frontier and, in the dark days of the war, had become a forester in Brittany.

Jean had no real home apart from his books and not many clothes either. He loved love, the sun, all women except Queenie, *pastis* and the oddities of human behaviour. He hated work but there he was, stuck, living with his wife and three children in four rooms belonging to the Auberges, charting the lives and loves of our numerous staff and pretending to take forward planning and maintenance seriously.

Jean and I worked together every day and ate lunch at the same table. As the season went by he talked about Provence, and I listened. I learnt some of its history, and some of its poetry. I found that I had entered a different country, a country of extremes: cool forests and bleak hills, waterless plains and deep torrents.

And there was magic too. Jean saw to it that I heard Saracen warriors riding in the woods, armour clinking, and he convinced me there were still elegant courts of love hidden in the mountains; turreted castles where the ghosts of wise and beautiful women listened, enraptured, to the songs and stories of the troubadours.

I toiled for over a year at the Auberges. It was hard work and the worst moments were down to lack of sleep, excessive venery and dealing with Garreau. I used to keep him sweet by always making sure that one of the chalet-rooms was left empty whenever possible, so that he could take his Belgian girlfriend there in the afternoons. She was even more rotund than Garreau, and their couplings could only have been achieved with difficulty and a certain amount of inventiveness.

But the chef de cuisine was a good man, an ally; he worried about me. While everyone else was suntanned, the long hours I worked made me look pale and poorly. On early five o'clock mornings, when I had to wake those clients going on excursions, the chef would throw open his walk-in refrigerator, cut me off a huge slab of steak, show it to the hot plate, and then make me eat it, raw and red, there and then, at dawn, between two chunks of bread, washed down with half a bottle of red wine.

And there was Paulette from Nice: a dark, soft-skinned waitress of about twenty, slight of body, with her black hair cut into a bob around a heart-shaped face, her muscles coiled – a cat ready to spring – her teeth white, brown eyes brimming with desire, a Saracen *houri* come down from paradise. She used to slip into my darkened room at siesta time and stroke me to sleep after she had made love to me. Alas, at the end of the season she disappeared, like almost everyone else from the Auberges, back into the rest of her life.

Like Ali, a tiny Algerian, one of the porters who did the washing up. He went crazy one summer's afternoon when the temperature in the kitchens must have been over 130°F, and he and only one helper had the plates and cutlery for 500 to deal with. He hunted everyone out of the kitchen with a long carving knife, threatening to kill any living thing that came within reach of his arm. And I was the only one there who could calm him, managing to get away with it because I ignored the knife, rolled up my sleeves and made a start on the washing-up. He watched me for a while and then decided that I needed help; he put down the knife, and we did the work together, sitting in the shade afterwards to drink a beer.

I saw my first and only straitjacket at the Auberges. I was called from a Paulette siesta to one of the pavilions where a massive and muscular Swedish woman was screaming endlessly and fighting off all comers. It needed five men to hold her down: Garreau, Jean, myself and a couple of miners from Yorkshire. It was two hours before the doctor arrived and we didn't dare relax our grip for a second. She was given an injection to sedate her, but it had no effect. We waited another hour for the straitjacket to arrive and, after a long struggle, got her into it. A straitjacket is a *camisole de force* in French. I've not used the word since, but I haven't forgotten it either.

I enjoyed the work while it lasted. I thought it was the high life. Lunch and dinner were served to me on a terrace overlooking the sea and I had the pick of the wine list. My nails were manicured and polished, my dance steps likewise, and every week the Blue Sky Express brought me a new woman.

Ocasionally I found time to visit Fréjus and St Raphaël; in those days they were quiet little resorts with none of the false glamour of Nice and Cannes. Even St Tropez had not been submerged by tourists or Brigitte Bardot, and the tiny museum of the Annonciade was a gem, with its paintings by Bonnard and Braque, Dufy, Matisse, Rouault, Utrillo and a favourite Vuillard – *Two Women Under a Lamp*.

It was all very well but there was no living with Garreau for long.

I soon came to understand why my predecessors had absconded with women or money, or both. He was small-minded, hot-blooded and repellent – a combination that made him dangerously envious of me and my friendship with Jean. He began to make my life unbearable.

It was fortunate that I didn't need the job that much, and it didn't take me long to decide, under Jean's tutelage, that I needed no job that much. One day there was a flaming row about nothing at all and I packed my bags. It was a relief, it was time to move on.

My idea was to return to London, but I had no set plan. While I was packing Jean came to my room and convinced me otherwise; it was good advice. 'Provence,' he said, 'is all round you. It is full of sun and waiting to be explored, a complete contrast to the life you have been living at the Auberges.' It was a contrast all right. Jean called a taxi and sent me along the coast to his mother's place. An hour later I was standing, exquisitely overdressed in white trousers and an alpaca blazer, at the end of a stony track in the middle of a baking vineyard, halfway up a rugged hill some several kilometres behind the town of Grimaud. Two peasants, a man and his wife, their eyes glinting through a bank of broad vine leaves, were staring at me in silent shock. I was surrounded by suitcases and felt acutely awkward under their scrutiny. I took off my jacket, hooked it to a branch and, as nonchalantly as possible, climbed through the blazing heat of the afternoon, and the noise of the cicadas, up to Madame Renoult's house. I was entering a different world.

7

1959

Grimaud and the Châtelaine of Rascas

Bonne Maman Renoult, Jean's mother, was as remarkable as her son. Her husband, an artist turned engineer, had died only a couple of years previously. All she had to live on was the minutest of pensions, and, after moving from one rented shack to another, had, for the time being, come to rest in a two-thirds derelict farmhouse; the house was called Rascas.

Like most Provençal farmhouses Rascas was tucked into a hillside in order to protect it from the mistral. Extensions had been added to each end of it at various times, but they were now in ruins. Bonne Maman lived in three rooms in the middle of the house: one down and two up. There was no electricity and water came from a well 100 metres away. Brambles grew up to the door and in through the ruined windows. There was no lavatory and the track from the valley was a vertical path by the time it reached the little plateau on which the house stood.

Bonne Maman must have been about seventy when I met her. I

fell in love with her and her house within seconds – but then so did everyone. Her living room was a treasure trove. On the walls there were at least a score of her husband's paintings, showing, as far as I could tell, undeniable talent. There were several fine pieces of furniture from her great days in Paris, books, silver oil lamps, and above the fireplace there hung a portrait of her husband painted by his cousin Raoul Dufy, done in dark browns and yellows – worth a fortune that she was determined never to realize.

Bonne Maman had no idea I was coming that day, just as I had no idea that I was leaving the Auberges. But she took my arrival in her stride. She showed me where the wheelbarrow was and I brought my cases up the hill and installed myself in the third room, happy to begin a visit (the first of many) that was to last three months. Rascas was a castle on top of a hill and Bonne Maman was the châtelaine, just waiting for troubadours to come by. She held court there and I was a fortunate onlooker. I threw away my gigolo shoes and my sea-island cotton shirts, and began to cut back the brambles. I found a broken bike in a nearby ruin and mended it. Now I could cycle down to St Pons les Mûres, on the coast road between St Maxime and St Tropez, climb a gate, cross a vineyard and come to a deserted beach and picnic alone; there where now the holiday apartments of Port Grimaud stand with their security gates, their breeze-block 'Provençal' towers and their fibre glass power-boats at the door.

Our social life, or rather Bonne Maman's social life, was a busy one. Although she lived on her own there were often fifteen people at her table. Visitors of all sorts appeared from everywhere; there was Edmond the sculptor, dressed always in a rough red shirt, who came from across the valley to lounge on the grass, his beautiful woman with him; and Émile Pélissier, a peasant farmer, a confirmed bachelor under the thumb of his mother, who used to escape to Rascas for dinner bringing bottles of wine from his own vineyard; the Abbé Persat too, an Avignon priest who brought under-privileged urban kids from high rise flats and camped behind Rascas in the summer months. There were cousins from Paris who couldn't understand why Bonne Maman stayed in such a place; the eccentric 'Tante Mimi', a sister who worked as a nurse helping old people to die; and Marie-Bernard, a young girl with a deformed back who drove alone across Spain in a *deux chevaux* every year to teach school in Morocco; and once a week Jean would arrive from the Auberges with Licette and their three children – Eric, Hélène and Annique. And there'd be a crowd of us at table, outside in the dying day, in front of the house, eating like kings, the Provençal wine a glittering red, the conversation never-ending, the songs and laughter coming as the sun went down.

Every three or four days I would trek into Grimaud for provisions, a knapsack on my back, learning the hillside paths, cutting across the vineyards and passing by Nani's shack, stopping for a drink of wine and water, kissing her on both cheeks, and her children – Martine and François – while in the distance her husband, Martin, pruned the vines. I'd take her shopping list with me too, and as I left she would halloo after me, half in her cups from the glasses of wine we had drunk, her voice echoing across the fields as I disappeared.

Often I saw a shepherd, Marius or Lucien, strangers to me then, hardly visible, unmoving in the shade beneath the trees, their flocks exhausted by the sun. I'd hear a shout: 'Get me a packet of *Gauloise*,' and I'd wave a yes, then I was across the footbridge and up the steep track into Grimaud itself, the ruins of the château perched high above me. And on to the baker's, the grocer's, the post office, and the butcher's, until I rounded off the expedition with a *pastis* in the café on the square, watching the old men play pétanque, with my eyes tempted away across the plain to the view of Cogolin and the village of Gassin, a silhouette on its hill, and beyond it the blue glint of the sea.

When there were no guests, bed times were early and I spent hours lying on my counterpane, reading by the golden light of the oil lamp; reading under Bonne Maman's direction: *Jean de Florette* – the heat of Provence bursting out of the pages; and the essays of Montaigne – absorbing the wisdom and the humour, my hoots of laughter keeping Bonne Maman awake late into the night. And our breakfasts – just two friends together in that cluttered living room, the Dufy on the wall, the early morning sun slanting through the shutters, the murmur of flies and bees outside. That sojourn at Rascas was a rare privilege, and I knew it was. I lived every busy and lazy second of it.

A couple of years after my first stay at Rascas, I rode a motorcycle from England to Afghanistan and then down the Khyber Pass and on to Calcutta. I was meant to return home by sea (Bombay–Southampton) but I was already two weeks late for my first term at Trinity College, Dublin, so I disembarked at Marseille and took a train to Paris, the idea being to save three or four days on the trip.

I was out of luck. A general strike had brought Paris to a standstill; no metro, no buses, no taxis. I stood forlorn on a street corner and stared at the brawling traffic. I was carrying my possessions in two huge leather camel bags that had been made for me in Isfahan; they each weighed a ton and there was no way I could carry them across the city from the Gare de Lyon to the Gare du Nord. There was only one train to Calais that afternoon and I was going to miss it.

In those days I knew only one person in Paris with a car, just someone I'd met at Rascas, sitting at Bonne Maman's table. I hadn't seen him for a year or two – a butcher who had his shop over by the Bastille somewhere, a friend of Bonne Maman's sister-in-law.

I'd been four months on the road, sleeping out in the desert and dossing in mud-walled caravanserais. I'd become pretty tough and single-minded during that time; to tell the truth I was as hard as nails. I didn't hesitate. I telephoned the butcher – I don't even remember his name – and told him I had only a couple of hours to catch a train to Calais, the only one for a week.

That man didn't falter. He walked straight out of his shop, leaving a queue of customers in the care of his wife, and drove through a jungle of traffic, right across the city. He found me on my street corner; shoved me and my camel bags into the back of his van – the smell was of sausages and sides of beef – and somehow got me over to the Gare du Nord in time to catch the train.

What can you say except that those people who had met Bonne Maman, and had sat at her table, were something special.

8

1959
The Shepherds of Provence

One weekend towards the end of May I was left in charge of
Rascas; Bonne Maman had gone off to Avignon with the Abbé
Persat and a dozen children. I was awakened early by strange
sounds: a kind of rustling by the door, a shout or two and the
clanging of small bells. I went out into the sunlight to find myself
surrounded by about 500 or 600 sheep. In the middle of this
flock, with two savage dogs at his heel, stood Marius Fresia, the
shepherd.

He leant at his ease on a stout staff and was clothed in a rough
flannel shirt and heavy corduroy trousers of dark brown. On his
feet were solid boots with soles an inch thick. On his head he wore
a broad-brimmed hat of olive green felt, while tied across his back
with a piece of cord was an enormous blue umbrella. Over his
shoulder was slung a large leather bag, the *musette*, containing his
food and drink for the day.

Marius was some fifteen years older than I was; his face had been
darkened by the sun and the wind but his expression was cheerful,
like the sound of his voice, though that was so coloured through
with the language of Provence that even when he spoke French it
was, at first, difficult for me to understand him. This was the man,

although he didn't know it, who was to take me with him on the transhumance.

The shepherd, constantly on the move, has always been feared by the sedentary peasant. In the popular imagination he was a stranger from beyond the horizon. He had seen many things, he was many things: doctor at best, magician at worst. He garnered and kept knowledge; he knew the names of poisonous plants and could make potions; he knew the spells to ward off the evil eye. Some said he was a descendant of the wandering gypsies and weren't they, if the truth were told, the Saracens who had failed to return to Africa and Spain after the fall of Fraxinetta, their castle at Grimaud? Whatever the reality behind these legends it was certain that the shepherd was the repository of much dangerous learning, and it was best not to cross him, just in case he pronounced the words that could do you harm.

There have been shepherds in Provence since pre-Roman times and Marius was little different, I imagine, from his forebears. He grazed his sheep near the coast in the winters, and in the spring set off on the transhumance, a trek of about 150 miles, from Grimaud to la Colle St Michel, leading his flock away from the burnt out grass of summer and up to the fresh mountain pastures of the Basses Alpes.

The shepherds travelled through the cool hours of the night, and they always chose to begin their journey at a time of full moon. Every morning, when the sun got high, they rested in the shade, leaving the sheep to lie exhausted under the trees, while the dogs slept, panting. It seemed to me that the shepherds never slept; instead they stretched their bodies on the ground, propped themselves on an elbow or against a tree trunk and talked the day away, drinking from time to time or tearing chunks of bread from a loaf, eating it with the saucisson that they sliced at with their knives.

Over a period of a few days I managed to cajole Marius into allowing me to go with him to the mountains. I wheedled and I pleaded but he wasn't keen on the idea to begin with. He was to travel with five or six other shepherds, joining their flocks together into one of 3,000; and herding that number of sheep, not to mention half a dozen spare mules and thirty goats, is hard work. He wasn't sure I could make it – my exertions at the Auberges had made me look thin and tubercular – there would be no hot food, no real sleep and, most important of all, Marius' companions did not know me, nor did they want to. I would be a nuisance, a tourist. But at last I convinced him. 'If I can't keep up,' I said, 'I'll hitch-hike back.'

'Be at the chapel of la Queste at midnight,' Marius said on the day. I shoved everything I needed into a large white sailor's sack that had belonged to Bonne Maman's husband – a sleeping bag, a change of clothing, a map and Montaigne's book.

On the evening of my departure, after dinner, Bonne Maman and I talked until it was almost time for me to leave. A last glass of wine, then we stood outside the house for a little while and the moon rolled up the hill as big as a melon, illuminating the ruins of Rascas and the narrow terrace that I had cleared of brambles. Bonne Maman and I walked to the edge of it and we embraced. She was pleased for me: 'It is a great adventure,' she said, 'come back whenever you want,' and with that I went down the path.

In front of the chapel, under the moon and by the side of the road, I sat on the duffel bag and waited. Opposite me was the black bulk of a farmhouse and all around me the silver vineyards. The air was still and I might have been the only person alive in the whole world. I looked towards the castle of Grimaud where it stood like a ghost against the sky. I could hear nothing save the trickle of the fountain a few metres away. Then, after a while, I became aware of a distant clamour, growing louder with each minute.

I distinguished the cries first, the voices of men, tense and angry, shouting at the barking dogs. Next came the bells, heavy ones that boomed and lighter ones that rustled more than rang, each one made by a shepherd's hands, scores of them filling the night. Then came the rattle of 12,000 hoofs on the tarmac, the bleating too, and soon I saw the hurricane lamps being waved from side to side to warn those who drove cars at night of the dangers that lay before them.

At last came the flock and the backs of 3,000 sheep caught the moonlight and sent it rippling from place to place like the shadow of the wind on water. Dark shapes of men went past me. I stepped forward and swung the white bag to my shoulder. I was ignored until Marius ran by, his two dogs leaping beside him.

'Throw your bag on the wagon,' he shouted, and then he too was gone. I did as ordered and followed the lamp that swung from the tailboard of the mule cart. I felt, as my brothers used to say, 'like a spare cake at a wedding'.

'Don't get so close,' a voice near me called out. 'You block that light and some tourist will drive right into us.'

We marched on, along the coast road to St Maxime. There the dawn came up as we passed by the grey sea, and the sheep filled the streets outside the dead night-clubs and the sleeping restaurants. We trudged deeper into the town, heading inland. The noise of the shouting and the bleating and the bells brought people from their beds. They came to their balconies and rubbed their eyes as we went by. Children ran out of doors still wearing their night-clothes, dragging their parents with them, and some families walked with us to the very edge of town before they fell away, waved and went back to their breakfasts.

But the shepherds could not stop and our road continued northwards and the sun came up and the air began to creak in the heat. The heads of the sheep drooped and they slowed their pace; the dogs padded behind in silence and I began to limp, not knowing if I could finish the day's distance.

It was not until ten o'clock, nine hours and 20 miles after leaving Grimaud, that we arrived at the Col de Gratteloup and the sheep were guided from the road and pushed in under the trees. The mule was unhitched and the cart manhandled into the shade of a ruined chapel. There we found another shepherd, with his flock, waiting to join us – Leonce Coulet.

I pulled my belongings from the cart, climbed into my sleeping bag and fell into a deep slumber, too tired to eat or drink. A few hours later I was awakened by Marius. The shade of my tree had shifted from me and I was lying in the full strength of the afternoon sun.

'Best move,' he said, 'or your brains will fry . . . Eat something . . . and drink too.'

I rolled back into the shade. The shepherds lay around me, their limbs sprawled in comfort, their hats tipped over their eyes, and Leonce Coulet was still talking, the sound of his Provençal lilting as if with the beat of a poem, though his voice was rough, like stones on a shovel. Leonce was a tall man dressed in a soft green shirt and waistcoat; his trousers were made from black corduroy. His wide-brimmed hat was also black.

I found his face remarkable, framed as it was with iron-grey hair and lined with dark creases where he grinned and frowned. It was a face that stopped you in your tracks and made you want to know the man and listen to him. Under well-marked brows his eyes were mischievous, and when they rested on you they made you feel glad to be alive. Troubadours must have looked and sounded like Leonce Coulet; perhaps he was a troubadour, one who had been lying in ambush at Gratteloup for centuries, just waiting for us to halt there so that he might tell his tale before we went on with our journey.

We went northwards, maybe ten days, stopping often and resting the sheep; le Muy, les Gorges de Pennafort, Callas, Bargemon, Castellane and St André les Alpes, then on up to the mountain tops, la Courradour, le Cordeil and la Chamatte.

It wasn't easy, getting accepted by Marius' companions. The food that Bonne Maman had given me ran out in twenty-four hours; I didn't have a cloak like the others to keep me warm at night, and I didn't have the enormous blue umbrella, the mark of the shepherd, to keep off the sun and the rain. In the first couple of days I was through the soles of my shoes and there were blisters on both feet.

I was on the point of giving up, just as everyone had said I would, when my luck changed. One of the hired hands fell ill and left us. He was the man who walked behind the flock, leading the mule cart which carried our provisions, our spare clothes and the newborn lambs when there were any. It was the most despised job of all, and he who had it walked forever in a cloud of dust and horse-fly, on call at every moment to run the length of the flock with whatever was needed: cloaks, leggings or a bottle of wine.

When the man had gone, driven away in a passing car, the shepherds looked at me and I looked at them. *'Je peux le faire,'* I said, and from the moment I showed that I was not a fool come along to gawp, everything changed. Someone lent me a spare cloak, ragged but warm. Someone else told me that I could buy a pair of the best shepherd boots ever made at Bargemon, and yet a third person gave me a broken umbrella. I was no longer a tourist.

Nothing could have been simpler than the work I had volunteered for, but I was no longer a free agent. No longer could I wander off the road to rest whenever I wished, or bathe my aching feet in a brook when I felt like it. Now I was obliged to keep the same slow pace as the sheep, waiting while they browsed at the side of the road. And I soon found that leading the mule was a struggle. I was never able to turn my back on it, for left to itself it would pull away in an instant, trying to tip the cart, and all our belongings, into some deep ravine where it fancied it could see fresher and greener grass.

So we went on, the cold and damp of low cloud soaking us at night, the dust parching us through the day. My clothes were engrained with dirt and sweat and I was as grimy as any shepherd, and like them I smelt of sheep. The ground rose steeper and steeper as the mountains came nearer, the evening sun pale over the vineyards. During the endless hours of walking I halted frequently to rest my feet, using the time to replace the pads of soggy cardboard and cloth with which I had attempted to mend the holes in my shoes. I was hobbling badly now and stealing rides on the cart whenever I thought I was unobserved.

One day, perhaps halfway to our destination, we halted in the grounds of the Château de Favas, on the banks of a river. We were in a delightful valley of wide fields, rich in good grass, with rounded hills on all sides. I unloaded the cart and laid our belongings under an oak tree where other shepherds must have rested, for I could see that large stones, much blackened by smoke, had been set together to form a fireplace. I only managed to stay awake a few minutes, just long enough for Leonce Coulet to make a thin soup of water, vermicelli, butter, salt and pepper. The moment I had swallowed it I crawled under the cart and fell asleep. It was the deepest and most dreamless sleep of my life.

Paul Graziani was a tiny man, about five foot nothing, and the most cheerful of the shepherds. From the very first day of the trek he had gone out of his way to speak to me, though his talk was not easy to understand. His mouth looked as if it had been kicked in by a mule and when he smiled it disappeared into his face, leaving nothing visible but a fold of skin.

When I awoke in the fields of the Château de Favas, and crawled out from underneath the cart, Paul was the only person still in our camp; the others were at the far end of the valley, grazing the flock in the surrounding hills.

In the afternoon's noiseless heat Paul and I lay in the shade and ate alone; at the distant edge of the field the cypress trees shimmered like obelisks in a mirage. When the day became a little cooler, the sun going down, Paul decided to take me to Bargemon so that I could buy a pair of boots.

The square at Bargemon was deserted. The fountain trickled with a gentle sound and the shade of the plane trees kept the water cool. For a moment Paul and I stood side by side, enjoying the peace of the place; one lanky youth, one old and stumpy man. Then he led me into a steep side street and we came to a door that seemed to open directly into an overhanging hillside.

As we opened the door a brass bell jangled. After the brightness of the sun the interior of the shop was all a yellowish gloom, though that did not prevent me seeing a short counter made from uneven wood with some bare and splintery shelves behind it.

A man, not much bigger than Paul, entered from our right and took up a position between the counter and the shelves. Paul began to speak in Provençal, tucking his shepherd's whip under his arm so that he might gesticulate more easily. The shopkeeper nodded and, when Paul had finished, came back round the counter to look at my feet. His face showed no emotion but he clicked his teeth when he saw the state of my shoes. Then he left the room.

'What did you tell him?' I whispered.

Paul sucked at his few teeth and the edges of his mouth folded inwards and then came out again. 'I told him that you have come from England to buy sheep and you will be taking them back with you, and as it is a long road you want the best footwear available.'

The bootmaker returned carrying only one pair of boots for me to try, boots that were truly magnificent, with a special folding flap instead of a tongue, and hooks on the outside instead of lace-holes so not the least drop of rain could penetrate to my feet. I knelt in the shop and put them on and they fitted me as if made by a magician.

As I tied my laces the bootmaker bent behind his counter and brought up a large black hat, just like Leonce Coulet's and just what I wanted. I left my old shoes on the floor and handed over the small amount of money that was demanded of me. Then Paul and I stepped into the sunlight and the bell rang again as we closed the door and walked away. I was tempted but I didn't look behind me once, being more than certain that the shop would have disappeared for ever by the time the bell stopped ringing – and in any event, I thought, why should I give reality the chance to triumph over imagination?

In the square at Bargemon I sat, immensely proud, on the terrace of a café with Paul. I tipped my new hat over my eyes and ordered *pastis* for us both, admiring my boots. Waiting for the drinks the shepherd stared at me, leaning forward to rest his elbows on the table and his face on his hands.

'You know, Michel,' he began, 'I think maybe you have been a shepherd before.'

'No,' I answered, 'never.'

Paul shook his head. 'What you say is difficult to believe,' he said. 'You do it well, you know.'

This was high praise indeed and I was touched by it, but I was totally unprepared for what was to follow.

'I have something to say,' said Paul as the drinks arrived and I poured water into the glasses, making the ice clink and the *pastis* go cloudy. 'You see, I am getting too old now to be a shepherd, walking the road, climbing the hills . . . but I have a good flock. I want you to help me keep the sheep this summer. In the autumn we will take them back to Grimaud . . . then through the winter I will teach you all I know . . . and next year I will give you my flock and you will take them to the mountains for me.'

Paul continued to stare at me and now I stared at him. I took a sip of my drink, astounded by the magnificence of this offer; but there was more to come.

'I also have a daughter,' said Paul, 'I will give her too, with the flock.'

I did not know if Paul's daughter was in his gift, but I could see that he was sincere in what he said. I took another sip of my drink. Perhaps it would be a good idea to become a shepherd and spend all my summers on the clear mountains and all my winters down by the warm sea. I smiled at Paul and shook my head in refusal, though many times since I have regretted it.

'I come from the city,' I said, 'and I don't know that I am capable of doing what you ask, or even if I am good enough to be a shepherd.'

Of all the places in Provence, Bargemon is the one I think of most; how difficult it was to leave, how full of shade the square is. And whenever I remember it I see Paul opposite me at that table, his glass held in two rough hands, his eyes looking at me full of hope, while all I could feel was a sadness at being unable to do what he asked; unable to become his shepherd and his son so that he might know that his sheep were safe on the mountains, even when he was too feeble to take them there himself; and above all unable, in the future, to help him remember the comradeship of the road and the ancient simplicity of the best days. Who, I wondered, would graze my sheep for me when I was old?

9

1959
The Road to the Mountains

In Castellane, where a chapel stands on the summit of a huge pinnacle of rock, our 3,000 animals blocked the narrow streets as if for ever; cars and buses were halted and pedestrians took refuge in doorways, marooned in sheep. The clamour of our bells was everywhere, echoing between the houses, but it was a scene and a sound that everyone loved, and there were smiles on every face.

At the back of the flock with my cart and my mule, I moved only slowly, a yard or two at a time. In a particularly narrow stretch of the road I came abreast of a Morris Minor bearing a British registration, a young man at the wheel, his woman beside him. They smiled and nodded and took a photo of me, enjoying the pastoral, enjoying the sight of a stained and smelly shepherd, a real Provençal with his battered hat and heavy boots, his face all tanned and unshaven.

It was difficult to resist. As I drew level with their open window I looked in at them and, speaking in an affected upper class drawl, apologized for the delay.

'It won't be long,' I said, 'we'll have you out of here in a jiffy.' I actually heard their jaws hitting the floor of their car, but I didn't feel too badly about it. After all they would have dined out on the story for years.

After Castellane we took the flock along by the lake and through St André les Alpes; this was the home town of three of the shepherds: Jules, Joseph and Jean Martell. As we moved slowly down the main street the Martells shook hands with friends and family at every doorway.

'And who is this?' the people of St André asked, nodding their heads at me.

'That,' answered the Martells, looking slightly ashamed of themselves, 'that is our Englishman. He is not the vagabond he appears to be, but be careful, he puts everything you say into a notebook.'

Leaving the town we passed through a gorge, crossed a bridge and all at once came into a soft-rimmed valley, protected from the wind. It was like going into a different country. This was the valley of Allons at last and the Martells owned it, and the mountain that stood at the end of it.

We made camp where Jean Martell's wife, Jeanette, was waiting for us. She was a good-looking woman wearing a simple blue dress. She had shoulder-length hair and fearless bright eyes. We were nearly home now and in celebration she had prepared a feast for us, brought down from the village. She unpacked it and spread it before us as we groaned with fatigue and sat on the grass.

The meal I had that day was one that I shall always remember. The first two courses came piping hot in black casseroles: soup to begin with, followed by rabbit and pasta; then some cold slices of *gigot*, cheese, fruit and wine. But it was not the menu that made that banquet so extraordinary. It was the company and the place, and the feeling that I had walked to Allons through a whole lifetime of experience, and had seen all the world on my way. I know now that never again will I eat such food, because that is what the gods eat and only carelessness on their part had allowed me to be called that once to their table.

I had not seen much of Lucien, one of the hired men, during the journey from Grimaud. Most of the time he had walked near the middle of the flock, and when we had camped he had said little. He was a big man and his chin was dark with the stubble of a black beard and his eyebrows, black also, were thick and well defined. He wore his beret flat on his head and under it his hair was shaggy. His clothes were ragged and dirty and his face was fat, but in spite of his appearance there was something genteel about Lucien.

I was asked to help him take Jules Martell's flock to the top of la Courradour, and halfway up the mountain we stopped to rest. From one of the mule packs Lucien took a bag and opened it in order to make me the gift of a sheep bell that he himself had fashioned. In that bag I glimpsed his small collection of books.

'This is all I own,' he said, pointing to the bag, and he made the statement proudly, as if this fining down of possessions was his greatest achievement, or indeed the greatest achievement of anyone. I turned the bell over in my hands.

'I make them through the summer,' said Lucien simply. 'I bring the wood for the collar with me and carve it, then I steam it and bend it round my knee to get the shape of the sheep's neck. Leather to hang the bell on and bone from the sheep's leg to make the clanger . . . I can't do much more than carve but I make sure that I carve well.'

At last one final step got us to the summit. Looking up I saw the wildest country I had yet seen, with peaks and ranges striding away into Italy, the ridges sharp, all mauve and dark blue like black, the sky as hard as diamond and lit from within by great splashes of sunlight.

'This is why I am a shepherd,' said Lucien, 'this is why.'

I stayed with the shepherds for another week or two, and before leaving I decided to climb to the top of Marius's mountain, le Cordeil. I wanted to make my farewells, to thank him for bringing me with him, and to see Argens, the tiny hamlet where he had his house.

The road from the valley was barely 2 metres wide and rose

abruptly, following the contours of a wooded hillside where the undergrowth was wild and impenetrable. Below me, on my left, the vegetation was no less dense and fell away down a steep slope that led, according to my map, to the bottom of a narrow ravine.

After walking for a while the weight of my duffel bag began to annoy me, so I concealed it, and all its contents, in the undergrowth near the road. Now I strode out and as my path rose my spirits rose also. All around me was silent and dark green with just one great band of blue above.

And then came the eagle, stopping my heart with the sudden beauty of its flight, its wide wings motionless and all its body poised on the air as if the air were solid. Perhaps it had been disturbed by the sound of my steps as it perched in the shade of some tree, or perhaps the bird had been drifting down the shape of the sky, searching for its prey. I do not know. All I do know is that for a moment it was close enough for me to smell, swooping within the stretch of my arm, and for a split second I saw every detail of it: the bright clean plumage and the imperious head, the curving beak and the hard eye which stared at me as if I lay in its power, body and soul, reminding me that eagles could kill whenever they chose. Then it skimmed away and for another moment I could look down on it as it soared below me, over the treetops of the valley, contemptuous, then it was gone.

Argens, I discovered, was nothing more than five or six houses built on an outcrop of rock. It was midday when I walked into its short and crooked street, a street deserted save for an old man sitting on his step, leaning back against the door, eyes closed, warming his lizard skin in the sun.

I woke him and although he hardly understood French he pointed me in the direction of Marius' house – two tiny rooms with a stable below for the mule. The door was unlocked – as it always was – and once inside I found the place a haven, cool and restful after my long march, the slatted shutters casting striped shadows on the dark, tiled floor.

I made myself a meal, removing my clothes for the pleasure of eating naked. Afterwards I warmed two large saucepans of water. Then I stood in a plastic washing-up bowl and scrubbed myself clean, splashing my body all over, and singing with the joy of it.

The English of the songs I sang must have sounded barbarous in the ears of the old man outside, for when I left the house a little later, to begin the climb to the summit of the mountain, he was nowhere to be seen.

Le Cordeil is nearly 7,000 feet high and was, for me, a good two hours' climb. At the end of it I came out onto a wide ridge about 5 miles long and I followed it until I spied Marius' cabin. I came to it silently over the grass, so silently that the dogs did not bark. I went to the rear of the hut and there was Marius lying in the sun, his head resting on his rolled up cloak and his eyes staring up at a silver aeroplane that was etching a vapour trail across the enamel sky.

The dogs growled and Marius pointed above his head.

'I was thinking about them up there, and whether I ought to be with them, flying to Paris or Rome . . . but then I thought – here I've got air as fresh as mountain water and mountain water as light as mountain air . . . you know, when all is said and done their days don't compare with ours.'

I stayed a week of those days with Marius and then began to think of leaving, for good.

'You did well,' he said, '*pour un anglais*. Perhaps you should marry Graziani's daughter after all and stay with us.'

Perhaps I should have done. I had been out of the world for what seemed like an age, but I had no desire to re-enter it. I was not the slightest bit interested in rediscovering buses or trains or hotels. My journey with the shepherds had changed me; Provence had worked a spell. I felt different and set apart, marked even.

I was unsure of my next destination. Back to Bonne Maman's for a while, certainly, but never back to the life I had lived before. All I knew was that I wanted to keep in my heart – for ever if possible – the elemental simplicity I had seen and admired along the way...that, I knew, I had to cherish. I had always wanted a pure adventure and now my wish had been granted.

I walked back down the mountain, through Argens and back to the valley. My bag was still in the undergrowth where I had hidden it, and the bell Lucien had given me clanged as I picked it up. The noise saddened me and even now it still does. That day I felt sure I was going in the wrong direction – sometimes I still do.

Jean Renoult took me to the station at St Raphaël, to catch the train to Barcelona. His family came with him: Licette, his wife, the twin girls, Annique and Hélène, about sixteen, and the son, Eric, nine. I had said farewell to the shepherds a month since and, troubled by the beauty and simplicity of the whole experience, had decided to go somewhere, though not quite sure why or where. My doubts about going had been resolved by Jean.

Imprisoned for years at the Auberges so that he might earn a living for his children, ground down by the awful vulgarity of the dreadful Garreau, he nevertheless managed to sound like Robert Louis Stevenson as we waited on the platform.

'Just go, Michel,' he said. 'Travel for the joy of it . . . It gives your life back to you, all new, like you've never seen it before.' Jean smiled his smile. He was a man who leant over the world like an angel, helping people like me who wandered into his life, helping them to become content with the hazard of their existence, making sure they enjoyed their minute of eternity.

10

1960

Avignon: Two Old Ladies and Treasure in Heaven

The Abbé Persat, when I met him at Bonne Maman's, was in charge of a poor Avignon parish whose inhabitants lived in the HLMs – tall tower blocks housing the lower paid.

He had been captured at the beginning of the war as the Germans poured into France. Priest to a regiment he had been offered the chance to return home, but chose instead to go into captivity with his comrades, and so spent the whole of the war with them. He didn't talk about it much.

He had two main desires. The first was to look after the under-privileged children in his care, making sure they got a trip to the seaside at least once a year. It was for this reason that he came every summer to Rascas, and why later he purchased a section of land nearby where he could pitch an old army tent with room enough in it for about twenty beds. His second ambition was to build a brand new church where he had only a prefabricated shed. Both projects needed energy and money; luckily the Abbé Persat had lots of the first, though hardly any of the second. It was a slow business but over a period of years the church was built and I attended the first christening there.

Every summer of the ten or so I spent at Rascas I was always delighted to see the abbé arrive, and every now and then I would accompany him on his excursions, taking the Avignon kids to les Baux or to Nice. I couldn't help but admire him; the Abbé Persat was a solid man with a fine face and a quiet determination about him, the kind of man you wanted next to you in the trenches.

One day in the early 1960s, out walking between Villeneuve and Pujat on the west side of the Rhône, the abbé stumbled on a hunter's track and followed it through thick gorse into a small valley. He soon became disorientated, turning first one way then another, back and forth.

The *maquis* is fierce and frightening; it is as hard and as unforgiving as barbed wire; it clutches at you like a thing bewitched. You cannot cut through it and you cannot see above it. The abbé was lost.

At last he came out on a low ridge and found himself looking down on the tiled roof of a Provençal farmhouse. Although large the house was barely visible, so overgrown was it with bramble and scrub. The abbé inched along the ridge and eventually found a faint path leading to the front of the building. Now he could see the house more clearly: square-fronted, high, with perhaps three floors. The whole was surrounded by a crumbling wall which held within it a garden that had run completely wild, so wild that it couldn't be distinguished from the unkempt countryside that stretched away on all sides.

To the left of the farmhouse was a long terrace, some stone columns and half a dozen rooms at the back, built against the hillside. And everywhere there were goats, perhaps a hundred of them: on the terrace, in the *maquis* and in the house, where the ground floor was covered in their droppings. The smell, said the abbé when he told the story, was enough to make him gag.

In the house lived two ancient and frail women, friendless, seeing no one. Even hunters did not come near them and they survived off what the goats produced and what they could grow. They dressed in ancient smock-like dresses, and old battered shoes with broken backs. Their hair was straggly, their fingernails broken, and an animal light gleamed in their eyes. They were fearful and untamed, but perhaps the abbé's cassock reassured them, for over a period of time he gained their confidence and became their friend and adviser.

Then one of the women died and left the survivor lonely. At last she decided to move into a small house on the outskirts of Villeneuve, and when she too died she left her farmhouse and its ground to the abbé. The property was called Carles.

It was a gift from God. The abbé marshalled the energies of his parishioners and those who wished him well, and gradually Carles was cleaned up; the *maquis* was cut back and a track laid from the road. Now the children of the tower blocks had somewhere to go at weekends, and their parents too. There were concerts and camping weekends, weddings and baptisms, and on feast days there were trestle tables erected along the length of the terrace, and everyone who could brought bags of provisions and bottles of wine; Carles became a very special place.

Not long after the property had come into the abbé's possession, and the land that surrounded the farmhouse was still a jungle, he led me into the wildest part of it. We climbed down a slope, through a cleft and into the first of a series of caverns that had been cut deep and square into the solid rock – that honey-coloured rock of the south. The spaces around me were vast, the roofs high. It was a dark and echoing place, stunningly beautiful; a place that would remain cool even in the heat of the Provençal summer. This was where the Romans had quarried, and where the stone for the pope's palace had come from.

'Oh, *Père*,' I said, full of enthusiasm for an idea which had that very second exploded into my mind. 'This would make the world's best night-club . . . I could open it, say, three nights a week – Friday, Saturday and Sunday. We'll share the proceeds fifty-fifty,' I went on. 'You won't have to lift a finger. Think of the money it would bring in for the parish, it would build your church . . . We'll make the devil do God's work.' It was an excellent thought and it would have worked. There was nothing like it in the Avignon of the time. We would have made a fortune, several fortunes.

I wish he'd agreed. Had he done so there is no doubt in my mind that I would have moved into one of those many alternative existences that I'm always dreaming of. This was pretty high on the list: living in Provence with only three days' work a week; more than enough money to live on; four days left for writing; bilingual children; glamorous French wife; a drink problem. Ah, well. It didn't happen. The Abbé Persat just looked at me and smiled a far away smile, saving me from myself. And he was saving something else too – treasure in heaven.

Twenty-eight years on the abbé invited me to a gathering at Carles. I went of course. It was in celebration of what would have been Bonne Maman's hundredth birthday, and there must have been 150 of us there, and all of us brought food and wine, just some of those who had known her and had benefited from her hospitality, up there on the hill at Rascas. The abbé said mass for her; then there were songs and talk and pétanque, and the meal went on from midday until the sun fell down the sky. I hope someone celebrates my hundredth birthday.

11

1961-6
Predicaments in Paris

I spent four years at Trinity College, Dublin, reading French and English. Every long vacation I went back to Bonne Maman's, cutting into the brambles that had grown in my absence and meeting more of her friends and her family. The abbé was always there with the kids from Avignon, and Jean and Licette came every Sunday to eat at the long table outside. The poets and peasants also appeared, just as frequently. And twice more I walked the road with the shepherds, accepted now by all of them without hesitation; after all, I knew the route and I knew what to do – I *was* a shepherd. Those summers were amongst the best moments of my life – simple, littered with books, close to the earth, rich and full of friendships.

At the end of my time in Dublin my professor of French put me in the way of a scholarship to the École Normale Supérieure in the rue d'Ulm, Paris, thereby ushering me into a year of self-indulgence. We *normaliens* were totally spoilt in an establishment that was designed to receive the intellectual élite of France. Each student had his own room; the food was free, and wine a-gogo came with it. And what was more, nobody cared how many women we smuggled into our beds; the authorities obviously working on the principle that wine and sex were good for the brain, and encouraging us to take full advantage of both commodities.

And there was icing and marzipan on the cake – I had no set studies, no lectures to give, and a generous grant for my upkeep. What I actually did that year was to lounge in cafés, jawing about love, life and literature, and loaf in cinemas, theatres and art galleries, strolling from one to the other, arm in arm, *bras dessus, bras dessous,* with Hélène, Solange, Claudine and Monique.

My closest friend at the École was a student called Jacques. He had long black hair, sallow skin, a moustache and brilliant brown eyes. He looked like a Mexican bandit, and the girls used to troop to his room in regiments, four by four.

I had been in Paris only a week or two when he took it into his head that I was lonely, that I was short of female company. I don't think he was being particularly generous, it was just that he always had more women than he needed. One night, in a café along the rue Moufftard, he introduced me to a Greek number called Anna, an attractive girl, slim, with eyes that were unreasonably black and bright, and white teeth that pointed forward out of a sensual mouth; something I have always found endearing.

Nothing happened that evening but a few days later I received a note from her at the École, inviting me to dinner at her place. The note gave the time and the address: an expensive flat on the top floor in the rue Lacépède.

When I got to Anna's flat, a bottle of wine in one hand and half a dozen yellow roses in the other, I found that I was the only guest. It couldn't be anything but a good omen, I said to myself. What a nice chap that Jacques was.

The meal was Greek and delicious, and Anna looked like something out of Andromache. Her black dress was simple and showed off her shoulders beautifully; her collarbones were carved ivory. At the end of the meal she made coffee and poured us each an armagnac. Then, leaving the table covered in its debris, the luxuriant *sobre mesa,* she took me by the hand and led me into her bedroom.

The night was warm and Anna exuded an odour that mingled

with the smell of wine, olives and garlic; I was Henry Miller and Laurence Durrell, and Anna was 'O'. The bedroom window was open and the lights of Paris glittered, discarded necklaces against a sky that lay just beyond the balcony and led all the way across the hexagon, down to Provence, down to the empty beach at St Pons les Mûres where the waves broke on the sand.

Anna caressed me for hours; I had never known such a touch, it was the touch of an angel. At the end of our love-making I fell into the deepest of sleeps, and when I woke she was still leaning over me, her eyes even brighter than before, bright in ecstasy. There was a knife in her hands.

At first I didn't move, I was convinced that I was dreaming, but when I felt the point of the knife nicking the skin of my chest I knew I wasn't; there was a trickle of blood running down the side of my right arm. I grabbed Anna's wrists and squirmed out from underneath her. I snatched the knife from her hand and threw it onto the balcony. She fought like a tigress and was as strong as I was. She wrapped arms and legs around me and spat and bit and scratched; from her throat came sighs of pleasure.

I escaped eventually, though I was obliged to fight every inch of the way and dress at the same time, hopping on one foot to get my trousers on, pushing her away as I struggled into my shirt, tucking my shoes into my jacket pocket. The socks I abandoned.

Back at the École I inspected my wounds in the mirror. They were superficial and I would live. When I saw Jacques I was angry with him, very.

'Well I thought you'd enjoy it,' he said. 'You haven't been to Paris unless you've been to bed with Anna.'

'She had a knife!'

Jacques shrugged. 'That's what turns her on . . . You're lucky . . . she has been known to go for the scrotum . . . Give me a break . . . I didn't know she was going to get to you so quickly, I didn't have a chance to tell you about her, she's harmless really. The trick is not to fall asleep . . . or you tie her up . . . she likes that too.'

*

One day I woke to find a strange stain on my sheets. I was petrified. I went to Jacques. 'It's nothing,' he said, 'just go along to the hospital, they'll give you an injection, it will be all over in no time. I've been there a score of times.'

'Hospital. On my own?'

He laughed at me. 'All right . . . I'll take you by the hand,' he said, 'show you what to do.' Jacques always found me very naïve.

I can't remember how we got there. I know that my embarrassment was almost choking me. We were put into a kind of waiting room, constructed out of dark wood and frosted glass panels that gave onto a corridor. On either side of the corridor were a dozen or so narrow doors, leading into tiny inspection booths, each about the size of a three-person lift. Every booth contained a doctor in a white coat. An orderly gave me a numbered disk and I held it tightly in my hand. 'Just wait till they call your number,' said Jacques.

I waited, dreading what was to come. I had never been in this situation before. The voices of the doctors boomed out occasionally – *vingt-quatre, cabinet numéro dix . . . vingt-cinq, cabinet numéro sept . . .*

I heard some high heels clatter down the corridor. There was a pause and then a genteel and calm voice called out my number – it was a feminine voice: '*Trente-trois, cabinet numéro quatre.*' Fate had decided that I was to un-zip, in the cold light of day, before a woman. Jacques was delighted. The story would be all round the École within five minutes of our return.

I opened the door to the cubicle and peered in, wishing I were anywhere else in the world. She wasn't even wearing a white coat and, I guessed, had not long graduated. She looked about twenty-five, and was blessed with sophisticated good-looks. There is no logic to it, but why couldn't she have been old and ugly?

Her hair was beautifully done, drawn back from a striking face; the lipstick, the eye-shadow were tastefully applied. She was dressed in a smart brown suit, and bangles of gold jangled on her wrists. She smiled.

I told her about my emissions. 'We'd better look,' she said and smiled again.

It is not the greatest of situations for a young man, standing, legs slightly bent, holding his trousers down by his knees, while a cool young woman bends forward in her chair and fingers his manhood, looking critically at that limp morsel of flesh, finally sticking something up it to take a swab.

I went back to the waiting room where Jacques still sat, now surrounded by a new assortment of patients, sheepish and self-conscious. Only Jacques was at his ease, a grin for everyone. It didn't take long, and I heard her voice again. '*Trente-trois.*'

'It's nothing,' she said. 'A strain. I know you are in Paris, but just try to take it easy.' She shook her head in amusement and I left.

Jacques and I went to the nearest bar. My hand was shaking as I raised my glass of white.

'I wonder how many cocks she's seen,' said Jacques and closed his eyes as he tried to imagine it. 'Rows and rows of them . . . I bet she's seen better things than yours hanging out of a bird's nest.'

12

1966

'Bing Crosby', Beauvais and Apricot Ice-cream

Towards the end of that academic year I saw a notice on a wall in the Sorbonne: a large travel company needed English-speaking students to show tourists around Paris. The man in charge of the operation was a Colonel Crosby, and without wasting any time I went along to see him.

Colonel 'Bing' Crosby had fought a very interesting war, eventually leading an early advance into Burma where, after the Japanese collapse, he'd found himself ruling over a large tract of the country as a kind of viceroy.

Bing was every Frenchman's idea of what an English colonel should look like, right down to the tweed suit and the monocle, which of course he allowed to drop from his eye at moments of surprise. He was something of a pasha too, being perpetually surrounded by doe-eyed nymphs got up in blue air-hostess uniforms. These were what he called his 'bunnies', girls who took care of the tourist groups that came to Paris on four-day visits. This

entourage and the business he brought made Bing popular wher-
ever he went; he got the best seats at the Lido and was fêted at the
Moulin Rouge. Every waiter panted to serve him, and every
sommelier wanted him to taste the best wines. So the Colonel
danced and skipped across the Paris skyline; everyone loved him
and he could do no wrong.

At the time I met him Bing was recruiting for a new scheme of
one-day tours of the French capital; up to twenty-five flights a day
coming from airports all over Britain – Southend, Manchester,
Newcastle, Bristol – all landing at Beauvais, 60 miles north-west of
Paris.

It was to be hectic work. The majority of our clients had never
been abroad before; they came from factories and mothers' unions,
and were on a 'good day out'. That meant they sang and drank a
lot, and were determined to get into trouble.

During the hour or so it took to drive to Paris it was each
courier's task to inform his tourists of the plan for the day – a
simple enough itinerary: lunch near the Gare du Nord, chicken
and chips; Notre Dame for an hour and into the souvenir shops to
spend more money than was reasonable, the shop-keepers passing
me a 10 per cent commission; then off along the river, past the
Invalides to the Eiffel Tower to take photos; on to the Arc de
Triomphe, down to the place de la Concorde then to the
Madeleine or to the Opéra where we parked for two or three
hours so the women could go shopping in the Galeries Lafayette
and Monoprix. We always left town by way of the Sacré Coeur and
Montmartre.

These tours went on for two and a half months and doing one
every day, as I did, eight till eight, was exhausting and boring. What
kept us twenty or thirty couriers on our feet was the camaraderie
that existed amongst us, and the friendships that developed with the
Beauvais bus drivers who drove our coaches. But there was something else that sustained us – alcohol.

The drivers were often up at five every morning, doing factory
and school runs. Three hours later, at the airport bar, they would

stand each other, and us, a coffee cognac, just to kick-start our hearts. At lunch there would be an aperitif and wine with the meal. At Notre Dame it would be a beer or two; then more at the Opéra, playing *quatre-cent-vingt-et-un* while we waited for the shoppers to return. Montmartre was more aperitifs, and then back to base for the evening meal and a bottle of wine.

We couriers were lodged in a tall and narrow cheap hotel called the Cygne, situated on the main street of Beauvais. Every year we occupied two, sometimes three, floors of the establishment. When the management got the bookings wrong we slept on each other's floors, and very often were obliged to share a bed with a girl, or a young man, we had only met for the first time that day.

The talk and drinking, and the laughter, used to go on to the early hours; we brought fruit and bread and wine back from the restaurants and had midnight 'dorm feasts'. And so, without too much imagination being used, we called the hotel, or our part of it, 'Beauvais Grammar'; we had a head pre, a headmaster, a gym mistress, Porky-Patters, Mugsy and Bugsy, and I was Sneaky-Larrabeiti from the fifth remove.

If the noise in the High Street below became too loud when the cinemas closed, especially when the boy racers revved their engines, we would lean out of our windows and hurl a rain of soft bananas down onto their cars, making their roofs echo and boom, then duck behind our curtains to watch while the drivers scraped smashed gunge from their windscreens, wondering where such a rain of exotic fruit had come from. And then it was a childlike sleep, lying in each other's arms, and up again at seven-thirty and the same mad day would begin again, and the day after, and the day after, and the day after that.

Occasionally, at the airport, we would eat a long leisurely dinner in the restaurant, a whole band of us, counting our tips and gambling them away at spoof. And the air hostesses and the office staff, as well as the people who worked in the control tower and the duty-free shop, plus the barmen and the waitresses, were all caught up in this *ambiance*: so Françoise fell in love with Angus; Henri was cuckoo over Arlette; Maité, when she wasn't flying, set her cap at me; Sebastien told everyone that he must have Geneviève or die, and Little Nick swore that he was going to sleep with every woman in the world.

We had our own language too. Every one of us spoke in a magic mixture of English and French, Franglais with a vengeance, or was it Englench? 'Es-tu off today?' 'Non, j'have to travail.' 'Quel wankère, qu'il est, ce bloke.'

Once in a while, if the gods smiled on us, there were hours of freedom, when a flight was cancelled and we found ourselves with time stretching empty before us, giving us a day as infinite as a summer day in childhood. If the sun was shining we would gather up whoever was loafing at the airport bar and squeeze into a car, driving off to Milly sur Thérain, a village by a lake some 6 miles distant. And by the water's edge, heads could rest in laps, and there was more food and more wine and more laughter.

And our drivers became part of this cavalcade; men who drove expertly, were *sérieux* but nevertheless enjoyed the kind of nonsense we couriers were good at, sharing our sense of humour. I had my favourites amongst them, those whom I would choose to work with when I could; Dédé Retel, Bertrand Dejonge and above all, Pierre Cilliez, who could turn his bus on a sixpence and back it into a gateway, hardly looking into the rear-view mirrors.

Pierre had deep-set brown eyes, pronounced eyebrows and curly black hair which lay flat over his forehead. I called him Caligula because he looked like my idea of a Roman emperor, 'Calig' for short. On many a night, when we had worked together, he used to invite me into his home. At his table we would eat a meal prepared by Camille, his wife, a large, warm woman with a smile that had so much love in it that it could have melted an iceberg. Such food too, fit for a king, and wines shining red in the glass. But before long I would fall asleep, rolling onto the long sofa, and Camille would put a pillow under my head and throw a blanket or two over me, leaving me to sleep until morning.

I did nine seasons of those one-day tours, each one of them more Homeric than the last, and whenever we meet, any of us *compagnons* from those days, French or English, we can hardly talk of anything else. You've got to be young for the kind of madness we practised at Beauvais – young enough to be immortal.

Beauvais Cathedral was begun in 1247 and was beset with problems, the design being exceptionally ambitious. The excessive distance between the supporting pillars caused part of the vaulting to collapse as early as 1284 and so more pillars were added to support the main structure.

In 1569 an immense stone bell-tower was constructed and was later surmounted by an oaken spire, the whole rising as high as 502 feet above ground level. Only four years later that part of the edifice came crashing down, bringing with it the pillars of the transept. War, the plague and lack of money prevented the completion of the cathedral, which consists today only of the choir, the transept and a single bay of the nave.

In August 1949, on my way back to the coast after that first trip to Paris, the 'Voyage of the Green Chartreuse', I cycled into Beauvais and got off my bike in front of the cathedral. In a shop that still exists, I bought myself an apricot ice-cream – I had never seen such a thing in England, and I have never forgotten the taste. Licking the ice-cream, and thinking only of that, I went through the church doors and, unknowing and unthinking, I stood in the transept.

It was as if the top of my skull had been lifted off and my mind was soaring free. I was tiny and insignificant, lost in a masterpiece, unique in its breadth and height, the most glorious Gothic choir in the world. And all these years later I cannot taste apricot fool, straight out of the fridge especially, without seeing the arches of Beauvais Cathedral rising out of sight, up into the sky. Such pictures to carry with me: apricot ice-cream, flying buttresses, and a skinny adolescent in baggy shorts with wrinkled grey socks around his ankles.

When I took my daughters to see Beauvais cathedral for the first time I covered their eyes with my hands as I guided them in through the south door. Once they were standing in the transept I let them look upwards so that they could discover the wonder of that space in a single glance, each of them holding an apricot ice-cream.

13

1968

Caligula, a Paris Bus and the Events of May

There were about ten of us tour guides eating in the restaurant at Beauvais airport. It was late when Pierre Cilliez appeared and beckoned me over to the door. He had a smug, very Caligula look on his face. 'I've got something outside,' he said.

I went into the car park with him and saw a Citroën light fifteen, black as anthracite, gleaming in the dark, its long bonnet panting, the engine tick-over relaxed and powerful.

I had driven through a lot of France with Pierre by this time and he knew I coveted one of these machines, so he'd gone out and found me one, buying it without telling me. His self-satisfied expression broke into a broad grin. I couldn't find the words to thank him. He was a star, that man.

By now some of the others had followed me out, and we took turns in driving the Citroën round the perimeter of the car park. It was front-wheel drive and as hard as a lorry to steer, it only had three forward gears and the gear lever was up on the dashboard, and when changing down it was a good idea to double declutch. It was a gem.

'Oh, Calig, how much is it?' I said, not sure I could afford such a pearl.

'*Soixante-dix milles,*' said Pierre, which was then about seventy pounds . . . 'You want it?'

Of course I wanted it, but getting it to Dieppe was not going to be easy. In the days before the European Union French insurance companies wouldn't insure a foreign driver if he didn't have a French driving licence; and my English company wouldn't insure a car that was registered in France.

It was Pierre who came to the rescue and when the time came he drove the Citroën – he called it *Fanfan la Tulipe* – all the way to the boat for me. Once in Newhaven I drove home on my comprehensive policy and in due course *Fanfan* was given an English number plate – EUD 260K. The following autumn I was given a job taking busloads of drinkers around the Bordeaux wine chateaux; *dégustations* everywhere and sample bottles for the tour guide. When the time came I drove south in *Fanfan*, as free as the air, and as proud as any peacock.

For quite some time I had been asking coach drivers and restaurant owners to find me light fifteens, and now that I had purchased one, in the way that such things happen, two more were unearthed. One came from St Emilion, the other from Beaune, purchased from a baker who was delighted to relieve me of £100. He thought it a great joke that I should pay so much, and he and his wife, when I met them in the bar of the Hôtel de la Cloche to hand over the money, had several drinks and a long laugh at my expense. I have rarely seen a woman so pleased with herself. But the car was perfect and the engine made a noise like a panther purring.

So there I was with three light fifteens to get home, two French-registered and *Fanfan* herself. I know he would have done it but I had no intention of asking Pierre to drive them on his insurance; St Emilion and Beaune were too far from Beauvais; besides, Pierre worked six days a week and couldn't spare the time.

There was only one thing to do and I did it. At the end of the season I drove EUD 260K from Bordeaux to Beauvais and left it in Pierre's back garden, behind a hedge. I removed the English number plates, shoved them in a haversack and hitch-hiked back to Bordeaux. In the quiet of a hotel car-park Citroën number two waited for me. I removed its French plates and replaced them with the English ones. Now at least I appeared legal, and I motored back to Beauvais at a leisurely pace, using only secondary roads and visiting any town or church that took my fancy.

As soon as car number two was parked in Pierre's back yard I took a train to Beaune and in the privacy of the baker's garage his Citroën became EUD 260K the third, and a few days later joined the others behind Pierre's house. I followed the same procedure to transport the cars to Dieppe and, once they were together on the quayside, I restored each Citroën to its proper identity, for as soon as they were loaded onto the ferry I would be insured to drive them all.

In Newhaven I waited until I was alone on the car deck before driving the first Citroën up and into the customs shed. Most of the officers had gone, believing the ship to be empty, but there was one uniformed man left and I pulled up alongside him. He stepped forward and looked me over.

'Yes?' he said. 'Anything to declare?'

I raised a hand. 'Hang on a minute,' I said. I turned, ran out of the shed, back along the dock and down into the boat.

The second car started perfectly and I drove it into the customs hall and parked in line behind the first car. The officer stepped forward again.

'Anything to . . . ?'

'Just a second,' I said, turned on my heel and ran away from him again. He looked peeved. I ran the course as quickly as I could and was soon parking the third Citroën behind the second.

The officer placed his hands on his hips.

'Well,' he said, taking a deep sigh, 'is that it?'

'It is,' I said.

'Spirits? Cigarettes?'

Pierre had given me a couple of bottles of illicit Calvados but I kept quiet about those.

'No, just some wine and these two cars. One is for my brother,' I lied, 'the other is for spares.'

The officer pursed his lips and half closed his eyes. He didn't believe me one bit, but he was a player, and he only charged me seven quid on each. I made the necessary three journeys from Newhaven to London, and kept the best car, the one from Beaune, for myself. I sold the other two at a disgusting profit. Eventually, and many years later, I sold the last one. I was sad about it, but the price cheered me up – £2,800. I sent the baker a postcard, wanting him to share in my good news. According to the barman in the Hôtel de la Cloche, the baker's wife didn't speak to him for a month.

It wasn't long after the summer of the Citroëns that Bernard, a friend from London, telephoned me at Beauvais airport and asked if I could get him a Paris bus. He had read somewhere that they were being sold off, and he wanted one of the old sort with the open platform at the rear.

I arranged the purchase by phone and, at the end of the one-day tour season, I met Bernard in Paris and we made our way to a large bus garage in a dusty suburb. Neither Bernard nor I had ever driven anything quite so big as a bus. It dated from the 1930s and had crash gears. We also had to drive the monster out of Paris, and to do this for us I had brought along another of my favourite drivers – Bertrand Dejonge.

Dejonge looked like D'Artagnan: fair hair swept back from his forehead, a pencil-thin moustache, and eyes that were too close together. He was tall and handsome in an untrustworthy way, and he had style. At the time he was sleeping with one of Bing's 'bunnies', an uppercrust girl who drove a sports car with the top down and occasionally fancied a bit of rough trade, especially when she was abroad.

Dejonge leapt at the chance of driving that green and cream bus.

He swept out of Paris full of joy; the driving wheel enormous, the foot pedals as big as snow-shoes. Bernard had brought his girlfriend with him and they sat, isolated in the back, on those dark brown rexine seats. I sat up in front with Dejonge, watching how he drove.

At Beauvais we went to the airport bar for a celebratory drink, and everyone came out, emerging from offices and airplanes: the customs, the police, the administration, the ground hostesses and spare bus drivers on their way to Paris. Dejonge loaded them aboard and drove them several times around the car park, the bell ringing and the hooter hooting, and we held our drinks aloft like a wedding party.

Then it was serious. Dejonge drove Bernard and me out to an old fighter airfield that had been used by the Luftwaffe during the war, and there we took it in turns to drive up and down for an hour or so. We had to be ready; the following morning it was Dieppe or bust.

As it turned out the journey from Beauvais and on into Normandy was a pleasure. We sailed high above the hedges, the roads were deserted, the sun shone and the blackbirds sang. People waved and called to us as we coasted through a dozen towns and villages – Troissereux, Songeons, St-Samson-la-Poterie, Gaillefontaine, Neufchâtel-en-Bray and Arques-la-Bataille.

But that wasn't it.

On our way across London I drove the bus into Battersea, to the street where Bernard and I had grown up together and where my mother still lived – Altenburg Gardens on Lavender Hill. I parked the bus outside my mother's flat, and ran up the stairs, full of excitement. I dragged my mother to the window: 'Look, Mum, a bus from Paris.'

'That's nice,' she said.

When Bernard and I were about to leave, my mother put on her coat and slipped her shopping bag over her arm.

'I've got some things to get,' she said, 'down the Junction.' It was maybe a ten-minute walk for her.

'We'll give you a lift in the bus,' I said.

She didn't bat an eyelid, but then she never did. Born in 1905, the eldest of ten, she'd seen Zeppelins fly, been a bookie's runner for her father who'd been badly wounded at Loos and then died of those wounds, thrown buckets of sand on incendiary bombs in the Second World War, given birth to five children and brought them up on her own, and had been prosecuted for shop-lifting, trying to feed us when times got hard.

And so, the happiest son in the world, I drove her down Lavender Hill to Clapham Junction in the Paris bus – her standing on the platform at the back, leaning out to get the air. I pulled up at the bus stop outside the Falcon where my uncles used to drink pints of Bass and get into fights. I watched in the rearview mirror as she stepped down into the road, stared at as she did so by the people waiting in the bus queue for an ordinary bus, and by the white faces at the windows of the public house. She glanced over her shoulder at me, smiled quietly to herself and then disappeared into the crowd, off to Leighton's the butchers to get a lamb chop for her supper.

I was still working as a travel guide when I became marooned in Paris in May, 1968. It was *les événements* that did it – the student revolt that led to a general strike. It began slowly – small demonstrations in the faculties – but then the unrest spread to universities across the country and became violent. Around the Sorbonne the heavy mob – the CRS – took over the streets in that menacing way they have, just waiting for an excuse to wield a truncheon and split a skull.

It seemed like fun to begin with, something interesting to point out to my clients through the windows of the coach. 'Look, there's the CRS . . . there's the Sorbonne.' But all too soon the fighting began and the barricades grew higher. Trees were felled, cars were set on fire and the roads were dug up and mined for cobblestones – dangerous projectiles. Now the CRS really got going: they attacked indiscriminately, men and women, demonstrators or passers-by, it didn't matter, and by decree, the faculties were closed.

The travel companies continued doing tours on the right bank, but even that became impossible as the strike spread. In no time at all there were no buses, no trains, no planes and no cross-channel ferries – I was stranded with a last contingent of tourists, and there was only one escape route. I had to take my bus across northern France and into Belgium, shipping my clients out from Ostend.

It was, in all honesty, an easy run, but when I stood on that Belgian quayside at last and thought about going home I found I couldn't. I would have felt like a deserter. 'Bliss was it in that dawn to be alive, but to be young was very heaven.' I hurried back: the air of Paris was too intoxicating to miss, a cocktail of champagne and tear-gas, one breath and you were tipsy with it. While I had been away the students had occupied the Sorbonne, the Odéon and most faculty buildings. They gave their own lectures, directed traffic, ran the commissariat and covered corridors and walls with superb graffiti: *L'imagination au pouvoir; Exagérer, c'est commencer d'inventer; Sous les pavés, la plage; Plus je fais l'amour, plus j'ai envie de faire la Révolution.*

I threw myself into the fray and played a small part on the fringes of one or two battles. I sat in lecture rooms and listened to speeches and debates. There were endless improvized dinners, the talk going on for hours. It was amazing – the tension, the adrenalin. Everything under the stars was possible.

I forget what night it was, but the CRS were attacking the great barricade in the rue Gay Lussac. I'd had enough and was trying to make my way to the friend's room where I slept on the floor, somewhere beyond the place Monge. The air was thick with gas and cries of fear and anger. A band of the CRS blocked off one end of a side street just as I entered it. I turned to retreat; more policemen coming towards me.

I attempted to merge into the shadows but I had been seen. I heard a shout. I was easy meat. I ducked into a deep doorway. Then there were footsteps, running. I was in for a serious beating; a foreigner sticking his nose in where it wasn't wanted.

Then the door behind me opened. A girl's voice said, '*Suis-moi.*'

We were all *tu* and *toi* in those days. It was a tiny room at the top of the house. A narrow bed, a Che Guevara poster on the wall. She had a face that I have always remembered as medieval: oval, Mediterranean skin, quiet eyes, and straight black hair.

She opened a bottle of red wine and we made an omelette. Her name was Kati and she found it amusing that I was English. The battle raged in the streets below, but we stayed where we were and after a while it seemed perfectly natural to go to bed, and we did.

She got up, naked, in the morning, and brought me coffee. I watched her move about the room, gathering her up for the future, remembering the things we had said. It was with Kati that, for the first time, I met that special texture of the flesh – a muscular glee that carried with it an ironic sense of disdain behind the physical enjoyment. I have never forgotten her. It is her body that I find beneath my fingers every time I dream myself awake, with her black hair and her breath as wholesome as witch-hazel.

'*Pourquoi?*' I asked her as I left, wondering why she had taken me into her bed. Her answer was perfect for that time, that place – so much so that later that day I borrowed a paint-pot and added her words to the hundreds of others that were scrawled on the walls of Paris: '*Il n'y a pas de pourquoi.*'

14

1969

Bordeaux Wines and Nights with Rapunzel

It was the time of the wine harvest and I was ordered to the Bordelais and put in charge of three buses, two tour guides and three drivers. My job was to show tourists around the vineyards and taste famous wines at every opportunity. I was lucky; I did it for three seasons and during that time I visited most of the major châteaux: Haut Brion, Léoville-Barton, Latour, Margaux, Cheval Blanc, Coutet, Yquem, and even Château Rothschild, where I was once shown round the museum by the Baron himself.

I worked with a Bordeaux coach driver called André (he had wide nostrils and I called him *Dédé la Narine*). He was quiet and gentle and had a tendency to disappear from time to time with the girls who frequented the streets at the back of the big hotels. Because he and I worked well together we were always allocated any group that was a little out of the ordinary – the difficult ones, the specials.

Neither of us had much time for the people who came in those groups; they considered themselves a cut above the rest of us, were arrogant and, worst of all, never tipped. One such group, publicans to a man and woman, was sent out to me by Charrington's brewery. They were loud, bad-mannered and vulgar, yet in spite of their coarseness a slap-up dinner had been arranged for them in the dining-room of the Château Batailley. The orders from London were straightforward: take them to the château, eat with them, be charming and then return them to the hotel. Dédé hated these evenings; they put him in a bad mood and were unpaid but, more to the point, they prevented him spending his free time with the ladies of the town.

It was dark by the time we drove the coach up to the front of the château and disembarked the clients. The building was out of a fairy-tale, with golden lights gleaming through the windows and a sweep of steps rising to the main door. The leader of the publicans led me to one side and, smirking like a gigolo, informed me that he had pulled certain strings to make sure that I could dine on top table with him. It was, he said, a great honour. As for Dédé, he would have to eat in the kitchen, with the staff.

I did a berserker. 'I'll eat in the kitchen too,' I said, and stormed off . . . but I stormed off to one of the best meals I've ever had.

The meal had been prepared by outside caterers – *les traiteurs*. I can't remember the menu but the *ambiance* was superb, a kind of medieval feast, all movement and joy, hard work and sweat, with odours from heaven.

The kitchen was a makeshift area set somewhere at the back of the château, behind the dining-room. There was a chef de cuisine and his mercenaries, pots and pans clanging, steam, the clatter of plates, and voices calling to each other, both in laughter and in anger.

Dédé and I were led to a tempestuous corner of the place and made to sit on upturned wine crates behind a trestle table. The waitresses – there were a half dozen of them – were fine flaunting girls with swirling skirts, their faces flushed with the heat, their eyes full of glances.

There was enough food to feed France, and Dédé and I had great platters to choose from before they were carried out, shoulder high, to the dining hall. And no small talk to put up with, no polite conversation to weave in and out of endless inanities. Best of all, the great wines of the Médoc were placed before us, whole bottles, without us being obliged to wait for a mean-spirited sommelier in white gloves to serve us, sneering over our shoulders. Not a bit of it: we poured each vintage so that it splashed into great goblets, and quaffed it down. Who cared about the king's ransom it cost – we weren't paying.

Slowly the meal drew to its end. There was no rush, it would be a long wait before the publicans were ready to climb into the coach and return to the hotel. I sat on the balcony and sipped a 40-year-old brandy. Dédé, as I knew he would, had disappeared into the dark with a waitress. I leant back in my chair and began to count the stars.

When we got back to the hotel and Dédé had parked the bus we took a night-cap together. When the last client was out of earshot Dédé let out a great sigh.

'They may not tip,' he said, 'but that wasn't a bad evening's work after all. I've got two crates of Batailley for us in the luggage compartment . . . one each . . . must be worth a fortune.'

I looked at him amazed, though I shouldn't have been. I had worked with French drivers enough.

Dédé explained. 'That little waitress with the blonde frizzy hair, and the . . . you know, the good figure . . . she took a shine to me, in the back of the bus. She didn't like our group either . . . so she showed me where they kept the wine. The rest was simple . . . and don't worry – the publicans will be charged for it.'

We hadn't finished with the publicans or they with us. There were more visits to be got through: St Emilion, the Graves, the Sauternes and a day trip to Cognac that was never easy.

We drove north via Blaye, and a town called Jonzac. There we stopped to try the local aperitif, a mixture of grape juice and cognac called Pineau de Charentes. It was a drink which was all innocence on the surface, but crept up on the unwary in the most treacherous manner. The publicans drank it copiously.

In Cognac itself we ate at an excellent restaurant, and the wine stained the lips and teeth of us all. Then Dédé and I gathered our charges together and herded them into Hennessy's distillery, where we spent an hour and a half wandering through gloomy warehouses, passing by row after row of oaken barrels. At the end of the technical visit, we were ushered into a large reception room where white coated waiters, looking like psychiatrists, invited the publicans to a tasting: cognac from every stage: white and raw, three years old, ten, then twenty.

My clients, and their wives, were greedy. How could they be otherwise – they were on holiday and the drinks were free. What they hadn't remembered was that brandy evaporates in great quantities as it ages in the barrel, and the demon spirit of it hangs in the air.*

An hour and a half in a cognac warehouse is enough to make all but the hardiest as drunk as lords; just inhaling does the trick. Then one drink in the reception room and the publicans were out of control; two and their health was seriously impaired. While they drank Dédé walked down the bus and laid sick bags ready on every seat.

Dédé was a man who bore a grudge; beware squalls if he took a dislike to you. On the way back to Bordeaux he lurched around every corner he could, and the coach swayed like an old lugger. Dédé knew he would have to hose out the bus the next day; but he knew it would be worth it, just to hear the publicans retching, just to see their pale faces and to gloat when they suffered, some twelve hours later, the torture of their hangovers.

I caught the group leader early in the morning, when he was at his most tender, sitting behind a breakfast he couldn't eat, packed and ready for the airport, the thought of flying tingeing his face with verdigris.

'I'll have to make a report,' I began, 'to your office . . . about the

---

*Cognac evaporates steadily throughout the ageing process and the barrels are topped up to keep them full. The amount that disappears every year in this way is calculated at something like 6 million litres. Those in the trade have a name that compensates for the sadness of such a distressing loss; they call it *la part des anges* – the angels' share.

state of the bus . . . it was disgusting . . . the driver's been up since
five this morning cleaning it out . . . not a pleasant job.'

The man groaned. 'A quid each from everybody would do it,' I
said. He paid up like a good'n – fifty quid on the nail. Dédé and I
split it between us.

The last day of the Bordeaux wine season ran, without a break, into
another tour – an up-market autumn jaunt that followed the
Dordogne river from one end of its course to the other: Bordeaux
– Rocamadour – Clermont Ferrand and then back again, one trip
every week for five weeks. Once again we were three travel guides
and three drivers – only this time the coaches were full of married
women taking a second holiday, but without their husbands. I
couldn't keep a straight face – the fox was in the chicken house, and
not only that, he ate in the best restaurants and he drank exquisite
wines.

Our clients for the second Dordogne trip arrived at Bordeaux
airport. As they emerged from customs the woman looked me
over and I knew in that second what was going to happen –
though it was she and not I who had made the decision.
Unfortunately her mother, the Black Widow, knew what I knew
and from that moment refused to let her daughter out of her sight.

They could not have been more dissimilar: the one dressed
totally in black, wearing a face of poison and distrust, the other, a
Rapunzel, willowy, blue eyes like dinner plates, slightly taller than
me – and I'm six foot – hair hanging down her back, hips of
elegance, neatly turned ankles and hands with fingers made for
stroking. She was a woman of sophistication married to a dull man
back in Cheshire, and there were two children. Passion glowed
through every pore of her skin.

The first day's journey took us from Bordeaux to Rocamadour,
and along the way and over lunch I discussed the situation with
Claude, my new coach driver. He was a handsome little brute,
blessed with an open, honest face that concealed a character of
great cunning and deviousness. He was a talented water-colourist

and a Casanova when it came to charming clients into his bed, though only with my help – his English was non-existent.

'*Tu peux m'embobiner la vieille,*' I suggested. 'Just keep the mother talking for an hour or two.'

Claude nearly drove off the road: he would have done a lot for me – but the Black Widow!

'Come on, Claude, she won't let the daughter out of her sight . . . we could do one of our special Rocamadour nights.'

Claude wasn't keen but he owed me a favour. The previous trip I'd swapped my room with his so that he could have the four-poster, and I'd spent hours translating and whispering his carnal desires into the ears of a dark beauty from Portsmouth.

Every time we arrived in Rocamadour we fell in love with it; it bubbled. Because it was the mid-point in our tour we spent more days there than anywhere else – on the way up and on the way down – and we'd farm out our laundry to the chambermaids know-ing that we'd find it pressed and folded on our beds whenever we needed it. We patronized three hotels and ate in them by turn, and organized black excursions to the underground river of Padirac and the ancient town of Martel. We pulled in lots of money and we spent it carelessly.

It is of course true that Rocamadour is designed for tourists – most of it is nineteenth-century reconstruction – but it does have a real allure, perched as it is on the rim of a cliff face. And we always timed our arrival to coincide with nightfall, stopping the coaches and getting everyone out so our clients could see the lights of the place twinkling all golden across a dark and deep valley.

There's not much to it; one narrow street, the souvenir shops and a few small hotels. Ours – le Beau Site – had a restaurant on the very edge of the chasm, and there, at the end of long and busy days, we used to install ourselves, the street lights floating like will-o'-the-wisps, the aperitifs poured, the dinner cooking and the Cahors breathing.

The owner of the hotel was a man of understanding and a good friend of mine. He knew about Rocamadour nights. He saw

Rapunzel arrive and, on his own initiative, he set up a table for a select dozen of us, and let me arrange the seating. I chose the jolliest of my clients to sit with me; I placed the Black Widow next to Claude and I sat next to Rapunzel. Gradually the warm night closed in; the moon came up and showed us the outlines of the valley below. The hors d'oeuvres were beautifully laid out, the *canard à l'orange* was perfection, and the sommelier, who was in on the plot, gave free rein to his imagination. Claude himself was airborne; assiduously attentive, he smiled all evening like a bar of expensive soap. And as he worked at his task, so the gleam of lust in the Black Widow's eyes began to reflect the moonlight that glinted in her glass.

After the champagne Claude took her arm and set off on a gentle stroll up the town. She hadn't by any means forgotten her daughter, or me, and she ordered us to follow closely, turning her head every now and then to make sure that we were. But Claude was a genius that night; he philandered for France and though the Black Widow understood not a word of it she surely must have heard the lilting music of his seduction. She turned her head less and less often, and Rapunzel and I dropped back into the shadows, until at last we ran for it and fled to the voluptuous and boundless countryside of my four-poster bed.

It must have been about three in the morning when she left me, shoes in one hand, underwear in the other, creeping along the corridor to the room she shared with her mother, both of us praying that the Black Widow would be fast asleep. We needn't have worried. At breakfast I took my coffee to Rapunzel's table.

'It was all right,' she said. 'Mother wasn't even there . . . she came in after me . . . Would you believe it, she says she's going out with Claude again tonight.'

Claude didn't appear until the evening aperitif, looking severely damaged, his eyes squinting, his face blotchy.

'You owe me,' he said, after the first *pastis*. 'That woman tore me to ribbons . . . *quelle tigresse* . . . Never again, never, never.'

I ordered another drink. 'Okay, I owe you, what do you want?'

He'd worked it out in advance. 'All the tips and percentages from this trip, and the four-poster bed for the rest of the season.'

I agreed without hesitation. I'd got off lightly. After all, he didn't know that Rapunzel and I had more plans for that very night. Nor did he know that the Black Widow had been waiting all day for him to reappear, and there would be no gainsaying her.

'That damn woman's fallen in love with me.' Claude was horror-struck.

'I know,' I said, 'they do it on purpose.'

Not far from the Cingle de Trémolat, about 35 miles south of the Dordogne, I drove into the *bastide* of Monflanquin one late after-noon, searching for a restaurant. The town looked like a film set for Cyrano de Bergerac, and I dawdled there three days. The arcades of the central square were floodlit and the evening stillness was broken only by good sounds: a *'Bonsoir'* from a window and a pair of shutters rasping on dry hinges as they were closed until dawn.

My intention had been to continue my journey the next morn-ing, Sunday, but the bells of St André drew me to mass. The offici-ating priest was tall and imposing in a cream robe, and below the shining dome of his head were tufts of white hair protruding above each ear.

A woman led the choir but the priest made sure she did not get too far ahead, pursuing her with a voice rich in wet gravel, diving in and out of the music like a seal hunting, mouthing his notes as if they had been marinated in Marsala. His gestures too were magnif-icent, his hands moving in the air like caresses. Here was a man who sang in the bath; he dwelt on melody, making it luxurious and plum-coloured.

At the elevation there was quiet and the church bells rang out over the town to castigate the irreligious. As the worshippers moved forward to take communion I stole away unnoticed.

Down the hill, au Bar le Rugby, Chez Gerard, there was a differ-ent congregation. Gerard had scant hair, a kind face and honest eyes. He served drinks rapidly, told jokes and took bets in a tiny office in a corner while his customers played *belote* or read the racing papers.

'But you can't leave without seeing the market,' Gerard insisted. 'This is a market that has been held every week since 1256, and besides you must eat at my house tonight. I make the best *omelette aux cèpes* in the Lot-et-Garonne ... and there are three bottles of Pomerol to go with it.' I was persuaded to postpone my departure.

On market day I rose early. The bright-hued awnings were already crowding across the square and a cool wind cut through the arcades. As I gave him a *Bonjour,* Roger the greengrocer pulled two horse chestnuts from his pocket. They were polished to a mahogany shine by years of carrying and touching, and they glowed with a far-away light. He held them up for my inspection.

'It can get very draughty in the arcades,' he said. 'Refreshing in summer, yes, but the winter! These chestnuts stop all that. I always carry them; they beat any other cure for rheumatism that I know of, and piles too – they never fail.'

That day the market took its time, but then a market that has been around for more than 700 years has no need to bustle or hurry. Such a gathering of human beings is more an excuse for continuing the previous week's conversation than anything else.

From the top of the square came the sound of a jazz singer and a quartet making music for their lunch on the terrace of a café – the Grappe de Raisin. I took a seat near them and ordered a *vin blanc sec,* then I leant back in my chair and stretched my legs.

I was soon joined by Jo-jo, an 81-year-old regular from Chez Gerard – a drinker of red wine. His glass was brought to the table and we talked of the war – the Hundred Years' War – with Jo-jo discussing the centuries as if they were but a short part of his own curriculum vitae.

'Lots of blue eyes and fair hair in Aquitaine because of that war,' he said. 'Those English soldiers were just like everyone else, when they made war they made love at the same time.'

He finished his drink to mark this sentiment and hauled himself upright so that we could cross the road to the market together, ancient enemies, arm in arm.

When we parted he shook my hand and tilted his head at me. 'We don't mind you English coming back,' he said, 'just as long as you don't take the wine away again – the Bordeaux and the Bergerac, that's ours.'

There was a pause while I smiled, then he said, 'By the way, I thought you were supposed to be leaving . . . you're not making much of a job of it, are you . . . ?'

The *bastide* of Monflanquin lies in Hundred Years' War territory, and for long periods was an English possession; indeed in the north-eastern corner of the square stands the house where the Black Prince, much cherished by the *Monflanquinois*, lived when he was Edward III's Sénéschal of Aquitaine.

Like most *bastides* in south-west France, Monflanquin was developed as an unfortified new town in which authority could group and perhaps control an increasing population, mainly for the purposes of taxation and good order. In the twelfth and thirteenth centuries runaway serfs, outlaws and those who were just footloose tended to gather together in these areas because they were under the protection of churches or convents.

The most powerful of local lords, including the kings of England, took advantage of these new towns to increase their power, and because they also marked the frontier between the English and French dominions, and as the Hundred Years' War progressed, both sides fortified them and made them into strongholds.

They were generally designed to the same plan: a central square with strong arcades on four sides to shelter troops, and also to house shops and the overflow from the market. There was also a covered market hall, and above it a large room for meetings of the town council.

The town plan was inspired by the design of the Roman camp, with streets and alleys cutting across each other at right angles. It was four sided, with ramparts and a fortified church to take the place of a redoubt or keep.

It is calculated that there are some 300 *bastides* in France.

15

1970

Across the Cévennes with Robert Louis Stevenson

Towards the end of August 1878 Robert Louis Stevenson stepped from a stagecoach in the little French town of le Monastier-sur-Gazeille. He was twenty-eight and had published nothing more than a few literary essays and one book, *An Inland Voyage*, a slight thing about a canoe trip on the River Oise.

He had come to this part of France to undertake another journey – across the Cévennes with Modestine the donkey as his companion, but why he chose le Monastier as a starting point is difficult to understand. Even the locals were puzzled: 'Why come to le Monastier?' they asked, 'when you could go anywhere?'

His description of the countryside tells us that the expedition he'd planned was dangerous, especially in view of the season. He didn't leave le Monastier until the 20th of September and his route would take him over high ground – between 3,000 and 6,000 feet – where it would be cold at that time of the year.

The *Monastiens* thought him mad. 'A traveller of my sort was a thing hitherto unheard of in the district. I was looked upon with contempt, like a man who should project a journey to the moon . . .'

In the hills there were ghosts, and wolves and bandits. People still disappeared in the forests, swallowed up by the Beast of Gevaudan. Nobody seemed to know exactly what the beast was, probably a large wolf; what was known was that it roamed the Cévennes quite freely and lived on a diet of people.

Stevenson had been told about it, with relish. 'For this was the land of the ever-memorable beast, the Napoleon Bonaparte of wolves. What a career was his. He ate women and children and shepherdesses celebrated for their beauty.' Many of the local peasants believed that Stevenson would be lucky to escape with his life. Even if he avoided the jaws of the beast, were there not strange people living in those outlandish farms and roadside inns? Had he not heard the story of the Auberge Rouge, where travellers stopped for rest and refreshment only to disappear with their purses, never to be seen again, save at meal-times, served roasted and garnished with garlic?

None of this dismayed Stevenson. 'The great affair is to move,' he wrote, 'to feel the needs and hitches of our life more nearly; to come down off this feather-bed of civilization, and find the globe granite underfoot and strewn with cutting flints . . .'

It was evening in le Monastier and across the valley the hills were smoking with cloud, remembering that they had once been volcanoes. I walked across a courtyard and towards the house with a tower on it, looking for Monsieur Pradier, the president of the *Syndicat d'Initiative*. 'He's too busy,' said Madame, angry. 'He's supposed to be running a garage . . . how do you expect him to make a living?'

Monsieur Pradier smiled like a bishop and took me into a large room built around a fireplace big enough to hold a double bed. There were books and files everywhere, in ranks, like armies. We sat down at a table covered with letters and cuttings.

He opened the visitors' book. 'Do you have a donkey?'

'No,' I said, 'a mountain bike.'

Monsieur Pradier turned the pages. 'There have been lots of

people on the Stevenson trail . . . there was a TV crew once. There are a couple of donkeys every year, of course, in August mainly. One day we'll have a statue in the square, Stevenson and Modestine . . . you'll see.'

Madame appeared with aperitifs and shrugged her shoulders like one who had given up the struggle a long while ago. 'Some *garagiste!*'

I set off to follow the route the following morning, but did not get far. The old road, a mule track in Stevenson's day, drops steeply from the town, opposite the church, and crosses the River Gazeille at the bottom of the valley, then rises on the far side in the direction of the next village, Courmarcès, and then on to St-Martin-de-Fugères.

At Courmarcès a man in his fifties, his silver hair cropped close, sat at a table outside his house, in the shadow of a spreading vine. He invited me to sit with him for a while and poured the *pastis*. 'My name is Auguste,' he said, 'and you have come from le Monastier?'

'I stayed at the Hotel Fayolle . . . .'

Auguste looked pleased. 'I was at school with Madame Fayolle . . . we all loved her.' His eyes went as cloudy as his drink. 'When she danced she was as light as her own petticoat.'

There were only ten inhabitants in Courmarcés and, attracted by the unusual sound of voices, two of them, old men leaning on sticks, appeared from their houses and joined us at the table. Their glasses were filled.

Aperitif time became lunchtime and I was invited to pool my food with theirs; a bottle of wine appeared, followed by another. Then lunchtime became the afternoon, and the sun began to sink and the conversation continued. Soon it was aperitif time once more. Eventually, when dusk began to creep down the hillside, I remounted my mountain bike and headed back to le Monastier, back to the Hotel Fayolle. I had covered maybe 6 miles that day, in a complete circle. Stevenson, a man who liked late starts, would have been proud of me.

Auguste shook my hand as I left. 'When you see Madame

Fayolle,' he said, 'make sure you tell her that Auguste still loves her . . . all she has to do is leave her husband.' And then with a smile, 'I suppose I'll see you for the aperitif tomorrow, it's not easy to get away from le Monastier.'

The next day I passed through Courmarcès and saw no one. The hens were warming themselves deep in the dust of the road, and barn doors hung open, the cows were distant in the pastures. The few houses straggled away from each other, their volcanic stone coloured grey, brown and black. The ground was soft and quiet with dried dung and broken straw. Nothing moved anywhere except for a pair of sparrow hawks, lazing in the sky.

But there was movement at *Fugères*, lots of it. Half a dozen donkeys had escaped from their field and an elegant woman of sixty or so, pearls at her neck, her grey hair neatly arranged on the top of her head, was trying to recapture them. Madame du Lac de Fugères had bright eyes, round apple cheeks and a fine aristocratic bearing, nicely touched with scattiness and plenty of mischievous energy. Together we rounded up the donkeys and I mended the fence.

'Well,' she said, 'it's reassuring to meet someone like yourself with a *de* in the name. My son writes his as one word now, doesn't want to offend people, he says . . . he makes Dulac sound like a tin of paint. The du Lacs have been here for centuries . . . Lancelot, you know, same family. He came here, from Brittany.'

I looked blank.

'Sir Lancelot of the Lake . . . du Lac . . . King Arthur . . . Guinevere . . . you should know all about them, being English . . . By the way, my son hires out his donkeys. He has about twelve of them . . . I don't live here any more.'

I followed her through a gated archway high enough to keep the rain off a stagecoach. We passed a covered wagon and a gypsy cart.

'He made those, he takes groups out across the hills. Some do the Stevenson trail, but most just hire a donkey to carry their tent and go off on their own, anywhere they fancy.'

We sat in the high vaulted kitchen for a while, a long dark room of stone where motes of dust hung motionless in the light from the door. There was a forest of furniture surrounding us, each piece abandoned rather than placed, and buried under a cascade of ancient paraphernalia, as if Sir Lancelot had left his belongings to hand so that he might return for them at any moment.

At the end of the afternoon Madame du Lac settled into her car for the drive home. 'My son needs a wife to help him,' she said, 'an English one would do, they're supposed to be sensible.' Then she engaged first gear and sped away, shouting as she went: 'Come and see me for lunch, when you've finished your journey . . . Mende, everyone knows me, don't forget.' And in the next second she was gone, in an explosion of noise and smoke, as magical as Merlin.

After two unpleasant nights, one in the open, Stevenson broke his journey at the Monastery of Notre Dame des Neiges. In the same place I enquired if I too might rest, but my shrift was short. I was not a serious religious person. I was directed instead to the video show and the gleaming souvenir shop where nuns on holiday chose between cuddly toys and three-dimensional pictures of the Last Supper.

There was also a bar, thirty paces long, with Brother Jean in his brown habit and blue apron, selling the monastery's own wine, a brew made from imported grapes. I bought a bottle of the red and drank it at dinner that night, in a rough and ready *gîte d'étape* on the banks of the River Allier, sharing a kitchen with a couple of girls who were riding their horses, by way of the long, high line of hill-tops, from Alès to the Vosges. As we sat chatting and drinking, my regrets for the monastery were few – like Stevenson, 'I blessed God that I was free to wander, free to hope and free to love.'

In the morning I went on along the valley of the Chassezac, and the sound of the river faded as I slowly struggled up the 4,500 feet of the Montagne du Goulet, where Stevenson had gone. I saw no one. Only the dog that lay by the three houses of the hamlet of Estampes raised its head as I passed, too indolent to bark. Now and then the woods fell back from the road to reveal the pastures below, bright and fresh, yellow and green, lying in curves where the river curved. When the woods came close the pines imprisoned the gloom like the pillars of a crypt, and only the rowan and the beech were cheerful.

On the mountain's summit I stretched on the grass and took time over my picnic lunch; then I put on warmer clothing and poured a libation in recognition of Stevenson's grit. All along the horizon to the south Mont Lozère lay like another continent. There was an awful lot of it to climb.

The village of Bleymard lies between the two mountains. I took a drink there and at three o'clock in the afternoon I pushed my bike across a bridge and began my ascent. It was a mistake; I had left it too late. The evening advanced, hastening like evil towards me. The storm that had been loafing around the hills all day now declared itself and went for the summit as I did.

When I arrived on that wilderness beyond 5,000 feet there was no space for me between the black turf and the monstrous clouds. In a moment the day became night, the spattering became rain, and the rain became a hail that was hurled into my face like hard coin. Then the thunder rolled over me.

Never in my life have I been so close to lightning. It came red out of the dark squalls, splitting the sky asunder with a sound like dry timber tearing. The smell of it was brimstone; my pride vanished on the wind like a rag and I prayed to be back at the monastery, warm and holy, for here I was, the highest thing in the world, riding into a freezing tempest and sitting astride the only conductor of electricity within a radius of 20 miles, an open invitation to hundreds of thousands of volts to rampage through my body. The moment I saw a ditch I abandoned my bike and hid in the ground until the worst was over.

On the southern side the sky lightened and the rain became softer. As far as the eye could see were ragged peat bogs, all a fearful and decaying brown and strewn with ungainly boulders, scattered here by a glacier that had once tried to scour the landscape clean. Now the ground lay under so much water that the streams themselves were submerged, and a rotting stench rose as a vapour in this false lull of the storm.

I saw only one habitation, deserted, a herdsman's hut, built in earth with slabs of schist for roof stone. Nothing stirred on these long slopes except where the skirts and tatters of the mist were hunted through the black outcrops of rock, and where a buzzard fought upwind through the gale. Then, as I moved on, dirt-coloured cattle surged up out of sunken culverts by the road and barred my way, their horns wicked, their eyes wild.

Rapidly now I advanced into the gloom of the valley and dropped towards the town of Pont de Montvert, 'of bloody memory'. It was just the weather for it, for in this place, during the religious troubles of the seventeenth century, the uprising of the Camisards had begun with the slaying of François du Chayla, persecutor of the Protestants. 'One by one . . . the Camisards had stabbed him; "This," they said, "is for my father broken on the wheel. This for my brother in the galleys. That for my sister violated and my mother imprisoned in your cursed convents." Each gave his blow and his reason; then all kneeled and sang psalms around the body till dawn. When it was over they filed away . . . leaving du Chayla's body pierced with two-and-fifty wounds.'

Dreadful persecutions were ordered: 'Dead or Catholic' was the cry. A terrible war began, producing, from among the ranks of the peasant Camisards, born strategists and wily generals. High in the mountains, where the paths were uncharted and dangerous to the soldiers of Louis XIV, the simple peasants performed wonders with night attacks and ambuscades. They were fearless and difficult to pin down – they could band and disband like starlings in flight. For years small guerrilla forces managed to pin down the Sun King's dragoons, but there was only one outcome possible. The villages that supported the insurgents, 460 of them, were razed to the ground and their men put to the sword or sent to the galleys. As for the women, they were imprisoned in the vilest dungeons until death should release them.

I came down the dark side of the mountain and arrived in Pont de Montvert, looking down into the garden where François du Chayla had been slaughtered. Only the gutters, overflowing with rain, gleamed in the yellow light that escaped from the edges of closed doors and shuttered windows.

I was shivering with cold and at the first hotel I came to I took three hot baths, a five-course meal and a bottle of Côtes du Tarn. That night, while all my clothes steamed in the boiler room, I lay safe in clean sheets and listened to the storm still raging on the mountain. All around me the lightning sought for a home, flickering – in the lamps, along the cables, across the roofs and through the branches of the trees.

'You were lucky,' the *patron* of the hotel had told me over dinner, 'last time we had a storm like that a man's car broke down and he tried to phone . . . there was a phone box on the road up there . . . A thunder-bolt struck it . . . there wasn't much left of your man after that . . . you and that bike could have fried . . .'

At Cassagnas I took a path that dropped down from the road to the level of the river and sat under the acacias with Madame Dumas who lives in the Café de la Gare, there where now there is no railway, only a bridge and a dark creek with golden leaves falling on to it. From her I heard the question that Stevenson must have heard so often: 'Protestant or Catholic?'

'A little of neither,' I said, for I was in real Camisard country, the Cévennes of the Cévennes.

'Hundreds of Protestants were tortured and killed in the forest,' said Madame, 'you can feel it. And during the last war there were runaways from the German factories hiding here, young people. They lived in the caves where the Camisards had hidden their storehouses, but they didn't live in them for long, they were too frightened . . . you see, they could sense that the Camisards were still there.'

I left her and followed the path upwards on the opposite slope, through woods of beech, ash and birch, walnut and wild cherry, poplar and chestnut. Under the branches the hooligan magpies were romping, but that was the only sound. On the windy crest I shared provisions with a walker who had tramped that day over the

Montagne du Bouges. I broke out the bottle of wine I had purchased from Madame Dumas.

'You know,' said the hiker, 'I thought that the old France of lonely tracks, chance meetings, cows in the middle of the road, all that, I thought it had disappeared altogether.' He raised his tin cup full of my wine and gestured northwards. 'But it hasn't.'

It was on the meridional side of this great watershed that Stevenson 'heard the voice of a woman singing some sad, old, endless ballad . . . about love and a *bel amoureux'*. The sadness of that unknown voice still lingers over the landscape and makes it, even now, a lonely place.

I went down into it, skimming without effort on my mountain bike, through an afternoon light that lay like a pale dust over everything. There weren't many farms and those I saw seemed abandoned, though each one had small terraced fields before and behind, every strip linked to the next by double flights of stone steps, as regular and formal as a château garden, but no farmers now and no crops growing, only tough grass for goats.

It was all downhill, many long miles of it, to St-Jean-du-Gard where Stevenson had sold his donkey, and it was a fine way to finish a fine journey – a Mediterranean evening, all golden, with gravity urging me forward. My spirits soared as I spun along and, like the woman Stevenson had once heard, I also sang, but out of joy, real joy, for if travelling doesn't make you sing sometimes, what good is it?

16

1972
Two Philosophers and Me

It was a morning that didn't know whether it was mist or rain. I went through an archway, and there was Montaigne's tower, something I had wanted to see since first reading his essays, lying in bed at Rascas.

I had come into a large courtyard that stood empty. There was a small office let into the wall, locked. Back through the archway I saw a young man wandering across the grass with a trug full of mushrooms in his hand.

'There's always mushrooms when it rains like this,' he said. 'Do you want a ticket for the tower? We'll wait a bit and see if anyone else comes. Why don't you walk along the terrace?'

I looked down on the landscape Montaigne himself used to contemplate. That morning the distance was half hidden in long lakes of transparent cloud, but all the more medieval for that: a wide valley, gentle hills, thick stands of trees and vines. I could see ploughed fields too.

At last the young man beckoned, took a huge key from his pocket and unlocked the door to the office. He went in, tore a ticket from the top of a thick pile and offered it to me. His hands were wet and grubby and a smear of mud appeared on the printed slip of paper. I am sure that Montaigne would have approved of the gardener and the curator being one and the same person. He smiled when I asked him about the difficulty of doing both jobs. 'Well,' he said, 'they are both culture of a kind.'

On the ground floor of the tower is Montaigne's chapel. On the first floor is the bedroom with a window and a niche in the thickness of the wall so that Montaigne could hear mass without going downstairs. The top floor, circular of course, like the others, was the library, the room Montaigne loved with all his heart – away from the noise of the farm and away from the attentions of his wife, who, legend says, was as tough as Xanthippe and lived in her own tower on the other side of the courtyard.

Nothing pleased Montaigne more than to lean back in his chair here and gaze around his literary domain, the apple of his eye. There were, in his day, five ranks of shelves covering the walls, the books laid out flat so that Montaigne could stroll from volume to volume and read the spines with ease. Above his head, written on beams and rafters were, and still are, words of wisdom taken from the Greek and Roman philosophers, and some extracts from Ecclesiastes.

I followed the young man back down the stone steps. He shoved the big key into his jeans and picked up his trug of mushrooms. The rain had stopped and the lakes of mist were sinking back into the earth. Nobody else was waiting to visit and the chateau was silent apart from the bombardment of horse chestnuts falling from high branches.

'Make sure you see the mosaics at Montcaret,' said the young man. 'There's more to the Bordelais than vineyards and wine châteaux you know.'

'It is wrong of women,' says Montaigne in his *Essay on the Imagination*, 'to receive us with pouting, querulous, and shrinking looks that quell us even as they kindle us.'

The daughter-in-law of Pythagoras said that a woman who goes to bed with a man ought to lay aside her modesty with her skirt, and put it on again with her petticoat . . . Married men, with time at their command, need not hurry, nor need they attempt the enterprise if they are not ready . . . Before possession is taken, one who suffers from the imagination should by sallies at different times make gentle essays and overtures without any strain or persistence, in order definitely to convince himself of his powers. Those who know their members to be obedient by nature need only take care to out-manoeuvre the imagination.

We have reason to remark the untractable liberties taken by this member, which intrudes so tiresomely when we do not require it and fails us so annoyingly when we need it most, imperiously pitting its authority against that of the will, and most proudly and obstinately refusing our solicitations both mental and manual . . . Be that as it may, nature . . . would have been quite justified in endowing our reproductive member with some special privileges, since it is the author of the sole immortal work of mortal man. For this reason Socrates held that procreation is a divine act, and love a desire for immortality as well as an immortal spirit.

Just beyond the limits of the Entre Deux Mers, across the Garonne where the wine region of the Graves has its frontier with the forests of les Landes, stands the château of another philosopher.

Charles de Secondat, Baron de Labrède and Montesquieu, was a man cast very much in the mould of Montaigne. He too wrote words of wisdom on the rafters, and like Montaigne, made his mark in the world, becoming a lawyer, president of the parliament of Bordeaux and wine exporter to the British. But he too, more than anything else, loved to return to his home and the study of his books.

The Château Labrède was built by Montesquieu's ancestors and is still owned by his descendants. It stands in 250 acres of parkland in the middle of a wide moat that is in reality a small lake. There is a watchtower and a *pigeonnier*, and across the moat a footbridge leads to the château. There are still 7,000 of Montesquieu's books in the library, and halfway up the right-hand side of the study fireplace is the worn stone where Montesquieu rested his foot when working, his manuscript on his knee.

I arrived mid-morning and discovered that the château did not open until the afternoon. I was annoyed at first, but then what is the point of visiting a philosopher if you cannot take his advice? I knew the saying of Montesquieu well enough and had underlined it in one of his books, though it was not written on my ceiling: 'There are few griefs,' he says, 'that an hour or two's reading cannot dispel.'

I made myself comfortable, stretching out on the grass, my back against a tree, and took out my book. What with that, the view of the château across the park, a bottle of Graves and some bread and saucisson, I was certain that I would be able to prove Montesquieu right – at least until lunchtime.

Not long after my arrival in the Bordelais I was invited to a wedding that was to be held in a small château which, like Montesquieu's, boasted a moat and an arched bridge. And there was more: extensive gardens with Greek statues hidden in the shrubbery, conservatories, honeymoon suites, private rooms, arbours and a large ornamental lake with wide steps down to it. An ideal place for celebrations.

I was staying for the week with friends in a village that lay about half a mile from the hotel. They had a house brimming with guests, some there for the wedding, and some to attend a party that had been got up to celebrate the publication of a book. It was going to be a jolly weekend, more particularly because the bridegroom was a Scot, and he, his best man and all his close friends, were to be dressed in kilts and little black jackets. Their sporrans swung at every step and daggers glinted in their socks. Oh my, but they were swanky.

Everything went well. The wedding ceremony was graceful; the meal was set in a long marquee and a string quartet played for us. The wine flowed and the speeches were mercifully short and entertainingly witty. Slowly the sun dropped down the hemisphere and the turrets of the château stood out against a navy blue sky, elegant with stars.

As the evening wore on the tables were cleared away, the marquee made ready for dancing and the wild Scots began performing their reels – whooping Caledonians at Hadrian's Wall. I soon found myself a comfortable corner and suborned a waitress into placing a bottle or two of St Julien under my chair, getting myself ready for some serious people-watching. Weddings, as everyone knows, are notoriously randy affairs: was there, I wondered, any action to be had?

In the event I didn't bother. Although the possessor, at that time, of a certain reputation, and although many beautiful and vivacious women were present, I had eaten and drunk too well that day. I remained quietly in my corner until I eventually felt the need for fresh air. It was time to take a stroll.

The night was exquisite. The air was warm, music floated over the purple lawns and a full moon floated in the ornamental lake. I made my way towards the water's edge, stepping god-like and tipsy in my evening dress, down the wide steps between the statues, and there, moored to an iron ring drifted a small rowing-boat.

How superb everything looked; how romantic, how velvety the breeze. Wouldn't it be wonderful to float across the lake under the moon, like a knight from an Arthurian legend? I knelt, a little unsteadily, on the steps and reached for the boat. It was a disaster; the mooring rope was far too long. As I leant forward the boat drifted away from me, my weight pushing it out, further into the lake. I was unable to get to my feet or to release my hold, so, as the boat left the land my body subsided into the lily pads. My evening dress, from patent leather shoes to crisp bow-tie, was soaked; even my head disappeared under the water.

I pulled myself onto dry land and skulked, in the shadows, across the château gardens and down to the village. I squelched up the back stairs of my friends' house, found my bedroom and changed into dry clothes. The swim had done me good; I felt refreshed and sober enough to return to the wedding. It was a bad idea.

During my absence the best man had misplaced his wife. I learnt later that she had disappeared about the same time I had left the marquee, and those separate exits had been spotted. Given my reputation that was enough. In the interim several clans of Scots had banded together, Glencoe forgotten, and were after me, claymores drawn. The grounds had been searched, so had the bedrooms, the shrubbery and the greenhouses – no trace of us had been found – and then I walked in, pink cheeked and in a change of clothes.

They had to pull the best man off me – none too hastily either. He hit me a couple of times and actually had his *skean-dhu* at my throat. That wasn't all. To satisfy their anger the Scots threw me back in the lake and left me to fend for myself. So for the second time that night I squelched through the village and back to my room looking for dry clothes.

The best man's wife? She had become even tipsier than her husband and was found the next morning, stoned out of her mind, fast asleep in a cupboard in the attic. I was innocent but no one believed me – despite all my protestations – especially not the sophisticated divorcée who was sleeping in the room next to mine.

'Ah Michel,' she said, 'you are wonderful . . . I'm going to take you to bed myself . . .' And she did, just as soon as she got me back to Paris.

After the disaster at the wedding perhaps it was just as well that my days as a tour guide were coming to an end. Two or three travel companies which operated in France had got together to make me an offer I couldn't refuse – a position as a kind of 'trouble-shooter', sorting out any problems that might arise with hotels and restaurants, and training new employees when necessary.

I didn't take too long over the decision. I knew that I would miss the camaraderie of the road – the coach drivers, the other tour guides, the restaurateurs – but the new job would give me the freedom to roam over the whole of France, almost at will, and there was still much I hadn't seen – the Canal des deux Mers for example, 300 miles from Bordeaux to Narbonne. I would bring my mountain bike over from England and cycle the whole length of the towpath. And there was something else. Before I took up my new duties I had a lorry trip to do, as a favour, with a man called Stewart. That was next.

17

1973

Terracotta Pots and Mediterranean Oysters

'There ought to be a good food guide to the greasy spoon caffs of Great Britain,' said Stewart in what was only the first of his many pearls of wisdom. I had arranged to meet him in the caff under the railway bridge opposite Battersea Park station, a caff where they served a builders' tea in which the spoon stood upright like Excalibur in its rock.

Stewart was five foot eight, stocky, about forty, with thinning hair, and he moved with a barely contained energy which showed in the way he spoke, like a machine gun: short and long bursts. Self-employed, Stewart had been hired by the flower and pot shop next door, owned by friends of mine, to haul terracotta from Aubagne near Marseille. He was taking me along to help with the loading and unloading; I was also meant to do some wheeling and dealing with the terracotta factory. He bit into his bacon butty and the brown sauce oozed out of the sides.

'I shan't be coming straight back. Some mates of mine have a house in Mèze, forty Ks on from Montpellier, and I always spend a couple of days there.'

Stewart was driving a ten tonner. 'I'm lucky this time,' he explained as we went for the M2. 'I'm not going out empty. I've got a load of furniture for this mad guy who lives in the hills . . . I think he's on the run . . .' He sucked his teeth when he finished speaking, but then I was to find out that he always did.

We came off at Calais into pouring rain and drove past the first of the many brown road signs telling us of the riches of France. 'The Field of the Cloth of Gold,' it said. Lifeless curtains of mist hung everywhere.

'It's where Henry VIII met François I,' I said. 'Each one trying to outdo the other; hundreds of courtiers and women, music. Henry VIII came off worst. His tent blew down and François knocked him off his horse in the jousting.'

'Henry always was a bit of a fart, wasn't he?' said Stewart and sucked his teeth again. The rain sprayed out from a thousand tyres and headlights flashed in the gloom as the brotherhood of lorry-drivers relayed messages to one another in the 'code of the road': 'beware coppers'; 'tacho inspection'; 'radar traps'; 'hitch-hiking hookers'.

'I first started driving part-time, now I love it. I was an actor for years. I got a lot of work . . . I even did a Yorkie commercial, leaning out the cab window and biting into the stuff . . . but acting died and driving gradually took over . . . now I wouldn't do anything else.'

At lunch the next day we came off the motorway at Vienne and on to the old Nationale Sept. There were half a dozen lorries parked outside a *restaurant routier* and we stopped beside them. 'If there's lorries,' said Stewart, 'there'll be good grub.'

Inside, Monsieur and Madame were behind the bar; the aperitif hour was noisy and the drivers raucous. In the restaurant the paper tablecloths were clean and crisp, and the litres of red, open, stood like sentinels in a straight line all the way down the room in a proper perspective. The smoke from black tobacco hung across the air in steady garlands, shifting only slightly in the draught between door and window. Best of all was the waitress.

She was out of a 1930s Jean Gabin movie – the superannuated tart with a rough voice and a loving heart. Pushing sixty, she had ginger hair permed into rusty coils like broken sofa springs, a flat face, a gash of red at the mouth and green fingernails. Then there was a pink, hand-knitted jumper that clung to low, swaying bosoms that skimmed the surface of my plate each time she leant over me. Her high heels clattered around the room and her skirt was so tight and short that she could walk in it only by keeping her legs straight, swinging them from the haunches in the tiny steps of a child. The meal was 55 francs, the litre 20, but she was worth her weight in gold.

When we passed by Valence the clouds soared into the heavens and the sky stretched to the end of Africa, blue all the way. Stewart took his hands off the wheel and raised his arms at the thought of arriving at Mèze.

'It's like St Tropez was fifty years ago,' he said. 'I tell you, coming down here is like getting into a sunshine overcoat!'

All along the Etang de Thau, opposite Sète and along from Montpellier, at Bouziques, Loupian, Mèze and Marseillan, oysters are sold in the same way that *frites* and ice-cream are sold elsewhere. We stopped at a little roadside place made from cane windbreaks and furnished with trestle tables. We took a dish of oysters each, with frosted glasses of a white wine produced from vines that grew on the edge of the hills we could see in the purple distance.

'Oysters are an aphrodisiac,' said Stewart. 'They were Casanova's favourite snack . . . and think what they did for him.'

That evening we celebrated our arrival by eating in a restaurant called la Brasucade. There were stone walls, dark furniture and an open fire of vine roots for cooking. It was a quiet place, dedicated to eating, without a note of music to be heard. The squid pie was delicious, and so were the kidneys in thyme. Stewart was still eating oysters, though he also took delivery of a large fish.

'It's the female of the species,' said Madame, her eyes akimbo, 'they're nicer to eat.'

With very little prompting Madame remembered Stewart from

May Day the previous year, the day when Mèze holds an annual parade, a procession that is an on-going peripatetic drunken party in which the men dress as women and the women as men, a kind of spring Saturnalia.

'We went from bar to bar,' explained Stewart, 'dancing in the street . . . I thought I was doing a dance called the *coucoulou*, but no one else remembers it. I fell over just outside here. I tripped over my skirt. I was so Brahmsed I never got to bed at all . . . I went fishing in the *étang* with Jo-jo, my neighbour, at five or six in the morning.

'So Jo-jo and me . . . we bought a couple of baguettes on the way down to the port, sailed out to the middle of nowhere, sat in the boat and had breakfast . . . the air smelt of seaweed. Jo-jo pulled up the oysters and I saw off a couple of bottles of wine . . . me with me skirt and my make-up still on. I tell you, if Casanova had made a pass at me, he'd have been in serious trouble. I'd eaten so many oysters I'd have killed him.'

It was barely light the next day when Stewart and I awoke. The smell of fresh-baked bread was on the air and an old man walked under the window with a long wooden box, full of oysters and dripping sea-water. The streets were cool and deserted as we left town, the sky starched clear of cloud by the mistral, and the landscape barren as we headed towards the southern foothills of the Massif Central, delivering furniture to the mad Englishman who lived on his own.

The truck climbed slowly up winding roads, out onto the great desolation of the *causses*, the limestone flatlands where the colours are pale greens and greys, a prospect fit only for goats and sheep, and a scattering of human beings who huddle in ragged and mournful houses. Some time before noon we arrived on a windy plateau, criss-crossed with stone walls that were crumbling back into the hard iron of forsaken pastures.

We had only the name of a village for address and we travelled a long way before we saw it written on a signpost, and then the village itself, rising on an outcrop, spooky, with nobody in the streets and an evil mistral tearing at the cornerstones of each building, making the ground shudder. On every door dried flowers as big as soup tureens were flattened out like amputated hands and nailed to the wooden planks.

We came to the house at last, an imposing mansion, tall, built, we learnt later, by a wool merchant in the eighteenth century as a summer residence. There were balconies all the way up, four or five floors, on double-fronted windows. The doors, also double, were made in walnut and large like a church's, and there was a *porte cochère* to the side, leading to the garage. The street running by the house was so narrow that it never saw the sun and its shadows were ancient and cold.

I pulled a brass knob and a bell, cranked by long lengths of wires and levers, clanged a couple of centuries away, though the noise died as soon as it had begun. I gazed upwards and noticed a long cord stretching up the outside of the house to the highest window.

We waited. After a long pause we heard footsteps on stone flags; a bolt was slid and the great door creaked opened like the first page of a Balzac novel. A face appeared – a young man in his mid-twenties, shivering. The face was grimy and fatigued, around it was a halo of black curls.

'We brought your stuff from England.'

The man nodded. 'Haven't got a cigarette, have you? Haven't had one for days.'

Stewart pulled a packet of *Gauloises* from his anorak and handed them over. The man placed a cigarette in his mouth and didn't move, just stared, waiting for a light. Stewart struck a match and the man inhaled a lungful of smoke, as deep as it would go, hoping, I imagined, that it would warm his body. 'You could put the stuff in the garage,' he said, and opened the *porte cochère*.

The unloading took an hour or so and when it was done I asked to be shown around the house. It was truly enormous, with huge rooms on either side of a central corridor, and with more double doors leading out to a great length of garden, overgrown and unkempt, gloomy, with mature trees that would murder the summer sun. From the unlit hall a marble stairway swirled upwards carrying wrought-iron banisters with it to the floors above. Everywhere, as we climbed, were shapes of darkness lurking in doorways and in corners. At the top of the house the man had constructed a kind of two-roomed flat, making walls out of plasterboard. For the rest, there was an unmade bed, a spavined armchair, a Formica table with an old loaf on it, breadcrumbs, a can of tomatoes and a can-opener.

'It was bloody freezin' up here in the winter,' said the man as we went slowly down the stairs. 'Eighteen below and I had no heating apart from logs and I didn't have many of those. My parents didn't send much money, you see. I got frost-bite in my toes. I got fed up with London and moved out here. I was supposed to do the house up for them . . . they're coming out in June, for good . . . I've been here a year, but I haven't done much. It was so cold I stayed in bed most of the time. The neighbours were nice . . . I'll say that . . . that's why I have that bit of rope out the window. My feet hurt so much I couldn't go shopping, the woman next door did it and I pulled it up in a basket. Once in a while she came in to see how I was going on.'

We came to the front door and Stewart handed over his second packet of cigarettes.

The man looked down the street like a famished fox. 'Are you going to eat? There's a restaurant along there, it's good, not expensive.' I looked at Stewart; we could have taken the bloke to lunch.

'Nah,' said Stewart. 'We haven't got time, we've got to get over to Marseille and pick up some terracotta pots.'

We were silent for a while as we drove away.

'You know,' said Stewart at last, 'that was like meeting Ben Gunn . . . "Got a bit of cheese about yer, matey? I dreams o' cheese o' nights, I do, dreams of it, toasted, mostly!" '

Twenty miles further on, across the same bleak desert, we found the village of la Couvertoirade. Once a stronghold of the Knights Templar, no one lives there now, except in July and August when a handful of hardy merchants make a living out of the tourists.

But that April, when we walked through the fortified gateway and under a tower built of a sombre stone, it was a Marie Celeste of a village, the narrow streets abandoned. The houses were blind, each with a set of steps at the side leading to a first-floor room where, in the old days, the peasants would lock themselves away from the blasts of winter, kept warm only by the animals that lived below in the stables and chewed the cud, turning hay into warmth through the digestive process, the steam gently rising – underfloor heating with an odour.

The village was silent and stark. The only sound was our footsteps disturbing the gravel. It is hardly surprising that la Couvertoirade lost its population, what with its rocky streets, the wind howling for ever out of the north and nothing but prayer to stop it.

'In 1880 there were 362 inhabitants,' I said, reading from the Michelin Guide, 'now there are none.'

'They were all waiting for the motor car to be invented,' explained Stewart, 'and as soon as it was – they cleared off out of it.'

The next day we loaded the pots and that night we dined at Mèze with Jo-jo and Josette, Stewart's neighbours. There were oysters, clovis clams and mussels from bottomless buckets; then bread and cheese and salad, and more wine from the Hérault, white and red. At the end of the meal Jo-jo brought out a golden bottle of Armagnac and raised his glass. 'To the Greeks and the Romans,' he said. 'The Greeks brought the oysters, and the Romans planted the vines – no men could have done more, and certainly not better.'

We left Mèze at five the following morning. The driver's cab was soon heavy with a garlic breath as thick and as blue as the smoke from a *Gauloise*. We slotted onto the concrete slab of the motorway and were immediately caught up in a rush of traffic, gaining glimpses now and then, as the sun rose, of the Canal du Midi, endless lines of plane trees showing through a thin mist.

'We're going via Bordeaux,' announced Stewart, sucking his

teeth. 'There's a girlfriend I have to visit, it's all them bloody oysters.' He pushed his arms straight, leaning back from the steering wheel. 'I'll tell you something,' he said, laughing. 'That house in Mèze doesn't belong to a friend of mine. That Yorkie advert paid for it, ten years ago. What a turn up! A lorry-driver with a house in France. There I was, losing my hair, and only five foot eight. And the best of it is – chocolate gives me migraine.' He laughed again and settled down for the long drive, aiming his lorry westward and northward, aiming it at the land of the brown-sauce bacon butty, determined, I knew, to talk and suck his teeth every mile of the way.

18

1975

Provençal Tales and a Forest Fire

During her lifetime there was hardly a year when I didn't return to spend a few weeks or so with Bonne Maman up on the hill of Rascas, and slip into the old ways, crossing the fields to do her shopping, walking with her to mass on Sundays. And Jean and Licette and their children still came on Sunday evenings, and we'd sit outside again, on the flat bit of the hill by the ruins of the bread oven, shouting to Marius as he took his sheep back to the *bergerie*. A little later he would reappear, his legs thrusting him up the slope, a bottle of home-made *pastis* in his *musette*, his dogs panting behind him.

Jean and Licette no longer lived at the Auberges, in those few miserable rooms where I had first met them. Out walking one day, some time in the early 1970s, up in the hills above la Gaillarde, they had found a ruined house with a hectare or two of land around it. The ruin stood on the flat top of a hill at the end of a rough track, perhaps 3 or 4 miles in from the sea. Jean had traced the owners of the property and, after some persuasion, they allowed him to erect, under the trees and out of sight from the air, a temporary wooden house, portable and made in sections. The Renoults loved it there: in the springtime the woods were smothered in mimosa, in the heat of summer the cicadas sang and the air smelt of pine resin, and in winter the spot was so sheltered that at midday you could eat in the sun. It was highly illegal, squatting of a kind, but that was how they wanted to live – on the fringe of things.

As soon as they could Jean and Licette got their furniture out of the barn where black cobwebs had smothered it. They made their wooden shack a joy to live in: there were divans covered in cushions, a long dining table, armchairs and rattan mats. On the walls were draped Polynesian sarongs: soft browns and yellows, bright scarlets and pale blues. And Jean hung his father's paintings everywhere, and made bookcases to fill with the books he had read as a young man; Giono, Aldous Huxley, Pagnol and Stendhal. Best of all, no strangers came that far inland; it was too hot for walkers to climb the hill, and expensive, low-slung cars would never attempt the rough track. Jean and Licette called the house Maeva – Tahitian for 'Welcome' – and they thought it perfect.

It was also highly dangerous. Living in a wooden house in an area given to forest fires, and putting into that wooden house all the treasures of your life, could not be described as the height of prudence. But Jean felt he had to take the chance: there was only one life and it was short; we all lived on the edge of a precipice anyway so he took the risk. He might just get away with it, and if he didn't, well it didn't matter too much – for the time being it was heaven. True he was still obliged to work at the Auberges, but he could get there and back in his *deux chevaux* and in winter, from October to April, his place of work was deserted: no Garreau and no clients for six months; all he had to do was paint doors and windows and tend to the gardens. There were worse ways of earning a living.

One end of summer, when the day was waning, up on the square at Grimaud where they play *pétanque*, a ground of dust and grit, a travelling troupe of actors gave a performance of Jean Anouilh's

Medea using the space under the trees for their dressing rooms.

The scene had been set in the light of two braziers, flames to hold back the advancing dark, but not strong enough for such a task, allowing the dusk to shape itself into arches of blackness, like the vaults of a dungeon. The backdrop had a grandeur all its own; starlight and firelight mingling, the houses rearing up towards the ruined towers of Grimaud, floodlit against the sky.

The whole town was there, full of excitement as they settled onto the benches that had been stolen from the school. Then came the story. Medea, to help Jason win the Golden Fleece, has betrayed her father and killed her brother. Ten years later Jason abandons her so that he may marry the daughter of Creon, the king of Corinth. But Medea is not the kind to be deterred by a little tragedy; she determines to poison Creon and his daughter and then murder her own two children, so leaving Jason bereft of everything he loves.

The girl who played Medea was strung as tight as a bow, every muscle taut, wearing a swirling frock and a scarf as red as blood in her hair. The frock flowed over her hips and thighs as she strode around Jason, mocking him as he stood there, stock still and stupid. She stalked him with disdain, her eyes mad in the light of the braziers, her bare feet careless, in her passion and hatred, of the sharp stones underfoot. Grasshoppers leapt from her path like sparks as she moved.

Then Creon came, stiff and regal in a robe of blue and silver, impressive behind a luxuriant beard of grey. He soliloquized grandly for a while then left, only to return a few minutes later as Jason; this time without a beard, though wearing a wig of curls and sporting yellow trousers and snazzy boots that were laced to the knee.

The nurse was solid and round, crouching in a long thick skirt, poking and feeding the fire, the smoke of it drifting upwards to spread itself into a thick canopy above the actors' heads. It remained there, unmoving, like clouds on a mountain, while just below the moths fluttered.

And beyond our theatre the dogs of the town were barking, and two or three goat bells clanged on the hillside, joining the tangible world to the world of the play in a rare combination. Then it was over and there was an hour or so to be spent in the cafés, and the travelling players came and drank with the audience, tired and elated, descending with reluctance from the high excitement of being on stage.

At about one-thirty in the morning we made our way home, on foot across the edges of the vineyards, a straggly line of us along the valley and up the hill to Rascas. In the sky the stars were clear and low; behind us the few lights of Grimaud were a constellation come down to rest, big and bright and golden.

The play had saddened me; all that betrayal and revenge. 'I suppose,' I said to Jean, 'it would be a kind of treachery to write about Rascas . . . all this, Bonne Maman . . . the shepherds.'

Jean smiled in the starlight and his teeth gleamed.

'If you do,' he said, 'I'll conjure up a Medea to hound you . . . to the death. This place and this time is secret.'

That same summer, one night when the moon was big and the light of it was strong enough to read by, Jean led me to a craggy hill above Grimaud where the locals said the Saracen castle of Fraxinetta had stood. There were five children with us, Jean's own and his niece and nephew, Martine and François. There we sat in a circle amidst the rocks, and Jean told us the most famous of the stories of Provence, the story of the golden goat.

Once upon a time a shepherd boy was sent by his father to look for some three or four sheep that had strayed from the flock. After searching for several hours the boy saw something glimmering through the trees and, going forward, soon found himself in a narrow gully where the light was so strong it almost blinded him, though not enough to prevent him seeing an elegant goat caught fast by her horns in a hunter's noose. She turned her face to look at the shepherd boy and her eyes were full of sadness.

The goat's fleece was smooth and well-groomed, but it was the colour of it that made the boy gasp. It was more than golden, and it flamed with a cold fire that was not a fire. Fear struck at the boy's heart. He had found the Golden Goat of Abd al-Rhaman, the Caliph, and on her head she wore the Caliph's crown of gold.

The boy drew his knife. The legends said that the Golden Goat meant despair and death. He who found her should cut her throat and seize her crown. The boy raised the knife, but to his astonishment the goat spoke, and her words were as golden as her coat.

'Do not slay me, shepherd,' she said. 'Do but cut me free and you may choose from the treasure of the Caliph three times, and take from it all that you can carry. One ruby alone would make you rich and your father rich, and your son and your son's son rich also.'

The boy hesitated, remembering the stories his father had told him, how, when the Saracens had been forced to leave Provence, Abd al-Rhaman had buried his treasure in a deep cavern, swearing to return one day, but in the meantime leaving his only daughter, the Princess Suha, to guard and protect his riches. Then he had commanded his sorcerer to change Suha into a superb mountain goat, so fleet of foot that it would be impossible for any man to capture her.

In return for her sacrifice the sorcerer vowed that the princess would live for ever, unless she quitted the cavern to live the life of an ordinary mortal. In that case she would regain her former shape, and become subject to age and decay as she had been before her transformation. But the Caliph never returned to claim his plunder, so for centuries men had sought the Golden Goat, though with little success; she had never been captured and only very rarely seen.

The shepherd boy pushed his knife between the goat's horns and cut the noose that held her. And the goat led the shepherd boy across the dark hillsides and as she ran she spoke to him, trying to deceive his senses with her soft voice, but the boy only tightened his fist in the golden hair and ran pace for pace with her. At last the goat halted before a wall of rock. She lowered her head and spoke in Saracen, and the granite rolled aside.

The goat stepped into a vast cavern and the shepherd boy was drawn in with her. He stumbled forward, his mind amazed. There was treasure all about him and the light from it so powerful that it dulled the sheen of the goat's golden coat. The floor was ankle deep in precious stones; there were ivory statues draped with gowns of silk, and orbs and sceptres, crowns and tapestries.

The goat stalked proudly into the cavern and the boy followed. She stopped by a huge throne, thickly decorated with diamonds; across its arms rested a two-handed sword with a jewelled hilt.

The shepherd boy pointed to the sword. 'That I choose,' he said.

'Oh, choose some other thing,' answered the goat, 'for that was the Caliph's sword. I would be disgraced if he were to return and find it gone.'

The boy pointed next to a caftan made of silver thread, heavy with rubies and pearls of matching beauty.

The goat stamped a foot. 'Fool, you cannot take the caftan of the Caliph.'

The boy felt pity for the goat and cast his eyes round the cavern for another treasure to bear away with him. 'I will have that turban,' he said. The turban bore a rich diamond at its front, a diamond as big as the boy's fist.

The goat's eyes filled with tears; 'My father wore this turban on his wedding day; he would punish me sorely if I let it go.'

The shepherd boy chose again and again, but whatever it was that he chose the Golden Goat refused. Finally the boy grew weary, realizing that the goat would allow nothing to be taken from her hoard, not the smallest diamond, nor the meanest silver pin. And he began to fear that he would never be free of that place and that he would die amongst all that treasure.

Nevertheless a sorrow rose in his heart for the Princess Suha, alone and without love. He took the goat's lovely head in his arms. 'Princess,' he said, 'leave this cave . . . better to be a shepherdess in the sun than live a thousand years alone. Come away and you will sleep under the stars and listen to the sheep bells at dawn.'

The goat shook her head. 'How could I leave? I am used to the feel of silk, the sight of gold and the glint of rubies. I could never live as you live, a barefoot shepherd.'

The boy was angered. 'Living as we live is better than living as you live,' he cried.

'And dying as you die,' said the goat, 'and how is that?'

'Dying a shepherd is better than living a goat,' said the boy and the tears ran down his face.

'Your tears are kind,' said the goat, 'and they make me wonder . . . I will try to come with you, but I will need your help . . .'

The goat spoke the Saracen word and the rock wall opened and the boy saw the pale starlight outside. The goat trembled and the boy held her tightly, but as they were about to cross the threshold he thought of the great wealth he was leaving behind, and how one pearl would shelter his father from the cold nights of his advancing age. So, hoping that the goat would not perceive his action, he squeezed the toes of his right foot around a small ruby that lay in his path, meaning to hobble with it into the open air.

But the goat knew at once what the boy had done, and she reared from his embrace, backing away, into the cavern.

'Do not take that ruby,' she cried, 'my father would search for it in the very moment of his return.'

The boy dropped the ruby to the floor. 'It is not your father keeps you here,' he said, 'it is your love of the treasure.' He leapt forward, seized the goat by the horns and dragged her stiff-legged through the doorway.

As he did so the goat vanished and the boy fell to the ground. In the goat's place stood the slender form of the Princess Suha, regal, beautiful and young, though her face was sombre and sad with centuries of loneliness. On her forehead glittered the Caliph's coronet of gold.

The Princess raised her hands and studied them, she touched her face, her hair, and then she screamed.

'How strange I feel,' she cried, 'how horrible this shape, this cannot be beauty. And how long would I live in this strange body?

I would grow old, unable to run sure-footed across the hills.'

At this she stepped back over the threshold of the cave and as Princess Suha disappeared the Golden Goat wheeled on its four fine feet in the doorway. The Saracen words were spoken yet again and the door of the cavern rumbled forward.

The shepherd boy leapt into the entrance and seized the goat's horns, but the goat was determined now. She lowered her head and shook it hard, flinging the boy from the cave, knocking the breath from his body. The door shut fast.

The boy recovered himself and began to grope his way along the gully, on hands and knees. He felt before him – it was still dark – and his hand struck something which rang out with an ancient sound as it moved against a stone. The boy raised the object above his head and held it against the stars. It was the golden coronet, fallen from the goat's head during her last struggle. The boy smiled. His dreams would come true after all.

But as he smiled there came a terrible sobbing from the depths of the hillside and the great door began to open and there came the sound of that voice which no man could resist.

'Ah, what will the Caliph say when he finds his crown stolen by a shepherd? Return it to me and you may choose what you will from this treasure.'

The door of rock had disappeared and the goat stepped across the threshold and took the form of the Princess Suha, holding out her arms to the shepherd boy.

'Return my father's crown and I will teach you the secret word that opens the cave, and you and your father will be as rich as Abd al-Rhaman once was.'

The shepherd boy tried to shut his ears but the voice of the princess was like the voice of reason itself. He felt soft lips whispering of wealth and power beyond belief, and gentle hands led him back into the cavern to choose what he would and the great door closed behind him.

Three days later the shepherd boy's father found his son lying on his back in a dry river bed and he wept. The boy's mind had gone and he never spoke again. All he could do was stare at the sky out of unseeing golden eyes.

And then Jean Renoult died and some half a dozen years later his house, Maeva, was caught in a forest fire and completely destroyed. Licette was in Corsica at the time, avoiding the crowds of tourists that holidayed on the Côte d'Azur – more and more of them every year. When she returned home the whole of her hillside was black; the undergrowth and the trees were cinders, the yellow mimosa gone, and only one or two twisted trunks stood stark like cadavers on the skyline; the little wooden house vanished.

Licette had been obliged to start her life from scratch yet again, setting up near Grimaud in another illegal dwelling much the same as Maeva. A month after the fire I went to visit her for a week or two, and one day, alone, I took the St Raphaël bus and got off at La Gaillarde – a pilgrimage to the place where the house had stood.

I went through the campsite that lies along the coast road, walked beyond it and up the track that Jean used to drive on his way to and from the Auberges. There wasn't one green thing growing between me and the horizon. The black dust was soft under my feet and rose to dirty my boots at every step in a smell of smoke. All around me branches and twigs had been tortured into grotesque shapes by the fire. After half an hour I arrived on the plateau where the German gun had stood, and came to the emplacement that Eric and his sisters, and the sons-in-law, had dug out of the earth to receive the contraband cottage.

It was an abandoned corner of hell, a gritty emptiness everywhere. The vegetable garden had gone, and the great stones, used as foundations for the house, had split open in the heat of a pitiless blaze. It didn't need much imagination to see the flames racing down the hill, playing golden leap-frog as the pine cones exploded like grenades and bore the fire on like a banner, down to the sea, faster than a man could run.And I saw those flames curling round the precious books, and the paintings of Jean's father, the frames and glass shattering, the picture in oils of Rascas gone for ever. It was hard to bear; that desolation, that smell of brimstone, that waste.

But the well was still there, cleaned out by the few hunters who came that way, and those who looked for mushrooms. They had left a rope and a bucket and I took a drink and the water was just as sweet as it had always been, and for a moment I could hear the laughter and see the Tahitian drapes and hear Jean's voice.

At the time of his father's death Eric was, by a strange and sad irony, one of those pilots who scoop up water in special planes, and then drop it on forest fires. A few days after the funeral he took his father's ashes up into the sky and scattered them into the sunlight over the sea, just off La Gaillarde where, in the winter when the beaches were empty, Jean and Licette used to picnic. He would have appreciated the cruel absurdity of it; both he and his house in ashes.

'To live like a flower,' I heard him say once. He came close to it in the winters; sole keeper of the Auberges, serenely painting doors, no dramas to deal with, no mad Swedish women to hold down until strait-jackets arrived; no flooded lavatories to unblock. Just tending the gardens and, in the cool of the evening, going back up into the hills, bouncing along the track in the *deux chevaux*, then a *pastis*, and a dinner cooked for him by Licette, whom he loved with his life, just the two of them, eating together.

Jean fought all his days to keep a clear and youthful perception; distinguishing between what was interesting and what was dull, between what was true and what was false. He busied his mind in getting rid of second-hand notions and false standards, searching always to recover that old fresh view of life, trying to make a distinction between what he had really and originally liked and those things that the workaday world wanted to make him simply tolerate.

In spite of his hideous summer work he managed somehow to avoid the squeezing out of the soul, the dryness that attacks most of us in middle age, as we slowly and imperceptibly get buried in custom, all daring gone. He taught me that travelling should be a love of the world, a warding off of death, as true love is – and more, it is a leaving behind, if only for a while, of those things we know too well, discovering ourselves anew as we journey, eager for those charged encounters with places and with people, those spots of time that burn in our minds with an inexplicable radiance, bright epiphanies that change our lives and bring us friends.

And the finding of those friends shows us what kindness is, and puts our lives in perspective, allows us to glimpse parallel worlds, and those alternative lives we might have led. This perception keeps us up to the mark. Even the bad times make us better than we were and help to remind us of the exhilaration of just being – an exhilaration I felt one night on Marius the shepherd's mountain, rolled in my sleeping bag on the close-cropped turf; a soft night, the wind dropping, and the stars coming nearer and nearer, and then even nearer, until in the end they were so close to the ground that the 15-year-old boy who always travels with me could reach up and touch them.

19

1978

Bordeaux to Narbonne:
Le Canal des Deux Mers

Monsieur Deloub shook his head when I asked him about the state of the towpath between Castets-en-Dorthe and Narbonne. A lock-keeper is not called upon to know much about what happens beyond the next lock.

'It's a long way,' he said unnecessarily, 'Narbonne.' He looked over my shoulder and gazed down the mirrored tunnel of plane trees. 'About four hundred kilometres, along the canal.'

'I don't mind,' I said. 'I'm going to Narbonne to see an old flame.'

'Ah!' Monsieur Deloub was wise. 'Then you'll be that much quicker getting there.'

Thirty miles south-east of Bordeaux, Castets-en-Dorthe is where the Canal des Deux Mers leaves the Garonne and sets off for the Mediterranean. We were standing in Monsieur Deloub's vegetable garden and discussing the canal and my plans to cycle alongside it. Above the trees the sun was warm and strong; by the canal everything was painted in the same gloomy green – the water, the shadows and the light.

To begin with – and when out of sight of lock-keepers and

beyond the secret places of fishermen and lovers – I found the towpath an abandoned place, the undergrowth mysterious and wild. I had cycled into a loneliness, but before long was surprised to discover a moored barge, brooding away on its own reflection. There was no breeze and the *tricolore* hung limp at the stern. The decks were covered with fresh blooms and creepers in terracotta pots. A man was tending to them, his thoughts so far away in his contentment that he neither saw nor heard me arrive or depart. Below the main deck there was a wide cabin with windows, all open. Here another man was dressing a table for two. It was a table you might have seen at the Tour d'Argent: a pastel tablecloth, napkins to match, folded like rose petals, cutlery enough to confuse a crown prince; wine on ice and the sunlight dropping through leaves to become captured in crystal glasses.

And yet only a half a mile away were the gypsies, two families living in tattered caravans on either side of a canal bridge. There were chairs and tables outside and children playing in the dirt. A grandmother, unmoving, sat and stared into the distance, still as death. A man with a broad moustache appeared, a wife and a small son peering out from behind him. On the opposite bank were two women, one washing herself and the other washing the family's clothes, elbow deep in a wooden tub, her dark hair wound all about itself like a tangled rope, hanging down into the suds.

I wanted wine for my midday meal and information about the towpath as far as Agen. They answered me in French and shouted across the canal in Romany: 'The "gajo" wants some wine.' The wine was poured from a demijohn into my plastic bottle. I paid and rode away while the grandmother continued to stare like stone, beyond us all.

In the town of Agen I crossed the bridge that carries the canal over the Garonne and found a museum that tempted me away from the towpath for a while. It was an excellent place, well laid out in four renaissance houses, thirty rooms, cool and free of tourists. There was a mad custodian too, leaning out from the door and bubbling with glee because it was Wednesday and no one had to pay.

'Bring your bike in too,' he said. 'Don't worry, I will look after it.'

At the end of the afternoon I crossed the Garonne yet again, searching for a place to sleep, on top of a hill in the village of Clermont Dessous. 'That's where I want to live,' the mad custodian had said, sending me back on my tracks so that I shouldn't miss it, 'that's where I want to end my time. The view, the quiet . . . and the food. I tell you, Clermont is halfway between heaven and earth, and not a bit expensive for paradise.'

He was right. I stayed in an *auberge* called As Tres Escales; its terrace hung from a cliff's rim, and out of my window I could see the wide spread of the river valley, and the canal beside it, ghostly with trees and tobacco plants, steaming with mist as night fell, like the background to a holy painting.

The canal goes right through the centre of Toulouse but I had no intention of stopping there; in the event my mind was changed for me. Arriving from the west along the towpath it was like cycling into the middle of a party. The place buzzes and moves – it must be all those students, 150,000 of them. Toulouse is rich in things to see but I wasn't allowed to enjoy many of them; I fell among thieves – buccaneers of time.

It started well enough; I left my bike and luggage in the hotel and strolled along the edge of the mighty Garonne. It was early evening and the red-rose buildings were turning to flame as the sun paled. Across the Pont St Pierre a great dome was reflected in the river. Downstream I could hear the sound of a weir, and the cries of sea-gulls echoing into the streets where the old brick frontages were worn rough from centuries of weather, the textures and colours of each house subtly different.

On the left bank, at river level, opposite the Beaux Arts building, there was a wide expanse of grass, a park really, and everywhere the party went on; old men watching the day go down into crimson water, jugglers practising, football with coats for goalposts, some-one playing bongo drums, students sitting in circles arguing, some painting, some kissing, and up on the level of the road, on the worn dirt, thirty games of boules were being played – endless and eternal.

It was on my way back to the place du Capitole, cutting through a narrow back street, the rue Mirepoix, that I discovered an English bookshop, Books and Mermaides.

I pushed open the door and went in. The bookshop was a strange shape, long but widening out at the back. Halfway down the room was a desk, with a man and a woman sitting at it, beyond that a large dining table with several people standing close by, talking; others seated, eating.

The man at the desk stood; he was square-looking, with a halo of grey hair and a beard to match – he looked like a cross between Karl Marx and Dionysus. His jeans were baggy and there was no belt to hold them up, and the crotch swung low between the knees while the waistband plummeted dangerously close to his plumber's cleavage.

I have always thought that the perfect way to earn a living would be to own a second-hand bookshop which had a wine bar at the back of it. It seemed that this man was on the point of achieving my ambition, so I was prepared to dislike him on sight. But that would have been difficult: John Sime sat me down and put a glass of wine in front of me.

'We haven't got permission for the café bit yet,' he explained, 'but we don't really need it, do we?'

'Why Books and Mermaides?'

'Well, there are fifteen thousand books . . . and nearly as many mermaides get in here from time to time.'

'And why an "e" in "mermaides"?'

He raised his glass. ' "Tell me where all past years are, or who cleft the devil's foot, teach me to hear mermaides singing, and to keep off envy's stinging . . ." '

A gentle whirlpool revolved around him that day, and I suppose, every day. People drifted in through the door, talked, asked what to read, and drifted away again.

As we talked and drank John sold a few books, but not enough to make a living, or even cover the cost of the wine – *The Picture of Dorian Gray*; *Brave New World*, Roddy Doyle and Titus Groan. A little later I was borne along to a nearby restaurant in the company of maybe a dozen people who had appeared out of the air of the bookshop. And then it was the next day, when I should have been bowling along the canal, 10 miles away. Instead I was in a food market, and once again I was astounded by how easily, in France, dinner can merge into the next day's lunch.

'It's the best covered market in France,' John said, 'long and wide and a hundred years old – le Marché Victor Hugo.'

I followed the others – it was the same play as the previous evening but with a different cast-list – climbing a flight of stairs to come into a long, narrow area which ran the length of the market but one floor up, a kind of gallery. It was full of noise and movement, warm with body heat. Along the gallery one restaurant ran into another, without a wall or partition to separate them, five or six establishments, each one with a bar, each one differentiated from the next by a coat of cheap bright paint: le Magret was blue, Chez Attila cream, le Petit Graillou yellow, all of them with menus between 65 and 110 francs.

The noise and bustle were medieval; it must have been where François Villon came to eat. At a rough count there were 300 or 400 people in the one place, eating and shouting, plates clattering, cutlery clashing. There were students, Moroccans and Spaniards, clerks and navvies, gendarmes and postmen, and between the tables waiters and waitresses ran like rabbits.

Every seat was taken. The menus were written on blackboards, the chalk smudged. Pitchers of wine were thumped down onto paper tablecloths, and the moment a pitcher was emptied a full one took its place. There was no thought of the morrow, and it occurred to me that I might never reach Narbonne, nor embrace the girl I wanted, the object of my journey. I could see lunch, like the lunch of the day before, stretching away into a shapeless afternoon, and on to dinner, and then on again to lunch the next day. They do it on purpose, the French – luring the unwary traveller into restaurants, undermining his best intentions, obliterating his intellectual pursuits, keeping him feasting until the museums are closed.

So I only made it to the cloisters of the Augustin museum a bare hour before its doors were bolted, and I fell asleep sitting on a wall, because the summer scents of the herb garden were drugged, and the harsh cawing of the crows was a witch's spell. But I dreamt a few things: a handful of Lautrecs and a Monet, Herod chucking Salome under the chin, a bas-relief of David tuning his harp; the curling hair of a St Sebastian, and above all a statue of Mary, the famous Notre Dame de Grasse, her face youthful and exquisitely sad – the draperies of her pale blue dress, its lace collar, her long tresses, and her strange posture – leaning away from the infant Jesus, looking away from him also, as if being the mother of God was too much of a responsibility for any woman.

Eastwards from Toulouse runs the seventeenth century section of the Canal des Deux Mers, the Canal du Midi, stately with oval locks and stone bridges. As far as Avignonet, 20 miles or so, the towpath has been covered in asphalt – a bad idea. On Sunday morning when I at last escaped from the city, the pathway was as brash as a market street, a Lowry or a Tissot where joggers and cyclists, dressed bright and vulgar like national flags, were shoulder to shoulder and wheel to wheel.

Then the asphalt disappeared and so did the fluorescent track-suits. To the north lay field after field of sunflowers, dying, their brown heads drooping like the heads of a defeated army. Soon the reach became gloomy, and lonely too, for the locks were closed between Toulouse and Carcassone. The trees joined their branches above my head and huge swaths of black weed encrusted the surface of the canal, solid islands of it.

As the day wore on the dark came down; so did the ghosts. For nearly 300 years this canal had been alive with toil, the towpath in commotion, the hostelries rowdy. In its heyday the Canal du Midi had carried more than 250 ships at any given time. Barges had travelled the 150 miles from Toulouse to Sète in eight days. In the mid-nineteenth century special craft had done the trip in thirty-five hours, without stopping, ostlers changing the horses every 5 miles.

Such a swearing of postilions there must have been, and such a thundering of hooves.

As I came into Castelnaudary there was no such movement or noise, and dusk lay under the bridges as I drew near the town's bright windows. In this place the canal widened into a great port that had once been a valley. More than a mile in circumference it looked deserted and forlorn as I passed. There was not a navigation light to be seen anywhere, nor a voice to be heard. Even the ghosts had gone.

I was on the road between Trèbes and Olonzac, looking for a hotel, when a *vendangeur* brought his tractor and trailer to a halt and insisted that I throw my bike aboard and keep him company for the 6 miles that lay between him and his destination.

It was a splendid way to travel, standing high up and gazing out over the landscape, like an aristocrat in a tumbril. In the vineyards around me the harvest was coming in: I was ankle deep in broken grapes and there was red juice under my feet. The warm air was heavy and moist, like a boozer's breath, and the whole world smelt tipsy.

The Hotel du Parc at Olonzac had the air of an establishment that had once fed and lodged a hundred travelling salesmen at a time – back in the 1920s, say – a place where the rooms were tall and the woodwork grain has been sculptured on over ridges of cream paint. I ate alone in a ballroom of a restaurant and had the waiter and the chef all to myself – glad of my company.

We talked of this and that through a menu of soup, *filet de porc*, aubergines in batter with a cream and mushroom sauce, wine, cheese and fruit. Occasionally the waiter and the chef left me to prepare and then fetch the next dish, acting in concert and with panache. One of these absences was longer than the others, and when the *plateau de fromages* arrived it was decorated with a full-blown rose that had been carved from an emptied tomato.

'*Après tout, je suis artiste,*' said the chef, and in the morning it was the sound of that artist playing a flute in the garden that awoke me. He mended shoes too, and he asked me to deliver some, recently repaired, to the lock-keeper at Roubia. 'He's a happy man,' said the chef, 'but everyone along this stretch of the canal is happy, come to think of it . . . He'll certainly give you a glass of wine.'

At the village of Homps there were half a dozen boats moored, one of them a hotel barge with a crew of two or three to care for a party of American tourists. As I free-wheeled past their gangplank they were sitting out on deck, waiting for breakfast, neatly dressed in pressed shirts and bright dresses, statuesque in armchairs, like actors in a play who had forgotten their lines.

At Roubia I delivered the shoes and drank two large glasses of red wine with the lock-keeper, sitting with him in the shade at the side of his house. 'It will not be easy,' he warned me, 'to stay sober on this towpath.'

I went on and passed another barge, a barge that was dawdling towards the Mediterranean with a young couple lying on deck, fondling one another, indolent in the morning sun – not a lock to negotiate for 34 miles, and nothing to do but drift and drink and stroke the skin.

And then another *péniche* with a complement of four couples on board, from Lyon, reclining on sun-loungers, contemplating the view and wondering how it was that the aperitif hour became earlier every day. My bike was hauled aboard and I was shanghaied for lunch: 'There's a restaurant along here called la Cascade,' they said.

I watched while Claudine massaged the big toe of Edouard's right foot. 'I'm learning reflexology,' she explained. 'He's got a sore throat, this'll get it for sure.'

'My knee hurts,' I said, 'from the cycling.'

Claudine didn't hesitate: she abandoned Edouard, undid my shoes, pulled off my socks and consulted her plastic map of the foot.

'Have some champagne as well,' she insisted, 'it helps.'

It was heaven. If the Reverend Sydney Smith could define paradise as eating *foie gras* to the sound of trumpets, then he never tried reflexology and bubbly on a barge.

I made a token effort to escape. 'If I stay with you for lunch,' I tried to argue, 'there'll be no afternoon.'

The others blinked at my stupidity.

'Exactly,' they said.

Not far from the restaurant I turned southwards onto the Narbonne arm of the canal, and headed for the Mediterranean at Port la Nouvelle. It was a good decision, for then I saw no boats at all, and had the canal to myself once more; just reeds thick at the bank and a ridge of black hills before me, leading to the Pyrenees. It was the best part of the day, calm and quiet with only birdsong to be heard; the sunlight was dying in the vineyards and the plane trees made green shadows across the water.

Beyond the city of Narbonne everything changed. It was like crossing into the Camargue; marshy ground stretching on all sides. There was even a field of white horses and black fighting bulls, running free. I left the level of the tow-path and climbed high onto a wooded promontory, the Ile Ste Lucie, and looked out towards the Mediterranean, feeling very much like stout Cortez, 'silent upon a peak in Darien'.

These were the last few miles of the 300 I had set out to cover. I crossed the last lock of all and came to a wide rutted road of dust that ran along by the canal where it comes, at the end, to the port. Factories and power stations crowded together here, cranes moved against the sky and rusty ships loomed behind and above the juggernaut lorries that were everywhere.

'Try the first restaurant after the bridge,' someone had said, 'for the best fish soup south of Narbonne.'

It was a fitting end to my journey, inside the Café du Port – twenty or thirty lorry-drivers eating and drinking, a smell of brawny men in dark blue singlets, stained with sweat, and the voice of Marie-Jo, the waitress, cutting clear across the mayhem as she ran back and forth. She was a big broad-shouldered girl, her long black hair tied in a loose knot behind her head, bearing the food, rough and ready, out of the steam of the kitchens amid laughter and the calls of the men as they offered love and marriage, and worse. But Marie-Jo was nobody's fool and she fought off all-comers with a violent sarcasm.

I sat at a long table with truckers who had driven in from the four corners of Europe.

'Where've you come from?' asked one driver, not seeing my bike outside and thinking perhaps that I drove a lorry.

'Bordeaux,' I said, proud of my twelve-day journey. 'I've just come all the way from Bordeaux.'

'Ah, Bordeaux.' the man nodded and reached for the bread. 'That's a nice little run. You'll be going back this afternoon then.'

I lowered my gaze. So much for stout Cortez.

Even in the seventeenth century the idea of a canal to link the Atlantic to the Mediterranean was not new. The Emperor Augustus long dreamt of saving his ships the perilous voyage through the Pillars of Hercules: and Charlemagne also became interested in the project. In 1539 François I examined the possibility of joining the river Aude to the Garonne, and in 1598 Henri IV supported research into a similar plan; but the project was always abandoned – there was not enough water available, said the experts, to fill such a canal. Luckily, one man disagreed.

Pierre-Paul Riquet came from fairly humble origins and spent the first part of his life as a tax collector. He was not a surveyor, nor a civil engineer, but he became interested in everything that concerned the movement of water and the nature of sub-soils.

As time went by he became convinced that there was an adequacy of water to be found in the Black Mountains, in small streams and rivers – the Alzau, the Bernassonne, the Lampy, and the Lampillon. After much reflection and experiment he built a great trench to obtain the flow he needed, channelling it into the river Sor, and then on across the plain to Naurouze, the highest point on the proposed canal.

Getting cash from the royal coffers was not easy and Riquet had to use his own money to get things going. After what seemed an age the king's proclamation granting permission for work to begin was read out in October 1666; by this time Riquet was sixty-two and had only fourteen years left to him – fourteen years of hell, fighting against fever and financial ruin.

But Riquet's faith in the ultimate success of the great enterprise never faltered: 'I regard this work with the same affection as I do the dearest of my children and it is indeed true that, even with two daughters to set up in the world, I prefer to keep them with me for a while longer and employ for the continuance of my work the monies previously set aside for their dowries.'

At Naurouze, the canal's watershed, stands Riquet's monument. Across a wide parkland passes a track lined with plane trees 140 feet high. It leads to a massive outcrop of rock on which stands an obelisk, raised in 1825, and all enclosed with a stone wall. On one side of the monument's pedestal is a profile of Riquet set within a garland of laurel leaves and supported by Minerva and Mercury. On the other side is a naked nymph, symbolizing the mountain springs. From an urn she pours water which divides at her feet into two streams, one flowing towards Neptune and the other towards Venus – the Atlantic and the Mediterranean.

'We must finish the task or perish in the attempt,' Riquet used to say to keep himself going – ironically he achieved both things, dying just seven months before the first ship sailed from Toulouse to the Mediterranean along the canal that without his vision would never have been constructed.

But I hadn't come all that way just to cycle the canal towpath and learn about Pierre Paul Riquet, fascinating as he was. I'd come to the Languedoc to see Maité again, remembering, through a romantic haze, the spring and the summer of the three Citroëns. She'd been an air hostess then, working out of Beauvais airport. Now she lived on her own in Narbonne, one marriage and one divorce later.

Maité was a Basque, dark haired and vivacious, her expression bright, her body bursting with energy. Cool and trim in her tailored uniform, she moved with a kind of electric grace; sparks flew out of her. During that airport summer we had spent time together whenever possible; starry nights in Paris and picnics in the fields and woods around Beauvais. I'd never wanted it to end, though it did of course, but we had remained good friends. Over the half-dozen years that followed our first meeting our paths had crossed occasionally, and when they did it was as if we had never stopped seeing each other. It was impossible for us not to fall in love each time we met.

A dog barked when I knocked. The door opened and there she was, Maité, her black hair cut like a flower round her face. She smiled and kissed me on both cheeks. Everything was going to be fine.

The dog was a Yorkshire terrier. It ran around as if on castors, zipping between my legs, tripping me up, yapping without need for breath. It was everything I hate in a dog: fuzzy, bumptious, egotistical, and noisy. I never saw such a fractious animal, and the hatred was mutual: we both wanted Maité to ourselves.

'It's called Pudding,' she explained. 'I bought it for company when my "ex" moved out . . .'

We went to a restaurant and left the dog at home. Our hands touched, her eyes grew large. I gazed at Maité through the candlelight and desire rose in my blood.

The Narbonne arm of the canal runs through the centre of the city and, after dinner, we walked along its embankment, past stone bridges and marble parapets, the dark waters reflecting the street lamps. The town was ours; just the two of us, hand in hand, the mood perfect. Maité leant into me, anticipating the hours of the night.

But Pudding had to be fetched out for his evening stroll, and so he was. He zipped and zoomed across the pavements, a clockwork maniac, skirting the canal, but Maité and I had eyes only for each other. We talked of the past, and strolled on, lost in thoughts of carnality.

Then Maité turned, her face a torn rag of white. Pudding had disappeared. We called, we whistled, we ran, retracing our foot-steps. 'He must have fallen in the canal,' she said. 'The poor little thing, he'll have drowned.' She was tearful, grief-stricken.

We ran back to her house. Nothing. Back to the canal. Nothing. Then Maité telephoned the dog sanctuary. Yes, he was there, some-one had found him drowning, swimming in figures of eight, only just visible above the surface of the water. I felt my heart sink as solidly as I wished Pudding had.

We took a taxi to a place on the outskirts of town. There he was, the darling, wrapped in a towel, pampered and spoiled.

Perhaps it was the guilt she felt but Maité gave £60 to the sanc-tuary, though there was no charge for the rescue, and what with the round trip in the taxi – another £20 – she'd spent twice as much on the dog as I had on dinner, which she'd insisted I pay for because her 'ex' had left her without a centime.

The atmosphere was tense. Finding the dog hadn't relaxed Maité a jot. The taxi dropped the three of us at her house. Maité turned on the doorstep, Pudding in her arms, his nose nuzzling into that lovely bosom of hers where my nose should have been. He snorted – he knew he had me beat.

'*Bonne nuit, chéri,*' said Maité. 'Try to understand, I'm so upset . . . There is a hotel on the corner . . . Come for breakfast . . . you can pick up your things then.'

I passed a miserable night: 300 miles from Bordeaux; 300 miles of ardent yearning, only to be eased out of bed by a Yorkshire terrier. I went for my gear in the morning but I had no stomach for breakfast. As for Maité, I never saw her again – after all, I have some pride.

20

1980

Corsican Patriots and Myself When Young

'Just work out an itinerary,' my boss had said, 'and choose a few hotels, we'll be sending clients over next year.'

I stopped for a hitch-hiker on the Bonifacio road, about five minutes after taking possession of the hired car at the airport – he was young, French and slopping over with confidence. He knew all there was to know about Corsica, life and literature. 'I come over every year,' he said, 'always out of season. It's like Provence was forty years ago' – he must have been about nineteen – 'the air is still scented here, like pages of Pagnol, smells like honey . . . A good lazy place too . . . as you probably know. They say the Barbary pirates only took Corsican slaves if they were really desperate . . . it's *la farniente*, which translated means a *douce et voluptueuse* indolence, and it's terribly catching. But they're right – work is bad for the soul.' He smiled, pleased with himself. 'Look, there's Bonifacio, the other Gibraltar.'

Bonifacio, to my mind, is more attractive than Gibraltar. It stands on a huge spur of rock with the sea on one side and the long narrows of the harbour on the other. High on that rock the old

150

town hides behind huge bastions and battlements and, to the south, hangs carelessly above the Mediterranean, which here seems as navy blue as a sailor's uniform and contrasts beautifully with the gold of the limestone cliffs, all sea-streaked and battered.

In the old town, through the Genoa Gate, the roads are narrow enough to be called alleys and in one such street, la rue des Deux Empereurs, there was a plaque on the wall announcing that Napoleon had stayed at No. 7 for five weeks in 1793. As I read the plaque Monsieur Stefani opened the door and appeared on the step.

'What's it like,' I asked him, 'living with Napoleon?'

Monsieur Stefani laughed. 'Napoleon's a nuisance,' he said. 'I can never get to sleep . . . busloads of people coming up here, in season and out, talking, shouting, especially after dinner . . . and the tour guides, you know what their voices are like – hacksaws. I know all about Napoleon – I lie in bed and listen to his life-story, every night.'

As we talked three women, faces in rigor mortis with make-up, jewellery clanking, stopped to give ear to him. Monsieur Stefani spoke to them in Genoese and they listened in Italian. 'We speak Genoese here,' he explained. 'They can't even understand us down the road in Porto Veccio, that's Corsican.'

'*Aie*,' the women cried, forming up and raising their hands to their shoulders like a tragic chorus. 'Do not complain about Napoleon, you fortunate man. We live in Mussolini's village and our trouble is worse – we have the *Fascisti* who come to worship him, they put notices on our doors "*Bravo il Duce!*" – and then there are those who come to hate him . . . what do they do? They piss on our walls. We too, we pay taxes and cannot get to sleep. We tell you, you know nothing.'

The next day I won a victory over Corsica's contagious indolence and was ready to leave Bonifacio by the crack of lunchtime. I put a picnic together and followed the road until it petered out on the shores of the Gulf of Santa-Manza. I was in a long, empty bay with a view to the sea. There were two or three dinghies moored, and some bits of bleached tree trunk. On the other side of the bay a white yacht, serene and unmoving, was anchored to another empty shore, and behind it the hills rose to become the jagged dark teeth of the central mountain range. It was heavenly peace.

I took out my book, unwrapped my food, uncorked the wine and leant my back against a rock that had been shaped by the waves over centuries for just that purpose. As I toasted my intelligence in finding such a haven a solitary pig, young and slim and sporty, came loping out of the *maquis*, obviously determined to spend the afternoon on the beach, scavenging, and grunting like me with a fathomless pleasure.

But up in the mountains, when I got there, I found no sun and the mist lay dead and cold along the highways. At Quenza, inside the Sole e Monti Hotel, Felicien Balesi was waiting for me, a huge log fire burning in the grate behind him. Felicien was a short man with a beaming and intelligent face, his body bubbling with energy. His eyes shone, his moustache had a life of its own and his trousers were rolled at the bottom. He switched from Corsican to French and back again like a man changing gears on a motorbike, and he spun through his hotel with the *élan* of an opera star on rollerskates.

'Oh, yes, we have lots of English here, they come for the walking, the quiet. Dennis Healey, he came, a happy man, went riding horses in the woods in shorts. Madame Thatcher came too, sad she seemed – no husband, no driver, she came alone and sat at this very table where you are sitting . . . planning her destiny, maybe.'

At dinner it was cured ham and saucisson, wild boar, half a dozen cheeses and apple tart and the wine was a Patrimonio.

'Did you know we had a King of Corsica once? King Theodore the First. That was kept out of our history lessons, and we got beaten if we spoke Corsican, everything had to be in French . . . and Pasquale Paoli, the father of the country, what do you know about him? Boswell came here to see him. He went into exile in England . . . you know, died there.'

Leaving Quenza the next day was no easy task: 'Just an omelette and green salad', that had been Felicien's promise. Oh really! There was a game pâté, jugged hare, some of the wild boar in cold slices, cheese, gâteau, wine of course and a coffee with a good measure of brandy tipped into it. Felicien was a gastronomic highwayman with no morals.

The clouds were still hugging the land when I set out for Ajaccio and the driving was dangerous and slow, the wheels crunching over fallen chestnuts in their spiky husks. It was an awful noise, like stepping on snails. But at last I emerged from the mist, the day lightened and I came upon my hitch-hiker resting beneath a tree. He made no sign but I stopped for him anyway.

'That King of Corsica,' he said, 'was a Westphalian, the Baron de Neuhoff, an adventurer. He was crowned in April and ran away in November the same year – 1736. He eventually died in the back room of a second-hand clothes shop in Soho. You're going to Ajaccio? Well, there's Napoleon's birthplace . . . then the Fesch Museum. Fesch was Napoleon's uncle, a cardinal, so the museum's full of religious stuff, a bit stolid, though there is a Botticelli, Virgin and Child, lovely colours, dark green; an El Greco kind of faded red and the angel's robe, grey but not grey . . . I think you'll like it.'

'Thanks,' I said.

'One of the curators will follow you around and get you to send him a postcard from abroad, he collects them, he's already got four thousand. You can't miss him, he has big round spectacles and a look of intense dedication verging on madness. Where are you going after Ajaccio?'

'Calvi,' I said.

In a restaurant in Ajaccio I sat at the same table as a cheese salesman from Marseille.

'It's impossible,' he told me, 'to make a living in Corsica. If you're not born here you can't sell anything. I don't know why my company bothers, really I don't. The only decent sale I ever made was when one Corsican introduced me to his cousin who ran a supermarket. There's only one thing to do . . . I'm going to get some WANTED notices printed, with my face on them, and I'll put one on every telegraph pole in the country. Then you'll see, I'll sell thousands of tons of cheese every week, you can bet your shirt on it.'

In Calvi the great mystery has been solved. For 500 years Calvi was a stronghold of the Genoese; Columbus came from Genoa, therefore Columbus was born in Calvi; and so, in a tiny street beyond the church there is a crumbling stone wall and a plaque to prove the supposition. *Dans ce lieu est né en 1436 Christophe Colomb ...'* Just below the walls of the citadel, 'to make assurance doubly sure' is a bust of the navigator, looking out over the town: a face that looks like a camp version of Charlton Heston, with his long hair floating free, bronze in the breeze.

It was no easier to leave Calvi than Quenza and I set off wilfully late, heading north towards the isolated villages that lie hidden in the mountains that look back towards the sea. In Calenzana I stopped to stretch my legs and an old man hurried out of the *bar tabac* and shook my hand, his own soft and gentle. He must have been eighty years old, but his voice was full of energy.

'Come in and have a drink,' he said, 'and when you get home tell your friends about the Germans and the bees.' Inside the bar there must have been a score of pensioners playing cards, their conversations loud, never ending, echoing around the bare walls. Between them they told me the story. It was perhaps the only thing that had ever happened in the town.

It was 1732 and a war of independence against the Genoese had been raging for three years. Eight hundred German mercenaries marched on Calenzana, intent on massacring the inhabitants, who had nothing to defend themselves with but a few pistols, some axes and knives and maybe a dozen arquebuses.

But the Calenzanais were nothing if not courageous. This was their homeland, their beloved Corsica. On their window-ledges and on their roofs were their beehives, for the town was famous for its honey. As the German troops advanced the hives were tipped into the streets and the swarms of bees they contained erupted into the air, covering the soldiers in dark clouds of anger, stinging in fury, making eyelids and lips swell with pain. The mercenaries screamed with the agony of it. They threw down their weapons, flapped their hands, and ran for the nearest stream or fountain. At this the citizens of Calenzana sped from their houses, gathering up every discarded gun and sword they could find, finishing off the work the bees had begun, slaughtering their enemies, giving no quarter. 'German blood,' they said, 'is this day better than Corsican honey.'

The old man led me from the bar and pointed across the road at the church. 'Over there,' he said and grinned a toothless grin.

At the base of the bell tower I found a plaque: 'Campo Santo die Tedeschi: Here died and are buried five hundred Germans, killed in the service of Genoa. Battle of Calenzana, 14 January 1732.' Inside the church the only sound was the sound of candles guttering.

I took a picnic on an open bit of ground that formed the side of a gentle hill. Ten miles to the west, across the bay, lay Calvi, glinting in the sun. I could hear sheep bells in the woods and as I ate the bells got nearer and the shepherd brought his sheep towards me and, coming close, leant on his staff and wondered who I was. I poured him a glass of wine and told him that I had once been a shepherd in Provence. He tipped the wine down his throat in one gulp, making it obvious that he didn't believe me.

There is a string of villages strewn across these mountains: Lunghignnano, Cassano and Zilia, each one higher than the last, each one clinging to a precipitous slope, their streets full of sun and empty of people, their grand churches boasting scrolled columns and Renaissance doors. At Montemaggiore I found a terrace on the edge of a crag and there in the distance was Calvi once more, beyond Calenzana, the mountains between all dusty with sunlight, and the air heavy with the scents of Corsica. I could still hear the sound of the flock in the valley, and in the pale sky the crows wheeled and quarrelled.

It had been an indolent afternoon and the distance I had covered had been insignificant, 12 miles in all, but every mile had brought me pleasure. And, by way of proof, as I sat with my back against a stone wall another ancient man of Corsica appeared through a gate and handed me a bunch of grapes from his garden. They were warm and sweet in the mouth. The man was sprightly and surprisingly well dressed, like a fashionable citizen from a large town. He wore a trilby and a jacket, and had a crease in his trousers that he could have sliced carrots with. He carried a stick in his hand and drew alien faces in the dust with it as we talked. His name was Reignier Antonini and I guessed him to to be about seventy; in fact he had been retired forty years – he was ninety-three years old.

He made me welcome in his house: three little rooms, a table, a rocking chair, a cupboard and a television set. He poured me a hefty dose of a syrupy Corsican aperitif, mauve in colour and as thick as oil.

'I started work as a guard at the Palace in Monaco,' he said. There was his picture on the wall, in an operetta uniform. 'But then I became Maréchal de Logis. Here's a picture of me with Prince Rainier . . . I knew him when he was so high.' He held out his hand at about the level of his knee. 'I was on my own here for a while . . . My brothers were killed in the Great War . . . and my wife wouldn't leave Monaco to come back to Corsica . . . she's still over there, but it was pretty easy for me to find another woman . . . so I did.'

We went back onto the terrace, our glasses refilled. The sun was sinking behind us and the evening shadow was creeping up the mountains opposite and the lights in the villages were showing gold in the dusk. On the horizon the line between the sky and the sea was indistinct; they were both one bluey-grey now. Even the sheep must have been back in their fold, for the bells were silent. Reignier Antonini clinked his glass against mine. 'It was good to meet you,' he said, 'someone from civilization.'

It was almost dark in Speloncato when I got there. Speloncato is the smallest of villages and sprawls across a ridge at the head of a wide valley that leads to the sea, a mere 12 miles away.

The central square was an odd shape, the houses thrown down with no plan and the streets not streets but irregular spaces between dwellings. In the twilight, two girls were playing hopscotch, three old men sat by the war memorial and a woman was bending over a potted plant. The fast set, four of them, were playing cards in the bar. And the church bells rang the hour twice, making sure everyone noticed the slow passage of time.

There was a hotel, the A Spelunca, but it was closed, the season over. I knocked anyway and Madame Josephine – 'Call me Fifi' – opened the door so quickly that she must have been standing behind it, waiting for me. Her grey hair was a halo and her smile a brightness in the gloom. 'It doesn't matter a fig,' she said, 'come in, come in, I only closed last week.'

It was more of a grand house than a hotel, once the home of a retired cardinal, with a fine stone staircase and a delicate iron banister that rose up three or four floors. Not only was I given a bedroom but a sitting-room as well, spacious and elegant – a painting of the cardinal on the wall, a parterre of octagonal tiles and good-looking carpets, a marble fireplace, a glass and gilt chandelier hanging from a moulded ceiling, velvet curtains, and stately chairs and cushions. With my hands behind my back I paced up and down and struck a few attitudes in the mirror: James Boswell, the Corsican traveller.

Madame Fifi invited me to dine with her that night in company with her husband and two friends, Italians from Guatemala. At coffee we were joined by Nuncio Colombani, Madame Fifi's brother, a man who had passed thirty years of his life as an engineer in France, but then at last had come home, loving Speloncato with a love that he had carried with him during all his exile.

'You can see the sea from this village,' he said. 'It shines in the sun and the moon, and yet I was more than ten years old before I saw it close to . . . It was like that for most villagers . . . you understand, the men used to take produce down on mules, from time to time, but some women never went to the coast . . . or maybe once . . . some from the village only got close to the sea when they crossed it to America. I remember touching the water, that first time . . . cool like silk it was . . . I never forgot it, I still touch it in my dreams. In 1900 there was a population of a thousand here, in 1935, seven hundred, now there are only one hundred and eighty . . .

'In the old days, before me even, they used to cultivate the ground right up to the sky, now the old terracing is broken, just old bulges under the turf, like buried bodies. We used to have gardens in every corner, anywhere where things would grow, scraping food out of the hardest bit of land.'

'And why do the church bells ring twice?'

'The first bells tell us to count properly the second time.'

'But you must have a watch.'

'Watches are not needed in Corsica.' The six people at the table showed their wrists and mine was the only one that wasn't bare.

For three days I was all Corsican indolence in Speloncato. Every morning the sun climbed over the valley's rim, woke me through my window, and then warmed the terrace where I took breakfast; and every morning the dogs barked without any enthusiasm, and the same woman went out to tend the same potted plant.

Then, when the clock had struck twenty-four, I strolled to the café where the men played cards, their voices raised in an on-going argument. Antoine was not meant to be drinking, for his health's sake. He dodged the prohibition by giving his *pastis* an alias, shouting loud to the barman in the hope that his wife across the square might hear: '*Un Vichy chaud, un Vichy chaud.*' After lunch I read in my sitting room. I was Boswell again.

I delayed the moment of departure for as long as I could. I had no wish to leave, but when I did Madame Fifi embraced me and thrust sweet tomatoes the size of grapes into my hands, and I ate them as I drove. Hail and farewell, Madame Fifi, *Ave atque vale*. Sadness at leaving, despair at knowing that I was never to see her again; joy at the prospect of another village.

I drove on to Morosaglia, out of the valleys rich with chestnut and oak, and through the honey-smelling *maquis*, across moorland and bare granite ridges. There were birds of prey wheeling on rivers of air, and cows camped on the road.

I spent an hour or two at the birthplace of Corsica's hero, Pasquale Paoli. There wasn't much to see: a statue, some soup tureens, a sword, an Italian translation of Boswell's *Account of Corsica*, and a photo of Paoli's monument in Westminster Abbey. As I came out of the house I found my hitch-hiker sitting on a wall.

'I always come up here,' he said. 'The houses are special, the forest is good for walking. That Paoli was some character, wasn't he? Did more for this island than Napoleon. He ran Corsica for fourteen years, fought off the Genoese but got massacred by the French.'

'And Boswell came to see him.'

'Well, Boswell went to see everybody, didn't he? Paoli gave Boswell a dog, which he lost, typically . . . but he did quite a bit for Corsica: wrote that book, wrote letters to Voltaire and asked him to help . . . raised money . . . there were even two years when Corsica was a dependency of the British Crown . . . not many people know that. Nelson lost his eye here . . . never been found.'

As I left I went to give him my address. After all, meeting him several times like that – an interesting cove.

'If you're ever in . . .' I began.

He waved me away. 'Life has too many addresses in it already,' he said. 'A full address book is a sign of failure . . . like too much furniture in the house.'

As I drove back down the valley, I suddenly remembered who the hitch-hiker reminded me of – myself, when young . . .

. . . I was hitch-hiking across France, about twenty-two years old and returning from a trip to Spain. The rain had been falling steadily all day. I had got as far as the outskirts of Limoges, the eastern side, making for Clermont Ferrand; from there I would head north and spend a few days with the Foulet family in Corbigny.

A Peugeot saloon pulled up and I climbed in. There was a balding man driving, in his forties I suppose, a kind and gentle face, a wry smile. He was going to Clermont Ferrand, where he worked for the Imprimerie Nationale, he said, something to do with printing bank notes. His name was Raymond.

A few miles further along the road the windscreen wipers ceased to function and we could go no further. We stopped at the first village we came to and found a small repair shop. It was the archetype of the provincial garage, run by *le vieux patron* and his wife. The floor was stained with the oil of decades and the double doors leant outwards at a crazy angle. The work bench was a litter of tools and the windows were thick with cobwebs and grease. The *patron*'s face and hands were shiny with grime. His overalls might once have been blue.

Yes, he could mend the windscreen wipers, but it might take some time; we'd do well to go to the bistro, or even better the restaurant . . . he knew the woman who owned it, of course he did, and the food was excellent – he ate there himself, didn't he? Of course he did – it was run by his cousin.

Raymond and I ate together and we chatted for a couple of hours – though I did most of the talking. I had seen bullfights, the Prado, walked the Ramblas in Barcelona, and in Bilbao had discovered cousins whose existence had been hidden from me. I had read Gerald Brennan and had left women weeping. We ate slowly and Raymond smiled his smile. I never asked him one question about himself: where he lived, was he married, what he'd done, where he'd been.

When we arrived in Clermont Ferrand I got out of the car and shook his hand. 'I'll look for the youth hostel,' I said. Raymond shrugged: 'This hotel is hardly more expensive,' he replied.

We ate together again that evening and talked for another couple of hours. He was one of the best-read, most modest and charming men I have ever met. His French was spoken with precision and grace and set a standard that I have always wanted to emulate. He was a marvellous companion and I felt then, albeit vaguely, that I wanted to mature into something like he was. His conversation, when he could get a word in, was fascinating and I have never forgotten it.

There was, he maintained, a passionate love affair going on between England and France, but it was clandestine, adulterous and, like some adulteries, was expertly concealed behind a mask of hostility, so well concealed in fact that the hostility had become more real than the love. And yet the truth of the matter was that the hostility between the English and the French arose from the fact that we were so similar, in history, in background and in ambition. We were feuding cousins – jealous of the other's success – tribesmen killing each other because we were so closely related.

And there were so many parallels: the Normans invaded the British Isles because they had every right to; the English legally occupied Aquitaine for 350 years and shipped every drop of Bordeaux wine to England – a tactic that would annoy anyone, let alone a Frenchman; and the Hundred Years' War was a civil war, a long quarrel between greedy relatives.

It was quite simple: France and England, being relatives, wanted the same things, so they fought each other all over Europe, not to mention the conflicts in North America and India. Albion was perfidious, and the Frogs were treacherous. Indeed so similar were we that the French ran away *à l'anglaise* and the English took 'French leave' – QED.

'There was more,' said Raymond. The French were mortified that the English had beheaded their king before they themselves had even thought of such a thing. Never mind, they would do something bigger and better. A hundred and fifty years later they treated themselves to a revolution of their own, and chopped off several thousand heads to prove their superiority. And out of that came Napoleon and the Duke of Wellington, and two railway stations, Austerlitz and Waterloo.

Both France and England had magnificent literatures, each one better than the other according to chauvinist critics, and each nation was convinced that it possessed the richest language in the world. And individuals of tremendous bravery, from both countries, had sailed to the ends of the earth to claim great chunks of it for their homelands, establishing empires on which the sun never set, and yet the descendants of those individuals have managed to remain impossibly insular. Why the mutual admiration, why the hatred? Envy of the lover, that was the answer.

We rose from table, and Raymond suggested that we exchange addresses. I waved the idea away. One should travel through life with as few possessions as possible, no excess baggage. Too many addresses was like too much furniture in a room . . . it showed bad taste – the memory of someone was better than their telephone number.

That was one of the most stupid actions of my life, and they have been legion. Only a few miles down the road the next morning, as I stood waiting for a lift, I bitterly regretted the things I had said – that overweening conceit of mine. I had not been able to find Raymond at breakfast; he had gone from the hotel before I'd managed to get downstairs – what was worse, he had paid for my room, the wine and the meal.

21

1983
Badinage in Burgundy

It was high summer and I took my Citroën light fifteen back to Beauvais. I wanted Roger Langlet, the best mechanic I have ever met, to go over it for me and get it into peak condition. I had known Roger for fifteen years; he'd been the chief mechanic for the bus company providing the transport for our one-day visits of Paris. To begin with we had become good friends because of the Citroëns, and then just because.

Roger was a portly person whose body burst with a mischievous energy – a doctor of divinity to look at, a Panurge to be with. He bubbled over with life, a man with no time to lose, an enthusiast who insisted that his companions and friends should enjoy life as much as he did: right away, no hesitating.

I knocked on the front door of his house, expecting to see his episcopal face, but that was not what I got. The door was thrown back and his wife appeared, spitting flame and brimstone. Roger had run away with a schoolteacher from Compiègne and dropped out of sight completely – silence, exile and cunning – pleasure bound, looking for a way of life that left his fingernails clean. His wife was now his ex-wife, and because I had been one of Roger's good-time friends and drunk *pastis* with him, I was deeply implicated in his fall from grace.

I tracked him down eventually without too much trouble. Pierre Cilliez, who knew everything, knew where he was.

'He's in Noyers-sur-Serein,' he said. 'That school teacher has a second house down there . . . Burgundy, just north of Avallon. He wangled himself a disability pension, what disability I don't know, self-inflicted cirrhosis, doubtless . . . bought himself a little vine-yard, a garden; she works in Compiègne still, gets down there at weekends . . . he's on his own the rest of the week, can you imagine? He doesn't have to die – he's in paradise already.'

My work was sending me south anyway and I needed no green Michelin Guide to tell me that Noyers was worth the detour – if Roger was there that was enough. He was a Panurge with taste.

Noyers turned out to be unspoilt and beautiful, neglected by tourists: a fortified village around which the river curled in a leisurely loop, two main gates, some remnants of walls and sixteen towers. Above all it was tranquil, hushed, like a ship becalmed. In Noyers indolence has been raised to the level of religion.

It was high summer when I drove into the empty square, and under a pale blue haze the whole of France was slumbering. Nearly all the houses were half-timbered, fifteenth- and sixteenth-century. The upper storeys jutted out over the uneven pavements; the corbel ends were carved into human faces and the beams were black with age. Roger's house was one of the most ancient, heavily timbered like the rest and standing on the shady side of a narrow street.

My knocking broke into the deep silence of the siesta hour, and it took some time for Roger to appear at an upstairs window, his face creased with sleep and heavy with lunch; but when he moved he moved quickly. Up steep steps I was dragged, through the kitchen and out on to a wide balcony that overlooked the river and one or two of the towers.

There we sat and drank a celebratory *pastis*, Roger smiling, hatching plans like a megalomaniac. Below us a man rowed slowly down the green weeds of the Serein, and in the water meadows the cattle stood as still as the statues in the song, not even flicking their tails at flies that were too lazy to move anyway.

First things first – lunch was in the past so it must be dinner next. But it was Monday; the baker's was closed and Roger was short of bread. It didn't matter, his friends would lend him a baguette or two.

We drove around the village and what began as a search for bread soon became a royal progression from one aperitif to another. No matter that Roger came on the scrounge; everyone was pleased to see him, the men laughing till they wept, and the women blushing till their faces burned. Every *pastis* we tasted was succeeded by another, obligatory – *on ne marche pas sur un pied* – and many were home made, strong enough to corrode stainless steel. At the end of it all we had gathered more bread than we needed and swallowed more aperitifs than was decent, and in this state we set out for Roger's garden to collect tomatoes and salad to round off the evening feast.

While Roger prepared dinner I walked around the village, following the river and the line of the fortifications. I tried to number the sixteen towers as I walked but some had disappeared, incorporated into various buildings or simply been allowed to crumble away and become overgrown. In any event, I lost count, my mind out of gear, the cogs disengaged, spinning in Pernod. But dusk was gentle and an end in itself: a cow stood cool in the water, udders submerged; house martins swooped low over my head; and through open windows I could hear the sound of tables being laid.

At dinner Roger drowned me in Burgundy; he cut thick slices of *gigot* and nostalgia and placed them before me. We drifted back to the days when we had worked together in Beauvais, getting up to no good and making the perfect Citroën even more perfect. 'Ah,' he said, 'what a car she was . . . what did we call her?'

'*Fanfan la Tulipe*,' I said, 'I was hoping you'd check her over for me . . .'

'Why of course.' Roger winked at me, and then he gave me the *quid pro quo* – when I was at my weakest, pickled in Gevrey-Chambertin and marinated in remembrances. 'I will lay hands on your Citroën . . . but you see . . .'

It appeared that Jean-Paul, the local garage owner, had put one over on Roger and it rankled deeply. I had arrived, fortuitously, to help him take his revenge. I heard the story.

'Jean-Paul asked me to rotovate a garden for an old lady on the other side of town, with one of those toy tractors. I drove it right through the village, everybody watching . . . a big man like me, sitting on that silly little machine – *j'avais l'air d'un vrai con*. When I got there the garden didn't need doing at all and the old lady knew nothing about it, so I had to drive the bloody thing all the way back again . . . and they were waiting for me outside the café, Jean-Paul and all his cronies . . . you can imagine . . . "Come and do my garden, Roger . . . how much do you charge?" I felt that big.' Roger placed index finger and thumb together leaving no space between. 'Michel, I've got to get back at him . . . you can think of something, I know you can . . . some of the strokes you pulled at Beauvais . . .'

The next morning I called on Jean-Paul at his garage and told him that I had just purchased a certain large house and garden 3 miles outside Noyers.

'I want to try one of your garden tractors,' I said, 'that large one, on the forecourt . . . bring it over at lunch-time. If I like it, I'll buy it.'

Roger rounded up a few of his drinking companions and, from a safe distance, we watched Jean-Paul load the tractor into his pick-up; then we followed him out of town in a couple of cars and watched him again as he unloaded the machine and, with great difficulty, manoeuvred it into the garden. We let him wait for fifteen minutes, then we joined him, taking with us a couple of bottles of Chablis in an ice-bucket, and half a dozen glasses.

Jean-Paul swore a great deal when he saw Roger, but as there was nothing he could do he stretched out on the grass with the rest of us and took his defeat like a man. The wine was poured and Roger rolled on the ground, lost in laughter and slapping his thigh – his honour had been satisfied, and in the days that followed he did a more than thorough job on the light fifteen, and didn't charge me a penny.

On the eve of my departure, late at night, Roger showed me some ancient postcards, views of Noyers between the wars, and they reminded him of the story of Monsieur Mossand.

In the 1920s the electricity supply for the whole village was controlled from a local substation in the charge of an engineer – Monsieur Mossand himself. Every evening after work he would set off to the bistro for an aperitif or two and a game of cards or dominoes. As often as not he failed to return home for his dinner – his house backed on to the substation – and the meal his wife had prepared would slowly dry to cinders in the oven.

But Madame Mossand was a resourceful woman. When her patience was at an end she would let herself into the substation and throw the main switch, and in that second all of Noyers was plunged into darkness, and it would stay that way until someone brought her husband home, very often in a wheelbarrow – she was never kept waiting for long.

Roger shook his head in admiration at such doings from a golden age. 'The mould has been broken,' he said. 'They don't make nutters like that any more.'

I looked at him over my glass, and shook my head. '*Mon oeil!*' I said, 'not much they don't, not much.'

22

1984
The Valley of the Drôme

I had driven south from Grenoble, across the mountains and into the department of the Drôme. I was a couple of days ahead of schedule, feeling indolent and, halfway up a range of high hills, I found a good spot to do nothing in, lying in the shade of a low-branched tree, recovering from lunch and smelling the hedgerows: soapwort, cranesbill and joe-pye-weed. Behind me the dusty blue of cornflowers, where they grew against a background of St Anthony's lace, looked as delicate as embroidery. When I sat up at last I saw, just across the road from me, a signpost pointing up a hill: *Autichamp – voie sans issue* it said.

Autichamp was nothing more than half a dozen stone dwellings. It was a hamlet asleep, baking quietly in the afternoon sun. I parked in a tiny square that was made dark by a couple of trees. After the glare of the road the shade was a total blackness to me and I could not see into it. I got out of the car and stepped into an immense silence.

Close to where I stood was a bell-tower with a pointed roof. Nearby, on the outside steps that led up and into her house, sat an ancient lady: opposite her, sitting on her own steps, was another. Neither of them moved but they stared at me, not with hostility, just staring, as if they'd been there for ever and I was too transient a being to trouble them. They said nothing.

I went towards the tower, thinking I might climb it for the view. I came to a kind of portal in its northern wall but it was fenced off by a mesh of wire on a frame. Behind the wire were a dozen chickens, an array of garden tools and a stack of logs for firewood. It looked private and I retreated.

I returned to the square and under a lime tree, in the shade that I had not been able to see into a few minutes previously, I discovered two middle-aged women sitting on a stone coping. Behind them, in an even deeper shade, lay three men on soft grass, enjoying an endless snooze. They must have devoured one hell of a lunch.

Solange was blonde, dressed in a salmon-pink blouse and a grey skirt. Odette was black haired in a blue and white dress. The two old ladies over the road were still unmoving, still staring.

'My mother and my aunt,' explained Odette. 'They're ninety-three and ninety-five. People say it's the air up here. We won't live so many years where we come from . . . down in the towns.'

Across the street another old woman showed herself and began throwing grain at the chickens.

'It was built a thousand years ago, our campanile,' said Solange with some pride. 'You ought to go to the top, the panorama is something you don't see every day.'

The two women got to their feet and took me back to the tower, stopped at the wire barrier and pulled it to one side. Odette shooed the chickens from her path, and led me through the tools and timber until we arrived at the bottom of a set of steps. We went to the very top of the building and, gazing past the huge bell that hung there, I could see right over the wide valley and back towards the peaks called *la Colombe* and *les Trois Becs*.

It was a magnificent prospect, with enormous cotton-wool clouds lying above the mountains and dwarfing them, rolling up into a great bulk. The escarpment itself fell straight down, vertical until it disappeared into the muted green of the tree line, the green changing to black in the ravines and hollows.

Odette reached up and pinged the bell with a fingernail and the sound stood solitary in the air for a moment, then echoed off the walls and died, dropping down into the heat of the landscape below.

'Flavie rings it twice every Sunday,' said Solange.

I looked at the solid size of the bell, several tons of it, then down at the massive rope which ran through a hole in the floor at my feet.

'Flavie,' I said, seeing in my mind's eye some olive-skinned Amazon in the prime of life, 'who's Flavie?'

'The woman feeding the chickens,' said Odette, 'she's only eighty-four.'

'*Vogue à Piegros-la-Clastre*', announced the local newspaper. *Vogue* in this sense was a new word to me, but the two-volume Larousse had the answer: '*Fête patronale dans certains départements du sud-est de la France.*'

I drove the ten miles from Crest and stopped the car by the side of the church, in a paved area that was, in fact, a car-park. A young man, well in his cups, put his face through my open window and asked me to put the vehicle somewhere else.

'*Pas stationner sur la place,*' he mumbled, '*bal, ce soir . . . à onze heures.*' With this he staggered and his head floated away leaving a sickly stench of beer behind him.

Not far from me I could see an articulated lorry – cab and flat trailer. On the trailer was a small shed, and in it a man wearing earphones. That was the disco.

Over the car-park three trees spread their branches; two plane trees and a walnut; coloured lights were strung between them. By the war memorial some youths were doing what youths do best – mooching.

I reparked the car and it now stood in front of a small café and épicerie. 'Chez Fred,' said the sign. It was two hours before the hop was due to start so I saved Fred for later and began by walking up the village; then I walked down the village and to the rear of the church. At the top of the little square was the smallest of town halls. In front of it, half a dozen responsible citizens were setting up trestle tables. Others were unloading bottles of pop and beer from a van. Fat was being heated on bottled gas for the frying of the chips.

I returned to Chez Fred's and went in. I sat at the bar and ordered a glass of wine. Four teenage boys came in off the street and flexed their muscles for a game of Baby-foot, a contest where lines of footballers, on a kind of table top and rigid on rods, are twirled at speed in order to propel a little ball into a goal. When the Baby-foot tournament had been lost and won I stood on Fred's doorstep, leaning against the wall.

The hop was beginning as all village hops begin. The DJ was chattering over every record, doing his best to get people dancing. Boys were standing in awkward clumps, shoving at each other and guffawing, stealing sly glances at the girls. The girls themselves stood in closer groups and swayed to the music, self-conscious under the scrutiny of their admirers. Only the tiny tots threw themselves whole-heartedly into the beat, twisting their hips and waving their arms, mimicking what they had seen their parents do at weddings and birthday parties.

Time passed. Old ladies emerged onto their balconies and shouted to friends below. The tribes of boys and girls grew larger, the fringe of one group mingling with the fringe of another. Two girls took to the floor, both fair haired, both dressed in exactly the same gear: blue jeans, black leather jackets, white trainers.

It was midnight before things really got going. The whole village must have been there, maybe 200 people. The two blonde girls formed a nucleus of action. They had hardly missed a number since the beginning of the evening. Sweat poured from their heads and darkened their hair; their faces shone with pleasure under coloured lights, and more girls joined them to make an exclusive circle, all chewing gum, jaws in harmony.

The lanky youths began to stir. One by one, they roused themselves, drawn willy-nilly into that clamorous whirlpool, pushing and nudging each other. Now not one of them wanted to be without a partner. The old women on their balconies smiled among themselves, remembering when.

Suddenly, from nowhere a wisp of a girl appeared on the scene, sixteen years old maybe, a waif with a strange triangular face, pale from smoking too much, yellow from the electric light bulbs. Her forehead was flat, her chin was pointed. Her black hair dropped straight to her shoulders, and her eyes were incandescent with a ravenous appetite for life, and devil take the hindmost. She looked fragile, a butterfly who wouldn't last the day – careless of what fate had in store.

Her bones had only the slightest covering of flesh; her legs were straight and skinny; she had no buttocks to speak of, and the bulge of her bosom was only the slightest of suggestions. She was dressed in the simplest of black shifts – the short skirt of it ending well above her knees. I was infatuated immediately.

She made her entrance like a creature from another planet, a different kind of human, her feet clad in clonking great wedges of high heel. She kissed every boy she passed, collecting men, looking for candles to burn at both ends, kicking one leg up behind her at each embrace, dragging on a cigarette between kisses. She was in a hurry with existence, impatient for everything. She rolled her hips to the music, a scrap of life eager to devour the world.

The coloured lights were flashing now, pulsing to the thump of the rhythm; the dance floor became crowded and the toddlers were banished. A young couple took centre stage, showing off, jiving in the old manner. He threw her up in his arms, into the lowest branches of the walnut; then she locked her thighs around his waist, clutching him tight.

I watched from the edge of the action. A woman in her fifties jigged round a tree trunk, mesmerized, eyes half closed behind gold-rimmed lenses that were as thick as the bottom of milk bottles. She wore a white pinafore dress that should have been buttoned tight from neck to hem, but more than half the buttons were undone, showing the skin of her belly, the curve of a bosom. And so she trod her light fantastic, not only alone but unaware of anyone else. She was as dedicated as a druid in her movements, but those movements were totally uncoordinated and they lived one beat behind whatever melody was playing. What did she care? She was spinning in an orbit of her own.

I thought about dancing too, just one before leaving – with that wisp of a creature in black. She was rocking with the two blonde girls now, her eyes burning as bright as madness, hair flicking over her face.

I made my decision, never mind that I was too old. I started towards her, determined to cut a mean caper. It was then that a lanky youth, a Baby-foot champion, guessed my intention and pushed in front of me. He seized the girl before I could, and bore her away. And there, together, they began their night.

There was nothing left for me to do but continue my progress across the floor, pretending, to myself and anyone who might be watching, that I was merely taking the shortest route to my car. Bad tempered and ill mannered, I pushed through the crowd: I should have spent the evening in the quiet of my hotel room, with a good book.

I switched on the ignition and put the car into gear. There was a quote from Horace lurking in my mind – I only know it in transla-tion: 'You have eaten enough, and taken sufficient wine. It is time for you to move on, for if you do not, then the young, who can play the game so much better than you, why then, they will mock you and elbow you aside . . .'

That's the trouble with Horace: he's always right.

On the D93 between Aouste and Blacons there was a sign by the side of the road, crudely painted on an old sea mine: '*Musée de Billes*' it said, the Museum of Marbles.

A man was sitting on the doorstep, right by the sign. He was slightly built, sixty maybe, with a moustache stuck in the middle of a face that looked like a bit of old rock. He looked a trifle the worse for wear, as if he was not too sure that his feet were in contact with the ground. His breath smelt like a brewery. His name was Maurice Guilhot.

'I was at a wedding yesterday,' he said. 'It went on all night . . . my great-niece.' He shook his head and looked at me with regret, wondering why he'd bothered to get out of bed that morning.

He dragged himself upright and we went into a gloomy, nondescript room that stood between two sections of a factory. There was stone dust everywhere; thin coatings and thick drifts. The room was furnished with a desk of sorts, a chair, and on the walls were pinned newspaper cuttings and photographs. Maurice Guilhot was famous.

He took me into a factory shed that had a high, hollow ceiling and very tall windows, all of them green with grime, giving a spooky, underwater quality to the light. It was like walking into a fairy tale and finding there was no escape.

In the corner to my right was a huge grooved disc, like a giant gramophone record; above that a vertical conveyor belt. Murderous tangles of electric cable cascaded out of cupboards, and at the end of the shed a row of cement mixers was drawn up. There were overhead belt-drives, wooden barrels with iron hoops, old ovens, wheels and rollers. It was the last marble factory in the world.

'In the classical era,' Maurice began, his voice cracking under the weight of a force 10 hangover, 'the Egyptians and the Greeks got their marbles from river beds . . . the running water did their work for them.' He blinked, swayed and held onto to a passing bench. 'We used to make marbles out of squares of onyx, put them in the grooves of this disc, and they went round and round for at least forty hours . . . wonderful marbles but too expensive and too slow to make. Now it's different, we start them off in these mixers, grains of sand, a mixture of clay and cement, then dry 'em and then bake 'em for six hours in a coke oven, polish 'em in kaolin, then we tint them.'

In the next shed Maurice showed me the paint shop and the great rectangular trays loaded with finished marbles. They glistened in magical colours: turquoise and maroon; pale blue, mauve and orange; scarlet and yellow. But his pride and joy was the crazy toy village he had built on the broad expanse of the floor; an obstacle course for marble champions, full of cul-de-sacs, bridges and intricate byways.

As I left he sold me a monster jar of marbles to stand on my desk. 'We have an annual all-comers competition,' he said, 'and a ladies' cup, and the winner takes the Golden Marble ... there's a few drinks taken then, I can tell you.'

'There are no glass marbles here,' I said.

Maurice's expression became dangerous and his lip curled. 'Don't mention glass marbles in this place,' he said, 'they're an invention of the devil.' And with that he slammed the door behind me.

In Romans-sur-Isère, in a convent building, several rooms have been set aside as a monument to those who fought in the Drôme for the French Resistance, and also to remember those who were deported – 238,000 of them. Only 35,000 returned.

During the German occupation hundreds of young French men and women came to the mountain wilderness of the Vercors to escape the forced labour that would otherwise have been imposed on them. Many more came to form base camps for armed resistance. In the summer of 1944, on the third of July, the *maquisards*, about 4,000 all told, felt secure enough to declare a free republic – the move was disastrously premature.

The German high command could not tolerate such a threat on their flanks and they ordered in a force of some 15,000 crack troops; airborne commandos and SS regiments. The battles were fierce and at least 600 *maquisards* perished.

The museum at Romans commemorates the period with old black and white photos of executions and torture, ration cards, swastikas, Free French armbands and transcripts of cryptic messages from the BBC. Most moving of all is the letter from a 22-year-old to his mother on the eve of his execution: 'The prison will send you my things, but I will keep father's pullover so that the cold doesn't make me tremble . . .' After that nothing would do but a pilgrimage to the Vercors itself.

I drove north from Beaufort, through an embroidery of alpine pastures. At St-Jean-en-Royans I bought saucisson and wine, then I followed the river Vernaison upwards through a narrow gorge where the road clung by its fingernails to the rock wall.

At les Baraques, a hamlet with a bar and a bridge, there was a commemorative plaque – twenty *maquisards* killed, holding back a German force of 300 in order to allow the main French force to escape. I went on across a wild upland to the grotto of la Luire: a cavern that was used by the Resistance as a hospital. On the car-park, another plaque – '27 *juillet, 1944. Les grands blessés soignés à l'hôpital du maquis furent transportés ici et achevés sur leurs brancards . . .*' then it gave their names – fourteen of them – and two doctors and a priest executed in Grenoble: the nurses deported to Ravensbruk. *'Passant, souviens-toi.'*

Inside the cave there were more plaques and there were fresh flowers lying on the ground, wrapped in transparent plastic and swathed in a *tricolore* sash, all damp with the condensation that dripped from the roof, the drops steady.

In the town of Chapelle-en-Vercors the old ladies sat on benches and laughed among themselves under the chestnut trees. The men played *pétanque*, and children splashed and screamed in the municipal swimming-pool, the sounds carrying into the farmhouse yard nearby where sixteen hostages had been lined up and shot in that same month of July 1944, all of them under forty, most of them under twenty-five.

And from high above Vassieux I could see only modern houses, showing that the original village had been put to the torch. I looked down on a wide valley where the Germans had landed their gliders. To one side was a war cemetery, its white crosses neat and orderly . . . and too numerous.

'These mountains of the Vercors,' said another plaque, 'are not mountains like other mountains; the martyrdoms undergone here have made them a symbol of all resistance against all repression . . . Vassieux is sacred.'

I set out to drive back over the Col de Rousset, a drop of 2,500 feet to the river Drôme, down through a frightening vista of peaks and precipices, all jumbled untidily together. In my rear-view mirror I could see dark clouds clambering up each other's backs, big and bulging with muscle, like bullies spoiling for a fight. But I didn't drive far, I couldn't – my eyes were full of tears.

Because the town hall of Die was about to close, the guardian of the door raised an eyebrow but allowed me in nevertheless. The mosaic lay a couple of feet below normal floor level, and was roped off so that it could only be viewed from the entrance. There was a fussy little man in there already, his face dark and big-eyed. He brimmed with enthusiasm and he knew his subject thoroughly. 'I go all round the world,' he said, 'looking for mosaics.'

We were talking so animatedly that the curator, out of the warmth of his heart, left us there an extra three-quarters of an hour. 'I have other things to do,' he said, 'I'll come back later.' He could see that we loved what he loved.

It was a twelfth-century mosaic depicting four rivers – the Tigris, Euphrates, Fison and Geon – and the four winds were also shown, cheeks puffed, and there were fish and mermaids in the background. The colours were fresh; black, yellow and green, dark reds, grey and salmon pink.

'See the different sizes of the stones,' said the little man, 'they're meant to be irregular, the idea is to give life and movement to the figures.'

Afterwards, in an ancient café with the bar topped in zinc, we tried some *pâté de sanglier* with a glass or two of lightly chilled Châtillon.

'The French,' said the little man, 'unlike the English, have no inhibitions about cooling red wine. In hot weather we drink it *frappé*, from Bordeaux to Burgundy. And how it goes down, all clean and refreshing; and how it burgeons in the stomach, releasing its colours there, a rainbow, a flower opening.'

'They buried Marie in the chapel,' said the woman. She was the local volunteer guide, and she called Madame de Sevigné by her Christian name, as if she were a friend she had known and loved and still carried in her heart.

'She was an extraordinary person. She was attractive, full of fun, and she was sensitive too . . . full of verve. You must read her letters, it's like having her in the room.'

I went down to the chapel, which lies just below the terrace of the château at Grignan, but I knew that Madame de Sevigné was no longer there. Her tomb had been pillaged at the Revolution, torn up in a frantic search for jewels, her bones scattered. But Madame de Sevigné lives in her writing. Over 1,100 of her letters have been preserved, more than 700 of them written to her daughter, and almost every aspect of the seventeenth century is in them – court news, military campaigns, scandals, love affairs and gossip, illnesses and deaths.

She was married early, gave her husband two children, then told him to find his sexual pleasures elsewhere – she considered she'd done her duty. Her husband was most obliging, making her a widow at twenty-five, killed in a duel protecting the honour of another woman. Madame de Sevigné was no fool and enjoyed her widowhood; she spent time at the court of Louis XIV at Versailles, at her house in Paris, and in Brittany where she had estates.

Françoise-Marguerite, Madame de Sevigné's daughter, was as attractive as her mother and was seriously propositioned by Louis XIV, but she turned him down. Impressed, La Fontaine wrote a fable for her – *Le Lion Amoureux*.

> *Sevigné, de qui les attraits*
> *Servent aux graces de modèle,*
> *Et qui naquites toute belle . . .*

The fable demonstrates to the lion, representing Louis XIV, that love leads him to do stupid things, and puts him in a position of ridicule, or even danger.

French Leave

'Amour, amour, quand tu nous tiens
On peut bien dire: Adieu prudence.

Louis was not a little peeved at having had his suit refused so Françoise was married off to the Comte de Grignan, who was made Lieutenant-general of Provence. It was not a bad appointment but it meant that the Comte, and of course his wife, were kept away from Versailles, and Versailles was where all influence lay: it was exile in all but name.

To compensate for his banishment the Comte de Grignan cultivated delusions of grandeur and incurred massive debts, so much so that his daughter was obliged to sell the château very soon after the death of her parents. She also edited the letters of her grandmother, but unfortunately destroyed the replies written by her mother, which in all probability were dangerously critical of Louis XIV and others at court.

The château was severely damaged at the Revolution and went for many years without a roof; much of its stone and most of its fireplaces were sold off to be used in the construction of other buildings. What is seen now is largely reconstruction, but it doesn't matter; for anyone who knows anything at all about the Marquise it is a must – her spirit walks the terrace just as it lives in her letters. 'She thought that all our days had been spun from silk and sunshine,' she says of someone somewhere. Now there's a woman who could turn a neat phrase.

23

1986
Rainstorms in The Pyrenees

My mountain bike was with me: it was June, I had two weeks to myself and I was standing near the customs post that straddles the border on the Col de Somport at the top of the Pyrenees. It was deserted, not a frontier guard to be seen. On the peaks above the pass there was fresh snow – unusual for that time of the year. The café on the Spanish side was shuttered and desolate; the brasserie in France was open so we took a stirrup cup together, my friend and I – he had driven me up from Toulouse, my bike on the roof-rack.

'The King of Spain comes here to ski,' said the barmaid pouring the beer. 'Incognito . . . nice bloke. The border runs behind that table on the terrace . . . see.' It was irresistible – my friend stood in one country and I stood in the other, we clinked glasses and then he left, and suddenly I noticed how lonely the place was, how lonely I felt.

I mounted the bike and it was off like a mustang, surging through the hairpins, all downhill. I was in the valley of the River Aspe which, according to the locals, is the most attractive of the Pyrenean valleys. It is dotted with tiny settlements that nestle in small splashes of pasture, a farmland that looks soft and woolly, a landscape as vertical and as pretty as nursery wallpaper. And the green of the grass that afternoon, under a dark sky, was strangely luminous, lit from within by an enchanted twilight.

It was cold, and shapeless, bad-tempered clouds sailed low and held the moist air close to the ground. But the thrushes and black-birds were singing, and the wagtails kept pace with me, darting back and forth, an escort of outriders.

I slept in the town of Urdos that night and the next morning, looking out from my bedroom, I saw shreds of mist lying in the street – scraps of soiled chiffon. The rain lurked between the houses like an assassin, and a group of serious cyclists got ready to attack the mountain passes, their buttocks pert in black lycra, their little tunics yellow, scarlet and mauve.

As I emerged from the hotel the rain declared itself in earnest and the gloom thickened, but the speed I reached on those down-ward slopes was exhilarating; the *route nationale* swooped from one bank of the Aspe to the other, and the sound of a hundred trib-utary streams was never out of earshot, rushing and tumbling through boulders black with moss, the light all dismal below the trees, a hiding place for trolls.

At an abandoned railway station I sheltered under the wide eaves. It was a ghost of a station, a beautiful ghost, built in squared grey stone, the shutters painted a pale turquoise. The platform was overgrown and a forest of weeds was thick on the line. The mildewy odour of the past rose from the sodden earth, and the rain dripped steadily from a broken gutter, ticking for the station's dead clock, bereft of hands, the stains of rust like grave marks on its face – *les marguerites du cimetière*.

In the village of Etsaut I stopped for a coffee. In the grocer's the woman of the place helped me make a ham and tomato sandwich.

'*Quel temps*,' she said, shaking her head. 'It's like the second flood . . . we must have committed some terrible sins to upset the Almighty like this.' She gave me an old-fashioned look, and I shrugged as if capable of all transgressions and proud of them.

An hour later I left the valley to follow a D-road that ran paral-lel to the *nationale*, halfway up the hillside, a road that connected a string of hamlets where white cows clanged their bells on sloping meadows, and the rain still fell. Above me a silent lightning was flickering over the cloudy highlands, ominous and Byronic. Two red-cheeked women in wrap-around aprons gave me a *'Bonjour'* from an open window. There were young apples in their orchard and dog-roses in the hedge, but the stone walls that bordered the highway were falling apart, slipping back towards the ground.

I took lunch in a bus shelter. My pannier bags were soaked through and my ham sandwich had become a cold mush. I ate it nevertheless and, with no modesty, removed my wet wet clothes and replaced them with some wet dry ones.

I waited for an hour, hoping the weather would improve; but this was no ordinary downpour, this had malice in it, it was out to get me, like the Basques snapping at Charlemagne's rearguard beyond Roncesvalles. Trouble is, I'm no Roland, no Oliver. I'd had enough, I wanted to surrender to the sun, I had no desire to be a hero, I wanted decadence and warmth.

It did no good. By the time I'd aquaplaned into the town of Oloron-Ste-Marie I was convinced that I'd spent more of my existence under water than Jacques Cousteau. I was at one with the elements and resigned to despair – man as coelacanth. Then everything changed – I crossed the threshold of the Hotel Aragon and was enveloped in the warm embrace of Madame Françoise Bordelongue: unruly hair, quick ironic expression, a forthright manner and nobody's mug.

She waved a hand and her husband disappeared with my bike. *'Vous êtes trempé comme une soupe,'* she said. 'Get your clothes off and we'll throw 'em in the tumble-drier. *Il a plu des hallebardes aujourd'hui.'*

I stripped in reception and, wrapped in a towel, went straight to a bath, turning on the hot tap and letting it run until I had created a sauna. If there is an argument for cycling endless miles in a cloud-burst, and I doubt there is, then the feeling of well-being that an excellent dinner affords might just tip the balance in favour of such an exercise.

So it was that I allowed myself to glow with satisfaction as I contemplated my glass of Jurançon, a golden wine as rich in colour as Tutankhamen's treasure. My storm-washed clothes, now dry, smelt of dawn and Madame Françoise flew like an angel across the restaurant, her garments flowing, her feet encased in winged slippers. On the walls were paintings of cupids and cherubim; there were fresh flowers everywhere and scatterings of polished stones were strewn across the damask to add sparkle to each tablecloth. A quiet country girl with innocent eyes waited on table.

There was *garbure* to begin with: a peasant broth that is made from whatever vegetables and meats happen to be in season. Then came a whole duck's liver cooked in a *vin doux*, with cherry tomatoes and slices of apple. This was followed by *magret de canard*, and, to help the digestion, a local Madiran, red, from the vineyards that lie between Tarbes and Pau. I finished with a *crème brûlée*, and an Armagnac. There was Mozart in the background and I was in the company of half a dozen other diners, a select band who were in on Aquitaine's biggest secret – a secret that not even the vilest of tortures would make them divulge.

I awoke, after a night of untroubled sleep, to find that the halberds were still falling and, out of the endless goodness of her heart, Madame drove me into Oloron, where I decided to cheat and take the train to my next destination – the city of Pau.

I had two hours to wait and so I cycled slowly up to the Eglise Ste Marie, a wet and wintry wind slapping me in the face. Under the porch was a beggar, a Quasimodo, his head carved from a block of stone. He was half crouching in an alcove, as if he had only just, that very minute, ousted the statue that should have been standing there. His fingers strummed on an old guitar but not a lilt of melody came out of it.

He must have been a regular, for on the way to their devotions the old ladies of the church stopped to comfort him. He took their money and grinned a crafty lopsided grin, a Sunday high mass of a grin, his eyes gleaming with avarice as the silver coins fell into his cap, while in the steeple the bells rang, loud enough to dislodge the tiles and send them clattering down the roof.

I stood there a long while, watching the worshippers gather, running to avoid the rain. Then, when mass had begun and even the late arrivals had taken their place, Quasimodo tucked the guitar under his arm and limped across the road and into the warmth of the café opposite.

It seemed like a good idea and I was about to follow him in search of a glass of hot rum, when a woman, who if appearances were anything to go by was also one of the Oloron fraternity of beggars, staggered from the church. Her eyes were opaque and looked diseased, like dead jelly-fish. She was mountainous across the hindquarters, and two hemispheres of flesh trembled in her bosom. What hair she possessed had been sawn off and left all ragged round a bruised face.

Looking neither to right nor left, but intent on what she was doing, she went around the corner of the porch, and, in the pouring rain, hoisted up her skirts and peed, her legs straddled wide as she stood there; the flesh of her colossal thighs and buttocks a pale and mottled white. When she'd finished she rushed by me at a loping trot, head down, making for the café, her body aching for booze.

'*Je suis pressée,*' she said as she pushed me out of her way and opened the door, '*ça donne soif, la ménopause!*'

In the café, at the bar, I sat next to Quasimodo who was drinking a glass of red wine and reading the racing papers. '*Il pleut partout,*' he said, '*mais heureusement le vin fait vivre.*'

'Who's that woman?' I asked. 'She just peed, right outside the church.' He shrugged his shoulders. His head, low over the counter, seemed to come from the middle of his chest without benefit of neck. 'I dunno,' he said, 'she does it every Sunday. It's her way of praying.'

The city of Pau is famous for being the birthplace of Henri IV – Henri of Navarre, *le vert galant*. The château where the king was born is a rectangular building with towers, pointed roofs, an arcaded entry and Renaissance doors and windows. The view from the gardens, looking out to the Pyrenees, is astounding, says the brochure, 'with snow-covered crags shimmering high in sparkling azure skies'. On a clear day, that is. Not with the rain I had.

'Henri was a strong man, amorous, with many mistresses,' said the resident guide as he explained the château's treasures to me. 'He had great sexual powers, that is because, as a child, his breakfast was a glass of Jurançon, and his lips were wiped with a clove of garlic. They say that when he was fully grown you could smell him from five hundred paces. It was fortunate that in those days women liked their men to be powerful . . . in every way.'

Towards the end of my visit the guide invited me to enjoy a collection of chamber pots in Sèvres porcelain. There were the usual round varieties in puce and white, and that special navy blue, but there were oval ones also, long and thin, shaped like gravy boats, though much larger. 'They are called *Bourdalous*,' said the guide, 'after a seventeenth-century Jesuit whose sermons were endless, reducing ladies of quality to embarrassment. So under the voluminous dresses went the *bourdalous*, and the servants would pass behind the pews, emptying what needed to be emptied into large buckets. *Je vous dis – autres temps, autres moeurs.*'

It hadn't gone away the next morning – the monsoon – and once more I cheated. My destination was Marciac, a journey of about 40 miles by the secondary routes I favoured, but that was too much for me to cycle in such a squall. I decided to do about a third of the day's ride in a taxi.

When the driver arrived she frightened the life out of me. She was as square as the Parthenon, about the same size, and looked as if she had been as equally ill-used by history. She stowed my bike in the boot and ordered me to sit in the front with her.

'It'll be one hundred and thirty francs,' she said as we set off. '*Quel bordel*, in the last ten minutes we've had a month's rain.'

'A year's,' I said. I was getting bitter by now.

When the miles were done she watched while I put on my waterproofs and fixed the pannier bags.

'I'll only charge you a hundred,' she said. 'I like crazy people.' I offered her a 20-franc tip and she got angry: 'I said one hundred.' Then she smiled, and it was like the sun coming out as we were wishing it would. I wasn't going to argue with her – she could have cleared an SAS pub in ten seconds.

She left me with a wave, and I went on, cruising by fields of wheat and corn, and over narrow byways where, on the asphalt, the moss spread undisturbed and the grass grew thick. From Abère to Simacourbe I suffered heavy rain, and down to Anoye where two women, one old, one ancient, talked under a fig tree and under an umbrella; '*Ah, non,*' they said, 'there is no baker or grocer's for twenty-five kilometres . . . not until you get to Maubourget.'

I saw no one else for a spell; only the dogs watched as I went by. There were distant spires on the hill-tops, fern and rowan in the rough ground. And on the outskirts of Luc Adou there was a shrine, all built in wood to commemorate the hundreds of thousands of pilgrims who had passed this spot en route to Santiago de Compostella, back up to the Col de Somport where I had started, and down into Spain.

At Maubourget, a real metropolis with shops and restaurants, I ate a sandwich and drank a glass or two of Corbière. I pressed on across a watery plain to Marciac, past more maize, lush as jungle, and past trees planted *en quinconce*, where the hollow wind whistled damply round the trunks, and the air was tinted under the vaulted branches – a murky aquamarine swirling in on itself. And the dull rivers I crossed were all pockmarked with flurries of hail, large like pebbles.

After a night at Marciac I maundered through the soundless villages of Laveraet, St Christaud and Poulylebon. At Montesquiou the heavens emptied themselves onto the roofs and onto me; cataracts streamed down the walls, over the paved streets and out through an arched gate. The whole planet smelt like the interior of some wild mushroom, with a tang of wood smoke to it as everyone alive hid behind closed doors and lit their fires.

At last I splashed through the puddles and entered the city of

Auch. The tempest exhausted itself and the battered sky hardened and took on the appearance of a bleak mountain range, all grey, white and black, with huge canyons of indigo lying behind.

In Auch the cathedral stands high above its surroundings, hemmed in by winding streets, and is famous for two things – both sixteenth century – its stained glass windows and its choir stalls, 113 of them, fashioned in an oak so hard that no worm can gnaw it, nor nail pierce it. The trees, I was told, had been felled at the full moon then seasoned for decades in the urine of cattle.

And while I made the most of being dry and warm, resting in a cathedral pew, the Orchestra and Choir of Toulouse rehearsed a requiem by Zelenka; musicians and singers of all ages dressed in bright sweaters and jeans. The conductor was a showman, bald on top with a pony tail behind, energetic and hopping on one foot when he wanted the music made joyful on the word 'Hosanna'. 'Hosanna,' he cried, and the music rose and filled every bit of space under the roof – 'Hosanna.'

I spent two days in Auch then made for Levignac, *en route* for Toulouse. Being my last stint on the road it was only to be expected that the rain should stop and that the clouds should liberate themselves from the earth and soar away into the stratosphere. Beyond the town of l'Isle-Jourdain, and to the north, a ridge closed in the horizon. Near at hand a field of unripe tomatoes gave off a powerful odour. A young girl, still in her pyjamas, explored the deep grass of her garden; an old woman crept on stiff limbs to her wood-shed. A field of beans went by; a château with a huge *pigeonnier*, and, high on the skyline, I could see the village of le Castera and the steeple of its church.

I went into the village through a stone portal and arrived in a tiny square; there was a bar, closed, and a house, half-timbered and finished in the red brick of Toulouse. A man in his fifties came through the front door. He had silvery hair and a good smile.

'For a Frenchman,' he said, 'I make a very good cup of tea.'

The house was restful and attractive: lots of beams, fine antiques, prints and pictures, and a grand piano. At the rear was a terrace that looked out towards the Pyrenees, and now that the sun was out I could actually see the bright peaks suspended in the sky.

I was invited to stay the night and did. We talked and drank late. I came awake to the smell of coffee, fresh bread and my host playing the first of the Forty-eight on the grand. Already, in the eighteenth century, Laurence Sterne had it right: 'They order,' he'd said, 'this matter better in France.'

24

1989

A Boat Trip in Brittany

Even as a youngster I knew that France began at Victoria Station. For one thing the Golden Arrow used to steam past the windows of my school every day, the smoke lying sleek and transparent along the fuselage of the Merchant Navy Class locomotive. On Saturdays I used to haunt Victoria itself, platform 8, staring snotty-nosed through the polished windows of the golden Pullman cars, with their girls' names painted flowery, yellow on brown: Aimée, Rose and Susan.

But I've grown up since then, though the child who lives in my heart has never deserted me. Under the high roof of the Gare Montparnasse that child was happy, staring at the TGV where it lay like a brand new rocket, grey and royal blue, panting to be away into the night. Twenty coaches long, with massive power sections at each end and two more in the middle, it was a mighty sexual shape born of desire out of wind tunnels. 'Three hundred kph as far as Le Mans,' said the *contrôleur*, 'then she drops down to two hundred . . . Floats like a butterfly, flies like a bee.'

I threw my bag into the first class, remembering how I'd pressed my nose against Pullman windows – as the song said, 'always on the outside, on the outside always looking in'. Now it was my turn.

While I waited I paced the platform in style. Here was a man complaining of the *courants d'air* that whistled across the platform. There, preceded by a mountain of luggage, a couple of aristocrats, both clad in ankle-length fur coats, he with an astrakhan hat, she with a scarf as long and as wide and as heavy as a chenille table-cloth. The woman moved with the grace and distinction of an Isadora Duncan, making me pray, as I watched her, that she did not meet the same fate, especially at 300 kilometres an hour.

The train's take-off was so smooth that I didn't realize we were out of Paris until we were. Around me the lamps shone; the sliding doors opened mysteriously before they were touched and then closed again, unbidden. The stewardess was chic in a dog-tooth check jacket, flared slightly at the waist, a grey skirt cut to her figure and a yellow blouse to blend in with the lampshades. Elegant court shoes clothed her feet and her black and seamless stockings were as sheer and shiny as the precipice of a slate quarry in rain.

She brought me smoked salmon, chump chop of lamb, sizzling hot, *courgettes et haricots verts, fromage*, crystallized fruit and coffee. I leant back in the armchair and sipped the Pauillac . . . I felt I had been elected to the membership of a genteel club, only this one was flying along on the threshold of escape velocity, heading for Brittany.

I can't remember now why I'd been sent to Vannes, probably to try out a few hotels and excursions. It was nearly midnight when I arrived and so I dived directly into a small *auberge* that stood opposite the station – two stars and two Ns. I was allocated a classic hotel room as designed by the French – taller than it was square with just space enough to edge around the double bed. In one corner was a sink and in another an upended plastic coffin that was a shower. It moved when I got into it and seemed attached to the floor by its waste pipe only, and as I washed it rolled and creaked like an old ship. But none of that mattered for I was totally content when I climbed between the sheets; I knew that the early-morning trains would see to it that I did not oversleep or miss a minute of the following day.

The notice chalked on the blackboard said there was a boat trip across the Gulf of Morbihan that afternoon; three and a half hours for 110 francs. A family of five were up on the top deck, undaunted by the fierce bright wind of February. They were all, down to the smallest boy, equipped with anoraks, binoculars and notebooks. I stood with them behind the wheelhouse, where three *matelots*, relaxed and casual, directed the expedition and continued a conversation they must have started as boys. Below decks two couples turned up their collars, folded their arms, ignored each other and stared through the windows at the empty bay. It was bleak.

'Here,' said the mother of the family, handing me her binoculars and, in the same moment, adopting me for the afternoon.

'Look over there,' said one of the youngsters who obviously knew more than I did about everything. He pointed to the cold mudflats where the cormorants stood up like black sticks. My skin froze as the boat wound its way through the islands but I couldn't let the flag down by going below, not while children were still on deck, their round cheeks burning with health.

At last we came to the place where the bay met the open sea and the boat swung into the wind and fought against the waves.

'It's the Atlantic,' the father said as if he and Columbus had a monopoly on it. Then he told his children, 'It's the ocean.' But they knew anyway.

I stared down into the water. The currents were terrifying here – swirling, muscular deeps, dark green and black with pits and scars in a surface that resembled a cold and murderous lava.

The mother saw me swallow my fear. She took my notebook from my hands. 'I'll tell you what you've seen,' she said to cheer me up, and shouted names into the wind as she wrote them down: 'Herons, egrets, grebes, lapwings, peewits, kingfishers, coots, sandpipers and whistling ducks.'

We sailed for another hour or so until the three mariners tied up at a jetty on the Isle aux Moines. The other passengers disappeared, most of them into a warm café, but I stayed with the sailors, standing at the open bar of a windswept shebeen. A woman called Jeanette ran the bar; red hair and a rusty voice went with her, and in that rust was a laugh that knew all about men, legions of them attracted to her body by the rough shipwreck of her voice.

I was shivering and ordered a grog. Jeanette narrowed her eyes at me. 'I will make you a grog the like of which you have never tasted,' she said. For the sailors Jeanette poured red wine.

'There was a courting couple off your boat,' she said. 'I sent them up to Lovers' Woods – you know, the woods where two go up and three come back.'

The men drank their wine and laughed. All around us the houses were shuttered and a winter crop of black seaweed lay flat across the sands like dead hair. There was a long line of wooden beach huts too, closed tight, their doors padlocked, each hut imprisoning a Proustian childhood that waited only for the summer to be free.

Just before we left I bought the sailors a round of drinks and pushed some coins across the counter. 'I'll charge you a sailor's price,' said the rusty voice, 'but don't come back in the summer, not for that money.' And the sailors laughed again, and drank my health.

25

1991

Arles: A Poem and the Nord Pinus

'You cannot,' said Daniel Ravel, 'you cannot write about Arles without quoting the poem, the one by Paul-Jean Toulet, the one about the Alyscamps.'

We were sitting in the restaurant of the Hôtel Jules César, where the waiters levitated above the Persian carpets and the duck was superb; so was the Moulin à Vent.

It was a reunion lunch. Twenty years had gone by since Daniel and I had worked together as coach driver and tour guide: les Saintes-Maries to Orange; Nîmes to Fontaine-de-Vaucluse. We'd pulled a few strokes, eaten superb meals and Daniel had learnt English from women whose holidays he'd vastly improved.

'We had to learn that poem at school,' he went on. He leant back in his chair and contemplated the ruby in his wine glass – coach driver turned breeder of white horses in the Camargue, and troubadour, reciter of verses . . .

> *Dans Arles, où sont les Aliscams,*
> *Quand l'ombre est rouge, sous les roses,*

193

Et clair le temps,

Prends garde à la douceur des choses,
Lorsque tu sens battre sans cause
Ton coeur trop lourd,

Et que se taisent les colombes:
Parle tout bas, si c'est d'amour,
Au bord des tombes.

He emptied his glass. 'You ought to translate it,' he said.

According to popular etymology Alyscamps, as it is now written, is a place-name composed of the same words that form Champs Elysées, the Elysian Fields of Greek mythology. Once the most revered burial place in Christian Europe, the Alyscamps was a necropolis of considerable dimensions. Many miles square, its sarcophagi, magnificently carved in marble, were piled five or six high, making an enormous city of narrow streets with more bodies in it than many a city of the living.

In the middle ages the Alyscamps was *the* place to be buried, prince or pauper; the holiest of holies. St Trophime had been entombed there, Roland and Oliver too. Dante had written it into his poetry, and a vision of Christ had confirmed its sanctity. The faithful wanted nothing more than to take their final rest in that hallowed soil, then no matter what the confusion on judgement day, they were sure of paradise. From as far away as Poland the defunct were dispatched, thousands of them. Even the poor wanted their share of heaven. All along the upper reaches of the River Rhône they put their dead into barrels or watertight coffins and committed them to the current, nailing a few oboli to the wooden lids. Then, when the corpses arrived at Arles, as they always did, those who transported them across the city for burial could take their reward.

As time went on this commerce declined. Towards the end of the middle ages the local nabobs, counts and kings, took to giving the best of the sarcophagi to their friends so that they might embellish their palaces and gardens with them. Perhaps they were filled with water and used as baths, or tipped upright to make wardrobes or sentry boxes. Gradually the great necropolis dwindled to almost nothing, and in the nineteenth century, by way of a final insult, the railway came to Arles and the main line from Paris was laid through the graveyard, carving it up into shunting yards and sidings.

All that remains today is one long double row of massive stone coffins and, straggling between, a dusty and stony path that used to be one of the main highways of the Roman Empire. But there is still a feeling of the supernatural in the Alyscamps, and there is no doubt that it is haunted, crowded with the dead. As I walked among the tombs, from sunshine to shadow under the tall trees, out of the touch of the wind but within its sound, the *mistralet* – the little mistral – was stirring in the branches; a cold breath from the under-world.

A young girl, slim, eyes closed, lay on one of the coffin lids, sunbathing, her head on her rucksack, her hair shining on the dark granite, her bare feet fragile and white. By the ruins of the church of St Honorat was a triangle of green, littered with open tombs.

The iron gates of the church were open, and inside an Italian tourist, convinced he was alone, sang an aria – for the echo and the joy itself of singing – his voice powerful and brimming with life, and while he sang, long and loud, the ghosts of the Alyscamps, centuries of them, retreated into the shades to listen: '*O lacrimae rerum.*'

I was up before the mistral next morning, and took a coffee in the place du Forum, the most attractive small square in Arles, perhaps in the whole of Provence. I could have sat there for hours, idling, peaceful under the plane trees. The cafe tables were piled high, one on the other, from the night before, the chairs stacked into barricades, their cushions of different colours: blue, yellow and cerise. The early sun was just high enough to clear the rooftops and it glittered in the leaves above my head, flickering on the hands and faces of the waiters and their two or three customers.

A road sweeper moved slowly along the gutter, tattered and tarnished, a victim of *vin ordinaire*. He bent to retrieve something and groaned. 'The ground's further away than it was twenty years ago,' he said in a meridional accent that was thicker than bouillabaisse. He prodded a pile of litter with his shovel. 'Rubbish,' he said, 'look at it.' Then he sighed and threw his broom across his trolley. 'I've done enough . . . I think I'll go down by the river and sit in the sun for a while.'

Daniel saw me off at the station. There was a plaque commemorating Van Gogh: '20 February 1888. Vincent Van Gogh arrived in Arles by the Paris train. He was to stay in our town until 8 May 1889. *C'est ici qu'il faut installer l'atelier de l'avenir.*'

I wrote the words down in my notebook while Daniel looked over my shoulder.

'That reminds me,' he said. 'Did you translate the poem?'

I brought out a grubby piece of paper, made soft by much handling:

> '*Down by the Alyscamps, in Arles,*
> *When, under the roses, the shadows lie red,*
> *And the air is clear,*
>
> *Have a care for the sweetness of things.*
> *And when you feel your more than heavy heart*
> *Beating without reason;*
>
> *And when the white doves are silent,*
> *Speak softly, if you speak of love,*
> *In Arles, down by the Alyscamps.*

It's not bad,' said Daniel, 'but you didn't do the rhymes.'

'Are you kidding? Look at the rhyme scheme: a, b, a, b, b, c, d, c, d. It's impossible.'

Daniel sniffed. 'Paul-Jean Toulet did it,' he said. 'But then, I know that French is a richer language than English.'

'Yes,' I said, 'you and the Académie Française.'

It was not my fault, the name of the hotel – the Nord Pinus, Arles. That had been the hotel assigned to me as a tour guide in 1970 and I'd been worried about the reaction of my clients, but they were delighted of course. As one of them said: 'You don't get luggage labels like that every day.'

I didn't realize at the time that Arles was to become one of my favourite towns, nor that the Nord Pinus was to become my favourite hotel. Three two-month seasons I spent there, a total of six months in the company of Germaine Bessière, the owner – an achievement, given the nature of the woman, that should have been recognized by the award of the Legion of Honour.

Germaine was wide and solid, stumpy where she had once been petite. Nobody knew how old she was, seventy-five maybe. In any event, the best of her life lay far, far behind her. She had been a singer and a cabaret dancer, one half of a music-hall act with her husband – Nello – a tight-rope artist and a performer on novelty bicycles. One of those bicycles, a penny-farthing, leant against a wall in the hotel's ground-floor cloakroom; it was all that remained of Nello and his life on the boards.

For Germaine was already a widow when I arrived on the scene, and she reigned like an empress, a moody and autocratic Catherine the Great. That first time in the hotel, when I arrived to organize the room allocations, she was waiting for me, shuffling about in soft felt slippers and trailing a diaphanous, pastel robe behind her. Her blonde hair had lost its lustre, and time had done its work on her face.

'These clients of yours,' she said, as if she'd never seen anything quite as vulgar as a paying guest, 'I trust they're civilized.' She looked at me like Medea about to poison the children.

The hotel restaurant was a nightmare. Germaine was far too patrician to bother with the running of the kitchens, and so they were inhabited by a bunch of castaways who just happened to have been marooned on that particular shore. They were sulky troglodytes who knew no master and owed no allegiance. Evening after evening my clients waited for their soup to appear, and when it did it was lukewarm and characterless. I myself spent every dinner-time between the hotplates and ovens, trying to wheedle and cajole those mutinous myrmidons into some kind of activity and, much to their amusement, carrying plates, opening bottles of wine and cutting slices of apple tart.

Why did I like it then? How did such a place insinuate itself into my heart? It was certain that the atmosphere of the Nord Pinus had something to do with it: dark-brown armchairs in leather, the wide windows and mirrors of the dining room, the bar where the ghosts of matadors and poets still lingered and the rooms where the stars had made narcissistic love to one another in the wide soft beds.

And there was more. The hotel stood on the north side of the place du Forum, with cafés all around and great plane trees giving a flickering shade all through the summer. There was a statue of Frédéric Mistral, too, grand and dignified in a wide-brimmed hat, leaning on a stick and carrying his overcoat in the approved artistic manner. To drink my coffee in a Gothic novel every morning and then stand on the hotel steps to survey a perfect little corner of the world made everything seem worthwhile: the rustics in the kitchen and the tantrums of Germaine – all that became as nothing.

But 'Tout passe, tout casse et tout lasse' as the poet says. I moved on and Germaine became even older and the Nord Pinus raced downhill. From being Catherine the Great, Germaine became Miss Havisham. People no longer came to stay and the debts accumulated. The rats deserted the foodless kitchens. Beetles crept behind the wallpaper, and spiders and mice moved into the rooms where the rich and famous had taken their pleasures. Meanwhile Germaine sat on the steps and fed the sparrows, and the ruins crumbled around her.

In due time she made her solitary way to that great music hall in the sky and the Nord Pinus was sold – the danger being that a fine old hotel might become part of a faceless chain, or a set of municipal offices even. Luckily the new owner, a woman, was the ideal person for the job and she set about the task of the redecoration with the spectre of Germaine standing at her elbow. When I walked into the Nord Pinus, that year I returned to see Daniel, and the first time for two decades, it seemed not to have changed at all. I fully expected to see Germaine shuffling to the bar, her pastel dress still wafting behind her, an apparition in her own dream.

The leather armchairs were still in the foyer and there were vases overflowing with red roses. The bar too was the same; the same stools, the same chairs and the same vermouths and whiskies; the same bull-fighter's costume in its glass case and the same enormous posters announcing ancient *corridas* and their matadors: Ordonez, Chamaco and Belmonte.

And they gave me my old room that night – the famous number 10 with three balconies overlooking the square, and from that vantage point I could peer through the branches of the plane trees, and through the leaves that, in the daytime, cast those flickering shadows across the café terraces where the waiters wandered. In the room itself there were two double beds with wrought-iron flora at head and foot, all curlicues and whirligigs, painted black with touches of gilt picking out the fruits and flowers. There was also a marble-topped table and a huge mirror, the surround of it in golden wood, carved into wavelets and foliage; and in the centre of the ceiling a cut-glass chandelier.

But pride of place in my sentimental soul went to the framed declaration on the wall, its paper wrinkled and yellow: '*Sa Majesté, Napoleon III, Empereur des Français a passé la nuit du 3 au 4 juin 1856 à l'Hôtel du Nord, dans cette chambre.*'

Inspired by that testimony I lolled on my eiderdowns and read through the visitors' book, page after page of it. This is where they all came then, to sleep in my bed: Dominguin and Ava Gardner, Picasso, Jean Cocteau, Odette and Peter Churchill, Pagnol, Mistinguett, Edith Piaf, Yves Montand, King Farouk (once a captive of Germaine's beauty, say some), Jean-Paul Sartre, Jacques Tati, and even Charlotte Rampling, whose nude photograph, taken in that very room, gazed down at me. Had she slept in my bed, too? Little wonder then, that my dreams in the Nord Pinus were, that night, so ardent.

26

1993

On the Yellow Train: Toulouse to Perpignan

Toulouse railway station was busy with flocks of children chattering like sparrows in their favourite tree. They were off to the mountains with rucksacks and teachers. The train was a real train with corridors and high steps and a grey-haired *contrôleur*. He sauntered by, chanting to himself: '*On va à la montagne, on va à la montagne.*' I settled back in my seat. Work might be taking me to Perpignan, but I was going the pretty way – up to the Spanish frontier, along the Pyrenees, then down to the Mediterranean.

We followed the valley of the Ariège river, flat country at first, but as we advanced the hills came near and grew steeper. At Foix the river was pent in, just below the track, a broken water hurrying over rough rocks. Above us, so close was the town, leant the balconies of tall and narrow houses.

It was my kind of train. It dawdled at stations and even at top speed was overtaken by cars, when there were any. Louring escarpments rose on either side of the line, and directly ahead were the great peaks of the Pyrenees. At Tarascon-sur-Ariège the river became a mysterious green, murky under the trees. At Ax-les-

Thermes the valley was sheer. There was pine and silver birch, and thin streams of white water running down swaths of shale, the deep scars of ancient avalanches. The only buildings to be seen were farmhouses, sombre, built out of mountain stone, the roof tiles too – everything the same colour, painted thick in verdigris.

Swaying, the train took us on over the Col de Puymorens at 6,200 feet, then we dropped back again to four thousand and into our destination, Latour-de-Carol.

'*Une gare internationale,*' said the *contrôleur*. He was singing now, anticipating his lunch in the station buffet, impatient for his aperitif. He waited for the children to gather their belongings and disembark. 'This is nothing, it takes half an hour to get Parisians out of their couchettes in the high season, God knows what they get up to at night . . .' He winked at me. 'Change here for Barcelona, and the Canari – the little yellow bird.'

The Canari is a narrow-gauge train with dinky carriages, each with an open platform in the middle that is fenced off with tiny red gates. There was a notice on the wall – 'Those passengers wishing to alight at request stops should get in at the front and inform the *contrôleur*.' I did as I was told and installed myself on a rexine bench seat, the only person in the carriage.

The driver, Jean-Luc, and the *contrôleur* welcomed me in and Jean-Luc propped the door to his cab wide open with a broom handle so that we could talk. The journey was 39 miles, two and a half hours. We were travelling into a high Pyrenean valley, la Cerdagne, lush and flat, dotted with fortified farms and villages – hamlets with names that rang with romance: Bena Fanès, Ur les Escaldes, Estavar and Bolquère Eyne – the highest station on the French Railways network – 5,174 feet.

These were isolated communities but Jean-Luc knew every villager in them and they waved to him as he passed. In return he gave a long blast on the train whistle – and three for an attractive young woman waiting at a level crossing. After only five minutes of conversation I was in the driver's cab and installed on the jump seat – a boyhood dream realized. At the next level crossing, where another young woman waited, I was encouraged to pull the cord that activated the whistle – another ambition fulfilled.

Jean-Luc had been six years a train driver. He was slim and angular with designer stubble; dressed in jeans and a check shirt, he was a good talker.

'I love this job,' he told me. 'It's so peaceful, unhurried. We always eat at table, either at home or at Latour. I get home most nights . . . I can watch my son grow. And I can use the train to go fishing . . . get off where I like, places you can't even get to by car, and the train picks me up in the evening . . . it's a real life, and I wouldn't change it to be president.'

We went further into the Cerdagne, and here and there on the flanks of the high peaks I could see more stone-built villages, their outlines softened by a summer haze. The train flew across gullies and plunged through tunnels, it rattled over bridges. A road gleamed, far below us at the bottom of the Tet river valley, and deep in some sunless gorge I glimpsed the ruins of an abandoned hotel. We rocked and we rolled; France to the left, Spain within spitting distance to the right.

'You're on a real TGV now,' said Jean-Luc, smiling at his own joke, '*Un Train Grande Vibration*'.

Gradually we dropped down to the level of the river, approaching the end of the line at Villefranche, a tiny town completely confined in its fortifications. Jean-Luc shook my hand in farewell, leapt from the train and onto the platform, into the arms of his wife. He kissed her and then swung his son into the air above his head. There was laughter from all three of them. Jean-Luc was a happy man who had made the right choices.

At about eight-thirty the next morning, I started up the dusty track that climbs from Villefranche railway station to the Vauban fort that sits on the hill and guards the walled town below. As I climbed I moved from the valley's shadow and out into the sunshine. There was nobody at the fort when I arrived there, it being too early for the *gardien* to be on duty. I sat on the wall of the dry moat and heard the whistle of the yellow train as the 09.05

rattled out of the station. A lizard sat on a rock opposite me and stared; the smell of thyme and mountain pine scented the air.

The fortress was a great slab-sided thing, a star shape with sharp corners. Built to defend the frontier with Spain, it had been designed by Vauban, a military genius of the seventeenth century; a man who, rising from obscurity, constructed thirty-three fortresses and repaired 300. It was typical of his work; every angle of attack had been covered and the enfilades would have been murderous.

I had given up on the *gardien* and was about to leave when he arrived in his car, surprised to see anyone at the fort so early and so far out of season. He led me high over the moat on a wooden foot-bridge, opened the gates and showed me round, as proud of Vauban as if he had been a near relative. 'A town besieged by Vauban,' said Marcel, placing his hand on my shoulder, 'was a town taken . . . a town defended by Vauban was a town they couldn't take.'

The fortress was as solid in as out; a firing step around the walls, a watch tower 60 feet high, a barracks for officers and men, and deep corridors carved into the rock so that if any attackers managed to get into the moat they would have died there, fired on from both sides.

But Marcel saved his *pièce de résistance* till last; ushering me into a dungeon in which four women had been imprisoned in the seventeenth century, banished from Paris by Louis XIV.

'It was the affair of the poisons,' said Marcel. 'An amazing scandal. The main culprit was the Marquise de Brinvilliers . . . she poisoned her father and two brothers. There was witchcraft, famous people dying unexpectedly, probably poisoned, including Henrietta, the daughter of Charles I of England . . . people at court implicated, even the King's mistress, Madame de Montespan, was suspected of consulting witches. She wanted love potions to make sure the King didn't stray too far from her bed . . . he was a lively number, that Louis. The whole affair turned very nasty, the king could have been assassinated, so he stepped in and put a stop to the legal proceedings, too much detail was coming out . . . too close for comfort. People were put away for life, under *lettres de cachet*, just for knowing too much . . . and that really meant life in those days. Four were sent here . . . one of them lasted thirty-six years – imagine, thirty-six years in this damp cell. But the ringleaders were hanged, broken on the wheel or burnt at the stake. There were thirty-four public executions . . . and those found guilty were tortured as well, their feet crushed, taken to confession in a tumbril, then covered in straw and set ablaze. Makes your blood curdle, I promise you . . . Madame de Sevigné writes about it in her letters . . .'

At last it is done, la Brinvilliers is blown away, her poor little body was thrown, after the execution, into a fierce fire, and her ashes to the wind, so that now we breathe them in . . . She was judged yesterday, and this morning her sentence was read to her, which was to make a public confession at Notre-Dame, and then to be beheaded, her body burnt and her ashes scattered to the wind.

Her interrogation began but she replied that there was no need as she would tell all. In fact she told her story until five o'clock in the evening, more terrifying than was thought. She had made ten attempts at poisoning her father, her brothers and several others . . .

At six o'clock she was taken, naked except for a shift and a rope around her neck, to Notre-Dame to make her confession, after which she was put back into the same tumbril, where I saw her, thrown backwards on a pile of straw . . . a doctor close to her, the executioner on her other side: in all truth a sight that made me shiver.

Those who saw the execution said that she went on to the scaffold with great courage. For my part I was on the bridge of Notre-Dame . . . never was such a crowd seen before, nor Paris so moved, nor so fascinated . . .

Mme Voisin was burnt yesterday. She knew her sentence since Monday . . . she dined and slept eight hours . . . She came by coach from Vincennes to Paris . . . At five o'clock she was bound, and bearing a flaming torch, she appeared in the tumbril, dressed in white . . . She was seen to push her confessor, and his crucifix, violently away from her. We saw her pass in front of the Hôtel de Sully . . . At Notre-Dame, she declined to make her public confession, and at the place of execution she fought as hard as she could to remain in the tumbril . . . she was dragged out by force and placed at the stake in a sitting position and bound there in irons; then covered with straw. She cursed a great deal and pushed the straw away five or six times, but finally the fire took hold and she was lost to sight, and her ashes are now somewhere in the air. So that is how Mme Voisin died, infamous for her crimes and her impiety.

Marcel had set up a bar in the fortress and after an aperitif or two he shoved me through an iron gate and into the Tunnel of a Thousand Steps, dug steep, almost vertical, with pick and shovel, through the living rock and down to the town; it was a tunnel that had been constructed so that the citizens of Villefranche might escape with their lives in times of siege.

It seemed to go down for ever in the dark and the cool, step after step. When I re-emerged into the daylight I found myself on the banks of the River Tet, and passing through a redoubt I crossed a high-arched stone bridge with walls on either side, and came into the town's narrow streets – and such a town, a town with a lazy spell to weave. An old woman stared at the morning; a man in a beret sat on a bollard, warming his bones in the sun. They called to each other in Catalan.

I wanted to stay but my conversation with Marcel had made me late for my train. I heard an announcement echoing in from the station; my connection for Perpignan was on the point of leaving.

On the platform, standing by the Canari, ready to set out for Latour-de-Carol, back across the valley of the Cerdagne, was Jean-Luc, his wife and child by his side. They kissed and again the child was swung high into the air and again he laughed with pleasure. As

I watched, the yellow train moved slowly away and Jean-Luc gave me an accolade of three blasts of the whistle. Above me loomed the Canigool, the sacred mountain of the Catalans, and all around it the high peaks of the Pyrenees danced in the sky, weightless, detached from the earth.

In the carriage I settled into a corner seat; I was leaving Villefranche with sadness, the way I leave most places, however short a time I have spent there. But I knew that I would soon be arriving at Perpignan, and Salvador Dali had spoken words of wisdom on the subject of its railway station, making me determined to go there: 'Suddenly I saw it with the brightness of lightning; in front of me I saw the centre of the universe.' Well, the centre of the universe, that would do nicely.

27

1996
Agincourt and Other Battles

My friend Laurie had fallen asleep one evening, face first into his soup. He had been working far too hard and so, with the encouragement of his wife and since I was now retired and had the time, I took him to France for a week. 'It will do you good,' I said.

We drove along secondary roads from Calais and made our first stop at Agincourt. There was no one in the main street, no one in the fields. On the edge of the village we found two gardeners: one an old man, the other a young girl with a wrestler's muscular body and steel teeth that gave her the smile of a piranha. They were tending shrubs, cutting and hoeing in the area around Agincourt's monument to the battle that had been Henry V's great triumph. There was a panoramic plan showing the disposition of the armies, and before us was the gently sloping hill up which the French men-at-arms had advanced.

On 25 October 1415, the terrain had been soft and sticky with mud, and the French troops had charged on foot, heading directly for the English archers, 5,000 of them, each one able to fire six arrows a minute – 30,000 missiles in sixty seconds.

It should have been easy for the French; they outnumbered their enemies by six or even ten to one – but the longbow more than compensated for the difference, and the flower of French nobility was delivered up to the English foot soldiers, who butchered them with daggers and axes.

Laurie and I had a rainy day for it too, and windy. We walked down the field of battle, silent – 10,000 skeletons lay beneath our feet. About an hour later, in Hesdin forest, cold and wet like soldiers retreating, we stood at a picnic table under high trees that swirled and bent above us, and talked about the battle, the piles of dead, the prisoners slaughtered. But sadness hadn't finished with us. We crossed the River Somme, east of Abbeville, at Pont Remy, and discovered by the side of the road, though hidden from it, a tiny graveyard in which lay the remains of perhaps a score of British soldiers from the First World War. Twenty, that was all, but it was a lonely and desolate place and its very smallness made the voices of the dead so very loud.

On the road south we stopped by a caravan snack bar and ate piping hot chips. The wind was still a hooligan and the caravan swayed as the proprietor poured our red wine.

'I'm sorry its not *chambré*,' he said. 'It's a bit difficult with this weather, but it'll warm up once it's inside you.'

At les Andelys Laurie did a number with the lady in the tourist office. 'I'm on holiday because I fell into my soup,' he began, 'and I'm achieving a lifetime's ambition. Ever since I was a little boy I have wanted to visit Richard Coeur de Lion's castle, the Château Gaillard. It was reading Ivanhoe that did it.'

The road to the castle was narrow and wound slowly upwards through black woods which were dripping a heavy rain.

'This castle had the first *machicoulis* in France,' said Laurie as I drove, 'and its walls are five metres thick. It was eventually taken from King John by Philippe Auguste, an attack through the latrines – dirty business, war.'

I parked the car and we looked across a shallow valley to where the ruins of the castle stood, grey against a grey backdrop. The rain swept over us like mist and we pulled on wet weather gear and wellington boots. We took an aperitif before setting out – there was half a mile between us and the castle. I placed a bottle of white wine, two glasses and a pound or so of prawns on the car's roof. Above us the sullen clouds quarrelled and thunder rolled down the sky. 'To hell with the weather,' said Laurie, and raised his glass.

At last we walked the track to the castle entrance and found the custodian and his woman smiling at us from the shelter of the gateway. There were no other visitors and they looked lonely, pathetic even, as if they'd been abandoned there by a witch and placed under a spell that made it impossible for them to leave.

We reached into our pockets for the price of entry only to discover that we had left our money in the car. The custodian and his woman laughed, pleased to keep us there as long as they could.

'It is of no importance,' they said, 'come in for free, and stay as long as you like . . . tell us where you are from.'

Some days later in Compiègne – we were visiting the château – we parked in one of the main streets and as we got out of the car I saw Roger Langlet, the Beauvais mechanic, emerging from a florist's on the opposite side of the road with a large bunch of flowers in his hand. Such a coincidence was hard to believe; I had thought him to be happily indolent in Burgundy, where I had last seen him. Then I remembered that his woman still worked in Compiègne and he must have come up to see her.

'You'll come to lunch,' he said, and it was an order.

We went with Roger to buy a roast duck. There were twenty of them on spits, turning slowly in one of those glass fronted cabinets outside a *charcuterie* – all free-range and corn-fed. Roger winked and chose his duck from the bottom spit. 'All the juices drop down onto it from the others,' he said. It smelt delicious; moist and glistening.

The meal was consumed at a leisurely pace and we left the debris of it on the table. 'We'll take you to the place where they signed the armistice in 1918,' said Roger, 'the railway carriage – and where Hitler made us sign the surrender in 1940.'

The armistice railway carriage is the main exhibit of a museum set in a clearing of the forest that surrounds Compiègne. The old postcards show that in 1918 the area was a nondescript railway siding, half-lost in an unkempt terrain. Now there are manicured lawns and the gravel paths are raked into good order.

The emplacements of the two carriages – the German delegation also arrived by train – are marked by great stone slabs, and there is a statue of a German eagle with broken wings: 'Here on 11 November 1918, the criminal pride of the German empire succumbed, conquered by the free peoples it wished to enslave.'

The carriage, located just inside the museum doors, is not the original – that was taken to Germany on Hitler's orders and destroyed. What stands there now is a twin from the same period; a wooden carriage with doors at each end giving onto small platforms, and steps to the ground with brass handrails. The interior is arranged as an office with a large table surrounded by leather backed chairs. The places of the generals and plenipotentiaries are marked by cards.

Roger peered through the window: 'It doesn't matter how many times I come here,' he said, 'it always saddens my heart.'

Laurie and I drove northwards to the towns of Albert, Bapaume and Thiepval, names that haunt the memoirs written during and after the First World War. It was the beginning of spring and in each vast cemetery there were men with mowers and hoes, clipping the grass and turning over the soil of the flower-beds. They stood aside for us as we passed, smiling in welcome and commiseration, as if we were looking for the headstone of a grandfather. The wind was bitter and the rain drove us along like a whip, the cold filling our eyes with tears and making it difficult to look across the low hills and shallow valleys where so many men had died, and died so young.

We stood in the middle of a white forest of crosses, silent. Two gardeners carried away a huge weight of grass cuttings in a roll of black plastic, and it swung between them like a corpse in a body-bag. By the gate was a visitors' book with a space for comments – but the place was beyond words.

Sitting in the car I read Laurie a page or two from *Undertones of War* by Edmund Blunden, a poet who had fought at Thiepval, and survived:

In double gloom the short day decayed, and the noise of shelling swelled until my colonel sent me up above to listen occasionally if there was any sound of rifle fire. For during this battle of the Somme, there must have been a hundred shells for one rifle-shot; and the cracking of bullets from the front trench in the general stormsong would have been a danger signal . . . From Thiepval Wood battalions of our own division sprang out, passed our old dead, mud-craters and wire and took the tiny village of St Pierre Divion . . . and almost 2,000 Germans in the galleries there . . . I set off with a runner called Johnson, a red-cheeked silent youth, to reconnoitre forward positions, seeing that there was a heavy barrage eastward, but knowing that it was best not to think about it . . . What light the grudging day had permitted was now almost extinct, and the mist had changed into a drizzle; we passed the site of Thiepval Crucifix . . . Crossing scarcely discernible remains of redoubts and communications, I saw an officer peering from a little furrow of trench ahead and went to him.

'Is this our front line?'

'Dunno: you get down off there, you'll be hit.'

His chin quivered; this night's echoing blackness was coming down cruelly fast.

'Get down.' He spoke with a sort of anger.

Through some curious inward concentration on the matter of finding the way, I had not noticed the furious dance of high explosive now almost enclosing us . . . Then I said to Johnson, 'The front line must be ahead here still; come on.' We were now in the dark and, before we realized it, inside a barrage;

never had shells seemed so torrentially swift, so murderous; each seemed to swoop over one's shoulder. We ran, we tore ourselves out of the clay to run, and lived. The shells at last skidded and spattered behind us. We went on . . . and climbed the false immensity of another ridge, when several rifles and a maxim opened upon us . . . we retreated zig-zagging down the slope . . . now running, crouching, we worked along the valley . . . then we plunged through that waterfall of shells, the British and German barrages mingling, now slackening; and were challenged at last, in English. We had come back from an accidental tour into enemy country . . . We lay down in the mud a moment and recovered our senses . . . The way to Thiepval was simpler. At the edge of the wood a couple of great shells burst almost on top of us . . . We were received as Lazarus was. The shelling of the Schwaben had been a 'blaze of light' and our death had been taken for granted.

The monument at Thiepval is set on a rise in the ground overlooking the valley of the Ancre. There are thin black woods all around. The monument rises above the trees, stark and solemn in brick, tall with arches on all sides, and the wind cut through them, as relentless as death itself. There are 73,000 names of the fallen on the monument, bearing witness to those who have no known graves. Laurie and I were silent once again.

On the boat that night we saw off a couple of bottles of wine, and drank to millions of dead men.

'Everyone,' said Laurie, 'should visit those places . . . at least once.'

'Yes,' I said.

28

1999
The Oise Canal

After a good woman, and a good book, and tobacco, there is nothing so agreeable as a river.

Robert Louis Stevenson

In the 1960s a taxi-driver from Paris called Pierre Perrin wrote a song called 'Moonlight in Maubeuge', and it went to somewhere near the top of the hit parade. Monsieur Perrin had fallen in love with a *pâtissière* from the town who worked in a shop called Le Clair de Lune – hence the song. The lyrics are satirical, the singer claiming to have seen many beautiful things in his life, but nothing that can compare to *'le Clair de Lune à Maubeuge'*. Given that Maubeuge lies in what was the heart of the industrial north, within a stone's throw of the Belgian frontier, even the opening bars of the song bring a wry smile to the face of any French man or woman who hears them.

The song was a good enough reason, for me at least, to visit Maubeuge, but not the only one: Robert Louis Stevenson went there in 1876. Two years before goading his donkey across the Cévennes, he paddled a canoe from the Belgian frontier south towards Paris, following the Sambre canal and then the River Oise, writing an account of his adventures which he called *An Inland*

Voyage. My first bike ride in France had been in 1949; now, exactly fifty years later, retired and in receipt of a pension, I set out on my last, following RLS along the towpaths.

It was Sunday when I arrived at Maubeuge railway station, one of those half-awake Sunday mornings that make provincial France so seductive. I had brought my prejudices and preconceptions with me: smoke, I expected, factories, maybe a derelict coal-mine, grimy back-to-backs. I found nothing of the kind. The streets were full of sunlight, the buildings no more than two storeys high; flowers hung in pots to decorate the lamp-posts; there was the smell of honey-suckle on the air, and the River Sambre ran through the centre of town, its pleasure boats moored along both banks.

At eight the next morning I pedalled down a gravel slope and came to the towpath. I was alone – not a fisherman, not a barge. I passed under the walls of a dead factory or two, one pink, one in black and brown – high brick cliffs of industrial architecture where broken windows stared at me. But in no time I was beyond them and on to Hautmont, the next town. The track widened and became covered with soft, springy grass, and I was protected from the dangers of the great outside by tall trees that stood close to me like incorruptible sentinels. A lazy heron took off from under my wheels, grey against the green, haughty, an aristocrat of a bird and far too proud to spare me a glance.

'After Hautmont,' says Stevenson, 'we went through a delectable land, the river wound among low hills . . . On either hand were meadows and orchards, bordered with a margin of sedge and water flowers . . . The hedges were high . . . and the fields were a series of bowers along the stream . . .' Nothing has changed very much. I bowled along and all was an enchantment of green; the trees grew in beautiful shapes, and the cows made congregations in their shade. There were water meadows, more herons rising and the sun glittered through an early mist. The air felt so tropical that I half expected to see banana plants growing.

'Everything was drenched in the scents of summer, the hedgerows were full of perfumes, the riverside meadows were full of the sweetness of new-mown hay, and light sparkled golden in the dancing leaves.' At Berlaimont, church bells struck; a man was painting the lock gates and a long, swoop-lined *péniche* was moored to the bank, its colours turquoise and white, its name – Amour. And two contented grandmothers sat on their balcony under a sky-blue parasol, their hands folded in their laps like books that have been read and finished with – all was right with the world.

At Sassegnies the lock-house was bedecked with flowers; the surrounding fields were empty of cattle, the poplars were stately. Behind an elbow of the river lay the strangest of dwellings, sprayed bright Chelsea blue and, as if there weren't enough flowers or leaves in nature, its walls had been painted over with them. Its doors and windows hung open and not even a cat was to be seen – a Hansel and Gretel of a house.

At the next *écluse*, the Hachette, there was an island lying between the river and the canal, and on it there was another brick cottage, painted white this time, and beside it grew great blossoms, vying with the washing on the line to be the brightest colours in the garden. And there sat two ancient fishermen, 'stupefied with plea-sure', statues, saints in green niches, perched over the water on small, personal jetties, side by side, staring ahead, not speaking, like figures on some magic clock that registered not time but content-ment.

I was off the next day before the sun had risen much above the horizon. The waters of the Sambre lay still like smoke, the reflec-tions of the trees faint and ghostly. Moorhens rushed to the far bank as I passed, fish were jumping and the towpath was shrouded in curtains of mist. It rolled in from the fields and dripped, steady, from branches and twigs, making a noise like half-hearted rain, all the way to Landrecies.

When Stevenson passed this way it was only six years after the defeat of the French in the Franco-Prussian war, and Landrecies was a heavily defended garrison town. 'It was just the place to hear the round going by at night in the darkness, with the solid tramp of men marching, and the startling reverberations of the drum.' Now there is nothing left of its military past, save the extensive barracks, abandoned and silent. The barbed wire has rusted away, and weeds have burst through the ground where conscripts once stamped their feet and shouldered arms.

I stopped there, nevertheless, to visit a small supermarket and purchase some provisions and a bottle of wine – something of quality for a very special purpose.

A mile or two further on I followed the towpath through a sharp left-hand bend; the tiled rooftops of the village of Ors came into sight, and the chimes of midday echoed across the fields. The sound of the wind in the trees was like the sound of water rushing over a weir. I studied my map – there I was, standing on the long stretch of canal where Wilfred Owen had been killed.

Sitting on the bank, in the green shade by the green water, were two fishermen, retired some years since by the cut of them. They sat motionless in an endless calm where shells and bullets and bodies and blood had been, and where one of our most gifted poets had lost his life only a week before the signing of the armistice.

'The Germans blew up the bridge,' said one of the men, as if the explosion had only just happened. 'Owen is in the village cemetery with the others.' He took a long hard look at the end of his fishing rod. 'It's a lot quieter here now,' he said. His laugh was hard and preceded a long silence.

The main alley of the village cemetery is lined with family tombs, heavy in dull grey stone. At the opposite end to the gate stands a tall cross, and to the right of it are sixty-two plain white tombstones bearing the names of those soldiers who died at Ors, most of them on that same day – 4 November 1918 – most of them in their twenties. In the left-hand corner, three from the end, three red roses in bloom, was Wilfred Owen, MC, aged twenty-five. Beyond the wall an empty field stretches back to the village and its church. There was not a soul moving in that landscape; I was alone, so I read the poem I'd brought with me, drank half the wine then poured the rest over the grave.

With an Identity Disc

If ever I had dreamed of my dead name
High in the heart of London, unsurpassed
By Time for ever, and the Fugitive, Fame,
There taking a long sanctuary at last,

I better that; and recollect with shame
How once I longed to hide it from life's heats
Under those holy cypresses, the same
That keep in shade the quiet place of Keats.

Now, rather, thank I God there is no risk
Of gravers scoring it with florid screed,
But let my death be memoried on this disc.
Wear it, sweet friend. Inscribe no date nor deed.
But let thy heart-beat kiss it night and day,
Until the name grow vague and wear away.

I arrived in Guise that night, on the eve of the national celebrations for 14 July, and the whole town was buzzing. My hotel, a fine nineteenth-century building in brick with stone facings at the windows, stood behind grand gates. The hall had parquet flooring and an imposing staircase swanked its way up to the bedrooms, all of which had high ceilings, plaster mouldings and tall double doors for sweeping through, dressed in knee-breeches and flared coats.

The *patron* welcomed me in: 'Got your letter,' he said. 'So where is this Stevenson fellow you're following? He didn't stop here last night.'

When I stepped out after dinner, at about ten o'clock, the streets were closed to traffic and thronged with people, and there were extra tables and long benches outside every café and restaurant. Waiters darted across the pavements bringing beers and ice-creams to mums and dads, infants and grandparents. On a stage in the centre of the square, large middle-aged men with silver hair made music for the town, music of all sorts – rumbas and rock, jive and javas, waltzes and pop. Pedlars sold electric candles and flaming torches, shouting their wares, burdened with baskets that brimmed with light.

Into this bedlam marched the town band, *la fanfare du village*, about twenty strong, dressed in white shirts and scarlet forage caps, their faces just as red, puffing trumpets and French horns, cheeks bulging, banging drums both big and little, young and old playing together, and skipping behind them came the town children, letting off fireworks as they advanced, like skirmishers intent on harm.

The two musics, the dance band and the *fanfare*, came together like the cutlasses of opposing armies, neither giving quarter to the other. The noise was a cloud of alarming discord. Dogs barked and girls screamed with pleasure as Chinese crackers were thrown towards them, making them lift their skirts to hop away from danger. And the *fanfare* strutted right behind the dance band's stage and the commotion put the teeth on edge; but no one seemed to mind. Both sets of artistes kept playing at full throttle until at last the *fanfare* executed a left wheel and marched away, leaving the air bitter with brimstone and cordite.

At eleven came the official firework display, and every inhabitant of Guise, all 6,000 of them, gathered in the square and craned their necks, staring upwards. Deafening explosions boomed across the black sky, and monster showers of gold and blue and green, with bright silver rockets above them, burgeoned into vast herbaceous borders. The spectacle lasted for half an hour or so, then it was back to dance in the streets till two in the morning. Everyone's glass was full and every child was sleeping on his or her father's shoulder.

I found letters waiting for me at Compiègne, just as there had been for Stevenson when he'd arrived there. 'No one should have any correspondence on a journey,' he says. 'The receipt of a letter is the death of a holiday feeling.' He was right as usual, but then he was a master at distilling the incidents of travel into a philosophy. Journeys for him, as they should be for everyone, were grist to the mill of his intelligence, not expeditions to be undertaken simply for the pleasure of movement – an attitude made evident by his reflections on being swept from his canoe by the turbulent tide of the River Oise and nearly drowned:

> ... For I think we may look upon our little private war with death somewhat in this light ... If a man knows he will sooner or later be robbed upon a journey, he will have a bottle of the best in every inn, and look upon his extravagances as so much gained upon the thieves ... So every bit of brisk living is just so much gained upon the wholesale filcher, death. We shall have the less in our pockets, the more in our stomach, when he cries stand and deliver ... When he and I come to settle our accounts, I shall whistle in his face for those hours upon the upper Oise ...

And so shall I, Louis, and so shall I.

29

1999
Adieu Dieppe

It was four o'clock in the morning when the night porter let me out of the hotel and, leaning against the wind, I followed a dervish of a plastic bag through the streets of Dieppe in the direction of the Halle aux Poissons. Five or six fishing boats were moored at the quayside, in from long days at sea, their crews using hoists to swing the catch onto the dock. Their colleagues, the shoremen, stood at high trestle tables and sorted the fish into boxes, packing them tight – streaks of silver on white beds of ice.

These men were thickset, tough looking, buttoned up against the wind and the flurries of rain that swept over the water in curtains of cold. They were dressed in flowing coats and long oilskin aprons that covered them to the ankle, elegant and romantic, piratical even. In the yellow working lights their clothes glistened with wet and the scales of fish, and the same light made their faces cadaverous; eye sockets black like burnt-out holes in a skull.

I peered into the boxes: sole, flounder and dab, conger eel, skate, whiting and dogfish, mullet and bass, all blind and staring up at me. At five-thirty, with still no light in the sky, the *mareyeurs* arrived, the merchants who buy and sell wholesale. They strolled from boat to boat, shaking hands absent-mindedly with each other, thinking only of fish.

I followed one through a narrow metal door and found myself submerged in a tempest of noise. I had come into an auction room that resembled a kind of lecture hall with nine or ten rows of benches rising steeply upwards. At the front of the room there was a low stage, above that a balcony ringed with a banister of iron painted grey. On a series of rails above the balcony hung maybe a dozen blackboards, arranged so that each one could be slid over and past the next.

A woman, slim in a wrap-around blue apron, motherly with white hair and grey stockings, wrote down in chalk the names of the boats that had unloaded that morning: the Swan, the Saint-Jacques, the Bijou, the Tiger and the Explorateur. Under the name of each boat she added the weight and type of catch. On either side of her stood a young man, the auctioneers, with rubber-headed mallets in their hands. Each time a deal was concluded, by a shout from a *mareyeur*, they banged their mallets on the metal banister. The blackboards slid from side to side, and the woman in the apron rubbed out each item as it was sold, and chalked up more information as pieces of paper were brought to her.

The noise rebounded off the bare walls. The incantations of the auctioneers never ceased and the *mareyeurs* shouted against them, carrying on two auctions at once, buying in and off-loading, selling to each other; crowing for a bargain made and swearing for a bargain lost; giving rein to their tempers and finishing off their rivals with a pointed and lethal scorn.

'It is forbidden,' said one of the fishermen, like the Pope deciding on a tricky question of faith and morals, 'to come to Dieppe and not eat the *marmite dieppoise*. *Voici* – a choice of fish in thick cream sauce; sole, brill, some mussels and *langoustines*, with *pommes vapeur* . . . all kept hot on little stoves as you eat . . . after that, hot apple pie and more quantities of cream with – and this I recommend – a light red wine, a little chilled, say a Bourgueil, from the Loire.'

At the restaurant I sat in the window seat and watched people go by, but it was lunch-time and there were more people inside eating than outside walking. Next to me sat a couple from le Tréport, retired and out for the day: he a hobbit of a man in a blue suit, with a mauve tracery of delicate veins on his wine-fed cheeks, she, an ancient fairy godmother from a story book, her skin as soft and as sweet as rose petals, with a touch of golden down on it too.

'We drive a little,' they explained, 'and then find a restaurant . . . two or three times a week.' The man sighed and tucked into some *pâtisserie*. 'When you retire, there is no time for anything, no holidays, no weekends, no time off. We are too busy, too busy.' He sighed again, but he was far from sad.

At the western end of Dieppe, where I stood on the walls of the castle, and where the museum is, the view waited patiently to be painted yet again. I looked down on grey slates and red roof-tiles; two great churches rearing high above the town; a stone beach and the wide, grassy esplanades running along by the edge of the sea, which itself lay placid in thick streaks of green. The inside of the sky was a pallid white, and over all raced a mottled shadow as the sun was beaten along by the winter wind. This was the light the painters came for.

The museum itself had a nice out-of-season solitude to it. Just a man laying cobbles, his nose dribbling over his work as I walked past him and under a brick arch, into a courtyard of quietness and calm. Monsieur Bazin, the curator, was a cheerful and welcoming man with a sharp brain and the sense of humour of a knowledgeable rascal. 'I've been here so long,' he told me, 'I'm my own ghost.'

Dieppe was France's first seaside destination, the nearest resort to Paris, and the museum reflects this, stocked with paintings of beach scenes, and with seascapes of luggers and privateers.

It is possible, Monsieur Bazin informed me, that Dieppe's sailors discovered West Africa before the Portuguese; consequently it wasn't long before the wood carvers of the home port turned their hands to elephant tusks. And so the museum is rich in ivory ships of terrifying intricacy, with delicate ratlines, and sails as thin as airmail paper.

And there are paintings by some of the more famous artists too: a Renoir, a Boudin, a Pissarro, a few Lebourgs, several Sickerts, a roomful of Braque prints and three small Dufys.

'Turner did a painting of Dieppe,' said Monsieur Bazin as I left, 'but you have to go to New York to see it . . . at the Frick. Turner's a bit rich, of course, a bit like *endives au gratin*, and certainly more *gratin* than *endives*.' He smiled, arched an eyebrow and closed the door behind me.

So there I was in Dieppe, exactly fifty years after my first visit as a 15-year-old cyclist; and I felt what I always felt when I went there; Dieppe would be good to me for ever, it would always remember.

It was lunch-time and I was walking back to my hotel along the promenade, looking down at the sea. There was a line of beach huts just below me, and in front of two of them was a large square table with about fifteen people sitting at it – a festive board covered with a white tablecloth that could hardly be seen, so closely were the dishes and bottles of wine laid out on it: *langoustine*, whelks, slices of cold pork, salads, mayonnaise, savoury rice.

As I stared down, one or two of the revellers looked back at me. Behind them the sea was crashing on the pebble beach; one or two kites were soaring into the sky and the sun sparkled on a sea too bright to look at.

I had been caught spying and was embarrassed by it. To acknowledge my fault I raised a hand and wished them well; '*Bon appétit*,' I called, '*Vous avez assez à boire?*'

The answer was frank and fast.

'More than enough, come and help us drink it.'

It must have been about midday when I sat down at their table. I left it at midnight that evening.

We drank, we ate, we played cards, we talked. Catherine, Jacques, François, Martine, Philippe, Véronique, Yvonne . . . just doing that French thing of making lunch become dinner.

At one point I attempted to leave in order to buy some provisions: some food, a few bottles of wine. It was out of the question. '*Mais non, Michel, tu vois bien qu'il y'en a assez.*'

I told them the story of my first visit to Dieppe and they were pleased that I loved the place so. They were all from the town itself or from Varengeville a few miles away. Between them they owned two of the beach huts, numbers 39 and 40. They had begun their friendships simply as neighbours, but over twenty years they had made themselves into a family, and now, at the end of each letting season they celebrated being alive with lunch, and of course dinner, on the beach, and their generosity had brought me to their table.

I sat in my car in a small queue of vehicles, waiting to board the ferry. On my right the town, on my left the sea, the waves picking up the stones and throwing them down, again and again – a dismal intake of breath:

> *Listen! you hear the grating roar*
> *Of pebbles which the waves draw back, and fling,*
> *At their return, up the high strand,*
> *Begin, and cease, and then again begin,*
> *With tremulous cadence slow, and bring*
> *The eternal note of sadness in.*

My car reeked of Dieppe: shrimps and mussels, spilt wine and strong cheese, dry cider and savouries, fresh bread and dark chocolate.

When it was time for the ferry to leave, I went out on deck to watch the town slip away, looking down into the street, the same street that I had first seen at the age of fifteen. The seagulls were screaming, arrogant on the wind, and people at lunch looked up from their restaurant tables and watched the ship drift from the shore, and the waiters came to their doorways, napkins folded white on their forearms.

On the harbour mole the fishermen pulled in their lines and retired couples, arm in arm, strolled out to watch the big boat leaving. On we sailed, past the esplanade and the hotels and the grass and the beach, the waves crashing creamy and thick. In a little while we were beyond the last fisherman, beyond the jetty and out into the flat calm of the green sea, with the sky a Dufy blue. Dieppe, and the whole hexagon of France, had remained faithful to me, all these years, and I to it. We were still in love.

OTHER NOVELS
BY LAURENCE SHAMES

Mangrove Squeeze

Virgin Heat

Tropical Depression

Sunburn

Scavenger Reef

Florida Straits

WELCOME
TO PARADISE

WELCOME TO PARADISE

a novel

Laurence Shames

 VILLARD NEW YORK

To Marilyn,
who laughs,
with love

PROLOGUE

"Was the clams," said Nicky Scotto.

"Ya sure?" said Donnie Falcone. Skeptically, he tugged on a long and fleshy earlobe. "Ya sure it was the clams?"

"Hadda be the clams." Nicky sipped anisette and looked vaguely toward the window of Nono's Pasticceria. Nono's was on Carmine Street, two steps below the sidewalk. Half a century of exhaust fumes had tinted its front window a restful bluish gray. People talked softly in Nono's. Never loud enough to be heard above the steaming of the milk. Nicky put his glass down, said, "Fuck else could it'a been?"

Carefully, fastidiously, Donnie broke a *biscotto,* herded up crumbs with the flat of his thumb. He hated when crumbs got stuck in the fibers of his big black overcoat. "How should I know? What else j'eat?"

Nicky winced just slightly and softly belched at the recollection of the catastrophic meal. He pictured the breadsticks, the drops of wine on the tablecloth. His fist still pressed against his lips, he said, "Minestrone."

"Minestrone," echoed Donnie. "Ya don't puke off minestrone."

"Hadda be the clams," Nicky said once more. He leaned back in the booth, smoothed the creamy mohair of his jacket. Dark and thickly built, he was handsome until you looked a little closer. The jaw was square but just a little heavy, the black eyes too close to the thick and slightly piggish nose.

Donnie kept his eyes down on his pastry plate. "Ya sure you're not just lookin' for a reason to get mad at Al?"

When Nicky was agitated, his voice got softer instead of louder. His throat squeezed down like a crimped hose and words came out with the razzing purr of a muted trumpet. "I don't need another fuckin' reason to be mad at Al."

Donnie thought it best to leave it right there. "Okay. What else j'eat?"

Nicky absently ran fingertips against the wall. The wall was covered with small white tiles, broken up with ranks of gold and black at shoulder level. "Broccoli rabe," he said. "Scallopini veal, lemon sauce. Some pasta shit, little hats, like."

Donnie said, "Orecchiette?"

"Fuck knows?" said Nicky. "Look, I didn't come here to discuss macaroni shapes, okay? I come here to tell ya what that fuck Al did to me."

"A few bad clams," said Donnie. "Happens."

"Look, when I had the fish market, I did the right thing. I didn't give bad clams to places where friends of ours was gonna eat."

"Nicky. How is Al supposed to know you're gonna be eatin' in some hotel up inna Catskills?"

The question slowed Nicky down. His fingernails tickled the grout between the tiles.

Donnie went on. "Truth, Nicky, I don't see you inna fuckin' Catskills either. It's a Jew place."

"Used ta be," said Nicky. "Now it's everything. Hotels for queers. For Puerto Ricans. Couple good Italian places, you know that."

"Okay, okay. But whaddya do up there? Play shuffleboard?"

Embarrassed, Nicky said, "Ya look at leaves."

"Leaves?"

"I tol' ya, Donnie," Nicky said. "My mother-in-law, it was her seventieth. My wife says, 'She loves the autumn. Let's take her to the leaves.' So I say okay. The old broad wantsta look at leaves, I'm tryin' to be nice. Wha' could I tell ya—this is who I am."

Donnie drained his espresso, motioned for another. From behind his arm, he said, "It ain't the clams. You're mad 'cause Tony Eggs took the fish away from you and gave it to Big Al."

Nicky tugged at the collar of his turtleneck, twisted his head around in a circle. "'Course I'm mad," he finally admitted. "Fuck wit' a man's livelihood, who ain't gonna be mad?" There was a silence, and when the stocky man spoke again he could not quite hide a real sorrow and bewilderment. "Why'd he do it, Donnie?"

Donnie shrugged. He had a long thin face and a long thin neck, and when he shrugged, his shoulders had a lot of ground to cover. His skin had a grayish-yellow cast and his usual expression was distantly amused yet mournful. "I ain't got a clue."

"Come on—the man's your uncle."

"Great-uncle," corrected Donnie, and came close to revealing some pique of his own. "An' ya see how close we are. Me, I'm still hustling window-cleaning contracts inna fuckin' garment district."

Nicky made a vague and universal griping sound.

Donnie sipped coffee and quietly went on. "Look, the market's Big Al's now. Ya gotta let it go."

"This ain't about the market."

"I wish I could believe that."

"What this is about is that he poisoned me. Poisoned alla us."

Donnie's flat lips stretched out and came close to smiling. He wiped his mouth instead. "The t'ree a you in that hotel room—"

"Suite. It was a suite. Two bedrooms. Two bat'rooms. I thought two would be enough."

There was a pause. Outside on Carmine Street, taxis went by, the clatter of trucks filtered in from Seventh Avenue. The milk steamer hissed and Nicky got madder. Revolted. Humiliated. "Well," he went on, "two bat'rooms wasn't enough. The wife, the old lady—disgusting. Dignity? Tell me about dignity when you're leakin' both ends, hoppin' to the toilet wit' your pj's down your ankles. When your wife has to crawl over ya to get to the bowl."

"Nicky, it was just bad luck. Coulda happened to any—"

But Nicky was not to be hushed. Air wheezed through his pinched windpipe. "Ol' lady ends up whaddyacallit, intravenous. Happy birt'day, Ma. Camille, skinny marink ta begin wit', she drops six pounds. Me, I ain't right for a week. A week, Donnie! Cramps, runs, white shit on my tongue. Taste in my mouth like somethin' died. I tell ya, Donnie, a week a hell."

Donnie had settled back in the booth, all but disappearing into his coat. When Nicky finished, he leaned forward, folded his long neat hands in front of him, and said very softly, "But, Nicky, why stay mad? I mean, where we goin' wit' this? Ya gonna ice a guy over some funky seafood?"

Nicky sipped his anisette. His face went innocent. "Who said anything about icin' anyone? You said that. Not me."

"I only said—"

"Look, I'm a guy that does the right thing—"

"You keep sayin' that," Donnie pointed out.

"—and all I want is that that fuckin' guy should suffer like I suffered. A week a total misery. Justice. That's all I want. Zat too fuckin' much t'ask?"

"Justice? Yeah," said Donnie. He blotted up some crumbs. "So whaddya want from me?"

"Help. Advice. Like, ways to ruin his life."

"Nicky, I don't want no part a this. Besides, it's gonna have to wait."

"What has to wait? Wait for what?"

"Big Al's goin' outa town I heard. Goin' on vacation."

Nicky rubbed his chin. "Hey, I was on vacation too. A guy can't be mizzable on vacation?" He paused. He brightened slightly and his small black eyes squeezed down. "Where's he goin' on vacation?"

"Flahda," Donnie said reluctantly. "Key West is what I heard."

"Flahda," Nicky intoned. He drained his anisette, wrapped hot hands around the glass. He lifted up one curly eyebrow. "Flahda. Far away. That's nice. That's like the best advice you coulda gimme."

"Hey—"

"Flahda. Vacation. Far away from everything."

"You never heard it from me," said Donnie.

Nicky said, "So happens I got friends in Flahda."

ONE

1

"*Why we gotta* drive?" said Katy Sansone, who was twenty-nine years old and Big Al Marracotta's girlfriend.

She was bustling around the pink apartment that Big Al kept for her in Murray Hill. It was not a great apartment, but Katy, though she had her good points, was not that great a girlfriend. She complained a lot. She went right to the edge of seeming ungrateful. She had opinions and didn't seem to understand that if she refreshed her lipstick more, and answered back less, she might have had the one-bedroom with the courtyard view rather than the noisy, streetside studio with the munchkin-sized appliances. Now she was packing, roughly, showing a certain disrespect for the tiny bathing suits and thong panties and G-strings and underwire bras that Big Al had bought her for the trip.

"We have to drive," he said, "because the style in which I travel, airports have signs calling it an act of terrorism."

"Always with the guns," she pouted. "Even on vacation?"

"Several," said Big Al. "A small one for the glove compartment. A big one under the driver's seat. A fuckin' bazooka inna trunk." He smiled. "Oh, yeah—and don't forget the big knife inna sock." He was almost cute when he smiled. He had a small gap between his two front teeth, and the waxy crinkles at the corners of his eyes suggested a boyish zest. When he smiled his forehead shifted and moved the short salt-and-pepper hair that other times looked painted on. Big Al was five foot two and weighed

3

one hundred sixteen pounds. "Besides," he added, "I wanna bring the dog."

"The daw-awg!" moaned Katy.

Big Al raised a warning finger, but even before he did so, Katy understood that she should go no further. Certain things were sacred, and she could not complain about the dog. Its name was Ripper. It was a champion rottweiler and a total coward. It had coy brown eyebrows and a brown blaze on its square black head, and it dribbled constantly through the flubbery pink lips that imperfectly covered its mock-ferocious teeth. A stub of amputated tail stuck out above its brown-splashed butt, and its testicles, the right one always lower than the left, hung down and bounced as though they were on bungees. It was those showy and ridiculous nuts, she secretly believed, that made Al dote so on the dog.

She kept packing. High-heeled sandals. Open-toed pumps. Making chitchat, trying to sound neutral, she said, "So the dog's already in the car?"

Big Al nodded. "Guarding it." Again he smiled. Say this for him: he knew what gave him pleasure. He had a huge dog gnawing on a huge bone in the backseat of his huge gray Lincoln. He had a young girlfriend packing slinky things for a weeklong Florida vacation—a week of sun, sweat, sex, and lack of aggravation. For the moment he was a happy guy.

Katy snapped her suitcase closed and straightened out her back. She was five foot eleven, and Al had told her never to insult him by wearing flats. Standing there in heels and peg-leg pants, she looked a little like a missile taking off. Long lean shanks and narrow hips provided thrust that seemed to lift the dual-coned payload of chest, which tapered in turn to a pretty though small-featured face capped by a pouf of raven hair.

For a moment she just stood there by her suitcase, waiting to see if Al would pick it up. Then she picked it up herself and they headed for the door.

His face was on her bosom the whole elevator ride down to the garage. Vacation had begun.

Across the river in suburban Jersey, on the vast and cluttered selling floor of Kleiman Brothers Furniture on Route 22 in Springfield, a ceremony was in progress.

Moe Kleiman, the last survivor of the founding brothers, had taken off his shoes and was standing, somewhat shakily, on an ottoman. He stroked his pencil mustache, fiddled with the opal tie tack that, every day for many years, he'd painstakingly poked through the selfsame holes in the selfsame ties, and gestured for quiet. Benignly, he looked out across the group that he proudly referred to as the finest sales staff in the Tri-State area. For a moment he gazed beyond them to the store he loved: lamps with orange price tags hanging from their covered shades; ghostly conversation nooks in which a rocker seemed to be conferring with a La-Z-Boy; ranks of mattresses close-packed as cots in a battlefield hospital.

Then he said, "Friends, we are gathered today to announce the winner of the semi-annual bonus giveaway for top sales in dinettes."

He gestured for quiet as though there'd been applause. But the fact was that, for all of Moe Kleiman's attempts to bring some pomp to the moment, there was no suspense. Everybody knew who'd won. Who won was who almost always won. It was a regular routine already.

Nevertheless, Moe Kleiman soldiered on. "The prize this time around is the best ever. It better be. We got a fancy new travel agent and we're paying through the nose."

At this, people could not help flicking their eyes toward Alan Tuschman, the guy who always won. Twenty years before, he'd been a big-deal high school athlete—split end on the Cranford football team, power forward on a hoops squad that made it to the state semis—and, in a circumscribed, suburban way, he'd been winning ever since, sort of. Got a scholarship to Rutgers. Married a cheerleader with blond hair and amazing calves, cut and sculpted from years of leaping. The marriage didn't last; the scholarship evaporated when the coaches realized that Al Tuschman's talents wouldn't carry him beyond JV. Still, a few semesters of college and matrimony felt right while they endured, lived on in memory like bonus chapters appended to the high school yearbook.

Those temporary victories had helped to keep alive in Al the mysterious habit of winning, and he still got pumped and rallied at almost anything that could be called a game. Sales contests, for starters. Already this year he'd won the giant television set, for bedding; the trip by train to Montreal, for living rooms. His colleagues, of course, were sick of him winning, but they couldn't really find it in their hearts to resent him. He was a nice guy. Friendly. Fair. He didn't hog the floor, he didn't show off, and he didn't try too hard. People just liked to buy from him.

"The prize this time," Moe Kleiman went on, "is nothing short of Paradise. . . . Paradise—that's the name of the hotel. In Key West, Florida. Seven days, six nights. Airfare included. And the winner is—"

The old ham paused, of course. And in the pause, Alan Tuschman's fellow salesmen tried to figure out, for the thousandth time, the key to his success. Some people thought it was his height, pure and simple. At six-three and change, he was by far the tallest guy on the floor, and people felt good dealing with a tall guy. Others thought it was his looks. Not that he was model material. His cheeks were slightly pitted, his lips thick and loose; but his eyes were big and dark, the features widely spaced: it was a face that gave you room to breathe. Then there was the way he dressed—a strange amalgam of old-time collegiate jock and working-man suburban slick. Cotton cardigans over open-collared patterned shirts; pegged and shiny pants leading down to desert boots; a pinky ring that clattered up against a chunky school memento, class of '77. In its careless in-consistency, Al's style gave almost everyone something to hang on to.

"And the winner is," Moe Kleiman said again, "Alan Tuschman."

Amid thin and brief applause that was swallowed up by mat-tresses and chair backs, someone said, "Surprise!"

"Alan Tuschman," Moe went on, "who in the past six months, *in dinettes alone,* wrote a hundred twenty-eight thousand dollars' worth of business. Ladies and gentleman, that is selling! . . . Al, have a well-earned rest in Paradise!"

The boss shook Al Tuschman's hand, discreetly used the clasp as an aid in stepping off the ottoman.

A couple of colleagues slapped Al's back, and then the group dispersed, spread out through the beds and the imaginary living rooms to the four corners of the premises. It was 9:55 and the store opened at ten. Every day. No matter what.

By a quarter of eleven, thinking of vacation, Al had sold a French provincial love seat and a wall unit made to look like rosewood. But then he grew troubled, and stepped around the low wall of frosted glass that separated the sales floor from the offices. He poked his head into Moe Kleiman's tidy cubicle. "Mr. Kleiman," he said, "I have a problem with this prize."

The boss lifted his head and raised an eyebrow. When he did that he looked a great deal like the old guy from Monopoly.

"If it's all the same to you," said Al, "I'm not gonna use the plane ticket."

"All of a sudden you don't fly?" Moe Kleiman said.

Al Tuschman looked a little bit sheepish. "Truth is, it's the dog."

"The dog?"

"Remember last year, I won that package to New Orleans?"

"I remember, I remember."

"The dog was, like, traumatic. Put her in the carrier, she looked at me like I was sending her to the gas chamber. Then the tranquilizers made her sick. Woke up shaking. Laid down on my shoe so I wouldn't go anywhere. Two days I stayed in the hotel, looking out the window with this shell-shocked dog on my foot. I couldn't put her through that again. I'll drive. That okay with you?"

"Sure, Al. Sure. Only, the reservation starts tomorrow."

"You don't mind, I could leave today."

Moe Kleiman stood up, took a token glance out toward the selling floor. A Tuesday in the first half of November. Very quiet. He said, "No problem, Al. If it makes things easier for the dog."

"Thanks," said Tuschman. "Thanks for everything. You'll see, I'll come back tan and sell my ass off."

He turned to go. He was not yet forty, but these days, when he pivoted, he felt old tackles in his knees; the small bones in his ankles remembered rebounds when he didn't land quite right.

He was just rounding the wall of frosted glass when he heard Moe Kleiman chuckle. "The dog. Hey, Al, ya know something?"

The salesman took a step back toward his boss.

The boss lowered his voice. "The other guys, it drives them nuts, they constantly wonder why you're always top banana. But I know. I could give it to you in a word."

Al Tuschman did not ask what the word was. He didn't want to know. Like everybody else, he had his superstitious side. Something worked, you didn't jinx it.

Moe Kleiman told him anyway. "Relief."

"Relief?"

"Relief. People see you, Al—big shoulders, chest hair up to the Adam's apple—they figure, Oy, I'm dealing with a tough guy. Their guard goes up. But it soon comes down, and then you've got 'em. Why does it come down? I'll tell you: because they're re-lieved to see you really are a softie."

Pleased with his analysis, Moe Kleiman smiled.

Al Tuschman tried to, but it didn't work. His mouth slid to one side of his face; he looked down at a swatch book, shuffled his feet. A softie. Softie as in pushover? As in coward? Was it really that obvious? Did everybody know? He briefly met his boss's gaze, made another bent attempt at smiling, and steered his aching legs toward the partition.

Moe Kleiman watched his best salesman edge around the frosted glass, and understood too late that he'd barged in on a secret, that he should have kept his mouth shut. A note of pleading in his voice, he said, "Al, hey, I meant it as a compliment."

2

"But, Nicky," said Charlie "Chop" Parilla, "I don't even know the guy."

"Perfect."

"Perfect? What perfect? Hol' on a minute." He pressed the phone against his hairy, sweating stomach and screamed across the garage at the two workmen who were using giant hammers to bang the doors off a brand-new BMW 740i. "Ya see I'm onna phone. Try a fuckin' wrench." He dried the receiver on his pants leg, put it back against his ear. "What's perfect, I don't know the guy?"

"Motive, Chop," said Nicky Scotto. He was calling from a pay phone down on Broome Street. It was starting to snow. Two weeks before Thanksgiving, and thin, defective snow like a confetti of waxed paper was already blowing sideways through the street. "Ya don't know the guy, ya got no reason to torment 'im. No one's gonna suspect."

Chop Parilla scratched his ample belly, flicked moisture from his fingers. In Hialeah it was eighty-six and muggy. The doors of the garage were closed. Had to be when you were doing unrequested autopsies on other people's cars. Lifting engines out like guts. Scalpeling away spare parts until sometimes nothing but the drive train sat there on the lift, forlorn as the excised backbone of a chicken. "I don't know. Sounds like trouble."

"Trouble?" said Nicky. Wet snow was tickling his Adam's

apple and putting evanescent sparkles in his hair. "Think of it as fun. Twenty grand for a week a trailin' someone you don't care about one way or the other, and fuckin' wit' his head."

Chop watched as the wheels were lifted off the Beemer. Very handsome wheels. Aircraft-grade aluminum. He said, "If this guy's a big cheese in New York . . . I don't know what you're puttin' me inna middle of."

"There is no middle," Nicky said. "This is strictly unofficial. A small, personal matter . . . Look, Chop, I know the fuckin' shithole where you work. Wouldn't you like a paid excuse to get outa there awhile?"

Parilla thought that over. It was true that Hialeah got depressing. All those sunburned beggars with signs around their necks, sitting at intersections clogged with smoking cars blasting "murder-Castro" call-in shows. But on the other hand, in Hialeah Chop was doing what he was put on earth to do. Stealing cars. Taking them apart. Sometimes putting them together again in changed configurations. Gaskets; fuel injectors; the snaking cables of clutches. He loved them all; they spoke to him. If a couple of breaks had fallen differently, he might have ended up a smiling, legit mechanic with a computerized wheel-alignment gizmo and his name embroidered on his pocket, a regular Mr. Goodwrench.

Nicky Scotto broke into his reverie. "Go down to the Keys? Sunsets. Margaritas. A little poontang, maybe?"

This made it pretty tempting. But there were problems. "Nicky, how I even find this guy?"

On the snowy New York corner, Nicky Scotto smiled. "Easy."

"Easy for you to say easy."

"He's a little guy wit' a big dog—"

"Oh, great," said Chop. "That really narrows it—"

"—and a vanity plate."

"Vanity plate?" said Chop. "The asshole's got a vanity plate?"

"Did I tell ya he's a putz or what? Tells all the world, BIG AL."

Chop Parilla shook his head. It was a small head on a large

body. At the back, neck became skull in one straight line; in front, the jaw barely lifted clear of the collarbones—it looked like he'd have to jack his chin up to shave beneath it. Vanity plate. "Make it thirty grand, I'll do it."

"Thirty," said Nicky. "Now you're gettin' greedy."

"No," said Chop. "In fact I'm takin' a cut. Ya want this job done like it oughta be, I need a second guy."

On Broome Street the snow was getting drier. Nicky brushed flakes of it from the lapel of his camel-hair topcoat. "Have someone in mind?"

The guys in the garage had started hammering again. In syncopation with the tapping, Chop said, "Only the perfect guy for this job. Sid the Squid."

Nicky Scotto smiled, narrowing his piggish eyes. Snowflakes tickled his gums. Squid Berman. Nicky knew him by reputation only. But what a reputation. A warped, perverted, morbid, and sickly artful madman; perhaps a genius. "But wait," he said. "I thought I heard that Squid was inna slammer. Heisting a racehorse or something."

"Not a racehorse. Couple greyhounds. Got caught red-handed with a can of Alpo. But that was like three hitches ago. He just got out again."

"Wha'd they get 'im for this time?"

"Stealing letters," Chop Parilla said.

"Letters? Squid? That's stupid. Federal."

"Not letters," said Chop. "*Letters*. Big, gigantic letters offa hotel signs. Ya know, South Beach, deco. Wanted to make a huge, gigantic billboard that said YOU TOO."

"You too?"

"Don't ask me," said Chop. "He got it in his head. Anyway, he could use some dough and he could use some entertainment."

"Squid Berman," Nicky said with satisfaction. Why hadn't he thought of him himself? "Okay, Chop. Bring 'im in, ya got your thirty grand."

Big Al Marracotta spent that night in a Holiday Inn near Santee, South Carolina. By the time he drove across the Florida line next day, Ripper's rawhide bone had been masticated into a gooey mess, the Jerry Vale and Al Martino tapes had been listened to so many times that even the harp parts had trickled into memory, and Katy Sansone was nowhere to be seen. Her face finally came up from underneath the steering wheel somewhere north of Cocoa Beach.

Around Daytona, polishing her toenails, which rested on the glove box with the little gun inside, she said, "I hate long car trips."

"Relaxing," said Big Al. He gestured left and right. "Look at the palm trees."

"I'd rather watch the license plates," she said. "Michigan. Ontario."

Alan Tuschman, meanwhile, was lagging a state or so behind, driving a cruise-control seventy in his leased silver Lexus, and mostly talking to his dog, Fifi.

"Feef," he said, scratching her behind the ears, "dogs have it pretty good. You realize that?"

The dog luxuriously lolled her head from side to side, blithely entrusting her knobby little skull to her master's enormous hand. She was a shih tzu with an attitude, immaculately groomed and wholly the coquette. Arching bangs lent mystery to her black and glassy eyes. Her small pink tongue, not much wider than an anchovy, was an organ of flirtation. Her walk was proud and bouncy—a cheerleader's walk; she had a way of looking back across her shoulder that created a distinct impression of Bacall. But for all her apparent frippery, she had reserves of steadfastness and courage that had never yet been tested, but simmered at the ready nonetheless. Now, at ease and intimate, she lay on her back and let herself be stroked.

"You're a dog," said Al, "people don't expect that much. Don't gotta be strong just because you're big. Don't gotta keep winning the same game over and over again. What ya gotta do? Not pee on the floor. Roll over. Sit down, ya wanna biscuit. 'Course, ya gotta be loyal."

He stopped petting her just long enough to wag an index finger in her face. She licked the finger then bit down lightly on the bulbous knuckle.

"Loyalty's big," he went on. "Then again, it's big in people too. But somehow it's more appreciated in a dog. . . . And look at the other advantages. Say it's the middle of the afternoon and you wanna go to bed. You curl up with a rubber hamburger and people say how cute. None of this wondering am I depressed, is something wrong? . . . Or even, like, with sex. You're young, you have a fling or two, a good screaming hump across a couple of backyards, then boom, ya get fixed and your worries are over. None of this wondering do I still look good, am I hip, if I get somebody in the sack with me, how's it gonna go? I don't see where being a dog is such a bad deal."

Fifi did nothing to change his mind. She scratched her supple back against the leather upholstery, kicked her manicured and carefree paws into the air.

Al Tuschman stretched his dully aching legs and let out a deep, unhurried sigh that filled the car. He was thinking something that he wouldn't say aloud, even to the dog.

He was thinking how odd it was to have worked so hard to win this contest, to have *had* to win this contest, when the truth was that he needed a trip to Florida like he needed a hole in the head. Oh, the sun would be nice. He'd enjoy people's envy of his tan. It would feel good to dunk in a pool, and maybe he'd get lucky in the bars. But he couldn't help believing, secretly, that all in all he'd be happier at home. In his neighborhood. In the store. Where he knew what he was doing and who he was.

On vacation, who was he? One more aimless, nameless shmeggegi in boxer trunks, getting a headache from drinking in the afternoon sun, desperately pretending to be loving every minute. A disconnected guy waiting for life to throw him an experience.

Whereas at home he was comfortable, recognized, embraced. A well-liked character who got warm hellos in diners. Who kibitzed with the car-wash guys, the cops. Everybody knew him, or as much of him as he wanted them to. Maybe as much of him as he knew himself. The schoolboy hero. The top salesman. The smiling, easy fella who'd started putting up big numbers at an early age, and was putting them up still. The kind of guy who had a nickname known even to people who hadn't actually met him.

Big Al. Slightly famous in his town, a legend in his neighborhood.

3

There is one road leading to Key West.

Like a muddy river draining many streams, U.S. 1 gathers up the suckers who feed the resort economy, and the seekers who refresh the town's battered and eroding soul, and funnels them into two thin lanes that hop from key to key between the ocean and the Gulf, between ranks of power lines and strings of pelicans, between dank motels and stalking egrets, salty bars and patient barracuda, porno stores and sweeping tides. There are exits from this road but they are all dead ends, incomplete, unsatisfying stoppings-short. Only one route leads through to the edge that is powerfully agreed upon as the finish to this part of the world. On that hurtling and constricted path there is nowhere to hide.

Which is why Chop Parilla and Squid Berman had positioned themselves on the shoulder of the highway just where it crosses Cow Key Bridge and enters Key West proper.

It was early afternoon when they took up their post. The sun drew steam out of the mangroves when it broke between the spongy clouds that were blowing westward, carrying with them some of the last of the prodigious summer rains. The day grew hotter and traffic rumbled on the bridge. Each sort of vehicle made a different noise. Mopeds buzzed like paper on a comb. Cars plunked over seams in the concrete. Trucks forced a groan from the trestles and sent forth walls of wind that whistled in the railings.

Sid the Squid, morbidly sensitive to noises, as to most things, was made jumpy by the cacophony. He kept getting out of Chop Parilla's Jaguar—a mosaic of extracted, reassembled parts—patrolling some yards of Florida, and climbing in again.

Squid was built to be jumpy. He was shorter than average, and small-boned, but with incongruously bandy muscles that swelled between his narrow joints; at moments it seemed like he might snap his arms and legs from movements too spasmodic. His elbows were pointy, like Popeye's, and his Adam's apple stuck out so far that it deformed the collars of his T-shirts. His eyeballs bulged, and an improbable expanse of white could usually be seen around his flickering hazel irises. Now he dove back into the idling, air-conditioned Jag and said, "Hey, Chop, y'ever do a job like this before?"

"No." Truth was, Parilla's career had cleaved to the mundane. Besides stealing cars, he collected loans, occasionally set insurance fires, broke fingers and noses when it was unavoidable. Straightforward stuff, conventional.

"Me neither," said the Squid. "But I like it. I'm psyched. Ya know what I like about it, Chop?"

He paused what was, for him, a beat, but for most other people was a quarter beat. Chop did not have time to answer, and Squid went on in his chronically humid voice, the voice of someone with too much wetness seeping through the blue strands underneath his tongue.

"It makes no sense. I mean, it's pure—it has no purpose. Not like, say, robbing something. Torching something. Vulgar ordinary shit. Where's the creativity in that? This is like . . . it's like getting paid to be a gremlin. Hired to direct a nightmare. Yeah! Ya see what I'm sayin'?"

The statement was a little high-flown and abstract for Chop. He answered, "Can we steal his car?"

Squid rolled his bulging eyes. "That ain't the job."

"We're s'posed t'annoy him," argued Chop. "Wouldn't that annoy him?"

Squid didn't answer. He sprang out of the Jag again, paced along the shoulder, listening to the orchestra of traffic.

Shadows started to lengthen, silhouettes of palms were pasted on the roadway. The sun went from white to yellow and revealed the fine grain of the inconstant air. After a time Chop lowered the electric window and yelled out, "Squid, let's get a cuppa coffee."

The bandy man hesitated. He was launched on a performance, bringing to bear on a campaign all his loony concentration. It bothered him to leave his lookout, and he bounced from one foot to the other, deciding whether he would stay or go.

"C'mon," said Chop, and he gestured toward a pink and orange Dunkin' Donuts sign a quarter mile away, at the point where the Key West coastline bellied out and the dreary commercial strip began.

Squid calculated. It would take ten, twelve minutes to get there, score some coffee and a box of doughnuts, and get back to his post again. What were the odds? Not without ambivalence, he climbed into the Jag.

And while they were standing at the doughnut counter, discussing the merits of glazed and iced and Boston cream, Big Al Marracotta slipped unnoticed into town, his carsick rottweiler clawing at the windows of the Lincoln, his girlfriend refreshing her mascara, now that they had finally arrived.

Sunset approached.

Clouds flattened into slabs, spikes of sunlight slashed orange and rose and burgundy between them, a different color for each latitude of sky. Downtown the event was being celebrated as the climax of the day and the harbinger of cocktails, but for Alan Tuschman, still on the highway, heading west, it was mainly just a nuisance. Stoplights disappeared against the glare. Cruel rays shot through the smeared and eggy corpses of a million dead bugs on the windshield. His sunshade just missed being where the sun was, as sunshades always did, and he had to pee so badly that his solar plexus burned.

But at least he was very nearly at the Cow Key Bridge, the stubby gangplank to Key West.

On the far side of that bridge, Chop Parilla, bored into a trance, his Jag backed partway into mangroves, was looking toward the road, coveting selected vehicles, noting the tricks the red sun played on the pebbly reflective surfaces of the license plates.

Sid the Squid, jazzed up on caffeine, grease, and sugar, was pacing along the boundary where road shoulder softened into muck, sniffing low tide and the residue of hot tires while he scanned the stream of traffic.

Then, suddenly, at the moment when the sunshine went woolly in horizon haze, there it was: the long-awaited license plate, a hundred yards away, its shining letters filling up Sid's bulging eyes. BIG AL. NEW JERSEY. GARDEN STATE.

Berman's neck locked and his haunches quivered like a pointer's. He dove into the idling Jag just as the target car passed by. Chop Parilla peeled onto the highway, compressing him against his seat before his door was even closed.

"Hot shit," Chop said. "Lexuses I like. Best Jap car there is."

But tailing Alan Tuschman turned out to be too easy to be fun. He was tired and he didn't know where he was going. He crawled in the right lane the whole way down the Boulevard, his brake lights flashing now and then for no apparent reason.

At White Street, the boundary of Old Town, he pulled into a gas station, not up to the pumps, but to the curb next to the convenience store.

Thinking fast, Chop Parilla nosed the Jag next to the air hose. Squid Berman, on the pretext of checking the pressure in the tires, got out and crabbed along the warm and oily ground. He stayed there, low, kowtowing, as Alan Tuschman unfolded himself from his Lexus.

The tall man exited the car in stages. It took a long time. Big feet and fibrous ankles touched down on the pavement; a head of curly black hair dipped carefully beneath the door frame. Then he rose and the middle parts filled in: muttonlike thighs in snug black pants, a stretched thick torso that pulled at the buttons of a purple shirt. Rippling neck sinews festooned with gold; a strangler's veined and flexing hands, the furry fingers bearing rings.

Squid Berman, his eyeballs almost on the asphalt, looked steeply up and thought, Christ, he's huge.

Al Tuschman kicked one leg out, then the other. Hitched his pants up, sailor-style, with his forearms. The shih tzu jumped down from the car, sniffed around a moment, and squatted underneath a fender.

Squid Berman slipped back into the Jag as the furniture salesman, searching for a men's room, went into the convenience store. Chop Parilla said, "Fucker looks really tough. D'ya see the fuckin' wrists on the guy?"

Fear and excitement made moisture pool beneath Squid Berman's tongue. Damply he said, "Ya don't get the New York fish market lookin' like a wuss."

"Wuss?" Chop said, with a slightly nervous laugh. "Hey, I asked around about this guy, shit he did to convince Tony Eggs he's the guy to run the market."

"Like what?"

"Cut a deadbeat's nose off. Hand-fed it to his dog."

Squid stared at the shih tzu. It didn't seem the sort of creature that would eat pieces of a person's face, but with animals you never knew.

"'Nother guy," said Chop, "he had a problem using Tony Eggs' trucks. Big Al shipped 'im back from Montauk packed in ice between two tunas." He paused, had a sudden misgiving. "Mighta been swordfish. He catches us, we're fucked."

Squid hotly rubbed his hands together, yanked on each of his thumbs. "He ain't gonna catch us. I brought disguises."

Chop nodded absently, then turned his attention toward the Lexus. "Lives in Jersey. Figures. Needs a place to chill. Bet he has a huge house, big gate, doctors and dentists all around. What a fuckin' world, huh?"

A moment passed. Dusk was deepening, the lavender of sunset being elbowed aside by the orange of streetlamps. Squid stared off at the shih tzu, who was investigating shallow pools of transmission fluid, windshield detergent. Then he said, "Hey, wait a second. Didn't you tell me the guy was little and the dog was big?"

Parilla scratched his stomach. Detail was not his long suit except when it came to cars, and he didn't like admitting that maybe he was wrong. "Nah," he said, gesturing vaguely. "The dog is little. The guy is big."

Al Tuschman appeared once again in the doorway of the store. His shoulders blocked the light and he towered above a clerk who was gesturing directions.

Squid quibbled, "I coulda swore you said—"

Chop Parilla cut him off, slipping the Jag into gear as his quarry moved back toward the Lexus. "Squid, hey—can ya argue with a license plate?"

4

Big Al Marracotta, fortunate and lusty, had arrived in time to stash his queasy rottweiler in the Conch House kennel, to lose his Lincoln in the hotel's dark garage, then to enjoy the sunset from the rooftop bar, seven stories above the middle of Duval Street.

He and Katy sipped champagne and nibbled the obligatory fritters as a lounge pianist labored bravely, and the sun was doused in the pan-flat water out behind Tank Island. Al was happy. Key West. The air felt great and there were cocktail waitresses in fishnet hose, and some of them were female. New York was far enough away that he could forget about the headaches, the arguments, and remember only the good things. Rolling trucks. Tons of ice. Lobsters, crabs, and money. Seafood was a beautiful commodity. Delicious and perishable. Like life itself, but more so.

Al had timing. He was draining the last of the bubbly as the last of the red leached out of the clouds, leaving behind a blanket of slate gray. Without lowering his upturned flute, still hoping that a final drop might sizzle on his tongue, he said to his companion, "Nice, huh?"

"Very nice," said Katy. "Maybe we'll go out now, see the town?"

Al said, "First let's go downstairs awhile."

Katy dabbed her lips on a napkin to hide the pout.

They rose, and thereby became a spectacle. Katy had her high-heeled sandals on; they boosted her like afterburners. A high-tech bra made architecture of her bosom; Big Al could have worn her boobs as a cure for whiplash. Her waist came to his armpits, her spiky raven hair drew attention to his quarter inch salt-and-pepper helmet.

People watched as the two of them went by.

Big Al knew they did. Let 'em look, he figured. He liked it. Let 'em eat their hearts out.

Chop Parilla kept his gaze locked on Alan Tuschman's vanity plate as the short convoy continued down Truman Avenue.

At Elizabeth Street, the Lexus took a right and headed toward the Gulf. After eight or ten uncertain blocks, with a narrow slice of the waterfront coming into view, the salesman found, on the left side of the street, the sign that he'd been searching for. It was made of cypress wood, discreetly lit by soft floods bedded in shrubbery below. Immodestly, the sign proclaimed a single word: PARADISE.

Squid Berman could not let that slide. "His own little corner of hell is gonna be more like it," he said.

They watched Big Al pull into the parking area that was open to the street and paved in gravel. Then, unnoticed in the twilight, they slowly drove away.

Al Tuschman, weary from the road, switched off his ignition, picked up his suitcase and his dog, and trudged toward the office.

While he was filling out the registration card, the desk clerk asked him cheerfully, "And how did you find us, Mr. Tuschman?"

Without looking up, Al said, "I won you."

"Won us?"

The tall man glanced up now, smiled winningly. The imminent mention of sales made him act the salesman. "Contest where I work. Selling furniture. Dinettes."

"Ah," said the clerk, and he tried not to frown. He had a shaved head and a row of ruby studs along one eyebrow. He'd worked at Paradise for five years, and derived a large part of his self-image from his job. It was important to him that the place was classy, that its clientele were of a certain standing. Promotional junkets for salesmen in shiny shirts and pinky rings—that didn't sit so well with him. He changed the subject, gestured toward the shih tzu sniffing quietly around the small but airy office. "The dog's okay as long as he's leashed—"

"She. Fifi."

"—as long as she's leashed in public areas."

"No problem," said Al.

"Breakfast is from seven-thirty till eleven, and clothing is optional at poolside."

"Excuse me?"

"Mr. Tuschman," said the clerk, allowing himself a note of condescension. "We try to give our guests a totally natural and relaxing experience. There are no televisions and no phones. No entertainment other than the sun and the beauty of the gardens."

"Any single women?"

The row of rubies quivered on the desk clerk's eyebrow. "Our guests are very mixed," he said. "We're proud of that. We don't believe in segregation. God forbid a straight person should witness two men kissing, two women giving each other back rubs. Here at Paradise we don't think that way."

Al Tuschman pursed his lips and blinked, put the pen down softly on the registration card. "Bear with me," he said. "I'm a little tired. Are you telling me that I broke my ass from the Fourth right through Columbus Day, worked extra Saturdays plus Thursday evenings to win a free trip to a gay nudist colony?"

Contemptuous of categories, the desk clerk held his ground. "We get a lot of Europeans," he said. "Now and then celebrities who just want to be left alone. This place exists so that people can be happy. That's our only mission."

"Mission?"

"May I help you with your bag?"

Big Al Marracotta's suite was on the top guest floor. It had a king-sized bed with canopy, two bathrooms, a slice of harbor view, and a giant television set.

As soon as he and Katy had trundled down from the rooftop bar, Big Al called the desk to rent a VCR. He suggested to Katy that she might like to put an outfit on.

"Which one?" she asked.

Big Al put a finger on his chin and a twinkle in his eye. "The calico, I think. Maybe we'll go Western."

She went to the bathroom to change. Big Al went to the satchel of porno tapes he'd brought down from New York.

The bellman hooked up the VCR, and when he'd left, Katy reemerged. Her outfit was a thong and a tiny bra that looked like they'd been cut out of a tablecloth from a rib joint. A frilly garter cinched one thigh, and she wore a big felt hat like Dale Evans.

Big Al got naked and they watched the movie, which prominently featured a horse. Katy was impressed, maybe even aroused, but she wasn't having that good a time, and after a while even Big Al noticed.

"Whatsa matter?" he asked as the horse and the heroine were contemplating something hard to believe.

"Oh, I don't know," said Katy, pushing back the wide brim of her hat. She pushed it with her knuckles, and the chin strap moved against her jaw, and for a second she looked like a real cowgirl. "Vacation. Ya know. I thought we'd see the town."

This hinted at a basic philosophical difference. Some people thought vacation was about the place they went. Others viewed it as respite, pure and simple, from the place they'd left behind. "We'll get to that," he said. "We'll see the town."

"When?"

Al's eyes were on the screen. Either it was trick photography or he hoped to shake that woman's hand someday. "Little while later."

Katy had been seeing Al around eight months now. Their average date lasted three, four hours. Usually it was dinner and bed. Sometimes it was drinks in places where everyone knew Al, came over in waves to say hello, to hold impromptu meetings, sometimes argue. Once in a while they spent a whole night together; very rarely, when he could concoct a story to tell his wife, a weekend. This was the first time they were traveling together. "Al," she said, "I know you're like, high-spirited, but I never realized you're an out-and-out sex fiend."

Big Al took this as a compliment. It showed. "And not just sex!" he said. "Food. Excitement. Going fast. Gambling. It's got juice in it, baby, I'm there!"

From the TV came a chorus of whinnying and human moans.

"Later?" Katy said. "Later can we see the town?"

"Sure we can. 'Course. Crab claws, beach, a little jazz, anything ya like."

The girlfriend pursed her lips. She knew that was as well as she was going to do. First what he wanted. Later what she wanted. Maybe.

Big Al's eyes were on the screen. His tongue flicked out to lick his lips. He said, "Next year, maybe, I can get away, we'll go out West."

"Next year, Al?" said Katy. It seemed improbable to her.

Above the moaning and the horse sounds, Al said vaguely, "Arizona. Colorado. Looks nice, no?"

5

A bewildered Al Tuschman, already wondering how to tell Moe Kleiman to fire his fancy new travel agent, followed the clerk out of the office, through the deserted courtyard, and around the pool, whose water glowed an unearthly blue from the soft lights beneath the surface. A mild breeze moved the shrubbery, drew forth dusty, scratching sounds and the melancholy smell of used-up flowers. Fifi stopped to investigate, wiggled her nose at the tang of iodine, the sharpness of salt. Her master barely noticed. Uncharacteristically, his mind was still sniffing around something the clerk had said. That happiness was a mission.

This was not the kind of thing Alan Tuschman generally thought about. At home, schmoozing, doing business, obeying habits and following routines, who had time? But here, now, on vacation and by himself, the notion somehow tweaked him. Probably because he thought it was ridiculous. Missions were about active things, challenges, dangers. Catching a pass in heavy traffic on third-and-six—that was a mission. Making the layup and drawing the foul when your team was down by three—that was a mission. But happiness? That was . . . what? An accident? A by-product? A prize? No—prizes, he'd won plenty. Prizes, trophies—cobwebs made bridges between the heads and elbows of his trophies; trophies were a different thing from happiness. He gave an audible harrumph that made the desk clerk turn around and look at him a second.

They continued down a path lined with philodendrons so enormous that a dog the size of Fifi could have hid beneath each leaf. At the end of the path was a whitewashed bungalow.

The clerk unlocked the door, turned on a dimmered light switch to reveal a tropically tasteful suite. Wicker this and rattan that and bamboo the other. Al the furniture maven knew it was cheap stuff, borax, from the Philippines, from Thailand, but in this room it worked. A huge ceiling fan turned lazily enough to slow the pulse. A cozy alcove held a fluffy sofa with rain-forest upholstery. There was an outdoor shower framed in thatch. On the bureau, a platter of ripe fruits. On the raw wood walls a passable print of greenish women with greenish breasts, and a couple of flower paintings, coyly lewd.

The desk clerk left, smugly declining to be tipped, and Al, exhausted, lay down on the bed, his heel against the mattress seam. He thought he'd rest awhile, then go out. Margaritaville. Sloppy Joe's. He'd never been to Key West before, but he'd heard about those places. Fabled joints where inhibitions melted down and fell away, and bad behavior was applauded. Where women sucked cigars and cakewalked in wet T-shirts. Rubbed strangers with their bare knees, showed off intimate tattoos. Bartenders poured liqueurs down chutes of ice, and mouths became acquainted as they shared the sticky stuff. Every day was Mardi Gras, and the neighbors back at home would never know.

Al Tuschman lay there, resting, thinking, imagining the noise and the crush and the smoke, and gradually he realized that he wasn't going out. Not tonight. Didn't have the strength, the will. Arriving someplace new, alone—it wasn't all that easy. Smiling, being friendly, looking for a pickup or only a smile in return—a lot of the time it just seemed like one more game to win, one more sales pitch to deliver.

He kicked off his shoes. The dog, understanding that he was now down for the count, jumped up and joined him on the bed. Happiness, Al Tuschman caught himself thinking once again. A mission? Well, maybe. Who knew?

He looked up at the ceiling fan. If he squinted very hard he could stop the motion of the blades. The effort made him deliciously sleepy, and he didn't fight it. A week in Key West, he thought. Contentment, relaxation, pleasure. He'd get with the program. Tomorrow, maybe. Tomorrow, in daylight. After a long and peaceful and refreshing sleep . . .

While he slept, sometime after midnight, Squid Berman and Chop Parilla wreaked havoc on the Lexus, whose lease had two years, three months still to go, and which assessed stiff penalties for excessive or abnormal wear.

The attack was Squid's idea, and bore the stamp of his malicious artistry.

It began with fifty pounds of calamari, purchased at deep discount because it was getting old and turning faintly blue. The calamari was packed in ten-pound plastic bags that had the sodden lumpiness of the internal organs of someone who was very, very ill. When the bags were opened, there issued forth an ocean smell that, at first whiff, was not unpleasant, but soon grew tinged with unwholesome odors of metal and ammonia.

With the seafood stashed in Chop Parilla's trunk, they drove back to Paradise, using the Jag to block the view of Alan Tuschman's car. The street was quiet but for the humming of the streetlamps, and it took Squid Berman about half a minute to pick the lock of the target vehicle. The alarm wailed for three seconds before Chop disarmed it, and, as usual, no one paid attention anyway. Then Squid slipped into the driver's seat and got down to business.

Most guys, of course, would simply have dumped the calamari in the car and bolted. This would have been adequate to achieve the minimum goal of stinking up the car. But such slipshod workmanship would have appalled Squid Berman. He was there to make a statement, feverish to create. His eyes were rolling and his knuckly hands were twitching as he opened the first sack of seafood.

He started with the passenger seat. Carefully, he laid out a squid, tentacles forward. Next to it he placed another, tentacles behind. The two squids interlocked like tiles, and their own slime grouted them nicely to the leather. He pressed down row on row of calamari, making an upholstery of seafood, a rank mosaic gleaming opalescent in the streetlight. When the passenger side was finished, he stood up to do the driver's seat. Calamari forward, calamari back. The gummy creatures seemed to wriggle like paisleys, and the morning sun would bake them on for good. Calamari on the seat back. Calamari on the headrest. Teach this scumbag to serve rotten seafood to his friends.

Sid Berman lavished so much time on his creation that even Chop was getting nervous. Two guys spreading calamari in someone else's car in the middle of the night; this would be a hard thing to explain. Although one bag of goods was still unopened, he said at last, "Enough already, Squid."

Squid was too intent to look up. With too much moisture underneath his tongue, he said, "I've got enough left to spell out 'Fuck You' on the dashboard."

"I think he'll read that on the seats," Parilla said. "Come on, we're outa here."

Berman hesitated, sighed. In this life nothing was ever quite perfect. Never enough time, enough resources. That's just how it was. Shaking his head, he dumped the last ten pounds of calamari on the gas pedal, the brake.

He rose and closed the door. He took a moment to admire his macabre and slithery work. The tubes of calamari looked somehow like ranks of condoms dancing samba.

Moving toward the Jag, he sniffed his hands and said to Chop, "D'ya bring the whaddyacallit, Wash'n Dri?"

"Ah, shit," Parilla said. "Forgot."

"Bummer," said Squid, and wiped his slimy fingers on his pants.

6

Big Al Marracotta, a little lost inside his one-size hotel bathrobe, rang down for extra salsa for his scrambled eggs.

It was pretty early for extra salsa, but he was eager to get that spice thing going, that burn. He slathered butter on his toast, slurped coffee, and watched Katy pout. Today she had a right to pout, he admitted to himself. He'd promised that they'd see the town last night, and then he'd fallen immovably asleep. Well, what the hell. It had been a long day. Lotta driving. Lotta drinking. Lotta sex. A man was entitled to get tired. He'd make it up to her today.

"Tell ya what," he said, his lips glistening with butter. "We'll finish breakfast, skip the A.M. workout, see the town. How's that? Pick up the dog, check out the beach, do a little shopping. Whaddya say?"

Katy picked at the edges of her mango muffin. "Fine," she blandly said. Mornings were not her best time. Her raven hair, brittle from the dyeing, stood up here and there in random curlicues. With only smears of faded makeup, her eyes looked rather small and waifish. Her breasts felt heavy in the morning; they pulled down on her collarbones and reminded her that she was twenty-nine, and being kept in only so-so fashion by a terminally married man who, no doubt, would dump her fairly soon, by which time she'd be thirty, thirty-one, and what then?

Maybe Big Al was reading her mind. Maybe just trying to regain lost ground. He reached out gently and held her chin. His hand was small and surprisingly soft, the heel of it like a pillow. His touch could on occasion be infuriatingly tender. He said, "Come on. You're beautiful. Ya know that?"

She blinked. She could have cried. Instead she tried to smile, and when that didn't quite work out, she made a playful and ferocious face and bit his hand, the pillowy part between the wrist and thumb. Selfish bastard. Selfish bastard who could also sometimes be a charming bastard.

Big Al squirmed and pretended to wince as she nibbled on his hand, her small teeth leaving shallow dents in his flesh. It almost hurt; it did hurt, in a way that got him going, and he began to calculate just how much hell there'd be to pay if he took back his offer to skip the A.M. workout.

Alan Tuschman also woke up early.

He'd managed to slip beneath his light blanket, though not to get out of last night's clothes. Now he smelled damp earth and chlorine, and gradually remembered where he was. He opened his eyes to see his slowly turning ceiling fan, palm shadows flickering against his raw wood walls, greenish women with greenish breasts staring down at him with no great curiosity.

He stretched, his long hands and feet overreaching the confines of the bed. The dog licked his face. She wanted walking. He got up, washed, and went outside.

From behind its thatch enclosure, the pool pump softly hummed. Otherwise the courtyard of Paradise was quiet. Dew was shrinking back on enormous leaves as the sun climbed higher in the sky. A large woman sat lotus-style on a towel near the hot tub. Her eyes were closed and she didn't have a shirt on. She inhaled deeply and raised her arms, displaying furry armpits.

Across the way, the breakfast buffet was just being set up. Al caught a whiff of coffee and realized he was famished. He went over to investigate. There were thimble muffins and miniature croissants curled up like unripe fetuses and dainty little ramekins of fruit cup. It was all very cute but it didn't look like breakfast. Not to Al, who was used to Jersey diners. Danish big as hubcaps. Omelets the size of shoes. Home fries bleeding paprika, piled to the very edges of the plate.

He decided to go out to eat. He went back to his bungalow to grab his car keys. Then, with Fifi in the lead, he rounded the pool, trod the gravel path, and exited the gate to the parking area.

He took no special notice of the old hippie nodding out behind a buttonwood hedge across the street—the red bandanna wrapped around the long and stringy hair, the small, round Trotsky glasses worn far down on the nose. It was Sid the Squid, of course. He hadn't been able to sleep. Too excited. Hungry, like every artist, for a reaction to his efforts.

So he'd left Chop snoring in the mildewed motel room that they shared, and strolled to Paradise at dawn. Now he struggled not to fidget as Big Al approached the violated, sunstruck Lexus. Moisture pooled beneath Sid's tongue; he swallowed and his Adam's apple shuttled up and down.

Al Tuschman, tunelessly whistling, used his remote to unlock the driver's-side door. He'd reached out for the handle before he realized anything was wrong. Then he froze and squinted, disbelieving, through the windshield.

Sunshine was skidding across the sweep of glass, making it half mirror. Sky was reflected, and the restless crowns of palms; but light also penetrated, and what Al Tuschman saw behind the glare mocked all understanding. Calamari. Stale, dry calamari, spoiled to a sickly mottled gray, glued in wavy patterns to the leased leather of his seats. Scallops of scum marked the places where dead tentacles had shrunk back in the tropic heat. The black dots of eyestalks stood out creepily against the tasteful taupe.

Across the street, Squid Berman squirmed and swallowed, trying not to wet his pants or let out a whoop of glee.

Al Tuschman opened the car door. Fifi, by long habit, jumped up toward the seat, then seemed somehow to reverse field, midair, and pulled away, whimpering, to the limit of her leash. She'd smelled a stink that seemed to be the vapor of death itself. Ocean turned to ammoniac poison. Nourishment corrupted to putrescent goo.

Al Tuschman sucked in a tiny sniff that brought tears to his eyes. He stopped breathing. Yet some compulsion, some need for confirmation, led him to reach out a thick finger to touch the calamari. The tubes felt stiff and starchy, like undercooked lasagna. The tentacles were dank and crusty and bore a disgusting resemblance to something secretly discovered in one's nose.

Al closed the door, wiped his eyes, turned in a different direction to inhale.

Across the street, Squid Berman rejoiced and waited for the inevitable explosion, the operatic tantrum. In his world, men had magnificent and primal tempers that gave rise to absurd and highly entertaining displays. When something bad happened to them, they screamed, cursed, turned red, kicked walls, punched doors, swore revenge, and railed at heaven. It was great to watch.

But Al Tuschman did none of these things.

He didn't have much of a temper. Not anymore, having spent so much adrenaline on the ballfields of his youth. Besides, innocent, clear of conscience, he had no reason to suspect malice. So he wasn't thinking about revenge; as his mind gradually cleared, he began instead to think about insurance. What was the deductible on calamari? What if he needed a whole new interior? He rubbed his chin, wondered how he'd schmooze the lease people on this one. He shuffled his feet in the gravel. As if it mattered, he pulled out the remote and locked the car again.

Squid Berman watched him from behind the buttonwood, and his disappointment at the absence of a show turned moment by moment to grudging admiration. He thought: Christ, this guy is really cool. Calculating; patient. Made sense. Tough and cool—that was the combination that brought guys to the top. The hotheads, they went just so far before burning out or making a fatal blunder. . . . Besides, this guy was probably so fucking rich— what was a brand-new Lexus to him?

Squid retreated behind the hedge, choked back a private embarrassment that his initial ploy had fallen short, that his masterpiece of seafood had elicited barely a grumble from his prey. He was let down but not discouraged. He liked a challenge. Big Al was cool and rich, unflappable? Fine. Sid Berman would find a way to get to him. No problem. He'd just have to get some rest and try a little harder.

7

There were times when shopping was about acquiring needed things, and times when it was a desperate search for comforts true or false, and times when it was first and foremost an exercise in spite. The expedition that carried Katy Sansone up and down Duval Street, Big Al and Ripper at her side, was of this final type.

She wasn't getting what she wanted from this trip. Not at all. She hadn't been on the beach yet, even for a second. She hadn't seen the ocean except for slices of it from the cocktail lounge or through the window of her room as she lay there on her back. It was his trip, his vacation.

Well, what had she expected? The question mocked her, but she couldn't let it go. How had she imagined it would be? What did she think or hope she might get out of it? The awful truth was that, if she was going to cut through the fibs and poses and excuses and just be deadly honest, what she'd really wanted from this trip was not about beach and not about ocean and not about a suntan.

It was about romance.

There, she'd admitted it. Romance. It was ridiculous, pathetic, and she knew it was pathetic. Of course she did. She'd wanted to feel special. Ha. With Big Al? Whose idea of romance, maybe, was to light a candle before he poked her. Clink champagne glasses before the porno films came out. Before he washed himself and combed his hair and went back to his fat wife in Bay Ridge. This was romance? This was what people wrote songs about? Katy wished she was either a little smarter or a whole lot dumber. Little smarter, maybe she wouldn't have got herself into such a jerky situation. Dumber, maybe it wouldn't gnaw at her so much. As it was . . .

As it was, she promenaded up and down Duval Street, shopping with grim and joyless fury. Designer sunglasses that made her look either like a European actress or a total geek. Wraparound skirts whose ease of removal caused Big Al to lick his sloppy lips. A dolphin brooch; fake Spanish coins set into earrings. With each purchase, she looked sideways at her sugar daddy, trying to determine if she'd succeeded yet in annoying him, had managed to spend enough of his money so that he would reveal discomfort, and she could feel that she was somehow winning.

The strategy failed utterly, as she secretly knew it would. Big Al, swaggering along, flanked by his big-balled rottweiler and his tall young squeeze, got only happier and more puffed up as they shopped. Buying power was a beautiful thing. A potent thing. There was sex in a wad of fifties. Throwing dough at his girlfriend's whims didn't bother him at all. It tightened his grip and therefore made him frisky.

At some point, with shopping bags chafing against her thin and still-pale legs, Katy understood she was just digging herself in deeper. She got depressed. The sun was high, the fresh part of the morning had been wasted, and what had she accomplished? Got some things that, after Al got bored and dumped her, she'd never want to see again anyway. "I'm ready to go back," she said.

Big Al, on a spending roll, was surprised. "Already?" he said. "There's nothing else ya want?"

"Nothing I'm gonna find here," said Katy.

Big Al blinked up at her, and for some part of a second she thought perhaps he'd understood. Then he said, "Where, then? Miami?"

"Al," she said, "I'd like to get out of these shoes."

That, he understood. He shrugged and they headed back toward the Conch House, Ripper's testicles bouncing proudly as they went.

Alan Tuschman, disgusted, baffled, trudged into the office of Paradise and asked the clerk to call the cops.

The clerk seemed unsurprised and maybe even pleased that the slightly thuggish-looking salesman was having trouble. Unctuously, he said, "Is something wrong?"

"Nah," said Al, "just thought I'd say hello."

This was exactly the sort of Northeast sarcasm the clerk had moved down from suburban Philadelphia to avoid. He averted his gaze and made the call. Al went back outside and leaned against the trunk of his despoiled car. The old hippie across the way was gone.

A motorcycle cop roared up in about ten minutes. The short-legged officer climbed off the bike like a pug addressing a fire hydrant. He looked at Al accusingly. "What's the problem?"

Al pointed through the driver's-side window of the Lexus.

The cop clomped over in his boots and squinted through his Ray-Bans. "What is it?"

"Calamari. Wanna smell?"

The cop said no.

"Crazy, huh?" said Al.

The cop didn't offer an opinion.

"Something like this," Al asked, "why would it happen?"

The cop scratched his head right through the helmet. Then he began an expert examination of the car. He determined that it was new and pricey and from a Northern state held in universal and profound contempt. "Town like this," he said, "there's a certain amount of vandalism against tourists. Resentment, ya know. Hate."

Al Tuschman gave a worldly nod. To be resented, detested,

mocked, and victimized—why else did anybody take vacation? He said, "Any chance of fingerprints?"

Sharply, the cop said, "D'ya touch the door handle?"

He had Al there. He pressed the attack.

"Anybody mad at ya?"

"I just got here."

"Hot climate," said the cop, "it don't take long for people to get mad. Ya look too long at someone's girlfriend's titties? Get talkin' politics with shrimpers?"

Al had not yet had food or coffee. He was hatching a headache and he wished he was home. He said, "Look, if I could just get a report. For insurance."

The cop produced a pad, began scrawling. Now he pretended to be helpful. "I was you, I'd call a dealer."

"Got one here in town?"

"Fancy car like this, closest one's Miami. Sun, I think it's called." He paused, and Al Tuschman tried to believe he didn't see a quick malevolent flash behind the Ray-Bans. "Towing cost ya six, eight hundred bucks."

The cop snapped the report from his pad and roared off on his motorbike.

Al Tuschman stuffed the paper into his pocket, went back into the office, called the dealer in Miami. The towing, as it turned out, would cost a mere five hundred seventeen bucks. Al left the car key with the desk clerk.

"Who should I give it to?" the man with the shaved head asked.

"Anyone that wants it," said Al disgustedly.

The clerk bit his lip. What a sarcastic guy, he thought, as his big, rough-looking guest pivoted on aching knees and left.

Back in his mildewed motel room, Chop Parilla was more than half asleep. A sweaty sheet clung to his hairy back; its wrinkles seemed to continue in the thick skin of his stub of neck. Fugitive shafts of light and the dull hum of traffic from the Boulevard were prying him out of the millionth version of his favorite dream—a dream of weightless sex amid the knobs and gauges of a stolen car, never the same car twice.

In his mind he copped a final feel of the dashboard and kissed the dream good-bye. Then he heard the doorknob rattle and he reached by reflex for the revolver underneath his pillow.

As the door swung open and a rude wedge of sunshine cut into the room, he came up on an elbow, cocked the hammer of the gun, and drew a bead on a greasy-haired hippie with a red bandanna and stupid-looking little glasses way down on his nose.

"Hey, don't fuck around. It's me."

Squid Berman was slurping coffee from one of a pair of Styrofoam cups. He handed the other to Chop, who put the gun down on the nightstand. Squid tore off the bandanna and the wig, polished off his java, and started pacing the narrow alley between the single beds.

"So how'd it go?" Parilla asked.

"Went shitty," Squid admitted. "Went weird. The fucker hardly flinched!"

Chop rubbed the pads of fat beneath his eyes. "I'm not surprised."

"Whaddya mean, you're not surprised? Bullshit you're not surprised."

Calmly, Chop said, "Ya don't get the fish market goin' off half-cocked."

Squid paced faster, pivoted more furiously. "He acted like it was, I don't know, a mosquito bite. Closes the car door. Doesn't even slam it. Rubs his chin. Fuckin' philosophical."

"Smart," said Chop. "Ya don't just get mad. Ya give it time. Ya get *really* mad. Ya find out who to hurt. Then ya let it out. That's the smart way to get mad."

"Watches the dog take a leak," said Squid. "Strolls back to the hotel. Like ho-hum, just another fuckin' morning . . . A gorgeous piece a work like what I did, and the fucker barely flinches!"

Chop sipped coffee, rearranged the damp sheet that lay across his butt. "Ya want I should call Nicky, ask advice?"

"Don't insult me, Chop."

"Hey, it's just that Nicky knows 'im better."

"Not half as good as I'm gonna know 'im by the time I'm through. I'm goin' to school on the sonofabitch. I'm learnin' every minute."

"And what ya learned so far?" Chop challenged.

"Possessions, which is money, he don't care about," said Squid. "So what's that leave? His dignity. His person. I'll find a way in, Chop. I'll make 'im nuts."

"Enough with the pacing, Squid. You're makin' me a little nuts."

The bandy man kept doing laps. "You'll see. You'll see. Have I ever let ya down before?"

0

Al Tuschman surprised himself by not being more upset. Maybe it was just that food and coffee sufficed to make a hungry person happy, brought life back to basics.

He'd found a good breakfast place down on Duval Street. A courtyard a few steps up from the sidewalk. Outdoors, he could sit with Fifi, and, even better, the place had the kind of stuff that he was used to. God bless the Greeks. They had one recipe for home fries, disseminated it around the globe. Used the same take-out cups in Florida as in Jersey: blue background with a white acropolis, the seam of the cup always slicing through a statue's crotch.

Comforted by these familiar things, Al felt himself becoming more receptive to the newness parading before him.

Drag queens who hadn't been to sleep yet. Homeless guys tying up their mildewed bedrolls. Miserable youths with baggy pants, rings through their noses and tattoos on their feet. And the inevitable mismatched couples. Slight men with wide women. Brassy women with mousy men. Here a tall and chesty babe weighed down with shopping bags, on the arm of a grinning short guy who might have been her uncle, leading a rottweiler whose fleeting nearness made Fifi tick her paws against the gravel of the courtyard. The woman met his eye, held it for some fraction of a second. He thought he saw a quick twitch at the corner of her mouth. But she didn't seem to be flirting; more like apologizing for something.

A funny town, Al decided. He went back to his eggs and tried not to think about his car. Or, if he had to think about it, to find a way to rationalize what the towing and the deductible would cost him. Less than a Florida vacation. So he was still ahead. Sort of. Then again, he wouldn't be on vacation, certainly not on this vacation, if he'd had to pay for it.

Was that good or bad, he wondered—that he wouldn't take vacation unless he won it? Did it mean he was a workaholic, or just cheap? Was it that he didn't have a lady to take vacation with? Or was he simply the kind of guy who didn't like vacations? And why did that seem somehow shameful to admit?

He finished his omelet, paid his tab, and rose to leave.

But that was another thing about being on vacation—now that breakfast was over, he had no idea what his next activity should be, or what it would accomplish.

For a moment, he stood there indecisive, slowly wobbling like a bothered compass. Finally an ancient instinct steered him toward the water and he joined the stream that brainlessly headed down Duval, vaguely aware that in so doing, he had become a part of the tourist show, a big, burly, lonely guy, still in Northern pants, his only friend a fussy and unlikely little dog.

"The beach?" Big Al Marracotta had said dismissively. "Who needs it? Sand in your crack? Riffraff all around. No place to get a cocktail . . . Come on. Right here we got the pool, the swim-up bar. Beautiful."

Katy Sansone had pouted but decided not to argue. If she was ever going to have her way about anything, she had to pick her battles. Besides, could she explain to him how she felt about the difference between the ocean and the pool? Something vast and alive as opposed to something filtered and contained? Something full of mystery and romance compared with something tourists' children peed in? A blue and infinite horizon instead of a view of the lanai rooms behind the towel kiosk and the row of lounge chairs? She felt those things but she knew she wouldn't explain them very well, and Big Al would look at her like she was crazy.

So she'd sighed, pulled on her thong, settled it between her buttocks, slipped into a shift, and gone down to the pool.

Big Al at least was happy there, as usual.

He had a boxer-style bathing suit with a mesh cup that left him room to breathe. A Knicks cap kept the sun out of his eyes. He could look at the water cascading down women's cleavages as they pulled themselves out of the pool. Katy let him rest his knuckles against her bare hip, as long as he was careful not to leave some bizarre handprint of a tan line on her butt.

Sunshine and near-nudity. For Big Al this was heaven. He lay back on his lounge till he was good and sweaty, then waded, thigh-deep, into the pool. Tepid water. Beautiful. The sun had made him thirsty. "Cocktail?"

Katy squinted toward him. She doubted it was noon and she didn't want a drink. Problem was, it was hard to say no without a reason, and reasons to say no got only harder to find.

She joined him in the pool. They waded to the bar. Water reached her navel and Big Al Marracotta's nipples. He ordered piña coladas.

When the drinks were made, he squinted down, pushed aside the paper umbrella, and sucked his cocktail through a straw. Then, almost boyishly, he smiled at the sweetness of it, the cloy of coconut, the slushiness of pineapple. Smiled as though he had a virgin conscience and not a problem in the world.

In fact he had at least one quite serious problem; he just didn't know it yet.

His problem was that, at that very moment, Benny Franco, the guy he'd left in charge of the fish market in his absence, was having his rights read to him as he was bundled into a government Plymouth and carted off to the Metropolitan Correction Center.

In New York, Benny's arrest was regarded as a slight surprise. There'd been rumors, speculation. The feds had been looking pretty closely at his pre-seafood careers in paving and trash carting. Had noted certain patterns—a consistent lack of gusto in the bidding process if Benny was involved; a tendency of determined competitors to undergo misfortune. These patterns did not place Benny in a flattering light.

But no one had expected the indictment to come down quite so soon; and even though Benny Franco would be out on bail before the sun went down, his arrest was a nuisance. It didn't do to have a guy who'd just been indicted on racketeering charges running, even temporarily, such a visible enterprise as the wholesale fish market. The connection might lead people wrongly to imagine that their seafood was tainted by the raunchy hands of organized crime.

This, at least, was the position taken by Carlo Ganucci, the gaunt and ancient *consigliere* of the Calabrese family. "Don't look right," he said to Tony Eggs Salento, the *capo di tutti capi,* as they sat on folding chairs in the back room of their social club on Prince Street. "Guy's name gets inna paper. Place of employment: Fulton Fish. People like put two and two together."

"Fuck is Big Al at?" Tony Eggs demanded. He was an old-style boss, though he'd risen to the top only recently, as the flashy, newer-style bosses became celebrities and, one by one, were put away forever. Tony Eggs knew enough to stay in the background. He didn't go to nightclubs and wasn't photogenic. He wore undistinguished suits and plain white shirts and let hair grow out of his ears and nose. He was so somber and so glum that nobody was jealous of his power. He was known for being starkly fair and unforgiving, and he had a work ethic like the guy who beat the drum in Roman galleys.

"Flahda," said the *consigliere.* The skin on his face was pale and paper-thin. You could see his skull move when he talked. "Took vacation."

"Vacation," said Tony Eggs with contempt. To him there was a dark satisfaction and a grim responsibility in a mobster's work. Since when did mobsters take vacation?

"Ya want we call 'im home? Might take a day or two to find 'im."

Tony Eggs pulled on his face. It was a long and fleshy face and it stretched considerably as he pulled it. "Who else we got could run the show awhile?"

Ganucci thought it over. Not that there were many people to choose from; not anymore. But it could be a headache if they put in the wrong guy, someone who was not respected.

The boss tugged his chin, fretted with the short black hairs protruding from his nostrils, and answered his own question. "There's Nicky."

"That's true," Ganucci said. "'Course, ya fired him before."

"Never said he wasn't good at what he did."

There was a pause, then the *consigliere* said, "Well, ya don't mind my sayin' so, I never quite understood why ya took it away from him then."

Tony Eggs leaned far back in his chair, interwove his fingers, stretched them inside out so that the knuckles cracked. "He liked it too much. *Capice?*"

Ganucci wasn't sure he did.

"He bragged about it," the boss went on. "Strutted. Gettin' in his mind like a fuckin' movie star. When I heard he's goin' ta Gotti's tailor, I said, *basta,* that's it."

Traffic noise filtered in from the street. In the front room of the club someone was shuffling cards.

The *consigliere* cleared his throat. "Tony," he said. "Nicky liked the job too much before. It worry you at all that maybe he'll remember just how much he liked it?"

The boss pulled on an earlobe.

"Ya know," the ancient counselor went on. "Like maybe make a problem between him and Al?"

Tony shrugged. In the shrug was the patient, durable malice that comes with disapproval. "No one put a gun to Big Al's head," he said, "and tol' 'im that he hadda take vacation."

9

Al Tuschman finally got into bathing trunks and sat out by the pool at Paradise. Sitting there, his dog splayed out in the shade beneath his lounge, he felt torn between looking at everything and looking at absolutely nothing.

He could not help noticing that everyone but him was rubbing someone else. Over by the deep end of the pool, two men were taking turns rubbing sunscreen on each other's shoulders; Al scared himself by acknowledging a certain elegance in their gleaming skins and leanly muscled arms. Nearer the hot tub, a topless woman was doing something mysterious and sensual to another woman's feet; he could faintly hear the rubbed woman occasionally chanting.

Then there was the naked threesome. Two women, one guy. Breasts everywhere; a tanned, confusing minefield of breasts. The threesome had towels draped carelessly about their loins, but face it, they were naked. They spoke a foreign language, which heightened Al Tuschman's feeling that he had somehow stumbled into one of those slow and moody European films that he never understood. Decadence: Good or bad? Seemed pretty pleasant—so why did someone always blow his brains out at the end? The threesome talked softly but with animation. They giggled a lot. Were they witty or slaphappy? Sophisticated or just plain crazy? And was Al a bourgeois prude, or was what he was feeling a thin mask for envy, pure and simple?

There was neither profit nor resolution to these thoughts, but at least they kept Al occupied while Chop Parilla, not fifty yards away on the far side of a frail reed fence, was hijacking the tow truck that had come to fetch his car.

It was an impulsive maneuver, totally unplanned.

Chop and Squid had been staked out in the shade, sitting in the Jag. Squid wore a paper hat and a white apron that looped around his neck and tied at the waist; it was the look he needed for his next assault on Big Al's sanity. While they were waiting for an opportunity to put this next phase into effect, the flatbed from Sun Motors in Miami pulled up.

The driver—lanky, sweating, and with a shirttail out—parked next to the ravaged Lexus, then went into the hotel office.

Chop eyed the spotless stamped aluminum of the flatbed. Then he turned to Squid, his face flushed and his voice breathy. "If he's here for the Lex, I'm stealin' it."

Squid frowned so vigorously that the paper hat shifted behind his pointy ears. "Stealin' cars," he said, "that ain't the job."

"Look the opportunity," Chop argued.

Squid maintained a solid silence.

"It ain't *botherin'* the job," Chop pleaded. "Take two minutes."

Squid swallowed; his Adam's apple shuttled up and down. He said, "How long it takes, that ain't the point. It's fuckin' with my concentration. Ya wanna do somethin' right, ya do one thing at a time."

Chop drummed on the steering wheel and sucked his teeth as he watched the driver come back from the office, a key now dangling from his hand. The driver opened the Lexus' door, quickly stepped back at the stench. He shook his head and reached in just long enough to put the car in neutral, then climbed into his truck and maneuvered it into a position from which he could winch the pillaged vehicle onto the flatbed.

Parilla was stewing. Whose gig was this anyway, and why was he suddenly taking orders from Squid? He squirmed as the greased piston lifted and the flatbed tilted down; he plucked the damp shirt from his armpits as the driver came around from the cab and grabbed the towing cables with their awesome hooks. Finally he said, "Wit' all due respect to your fuckin' concentration, fuck you, it's meant to be, I'm goin' for it."

Squid just rolled his bulging eyes. Chop reached across and moved his gun from the glove box to the waistband of his pants.

He waited until the driver had laid down on the gravel to attach the cables to the Lexus, until he was helpless and in shadow.

Then he sprang from the Jag, walking quickly but not running. He dropped to his knees next to the prone driver, down at the level of axle grease and undercoating and the smell of tires. He hid his revolver with his body as he freed it from his pants, and stuck the muzzle of it in the driver's ear.

Softly he said, "Don't make a sound and don't move a muscle."

The driver flinched, then went rigid as a fish beached in sunshine.

"This is my car you're fuckin' with," Chop whispered.

"You make mistake, I think," the driver managed. "I have order to pick up this car."

Chop pushed the gun a little harder. "You don't understand. All cars are my cars. What's your name?"

"Ernesto."

"You a Teamster, Ernesto?"

"*Sí.*"

"Good. I get along with Teamsters." He put some fresh pressure on the muzzle and dug a knee into the small of the prone man's back. "This can be easy or this can be hard, Ernesto. How would you like it to be?"

The driver didn't have much breath left. "Eassy," he wheezed.

"Good man. Tell ya what. I'm gonna give you three hundred dollars and hurt you just enough to make you a fuckin' hero. That okay with you, Ernesto?"

"Hokay."

"Now be a pro. Jack the fuckin' car up and let's get onna road."

Squid Berman watched them pull away. Chop was good, he had to admit it. The gun never showed. Anybody passing would have figured he was down there helping. The whole move was crisp, efficient, practiced. Now Chop would call his boys in Hialeah for a pickup. The flatbed would drive down some deserted road. Chop would give the driver his cash, a black eye, and a shallow slice that would hardly need stitches. Neat.

Neat but conventional, thought Squid, pulling on his knuckles, straightening his apron. A formula. The work of a craftsman, not an artist. He resettled his paper hat behind his ears and refocused his attention on the entrance of Paradise.

What he himself was doing with this caper was on a whole different level, of course. The level of real invention, true improvisation. It was jazz to other guys' whistling. Did Chop realize that? he wondered. Did anybody?

By the time the afternoon shadows overtook the Conch House pool, Big Al Marracotta had had four piña coladas, and was in the grip of a salacious mix of wooziness and lust. His shoulders were sunburned, and he liked the heat. The cup of his bathing suit was damp, and he liked the cool. He liked the thighs of other men's wives and girlfriends as they scissored and lifted on their lounges, he liked the bare nearness of Katy's pinkened behind, and he was ready to go upstairs awhile.

Up in their suite, before he'd even got out of his wet trunks, he went straight to his satchel of tapes. He riffled through the black plastic boxes, lips pursed as he considered. Discipline? Chinese? Finally he said to Katy, "Feel a little . . . futuristic?"

She looked at him a moment before she answered. Drained and mellowed by the sun, she made an effort to think kindly of him, and gently of herself for falling in with him. She tried to remember his good points. That twinkle in the eye. A certain generosity that every now and then seemed separate from strutting or control. An unflagging and unthinking zest that amused her and that she envied. Who wouldn't? She managed a somewhat weary smile and went off to the bathroom.

She returned looking like a sunburned outtake from *Barbarella*. Reinforced conic bra in space-age silver. Strapped and shiny panties that suggested something gladiatorial. Arm-cinching bracelets from which dangled disks resembling electrodes.

"You are something else," Big Al said, flicking his tongue between the gap in his front teeth.

The movie was called *Sex Trek*. Its premise was that the future would be a very phallic era, and that technological advances would largely focus on bold new designs in marital aids.

Leaning back on stacked-up pillows, his hand on Katy's thigh and his eyes glued to the screen, Big Al Marracotta said, "Jesus, will ya look at that? Solar-powered. Gets 'er everywhere at once!"

Katy looked from the TV to the stymied golden light captured in the curtained window, and wondered if they'd finish up in time to see the sunset.

10

Dusk. *Al Tuschman* stood in the outdoor shower, which was framed in thatch and ended at his knees. He soaped his armpits, watched sudsy water slide off the slatted boards beneath his feet. The light was soft and violet; the air was the same temperature as his skin and smelled of fruits and flowers.

Al shampooed his coarse, curly hair and finally let his mind acknowledge what his body already knew: Key West was getting to him. All that bare skin. All that rubbing. All those pretty sunburned necks and unfettered pendant breasts with tan lines halfway down them. The lack of hurry. The lack of purpose, except for the staunchly unembarrassed purpose of feeling good. Happiness as mission. All this had been sexing him up from the moment he arrived.

Now he no longer had excuses for failing to get out there and do something about it. He had his bearings. He was rested. This was the evening he would do the bars and try to meet a woman.

He rinsed, turned off the shower, and stepped into the bathroom, where he dried himself and shaved. Shaving, he appraised his face. The pits and bumps of adolescent acne; the scattered crescent scars of energetic youth. The very first gray hairs just now sprouting at the temples. A face that had seen some life, that had some life to offer in return. It worked for him on the sales floor.

But in bars? In bars the salesman tended to get shy. Flinched sometimes at soulful stares. Needed help to jump-start conversations. Sometimes drank too much to loosen up, then got morose instead of suave. Or, very occasionally, suave till he couldn't stand himself. Still, a person had to try. . . .

He dressed. Pulled on snug pants that showed the contours of his athlete's legs while revealing nothing of the aches and creaks. A tight blue shirt, the creases where it had been folded soon stretched and steamed away by the bulk of his chest. Chain; rings; loafers. A last tousle of his hair, and he was ready. He put Fifi's leash on, waved to annoy the dozing desk clerk as he passed the office, and headed out to start the evening with some solid food.

Squid Berman, still, with obsessive patience, waiting in the Jag, watched him head off down Elizabeth Street, teased himself with the danger implicit in the tough guy's wide shoulders and his rolling gait. He sat tight until he saw Big Al round the corner.

Then, opening a cooler in the backseat, he grabbed a shopping bag, smoothed his apron and straightened out his paper hat, and walked through the gate of Paradise as if he owned the place.

He went into the office and told the clerk he had a delivery for the gentleman who just went out.

The clerk blinked himself out of his catnap, studs quivering on his eyebrow. "I'll hold it for him here."

"He asked me special to leave it by his door," said Squid.

"That really isn't necessary."

"It is."

"Is what?"

"Necessary."

There was a momentary standoff.

"What I'm delivering," Squid resumed, "it needs, very important, it needs, uh, moonlight."

"Moonlight?"

"Orchid. Very rare. Expensive. Real expensive. Needs moonlight or it dies. In minutes. Said I should leave it in the moon-light by his door."

The clerk furrowed his brow. The wrinkles went all up his shaved head.

"So please," Squid said, "point me to the room. You wanna be responsible it dies? Come on, it's too long in the bag already."

The clerk frowned at the bag, which, oddly, made a sudden paper sound, a scratch. He wondered why it was always the least classy guests who made the most trouble, then sighed and did as he was asked.

Squid skirted the blue pool, went down the path that led to Big Al's bungalow. Hidden by foliage, he slipped around to the side, crawled under the thatch of the outdoor shower, scrabbled along the still-damp slatted boards. He prepared to shoulder in the bathroom door, but Big Al hadn't bothered to lock it.

The gremlin sniffed at his quarry's aftershave, worked a splinter into his bar of soap, then slipped into the bedroom and made himself at home.

Al started with a beer or two, tried a frozen margarita, then switched over to Sambuca. But it was one of those nights when he couldn't get comfortable with a drink, and he couldn't get comfortable with a place.

It wasn't even eleven yet, and he was already in his third joint. The first had been cheesily festive and way too loud, with amplifiers hanging from the ceiling, sound waves seeming to blow the smoke around. The second featured the music of his youth, which didn't make him feel young or nostalgic, but rather anxious and sad and weighed down with a secret. Made him think about football games, the shameful thing that no one ever knew. He was scared. Scared every time the ball was thrown to him. The pressure not to blow the catch. The inevitable impact, the skidding, scraping collision with the cold, damp ground. Same with crashing the boards in basketball season. Smashed fingers; elbows in his nose and eyes. Scared every time. Big tough guy. Schoolboy hero . . . A softie. He didn't need to hear seventies music ever again.

This third place suited him better. It was dim and moody. Grown-up. It didn't pretend to be a party. Jazz was playing, and jazz was different every time, it didn't freeze you in a moment like pop songs, which never changed, which were stuck in their old neighborhood forever. He started to relax.

Relaxing, he felt sexy again. Feeling sexy, he was frustrated. Frustrated, he kept drinking. Drinking, he wavered between gloom, excessive confidence, and an increased capacity to be smooth, silly, or both together.

That's when the two women came in and sat down near him. They were no younger than himself, possibly a few years older. He smiled at them as they sat and they sort of smiled back, then pulled their eyes away. They ordered vodkas, lit up cigarettes, and started talking.

By their second round they were talking louder and Al was leaning subtly toward them.

"Don't get me wrong," one of them was saying. She had wonderful thick hair that rose up in a single wave, dark brown with unapologetic flecks of gray. "I don't hate men. I like men. In fact, I prefer men, all in all. It's just that men are kinky."

The other woman rattled her ice cubes. She had a tan and bony face closely framed in lank pale hair. Al didn't like her nostrils, which were flat as the nose holes of a skeleton. "You can't just generalize like that," she said.

"Oh yes I can," the other woman answered and lit another cigarette. She squinted at the smoke, which made Al realize how big and round her eyes had been when they were fully opened. "Look, I know the pattern," she went on. "At first it's lovey-dovey, aiming at the conquest of the body. You know, straight from high school. Getting in. But then right away it's head games, toys—"

"Hey," the lank-haired woman interrupted with a soft but bawdy giggle, "women too, there's a lot of . . . let's say improvising."

Al Tuschman sipped his 'Buca. He was dying.

"That's different," argued the woman with the wonderful thick hair.

"What's different?" said the woman with the nose holes, gesturing for more drinks. "The body's the body and the mind's the mind."

The thick-haired woman was groping for an explanation. She ran a hand through her hair and her fingers disappeared entirely. "It's about intimacy."

"Agreed."

"If the . . . improvising . . . if the improvising makes people more intimate, then it's, like, exploring. Less intimate, then it's just kinky."

The pale-haired woman nipped into her fresh drink. "So you're saying women explore but men are kinky?"

"I'm not kinky," Al Tuschman said.

He had no idea he was going to say it and he could not believe that the words had actually passed his lips. He inhaled sharply, as if to suck them back. An agonizing moment passed. The two friends might ignore him or call him an asshole or simply move away. He tried to look friendly. Not pushy, not leering, not drunk. Above all, not desperate in his loneliness.

The lank-haired woman glanced at him sideways. Blow him off or humor him? She gestured toward him, lifted an eyebrow in what might have been some part of a smile, then turned toward her friend as though she'd proved a point. "You see?"

The thick-haired woman looked away, seemed bothered and hard. Up until that moment, she'd seemed the cuddlier of the two; in fantasy, she'd been the one that Al Tuschman was going to sleep with. Now he realized the light-haired woman was really much more spirited, appealing.

"You see?" she said again. "Not all men are kinky. Some men know what simple pleasure is. No games. No bullshit. Pleasure and comfort. Am I right?"

Al Tuschman sipped his 'Buca, dared now to look full at her, soulful. She had high cheekbones, cat's eyes; the nostrils weren't really so bad. He told himself, Don't say too much, don't try too hard, don't blow it. "For me," he said, "that's what it's always been about."

That was good. He was pleased with that. The lank-haired woman smiled, opened up her shoulders, showed some teeth. He could almost taste her mouth. He stopped himself from reaching out his hand, draping his palm across her wrist. Too bold, too soon.

The thick-haired woman reached forward over the bar and roughly stubbed out her cigarette. She tossed back her vodka like she was ready to leave. Al thought: Good friend, she knows when to get out of the way.

Then she propped her chin in her hand. She fixed Al Tuschman with a stare that cut right through the smoke and through the other woman's gaze, a stare that was half defiant and half imploring. Her lips puckered and breath moved between them in the instant before there was a sound. "Prove it."

Not till he was bending over on the sidewalk to unravel Fifi's leash from the parking meter where she'd been tied did Al Tuschman realize he was very tipsy. Blood rushed to his head, stars burst at the edges of his vision, annexed themselves to the insane glare and flash of Duval Street.

But the thick-haired woman was impressed with and reassured by the little shih tzu. So unlikely, so unmacho. She petted the dog, made faces at it. Then, cuddly once again, she leaned against Al, her side warm along his flank, as they strolled together off Duval and through the quieter streets toward Paradise.

They went through the gate, around the pool that shimmered blue in a mild breeze.

"Nice place," the thick-haired woman said.

Al nodded modestly. "Where you staying?"

"Me? I live here."

Al felt dumb for asking. But impressed with himself too. And flattered. Sleeping with a local. More exciting, memorable, more legit, somehow, than just colliding with another unmoored tourist far away from either person's life.

He unlocked the door of his bungalow. Inside, they had their first kiss, peppery with the taste of her cigarettes.

"I'm glad I'm here with you," she said.

"I'm glad too," said Al.

"You don't talk much, do you?"

"Sometimes I do, sometimes I don't."

"Strong silent type," she said.

"Not really," he admitted. "Sometimes, to the dog, I ramble on and on."

She laughed, and the laugh became a long kiss. They pressed and petted. Loins together. They had their clothes on and they were four feet from the bed. An awkward moment.

"You a little nervous?" the thick-haired woman asked.

Al tried to answer, could only nod.

"I am too. I think that's nice, don't you?"

She led him toward the bed, undid the buttons of his tight blue shirt. Lifted off her loose, thin blouse, stepped out of her soft and draping skirt. He looked at her. She was bluish in the moonlight. Fleshy and candid as the women in the painting on the wall above the bowl of fruit. He kicked off his shoes and wrestled with his pants and pulled back the thin blanket.

She lay down. He was in love with her hair by now. It was so thick and springy that it made a second pillow for her head. He settled in next to her and they embraced. Mouths together; chests together. Kinky? Al thought dimly. Who needed kinky when there was such delight in lips and arms, such unfailing suspense in the surge of bellies and the wrapping of thighs?

That's when he felt the first pinch on his scrotum.

It was a harder pinch than was really necessary. There was a certain excitement in it, though he couldn't honestly say it felt that good.

Then the thick-haired woman made a soft and teasing and catlike sound. It might have been *meow* or maybe only *ow*.

He liked the sound but didn't know just what to make of it. Was she goading him to pinch her in return? Where?

Then she pinched down really hard, so hard that his testicles seemed to flash forth a pulsing red and green like Christmas bulbs.

Through the pain he noticed that both her hands were on his chest.

And her soft and playful *ow* rose to an enraged and screeching *OUCH,* and she belted him across the temple with her forearm.

Wrestling with the bedclothes, thrashing and struggling to free herself, she hissed out, "You're not kinky, you sick bastard? Just one more sick bastard!"

She managed to rise, clutching at the inside of her thigh. As she did so, something clunked onto the floor and seemed to drag itself away. Fifi, her neat paws skidding on the varnished boards, ran in circles until she'd tracked it down. There was a scuffle, then a yelp.

A befuddled but tumescent Alan Tuschman scrambled up from bed. He watched the thick-haired woman quickly climb into her skirt. The anguish of losing her briefly overwhelmed the searing pain in his groin, and it was a heartbeat or two before he focused on the unnatural weight and appalling pressure he was feeling there.

Then he looked down and he screamed. Loudly. He had a two-pound lobster dangling from his nuts. Its antennae were exploring his stomach hair and its tail was curling upward toward his asshole. "Help!"

The thick-haired woman was not inclined to get that close. She pulled her blouse on and turned her back. "You fucking pervert," she said across her shoulder. "I feel sorry for the dog!"

Al reached down and grabbed the two shells of the lobster claw, tried with all his strength to pry them off his scrotum. "You think I had this planned?" he yelled.

There was no reply. The thick-haired woman was out of there. Hadn't even closed the door behind her.

Hopping madly, fighting with the lobster and fondling his dented balls, Al Tuschman stared out at her sudden absence, at the giant philodendrons and the faint blue shimmer of the pool beyond.

11

In a clean and quiet Long Island suburb, Nicky Scotto climbed out of the bed he shared with his skinny, late-sleeping wife and padded off to the bathroom. He showered and carefully shaved, paying particular attention to the difficult places at the corners of his mouth. Then he found scissors and trimmed the overly luxuriant fringes of his eyebrows.

Standing now in his underwear and knee-high cashmere socks, he buffed his Bruno Maglis till they gleamed. He pulled on a black silk turtleneck and a pearl-gray worsted suit, and headed off for his first morning at his former job, now very temporarily his again.

He didn't have to dress this fancily for work. In fact, it was totally impractical. The thin soles of the loafers barely cleared the streams of fishy ice water that trickled over tile floors toward half-clogged rusty drains. The silk turtleneck didn't keep him warm enough as he made the rounds of reefer trucks and seafood lockers, which steamed a frosty fog when their doors were opened.

Still, he dressed rich because it reflected how he felt. Walking through the clamor and the echoes of the market, making his presence known, waving benignly to the little people in the stalls as they shoveled ice, uncrated octopus, he might have been an old-time duke parading through his village. People called his name. There was a friendliness in it, almost a hurrah, though it was not the friendliness of equals. It was the friendliness of happy subjects, supplicants who were rewarded as long as they paid tribute and obeyed the rules. Pete, Luigi, Tony, Fred—beyond the confines of the market, they would casually make it known that they called Nicky by his name, and this would give them standing in the wider world.

So, quietly thrilled to be back, he did his circuit, shaking hands, slapping backs, then headed down a chilly corridor toward what used to be his office.

An absurd and salty sorrow tweaked him as he neared the door. Not that there was much to have missed about the place. The lighting was lousy and it smelled of fish. The furniture was cold, cheap metal, and the one, dirty window faced out on a loading dock and a mountain of cracked pallets. Still, when he stepped across the pitted threshold and pulled the string that worked the lights, Nicky Scotto felt a pang. He'd been happy here. It wasn't just the money and the power. He'd felt like he was where he ought to be. And if happiness and belonging didn't give someone a claim, what did?

He went to his old desk. On it, in corny frames, stood pictures of Big Al Marracotta's fat wife and ugly, spoiled kids. He flipped them facedown against the metal, buried them under a phone book. He sat in what used to be his chair, and drummed his fingers on the arm, and told himself not to get too comfortable.

He was there only as a fill-in, a pinch hitter; his pal Donnie kept reminding him of that, as gently as he could. Tony Eggs hadn't changed his mind about who should run the market. Carlo Ganucci had been very clear: when Al Marracotta got back from vacation, he would take over once again.

Well, that was life, thought Nicky Scotto. You're up, you're down; you're in, you're out. But he didn't have to like it, and he didn't have to pretend it felt right. Sitting there as Big Al's sub, guest host on the show he used to run—it felt wrong as hell, wrong as a bad clam beginning to break down and spread its poison through his churning gut.

•

Al Tuschman didn't wake up happy.

His tongue was dry and swollen; there was a deep, slow throb where his spine plugged into his brain. He ached between the legs, and couldn't tell how much of the ache had to do with thwarted sex, and how much with the depredations of the lobster. In a feeble attempt to cheer himself, he remembered that most people paid two hundred bucks a night to be here.

He got up from the sweaty sheets, threw water on his face. He collected Fifi, whose nose bore a deep scratch from a flailing claw, and they headed out for breakfast.

As they rounded the blue pool, Al noticed a tangled and inert lump of something at the bottom. Turned out to be a pair of suffocated lobsters, strangled by chlorine. Al felt a moment's thin revenge, followed quickly by remorse. Poor guys. Try to see it their way. Could they help it they were lobsters? They'd survived bizarre adventures, endured the weight and heat of human crotches, then made a bold break for freedom through terrain as dry and foreign as the moon, only to end up in the dread gravity of the sucking drain.

Then he recalled the thick and springy hair of the woman he almost had, and thought, The hell with 'em, let 'em smother.

He passed the office, and the desk clerk called to him in a tone of mock politeness. By now it was war between the two of them. The passive, insolent employee smirking behind a charade of cheerful service. The disgruntled guest whose grumbling would have to ripen into bodily assault if he ever hoped to express his full dissatisfaction.

"Important call for you this morning," said the clerk. He handed Al a slip of paper, serenely confident that it contained bad news.

Al read it and his headache instantly got worse. Sun Motors in Miami. He asked the clerk for the phone.

The clerk moved grudgingly away to eavesdrop.

He heard Al say, "What? . . . Stolen? . . . Hijacked?! . . . What kind of craziness is hijacked? . . . Now, wait a second. I deal with the public too. So let's make sure we have this clear . . . we're not saying *we'll* work it out. We're saying *you'll* work it out. Right?"

Al slammed the phone down, pushed it across the desk in the direction of the clerk hard enough so that its rubber feet squeaked against the varnish. "What the hell kind of town is this?" he said.

The clerk allowed himself a hint of a smile. "Most people find it a very pleasant and relaxing town."

Al ran a hand through his hair. The motion pulled a throb behind it, as if something were stuck and crawling between his scalp and skull. "And another thing," he said. "Someone put lobsters in my room last night."

The clerk fingered the row of studs above his eyebrow. "You mean orchids."

"Whaddya mean, I mean orchids?" Al demanded. "If I meant orchids, I'd say orchids. I'm saying lobsters."

"Lobsters," the clerk said numbly.

"Lobsters," Al repeated. "In my room. Now they're in the pool."

"Mr. Tuschman. You shouldn't put lobsters in the pool."

"I didn't put them in. They ran in. They dove in. They're dead."

The clerk scratched his shaved head.

"And what's this crap about orchids?" Al asked him.

"Orchids?"

"Yeah, orchids. I said lobsters, you said orchids."

"Right. Someone came last night to deliver orchids."

"And you let him in my room?" said Al.

"I didn't let him in your room. He said he'd leave them by the door."

Al Tuschman bit his lip. "This guy, what did he look like?"

The clerk bit his lip too. "He looked like . . . he looked like . . . who remembers? A delivery man. Apron. Paper hat."

Al drummed his fingers on the counter, thought that over. At last he said, "Where I'm from, florists don't wear paper hats and aprons. Seafood guys wear paper hats and aprons."

"Gee," said the clerk, "I never thought of that." He stifled a yawn.

Disgusted, Al Tuschman turned to go. Halfway to the door, he was struck by something else. "Don't you ever leave here?" he asked the clerk. "Don't you ever sleep?"

"Rents are high. Not everyone appreciates," he whined, "just how hard we work."

"Batt'ries included?" asked Big Al Marracotta.

The clerk shrugged then took back the latex gizmo, tried to figure out how to unscrew the base. The gadget was not as technologically advanced as the ones in *Sex Trek,* but it had a raffish design and a certain ingenuity. Katy Sansone rolled her eyes.

"Yeah, batteries are in there," said the clerk. He sniffled, ran a finger under his nose, then added, "Or you can use the crank."

"And the hot water goes in here?" said Al.

"Hot water, margarine, whatever."

"Would feel good, no?" said Al. He'd taken the thing back and was cranking it in Katy's direction so that it wiggled like a spastic cobra.

"Al," she said, "isn't it a little early?"

In fact they'd just had breakfast. The porn store had been open fifteen minutes. The clerk's first cup of coffee still stood on a display case filled with ticklers and extenders and things with leather straps.

"All of a sudden you're inhibited?" Big Al teased. He flashed that surprising boy-devil grin, the grin that moved his hair and showed the small gap in his teeth. "Like *amore*'s only for the dark of night?"

"I guess I didn't realize it was *amore,*" she said. "Seemed more like Roto-Rooter. I'm going to the beach."

"The beach?" he said. "We been through that."

"Right," said Katy. "You don't like sand and riffraff. So you go to the pool. I'll see you in a couple hours."

Big Al fidgeted, took a moment to decide if he was mad. He felt a little silly with the pleasure unit in his hand and his girlfriend leaning toward the door. Plus, he didn't like her tone. A little bratty and ungrateful. Then again, some spunk, some spirit—it kept things fresh, a little bit on edge. "Fine," he said at last. "I'll see ya later."

Half surprised to be sprung, afraid that Al might quickly change his mind, she pivoted on her tall shoes and bolted from the store.

Breaking out into the clean, hot sunshine of the sidewalk, she inhaled the smells of softening asphalt and sunblock spiced with coconut, and realized all at once that she hadn't had a moment to herself in days. Just to walk at her own pace; to look at what she chose to look at; to breathe.

She walked fast for half a block, as though pursued, then started to relax. Slowing, using her own eyes, she saw and did small things that exhilarated her beyond all proportion to their actual significance. Twirled a postcard rack; smiled at plump twins in a stroller. Took a color brochure from a young woman hawking snorkel trips; listened hungrily as she rhapsodized about coral and striped fish. Paused at a booth promoting sunset sails, and let herself imagine that someday she would be aboard a sailboat. Why not? If she were on her own? Or had a friend to travel with?

Or was with a different sort of man?

There, she'd thought it. For a moment it felt great to think it, but then the feeling backfired, and she felt disloyal, guilty. Undeserving. How shallow could you get? Three minutes out of Big Al's grasp, and already she was fantasizing life without him. After him. Like he'd died. While she was still riding on his ticket, blowing his money, sharing his bed. It was wrong.

Then again, what was wrong with wanting to be treated right?

Okay, she thought—she'd made certain choices, choices that she wasn't very proud of. Well, so what? Did that mean she was disqualified forever from a little happiness, a little dignity? Wasn't she allowed at least to wonder if there were still men in the world who weren't married, and weren't outlaws, and weren't maniacs? Men who might see in her something more than a sex toy to be visited by other sex toys?

She strolled past T-shirt shops and jewelry stores and new construction. She wished she could do life over; then quickly shuddered at how much trouble that would be; then admitted with something like relief that there was nothing to be done except to go from here.

At an open stand she leaned across a cool chrome counter and ordered up an ice cream cone—vanilla with chocolate jimmies. Her mouth watered as she watched it being made, and she licked it happily as any kid as she headed toward the beach, wondering how long she could dare to stretch these clean, empty hours that were her own.

12

Squid Berman, happy and fulfilled, had just awakened from a beautiful and long night's sleep.

He'd needed it. Two nights ago he'd hardly rested, then he'd done an endless stakeout across the street from Paradise. He'd still been there, skulking in the buttonwood hedge, when Big Al and the thick-haired woman wobbled home together from the bar. He was still there some fifteen minutes later, when the woman, furious and suddenly sober, stormed right out again.

Now he was leaning on a pointy elbow, underneath a tortured sheet, and telling Chop about it.

"Ya shoulda seen the kisser on 'er!" he was saying. "Freaked or what? A masterstroke! I ruined it for 'im, Chop. I ruined it for 'im good."

Chop couldn't get that excited about it. Wacko mischief that no longer involved cars. He was thinking about the silver Lexus. Rip out the seats and you had a fine vehicle. He scratched his neck. Something was making him irritable. Probably that it was clearer all the time that Squid was enjoying this gig a whole lot more than he was. Grudgingly he said, "So what next?"

Squid thought. Thinking made his mouth water; he swallowed and his bony Adam's apple shuttled up and down his neck. Truth was, he didn't know what next, knew only that it had to top what he had done so far. This was the unremitting pressure on the artist, the thing a lunk like Chop would never understand. "Jeez," he said, "lemme savor this one for a while."

"Isn't time," said Chop.

Squid frowned. He knew the other man was right. There was never time. The next hurdle was always in your face before your feet had even reconnected with the ground.

Without getting out of bed, the bandy man bore down, started thinking once again. His eyes bulged, water pooled beneath his tongue, and he dug deeper into the cackling mysteries of making someone miserable.

Big Al Marracotta strolled back to the Conch House weighed down with two big bags of goodies. He had probes and plungers, harnesses and clips, lingerie and jellies. He had extra batteries and a video shot entirely from underneath a glass coffee table. He was ready for more vacation.

But back at his hotel, with Katy gone and nothing else to do, he let his mind flit just briefly to his business. In truth it had been days since he'd thought at all about fish and payoffs, ice and trucks, no-show jobs and haulers' kickbacks and soggy cartons full of halibut and crab. Now a sudden nameless qualm made him feel that he should check in, at least, see how things were going.

He put the goodies by the TV set and sat down on the edge of his giant bed to place a call to Benny Franco, the guy he'd left in charge.

This was a somewhat complicated procedure. There was a phone in the fish market office, but it was used only for the most mundane chitchat with outsiders. Real business calls were routed through a pay phone bolted to the loading dock across the yard. This meant that an underling would have to take the call, determine if it was worth a bigger man's attention, then trudge through slush and slime to fetch the boss. The boss, in turn, would have to put his topcoat on, his scarf, and tiptoe through the oily puddles.

Sitting there in Florida, Big Al remembered how freezing cold the receiver usually was against his ear. He dialed.

In Manhattan a guy picked up the phone, said, "Yeah?"

"Lemme talk ta Benny."

The request made the underling suspicious. Everyone who mattered knew that Benny wasn't there no more, had been led away in handcuffs. He said, "Benny ain't here. Who's iss?"

"Who's iss?!" said Al, and put a little menace in it. "Who's *iss*?"

"Lefty."

"Lefty, you putz. It's Al. Go get Benny."

Lefty hesitated. He was a cautious guy and not good at explaining things. He knew there was no percentage in carrying bad news. He said simply, "Hey, Al. Hol' on a minute."

He left the phone dangling like a hanged cat and trudged through the slush and slime to fetch Nicky.

"Who is it?" Nicky wanted to know before bothering with the topcoat and the scarf.

Lefty didn't want to say the name. No percentage setting up a meet between two guys who were never gonna like each other. "I think y'oughta take it" was all he said.

Nicky slid into his coat and stepped outside. The yard stank of diesel fumes and fish. Gross water seeped into his loafers. He picked up the phone, which was achingly cold against his ear. "Yeah?"

On his giant Key West bed, Big Al Marracotta yanked in his eyebrows so that his salt-and-pepper helmet crawled. Benny's voice he knew. "You ain't Benny."

"Did I fucking say I was Benny? All I said was yeah. Who's iss?"

Big Al puffed up a little, gave his neck a twist. Whoever this guy was, he didn't like his tone. "This is your boss, asshole."

The words chafed Nicky badly. Boss? Big Al? He said, "I ain't aware I got a boss."

The insolence, in turn, made Big Al wary; he did not want to admit that he had no idea who he was talking to. He wiggled his butt against the sheets and decided to seek more information. "Where the fuck is Benny?"

Nicky stomped his feet to keep the blood from freezing and tried to have a little fun. "How's the weather down in Flahda?"

"Fuckin' gorgeous."

Nicky thought about Chop and Squid, who were costing him several grand a day to make this guy's life a living hell. "And things are goin' good?"

"Beautiful," said Al.

Nicky smiled to think he must be lying through his teeth. Sure he was. Nobody ever admitted that vacation turned out lousy.

Al had finally put two and two together. "This Nicky?"

"Bingo."

"Fuck you doin' there?"

"Runnin' the place, that's all."

"Where's Benny?"

"Prob'ly at his lawyer's," Nicky said. "You picked a loser, Al. Benny got indicted."

Al sprang off the bed and pirouetted. Wistfully, he looked across the room at his trove of unsampled sex toys. "Shit. I'm comin' home."

"Don't let it fuck up your vacation, Al."

"I'll be there tomorra."

"Al, hey, market's inna best hands it could be in. Best hands ever. Least that's Tony Eggs' opinion."

Nicky was pleased with that remark, so pleased that for a moment he forgot how cold he was.

Al said, "Yeah? So why'd he kick you out and make you one more pissant onna street again?"

Nicky shivered. "Listen, pal—"

"I'm coming home," said Al. "I'm calling Tony."

Nicky shuffled his stinging feet. Too late he understood that his ballbusting was utterly misfiring. He should have made nice, been reassuring. Now he would be shortchanged even in his brief, false tenure back on top. His voice took on a wheedling tone that galled him, and he tried to patch things up. "Al, hey, don't get your bowels in an uproar. I'm just kiddin' with ya. Everything's fine. I'm just fillin' in. Temporary, like."

In Key West, Big Al Marracotta paced to the limits of the phone cord and considered. "I'll check that with Tony, Carlo."

"Yeah, okay, check," said Nicky, his voice still more conciliatory and chagrined. Bending over just to have a few more days in charge, pretending.

Al Marracotta hung up in his ear.

Nothing was more bitter than knowing that you'd lost after thinking that you'd won. Nicky Scotto stared at the phone a couple seconds, like he was blaming it for how things went. He slapped his arms for warmth, wiggled toes inside his squishy shoes, and trudged back through the oily puddles to what used to be his office.

13

Nothing stays strange for long. Normal is what's there.

Al Tuschman sat out by the pool at Paradise and looked around. Bare-breasted lesbians with boxer shorts and hairy armpits. Sleek gay men glistening like basted ducks in Chinatown. The Eurotrash ménage à trois with their stacks of fashion magazines, their ceaseless chattering and giggling. So what else was new?

Al was getting to feel so blithe that he seriously considered getting naked. Told himself it wasn't prudishness that held him back, but concern that his dented and distended scrotum would appear deformed, grotesque. He promised himself he'd strip as soon as the tortured sac resumed its accustomed shape and size.

In the meantime he tanned. At the very least, he would go home brown and make other people jealous. He lay back on his lounge and offered up his face. Hot sun scratched at his hairline and seared right through his eyelids.

It was pleasant for a little while. But Al was dark to begin with and tanned easily. No challenge; not a mission. He was soon bored.

He sat up, then stood. Light-headed, he blinked until the colors returned to flesh and flowers, and decided he would go check out the beach. He put on sandals, fetched a shirt that sort of matched his bathing trunks, and put Fifi on the leash. He got directions from the drowsy and mock-helpful clerk behind the desk and headed out.

The walk was a great deal longer than he'd been led to believe. Still, it wasn't long enough for him to notice the Jaguar that crawled along amid the traffic of rented convertibles and whining mopeds and clunky bikes, now lolling half a block behind him, now pulling ahead, then discreetly circling back.

Al's route wound through town streets full of bars and fishing stores, past a misplaced brick enclave of courthouses and county offices, through an apartment complex whose faux-Bahamian motif was the only thing that prevented it from looking just like Jersey. Beyond the complex was a half-abandoned navy base penned in by a rusting chain-link fence, and past the bunkers and scrap heaps of the base was a narrow road that finally got sandy at its edges.

Along this road, his throat parched, his headache returning, and his heels beginning to blister, Al Tuschman saw someone he vaguely recognized.

She was moving toward him on silver high-heeled sandals. She was long-legged, slim-hipped, and bosomy, with a rather small-featured face behind big sunglasses, topped by raven hair that salt air and dyes had made a little stiff and spiky.

Their eyes met, then tried to slide politely apart but stuck, as happens between people who look half familiar. Al finally remembered where and when he'd seen her. Breakfast yesterday. Promenading with a short guy. "Hey, there," he said. "Where's your dog?"

Katy could not help frowning at the mention of the slobbering and thankless rottweiler. "Oh, hi," she said. "It's not my dog, it's my boyfriend's."

She regretted the words before she was finished saying them, but there it was, she'd said them. Why did she do that to herself? Fact one: I have a boyfriend. A possessive, maniac boyfriend who takes care of everything and holds me back from anything decent while I play right along.

Al had to say something, so he said, "Ah. How's the beach?"

"Nice," she said. "Once you get to it. Water's really green. Wonder why that is?"

Al wished he knew. He shrugged. The Jag squeezed past them on the narrow pavement, considerately slowing as it headed toward the beach. Its effect was to push them to the margin of the road, moving them closer together.

The woman crouched to pet the shih tzu. It was a long way down for her but she descended very smoothly, ankles and knees and waist compacting like a closed expansion gate. To the creature she said, "And what's your name?"

"Fifi," Al told her.

"Fifi," she repeated, rubbing the shih tzu's knobby head.

"Mine's Al," he volunteered.

She kept her face down and gave a quick and mordant chuckle. "So's his." The disembodied pronoun sounded strange, and then again it didn't. It was the way unhappy people referred to their partner when their partner seemed less like a person than a blank but overwhelming fact. Almost as an afterthought, she said, "Mine's Katy."

She straightened up. She was nice and tall. Her forehead was as high as Al's nose. She leaned forward like she was ready to start walking. Al hoped that she would stay a little bit. "You having fun down here?" he asked her.

"Pretty nice," she said. "You?"

He thought a moment, scratched his ear. Then he said, "Not really."

This was so wildly and gauchely honest that both of them held their breath a heartbeat, then let out a giggle. No one ever admitted that vacation was going lousy.

Laughing was a great relief, a godsend, so Al went on. "I'm staying at this weird place. Paradise, it's called."

"Not exactly modest," Katy said.

"No. And like, weird stuff has been happening to me from the minute I arrived."

"They say Key West is like that."

"No, I mean really weird," Al said.

"Okay," she gave in. "How weird?"

"Like someone filled my car with calamari. Then someone put lobsters in my bed."

Katy's eyes screwed down behind her sunglasses. She figured he was bullshitting but she didn't see the harm. "You must have some wild and crazy friends."

"I don't have a friend within a thousand miles," Al said. He said it a little louder than he meant to, and the words seemed to hollow out a lonely capsule in the air.

Katy didn't see it as lonely. She saw it as free and exotic and bold. "You often travel alone?"

"Depends." Depended on whether he had a girlfriend when he won a selling contest, which usually he didn't, in part because he spent so many evenings on the selling floor.

"I bet," said Katy, "that's really when you see great stuff, when you get to do exactly what you want."

Al pursed his lips. "If you can figure what that is."

"Me," she said, "I'd go out on a sailboat, look at coral, look at fish."

Al finished his own thought. "And, like, if no one steals your car."

"Your car got stolen too?"

He nodded, shrugged.

She gave her head a sympathetic though not totally persuaded shake, then began to move away. She didn't really want to move away, but they were strangers, and she had a boyfriend, and what else was there to do? "Well, I hope things go better here on in."

"Couldn't go worse," said Al. He looked for some wood to knock. There weren't any trees along the narrow road. He wished he hadn't said it.

They moved off in opposite directions. After a few steps Al looked back across his shoulder. He'd had a fantasy that the tall woman was looking at him too.

She was not, of course. She was going back to the man who'd brought her here.

Al continued toward the beach. Without admitting he was doing it, he counted up the days until vacation would be over and he could go back home. In the meantime he looked forward to the yielding crunch of sand and the cooling sting of ocean water against his blistered feet.

14

From where the road finally ended, it was another third of a mile to the water's edge. Through a scorching asphalt parking lot. Beyond a grove of Australian pines whose feathery needles imperfectly screened the blaze of mid-afternoon sun, and where dog and master drank greedily from a lukewarm fountain. Down a slope of coral rocks that challenged ankles and clawed at heels. Then past a swath of trucked-in sand that gave, at last, onto the ocean.

By the time he got there, Al Tuschman was really ready for a swim.

Squid Berman had figured that he might be.

He'd stationed himself—in a loud and baggy print bathing suit that came down to his knees, bug-eyed goggles, and a pebbled shower cap—in a shadowed cranny of a pile of rocks that rose up from the green water thirty, forty yards offshore. Kids with snorkels climbed up on the rocks, yipping like a pack of seals. But Squid's weirdness enforced an empty space around him, and from his private grotto he had a panoramic view of the life on land—the gay trysting grounds over near the jetty, the picnic area with its whorls of charcoal smoke, the occasional topless European with teenage boys walking casually back and forth around her.

He saw Big Al swagger toward the shoreline, his water-shy dog quailing behind, sniffing sand. Watched as he kicked off his sandals and stepped into the first cool lick of the ocean. He imagined he heard a sizzle come off the tough guy's feet.

He willed him in farther, deeper.

But Al Tuschman stayed right where he was. He still had his shirt on, his sunglasses. The water felt great but he wasn't sure how much of it he wanted. He was an okay swimmer, not terrific. Besides, it was a commitment, going in the ocean. The adjustment in body temperature. The inevitable dried salt itching in the chest hair. The wet bathing suit that was sure to chafe the inner thighs on the long walk home.

Then again, there was the widely known effect of cool water on the scrotum. Given his stretched and irritated state, it might be very therapeutic. He pulled off his sweaty shirt, laid it on the sand with his sandals and his shades, told Fifi to be good and stay right where she was.

Squid Berman watched him stride into the ocean, big legs fighting off the suck of sand and the weight of water. Squinting through his goggles, he firmed his concentration and thought, Come on, you bastard, dive. Swim!

Al Tuschman took his time. Strolled in up to his calves, his knees. Stared off at fishing boats returning to the harbor, pleasure sloops just heading out. Felt the faint and ghostly pull of an undertow that was stifled by the reef.

Finally a wavelet lapped against his bathing suit and wet his nuts. The water wasn't cold but still he shivered. Ravaged skin contracted, inhaled into corrugations. He rose up on tiptoe, did a little dance.

The crisis over, he took another step, feeling now a primordial delight and wondering, as people always did, why he'd hesitated plunging in. A resolute stride brought the water past his waist, and he made a less than graceful lunge that soaked his head and started him swimming toward the far horizon.

Crouched in his cranny of the rockpile, Sid the Squid swallowed hard, licked dried salt from his twitching lips.

Al swam ten strokes, twenty, scudding even with, then past,

the outcrop. The exercise chased away the remnants of his hang-over. Not as fit as he wished he were, he yet reveled in the strength of his arms, the scissoring force of his kick. The ocean blotted out sound, turned the searing sun into a gentle blanket tickling his back, and it dimly dawned on Al that, for the first time since he'd got here, he felt like he was on vacation. Away from everything, including his usual self. Refreshed by strange-ness. Not so much feeling as being the plain, gut happiness that some people insisted was a mission. Joyfully, he swam another dozen strokes.

Then he saw the shark.

The shark was around the same size he was, but half of it was mouth. Behind the fearsome maw was a rank of gill slits like the airholes on old Buicks, and behind the gill slits a miraculous ma-chinery of fin and muscle that gave swimming the suave weight-lessness of flight.

The beast was fifteen, twenty feet ahead of Al, swimming slowly with fluid wiggles, crosswise to him. Al fixed on one beady, sleepily malicious eye and froze. His body lost its buoy-ancy, helplessly went vertical. His feet groped for, and couldn't find, the bottom. He held his breath, treaded water, and watched.

It seemed the shark was easing past him. Then it turned. Maybe it had caught a glint of pinky ring. It banked with the merest flick of fin and tail, and torpedoed straight toward Al. Its mouth was slightly open, crooked rows of incurved teeth just barely visible. In the instant before he screamed, Al imagined he saw water sluicing through the gills.

He screamed before his face was quite clear of the ocean. He sucked in a mouthful of water and choked on the stony taste of salt.

Still spluttering, he swam like hell for land, arms thrashing, neck craning. Even as he kicked he tried to pull his legs into his torso, hiding his feet and knees from the ripping pull of triangle teeth.

Terror made him forget about the need to breathe; he was winded after half a dozen strokes. For a while, fear filled in for oxygen, and he kept pumping with his arms although his ears were ringing and his vision had narrowed into a hellish tube of glare.

He was even with the rockpile when he saw that the shark had changed its course, had circled up ahead of him. Had cut him off from other swimmers the way a lion cuts from the herd a single antelope. Was blocking the salvation of the beach and forcing him seaward once again.

Al skidded against the scant resistance of the water, begged his body to pivot, somersaulted outbound. His lungs burned; his arms screamed in their sockets. Confused and piteous thoughts raced through his mind: the orphaned Fifi, never knowing what terrible thing she'd done to be abandoned on the beach. Old Mr. Kleiman with his opal tie tack, standing on an ottoman to eulogize his favorite salesman . . . He swam, waiting each moment for the clamping bite and the nauseating rend of flesh, the iron smell of his own blood spilling in the ocean. He couldn't tell if he was crying or if his eyes were simply melting into the salt water.

Ahead of him the blank and bright horizon was suddenly sealed off by the gray flank of the shark.

It had circled once again, bands of muscle folding back upon themselves with humiliating ease. The red cave of the open mouth was like a door to hell. Once again Al did a desperate one-eighty. His arms would no longer lift clear of the water; he paddled like a hound dog throwing dirt. His hip joint scraped, his pumping legs abraded sinew with each kick.

Sucking spasmodically at the soup of air and water, his lungs heavy and puffed up like a mildewed sponge, he flailed toward the impossibly distant shore. Flailed until his sinking feet miraculously touched bottom.

Leaning forward on numb hands and jelly knees, droplets flying from his heaving chest, he rose up and stomped through the cruel knobs of coral that floored the last fringe of the ocean, escaping at last from the horrors of the sea and collapsing full-length on the beach like a shipwrecked, sun-mad sailor.

Fifi ran over and licked his face. He turned on his side and burped up salt water, gurgling and wheezing as he strained to breathe.

In the shadow of his rock, Squid Berman's brain was itching underneath the shower cap, his eyes tearing with squelched laughter inside their glinting goggles. He fiddled with the radio control and steered the toy shark back to him, then pulled the little air plug and deflated it at leisure in the privacy of his grotto. No one but Big Al had seen a thing.

The tough guy writhed on the beach a couple minutes, coughing, spitting. Then he sat up, shaking his head, groping for his sunglasses.

When he finally stood up on shaky legs to leave, Squid noted with satisfaction that he was too freaked even to go to the water's edge to rinse off the coarse and salty sand that coated him from feet to cheek.

15

Katy Sansone knew what she would find when she returned to the Conch House.

She'd find Big Al either sprawled out on a poolside lounge or chest-deep at the swim-up bar. Either way, he'd have had a couple drinks. That boy-devil look would be stretching the corners of his eyes, and he'd be getting horny. He'd make some teasing cracks to stoke himself along. Ask her if she got picked up by any bulging Cuban studs at the beach. Offer comments on the breasts and backsides of the women at the pool. It would all be flip and crude—and also, Katy could not help but admit, comforting in its familiarity. Al had his routines. He was predictable. A man in whom habits cut an instant groove. Blunt in his wants, consistent in his appetites. And, no matter what else was right or wrong or crazy or impossible, it was nice to be consistently desired.

So she was surprised and, in spite of herself, a little disappointed when he wasn't where she thought he'd be. She walked the whole perimeter of the pool, skirted the lanai rooms, the towel kiosk. Scanned the flushed and vacant faces at the bar. No Al. She took a moment to decide what she should do. His absence, she felt, gave her permission to go off on her own a little longer. That might be nice, and yet . . . and yet she sort of didn't want to. This embarrassed her. Did it mean, she wondered, that she actually missed the sonofabitch? Or only that she'd had all the independence she could handle for one day?

She went up to their room, found Al in the same long pants he'd been wearing when they parted. He was pacing between the TV and the window, and his expression wasn't playful. Katy's first thought was that she'd stayed away too long and he was mad. She waited for him to talk.

"How was the beach?" he asked. He said it with neither interest nor blame, and Katy felt relieved.

"Fine. Nice," she said. No reason to elaborate, since he wasn't listening. She watched him pace. The skin was drawn and gray around his eyebrows, the stubble on his chin was flecked with silver, and she realized that he truly wasn't young. Not young, not happy all the time, not free of worries and responsibilities. "Something wrong?" she asked.

Big Al paused in his circuit, briefly stared up at her. The question gave him a dilemma. You didn't talk to broads. That was elementary. But up North he would have had pals, goombahs, that he could bitch to. Here there was no one else, and keeping silent gave rise to stomach acid. Laconically, he said, "Guy I left in charge . . . aw, it's all fucked up."

The answer, in turn, put Katy in doubt as to how much further she should go. Left in charge of what? She pretty much knew that Al was Mafia. He carried guns and knives and large amounts of cash; his New York friends all talked like they were eating crackers. But as to the specifics of his business, she was serenely in the dark. She had noticed that, when they dined out in the city, it was almost always seafood, and Al got fawned over shamelessly. The best tables. Free champagne. But that was as much as she knew. Now she tried to steer a middle course between showing concern and seeming to pry. "Fucked up how?" she asked.

Al was wearing a loose-fitting shirt, but he twisted his neck like his collar was too tight. Fighting back each word, he grunted, "Guy they replaced my guy wit'—worst guy they coulda picked."

Katy sat down on the bed, tried not to notice the two big bags of sex toys leaning up against the television cabinet. "How come?"

"How come what?" said Al, his throat closing down around the rising question.

"How come he's the worst guy?"

"'Cause we hate each other's guts."

"Why?"

"Why?" Al echoed, and stopped to ponder. Up until that moment it hadn't dawned on him that there had to be a reason. "He hates me," he said at last, "'cause he thinks I took his job away. And I hate him 'cause he hates me."

Katy said, "If that's the only—"

Big Al, suddenly impatient, annoyed with himself for blabbing, waved his arms, started pacing once again. "I don't wanna talk no more," he said. "What I said, fuhget about it."

Katy watched him pace, the short legs seeming disconnected from the barrel chest, the skin of the face pulled back taut as that of an astronaut. He went from carefree to wretched with almost nothing in between, and Katy had to acknowledge that his seldom-seen unhappiness gave a new dimension to his carnality, made of it a kind of victory. He stole pleasure between fits of misery. The pleasure had to be as extreme as his anxieties, and his greed for it was in proportion to his desperation. Knowing in some corner of her being that she was being suckered, was suckering herself, she felt a surge of tenderness for her thug of a boyfriend. He had his problems too. "Hey, Al," she said. "How 'bout a back rub?"

"A back rub?" he said, and he gave a little snort. The snort was not derisive, just surprised. A back rub. A simple kindness. Unselfish. "Katy," he said, "you're really a good kid."

"Come on," she said, and motioned him off his circuit to the bed.

He threw himself facedown at her feet.

She got up on her knees and worked his knotty shoulders. He

moaned, he sighed, and after a few minutes, not really meaning it but feeling it was called for by the moment, he said, "I don't deserve a girlfriend good as you."

Powered by a stubborn reflex sympathy, she leaned into his flank and vaguely wondered why it was so hard for her to accept that he was absolutely right.

The knots were somewhat letting go until the phone rang.

But at the first clang of the instrument they came cramping back all along his spine. Big Al quickly scrambled onto his side and told Katy maybe she'd like to take a bath. He didn't pick up the receiver until she'd closed the bathroom door behind her and started water running.

Then he finally squeezed the thing and said hello.

"Al? Carlo."

He knew it would be Carlo. He'd tried to reach the *consigliere* an hour or so before. It took the frail old guy about that long to drain his silty bladder and shuffle to a safe phone he could use.

Now Big Al got straight to the point. "What's this bullshit Nicky's in charge?"

"Someone's gotta be in charge," said Carlo calmly.

"Why him?"

"Who else is there, Al?"

Big Al knew this argument, and for him it didn't wash. Sure, the ranks had thinned. Sure, it was tough to find a colleague who was halfway competent and not in jail. But it wasn't *that* tough. "Come on," he said. "There's Rod the Cod. There's Big Tuna Calabro. Guys I trust. Guys I can talk to, for Chrissake."

Carlo didn't answer. Air wheezed through his nose.

"Somethin' else is goin' on," Al said.

Carlo came forth with a soft and weary sigh. "Don't make more a this than what's there."

"So what's there?" pressed Al Marracotta.

Ganucci sniffled, said at last, "Al, ya want the trut'?"

"Nah, I want more bullshit."

"I think Tony's p.o.'d ya took vacation."

Al sprang up from the bed, wrapped himself in phone cord. "P.o.'d I took vacation? This is fuckin' rich. Once every t'ree, four years a guy can't go off wit' a broad a lousy week or so? This is fuckin' America, Carlo!"

"I'm not takin' a position," the *consigliere* purred. "You asked what's goin' on, I gave you my opinion."

Big Al thought that over. He hoped that thinking would calm him down, but for him it didn't work that way. "So lemme get this straight," he said. "I'm forty-six years old. I been workin' wit' you people thirty years. An' I'm bein' punished, like a fuckin' kid, for goin' on vacation?"

"Al, don't look at it like—"

"I mean, if Tony wants me so bad to be home, he can't call me, man to man, and ask me ta come back?"

"He doesn't want you to come home," the *consigliere* said. He said it softly, and he meant it to be soothing, though of course Al heard it just the opposite. Defiance and insecurity were inseparable in Big Al. You couldn't tell him what to do and you couldn't tell him you didn't much care what he did.

He said, "That preening fuck Nicky's doin' my job, and Tony doesn't want me to come home?"

Ganucci sighed. These logical tangles—they happened more and more as he got older, and he never quite knew where the confusion started. "Al, he'd love to have you home. Tell ya what. I think I got it, a way that everybody's happy: have vacation, *then* come home."

Stubbornly, Al said, "Like I could be happy, this bullshit goin' on?"

"Al," the *consigliere* urged, "relax—"

"Well, I'm gonna be happy," Big Al insisted, his feisty side once more rearing up to defeat his paranoia. He thought about Katy, naked in a fragrant bath. He glanced off at his brand-new stash of gizmos. "I'm gonna have a fuckin' cabaret."

He almost knew that he was lying. His body was still in Florida, there was still sunshine and champagne and sex, but his vacation was basically over, and in the pit of his stomach he knew it. Nicky Scotto, after all, had succeeded brilliantly in spoiling it for him, if not quite in the manner he'd intended.

"Fine, Al, fine," said Carlo Ganucci. His bladder was burning and he wanted at all costs to end this no-win conversation. "Have a great time and come home when you're ready. We'll be thrilled to have you back. Goo'bye."

16

Lungs sodden, legs heavy and chafed, Al Tuschman trudged slowly back toward his hotel. Salt simmered in his belly; he coughed if he drew air too deep into his chest. Late sun baked his back, and he was barely aware of Fifi tugging at her leash, urging him along the sandy road between the navy's chain-link fences.

He was thinking about his luck.

There were perhaps two dozen people in the water near where he'd been swimming. Why had the shark selected him to chase? For that matter, why had some crazy, tourist-hating vandal picked his car to trash? And what about the freak hijacking? And what about the faceless delivery man putting lobsters in his bed?

Coincidence? Up until that moment he'd assumed so; his misfortunes had come too thick and fast for him to think about them in any other way. Luck, after all, good or bad, was famously streaky. He'd seen that on the selling floor, the ballfield.

But there were limits to what could be ascribed to luck alone, and now, finally, it dawned on Alan Tuschman that perhaps there was some other cause for his misfortunes. A pattern. The shark, okay, that was an act of God. But the other disasters—they were bizarre, ridiculous, but maybe there was a pattern to them nonetheless.

He pondered as he strolled. Was someone mad at him? He ran a catalog of those he might have wronged. Salesmen were not above exaggerating the merits of their wares—might there be a seriously disgruntled and deranged customer lurking out there somewhere? Possible; not likely. His ex? She was happily remarried, their relation cordial though distant. For better or worse, there were no scorned women in his recent past, still less jealous husbands. Who then?

Strolling now along streets lined with hibiscus shrubs and shaded by enormous banyans, he scanned his conscience and found it basically clear. He was an okay guy, not a saint, but a person of average virtue, ordinary decency. He was gentle with animals and would return a wallet if he found one. Essentially honest. Peaceable. Preferring to be kind than otherwise.

Such people were supposed to be rewarded. By God, or the universe, or however you wanted to put it. If not with gaudy gifts, then at least with neutral fortune and peace of mind. This Al had been taught, and this he still believed.

So why did he have less peace of mind than he'd had three days ago? Either the universe was out of whack, or he was looking at it wrong.

The universe, he couldn't fix. So he finessed his point of view.

These calamities that kept happening to him—maybe they weren't what they seemed. He'd been seeing himself as chosen victim, singled out for misery—but maybe that was a mistake. This unlikely, pinpoint malice that found him time and time again—maybe the real intention was something altogether different.

He walked, he pondered, then suddenly it hit him.

Hit him so abruptly that he laughed out loud from the bottom of his burning lungs. Of course! Of course that's what it was! No one was out to get him. He wasn't targeted for torment after all. A great wave of relief swept warmly over him, coupled with humble amusement that he hadn't caught on, solved the riddle sooner. He shook his head, and laughed some more, and wiped his eyes, and his dog looked back at him across her shoulder as though he'd lost his mind.

"Nicky," said his friend Donnie Falcone, "don't even think about it."

"How can I not think about it?" Nicky said, fingering the collar of his turtleneck.

In New York it was already dusk, one of those brown dusks that buries a gray day with people barely noticing the fade. They were having a cocktail in Tribeca. This was no dim and somber Mob joint but a hip place with an artist or two crammed in among the brokers. The waiter for their miniature table was skinny and wore black. There were women at the bar with straight, lank hair and bags under their eyes. Donnie, lean and lugubrious in his big black coat, almost looked like he belonged.

"I'm there," Nicky Scotto went on, "I'm runnin' things again—how can I not think about it?"

Donnie rubbed his long and concave face. "Find a way," he urged. "Be practical, Nicky. Skim your twenty, thirty, whatever you can manage in a week, and let it go."

"Twenty, thirty," Nicky said dismissively. "It's not about the money."

Donnie sipped his martini. "Don't make me laugh, I got chap lips."

"Okay, it's not just about the money. It's about who's the right guy—"

Donnie was rolling his cocktail napkin up around the damp base of his glass. "Nicky," he broke in, "lemme ask you somethin'. How'd you get the job?"

Nicky leaned in closer across the table that was barely big enough to hold two sets of elbows. "I tol' ya. Tony decided—"

"Fuhget Tony decided. How did you actually get the job? Who tol' you you had it?"

"Carlo," Nicky admitted. "Carlo called me up—"

"Exactly," Donnie said. "Carlo. Not Tony. Carlo. Zat tell you anything?"

Nicky looked stubborn in his bafflement.

"Here's what it tells me," his friend went on. "It tells me that who runs the fish market for one lousy week is exactly the kinda piddly bullshit that Tony don't wanna be bothered havin' a sit-down about."

"But if I just explain to him—"

"Explain what? Look, you want my advice, here it is: fuhget about lookin' ta sit down wit' Tony."

Nicky pouted, chased condensation down to the bottom of his glass of scotch. "Ta you it's piddly bullshit," he complained. "Ta me it's like a whole new chance."

"Fine. Except it isn't."

"How you know it isn't?" Nicky challenged. "How you know it isn't a tryout, like, a test."

Donnie raised his neat hands in surrender. "Okay, okay, I don't know nothin'. I only know that Tony's gonna be aggravated, ya waste his time wit' this."

"Waste his time? It's an opportu—"

"Nicky, you're makin' a mistake."

Nicky Scotto, annoyed but not dissuaded, gestured for another round of drinks. The waiter, more than cool, answered the gesture with the most elegant of tiny nods, and wove toward them through the crowded place as silent as a fish.

Al Tuschman was still chortling off and on when he walked into the office of Paradise and asked to use the phone. He was flushed and disheveled, and the desk clerk with the eyebrow studs looked at him with politely smiling disapproval.

"Been drinking, Mr. Tuschman?"

"Only half the ocean. If you'll excuse me, this is gonna be long distance."

He dialed, leaning on the counter. The clerk moved off just to the edge of earshot.

Waiting for the call to be picked up, Al got giddy once again. It's what happened when a man was allowed to crawl back from the precipice. Relief became a species of dementia. His chest heaved, his nose ran, and when Moe Kleiman finally lifted the phone and said a friendly, salesmanlike hello, Al had no breath to speak.

"Hello?" his employer said again. "Hello? Kleiman Brothers Furniture."

"You guys," Al Tuschman managed between snorts. "What a buncha kibitzers!"

"Who is this?" asked his boss.

Al wheezed through soggy passages. "The lobsters. The calamari. Jesus, howdya manage?"

"Al?"

"Really had me goin'. Thought . . . Christ, I don't know what I thought."

"If this is Al—"

"And about the car, I mean, jeez, the trip was prize enough. Ya didn't have to glom the car—"

"What car?"

"—pay off the lease—"

"Are you *meshuga* altogether?"

"Come on, Mr. Kleiman. Joke's over. Time to let it go."

"Are you okay, Al? Let what go?"

Al hesitated, cleared his throat of salt. Belatedly, it dawned on him that he must be sounding like a lunatic. He tried to cling to his giddiness, which was also his hope, but it was going, fast; emptily he watched it slip away like a loved one at the airport. Desperate now, he said, "Really, Mr. Kleiman, about these pranks—"

"Pranks? Al, trust me, I don't know what you're talking about. Is something wrong?"

He struggled for a normal breath and strove now for a sober tone. "Wrong? Oh, no. Coupla funny things have happened. I just thought maybe . . ."

"Yes?"

"Really I'm just checking in. Things okay up there?"

"Fine, Al, fine."

"Checking in, and thanking you again for the trip. This is quite a place."

"You like it?"

"Love it. Thanks again."

"You're welcome, Al. You earned it," Kleiman said, and Al could picture him kindly smiling, the thin mustache stretched into gray rays across his lip. "Enjoy and get home safe. We miss you here."

Al almost said he missed them too, but then was stopped by the galling and ridiculous sensation that if he said it he would start to cry.

Instead he said, "Hey, I'll be back soon. You'll see, I'll be tan and sell my ass off. Better than before."

17

"So what now?" asked Chop Parilla.

"I wish you'd quit askin' me that," said Squid. "Every time I'm baskin' inna glow of something, you're already buggin' me what's next."

They were sitting at a beachfront restaurant at the south end of Duval Street. It was a seafood joint but they were having burgers; ever since the calamari they hadn't felt like fish. Chop looked off at the ocean. The last light was skimming across it, making it look both thick and glassy, like if soup could be a mirror.

"Somethin's up my ass about this job," he finally admitted.

"Yeah," said Squid. "You only got to steal one car." He was eating french fries. He ate them one by one, the long way. He blobbed the tips in ketchup then held them up above his mouth like a trainer dangling herrings to a seal.

"Nah," Chop said, "it isn't that. It's . . . it's . . . ah the hell with it."

Squid wiped ketchup from his lips. He found it entertaining when Chop tried to explain himself. "Come on," he urged. "What?"

Chop took a bite of burger, slowly chewed. "It's that . . . it's that ya got no waya knowin' when you're finished, when ya've done the job. Ya see what I'm sayin'?"

Squid sucked his Coca-Cola through a straw.

"I mean," said Chop, "ya torch a place, the place burns down, ya've done the job. Ya hurt a guy, he's inna hospital, ya've done the job. But this? Ya bother 'im, ya bother 'im some more—how ya know when ya've bothered 'im enough and the job is really done?"

Squid folded his hands and serenely smiled, confirmed in his most basic belief—a belief that allowed him to feel his efforts did not go totally unappreciated. He'd always held that an intrinsic sense of art, however rudimentary and inarticulate, existed even in the densest dullard. "So you're saying it's about the structure of the thing?"

"Fuck structure. What I'm sayin'—"

"Is that you want a rise and fall, a climax."

"What I want," said Chop, "is to know when the fuckin' job is over so I can go home to Hialeah and play wit' motors."

Squid went back to eating french fries. "S'okay," he said, "in your own mind, what would it take for the job to be over?"

"Fuck difference does it make?"

"Come on," said Squid. "We're talkin' hypothetical."

"Fuck hypothetical. Lemme eat my burger."

Berman sighed. "Chop, ya know what separates us from monkeys? We converse while dining, we make witty conversation. So come on. What would convince you that we did enough, the job is over?"

Parilla put his burger down. "Okay. Okay. The fucker's hauled off in a straitjacket. Or better yet, he dies."

Squid clasped his hands together, looked up at the deepening violet sky. "Beautiful! Perfect classic endings. Except that ain't the job."

"I kinda wish it was. Now lemme eat my fucking dinner."

He'd had one forkful of coleslaw when Squid was at him again.

"What this job is," the bandy man said, "the beauty of it, it's modern."

"Fuck modern."

"It doesn't finish. It's just there. Like one a those paintings that's just dribs and drabs and slashes all the way to the edge. Forces you to deal with tension."

Chop put down his fork. "Keep talking and you're gonna deal with my foot up your ass."

"Ya see the power of that tension? I mean, it even gets to you!"

"One more word, Squid. One more word."

The bandy man swallowed viscously and finally shut up. Eating french fries, he stared off at the ocean, which had given up its copper tinge and turned a nighttime indigo. With neither rise nor fall, it spread to the horizon, and was everywhere a climax, since it had no start or finish. The most ancient and most modern picture. He wished he could make Chop see it. He knew he never would.

Big Al Marracotta, an all-or-nothing guy, could not accept that his vacation had been tarnished, that his carefree, sex-dazed time in Florida should be anything less than perfect. It offended him that problems dared intrude; it frustrated him that he could not shut off the world; it made him bitter that pleasure wasn't simple.

So his attitude got lousy and he did everything he could to make things worse. The change was very sudden, and understandably baffling to Katy Sansone.

Things had been going pretty well. She'd been giving him a back rub. They'd been talking about things, he'd been almost revealing. She'd felt like she was helping him, that they were getting close, almost like a real couple. Then the phone rang and she was banished to the bath.

Now, three quarters of an hour later, she was out of the tub, swathed in a robe, a towel turban on her head, and everything was different. Al looked mad again. "Things okay?" she innocently asked, shaking water from her ear.

He didn't answer and didn't look at her. He wasn't pacing anymore, just sort of wandering around the room.

Trying to be helpful, she said, "That phone call—?"

"There wasn't any phone call," he cut her off. "Remember that." He kept wandering, seeming to look for places where his small feet hadn't yet flattened the carpet.

"Al, is there anything I can do?"

There wasn't, and he held it against her that there wasn't. He stared at her from under his eyebrows, and in the stare was an unreachableness that was not very different from hate.

Katy still imagined that she must have done something to deserve that look. "If you're mad about how long I stayed at the beach—"

"I don't give a shit how long you stayed."

He went to the phone and ordered a bottle of scotch. Katy rubbed the towel against her scalp.

"Why don't you put an outfit on," he said.

At first she was happy he said it. Sex opened him up, if anything did. She scanned his face for some hint of the boy-devil grin, the wry, untempered zest that welcomed her into his selfishness awhile. But he didn't look zestful, just craggy and mean. She got worried in her stomach. She tried to sound playful. "Which one would you suggest?"

"Black."

She got some things from her suitcase and went back to the bathroom.

The liquor arrived while she was in there. Al poured himself a tumblerful and picked out a porno film. He pulled down the window shades; the last, dusky light put a lavender gleam around their edges, then faded, squandered, into night.

Katy emerged, walking stiffly on spike heels.

She wore a bra that lifted her breasts but didn't cover them, and panties that cinched her waist and thighs but left her sex exposed, made a lewd frame around a picture rendered vivid and obscene by lack of context. With effort she approached the bed.

She didn't mind being looked at; usually she enjoyed it. There was a kind of power in what she had to show. But now it didn't feel right.

It would not have taken much to put her at ease—a compliment or even just a smile would have sufficed. But Big Al couldn't manage it. He seemed aroused yet annoyed that she was there. Dressed but for his shoes, he leaned back on a stack of pillows and gestured for her to join him in the bed. Then, without a word or a touch, he used the remote to start the movie.

In the film, a man with muscles and a pointy beard was teaching a woman to submit. Leather straps bit into flesh. Wrists stretched in metal rings. Buttocks were pinkened as slaps combined with whimpers on the soundtrack. Cruel things were done to nipples.

Above the tinkle of chain and the crescendo of moans as pain imitated pleasure, Katy said, "I don't like this, Al."

He watched the film. He didn't answer.

"Come on," she said, "let's watch something else."

Al made no reply.

On the screen the woman's hair was being pulled, her loins assaulted with a device that looked medieval. Katy wondered if Al would notice if she closed her eyes. She didn't want to watch but she didn't want to make him angry. She narrowed her lids just far enough to make everything a blur, and amid the sounds of cursing and slapping, she watched a movie of her own. She saw the beach, a bright horizon flecked with distant sails. Green wavelets topped by tiny curls, silver foam sizzling and disappearing through a sieve of cool coarse sand.

When the film was over, Big Al took off his clothes and climbed on top of her. He wasn't kind; he wasn't unkind. He just started, then he moved awhile, and then he finished.

Katy Sansone surprised herself by feeling nothing. Nothing bad, nothing good. Still, the nothing that she felt had content. It was made of shame and frustrated caring and a tardy anger that was finally starting to ripen.

When he was done with her and had rolled aside, she walked slowly to the bathroom to wash. She faced herself in the mirror, regarded herself with curiosity but no expression. She realized after a moment that what she was looking for was something to be proud of. She studied her own eyes, she firmed her jaw. Then she took off the things that Al had bought her, the cupless bra and the panties that put her on display, and dropped them in the trash.

18

Alan Tuschman didn't leave his room that evening.

He was wrung out, his chest hurt, and he was half afraid that if he showed himself, yet another ludicrous and dreadful thing was bound to happen. His confidence was badly shaken, and in some primitive, unreasoning way, his feelings were hurt, as if he'd been cast out by all the world, turned into a pariah. He felt like he'd forgotten how to get along with people, how to do the simple things that got a person through the day. Like a voodoo curse, his run of bad luck spooked him, and thereby brought on more bad luck.

He took a shower, scraped his belly on a splinter that had somehow become embedded in his bar of soap. He ordered in a pizza, burned his mouth on cheese. He cut up a slice for the dog, and the two of them ate in mopey silence beneath the picture of the greenish women with the greenish breasts. Then they crawled, defeated, into bed. Al watched the slow and mollifying rotation of the ceiling fan, and let his mind go numb. . . .

But there's no medicine like sleep, and in the morning everything looked cheerier.

The salesman blinked through his window, saw giant philodendron leaves, pendant coconuts turning yellow, soft mist rising from the hot tub. Perspective returned. Pariah? Come on—he was a well-liked, friendly guy who'd had a few bad breaks. His luck would turn; he knew it. He was on a mission to be happy—Jesus Christ, he thought, when did I really start believing that?—and one way or another he was going to pull it off.

Exercise, he decided. In sweat was sanity and peace. Always had been; always would be. He'd take a good long run.

He pulled on a jock; there was youth and vigor in the feel of the straps against his butt. He almost touched his toes a couple times, then put Fifi on her leash and headed out the door, past the topless woman doing yoga on a towel, past the European threesome already giggling over thimble muffins, past the desk clerk, dozing with his hand around a mug of coffee.

He ran up Elizabeth Street, crossed the road that had brought him into town. He tried to think of his grimace as a smile, tried not to notice that none of this was easy anymore. His knees and spine didn't cushion his brain the way they used to. His eyeballs bounced. He sucked air past the lingering tickle in his lungs, past the weight of last night's pizza, and kept on going.

He reached the county beach, traced out its zigzag path, then headed north along a row of condos. Fifi's paws made a pleasant ticking on the pavement, and, for a while, it hurt less as he went. He remembered what it was to win, to break into the open with a football spinning toward him and the goal line chalked on matted grass. The sun got higher and seared his hairline. Without breaking stride he pulled off his shirt.

At the beginning of the long promenade that led on to the airport and the houseboats, he began to feel that he should turn around. His temples throbbed; there was a squish in his sneakers that might have been blood from his blistered feet. But his course was just reaching its most beautiful, with the green water of the Straits stretching away toward Cuba, and emerald-tinged clouds stalled above the Gulf Stream.

So, mouth parched and ankles clicking, he pressed on. Young women passed him effortlessly on Rollerblades. Old hippies scudded by on junky bikes whose fat tires hummed against the concrete. He plodded along and his thoughts whooshed by like distant traffic. Sex. Archaic ball games. Sales pitches finding their apotheosis in commissions. Mostly he just wanted to keep on moving. Beyond worries, explanations. Past the need to figure stuff out. Onward to the time when this eerie and unsettling vacation would be over and he could ease himself again into the womb of the familiar.

It wasn't that Big Al Marracotta didn't know he'd been a prick. He knew; but he'd started on a downward spiral and he just couldn't turn the thing around.

Over breakfast in their room, he watched Katy sulk, and he dimly understood that something different had come into her sulking. It was no longer a ploy. She wasn't doing it for attention or to get her way. She was doing it because she felt lousy and wanted to be left alone. She sat there with her bathrobe pulled in tight across her collarbones. She hadn't bothered to smooth her spiky hair, and her gaze floated without focus toward the curtained window.

Big Al looked down and stabbed his eggs. He knew the situation could still be rescued. He could apologize, and she would understand. But there's no way he would do it. An apology conferred status, gave a certain power to the person receiving it. He wasn't starting down that road. What about the next time he acted like a scumbag—would she throw it in his face? Would he have to apologize again? Till respect was whittled away to nothing? No way . . . Not that he absolutely had to apologize. Not in so many words. He could probably get things back on track and still stop short of that, just sort of slide around it. Tell her he had a lot on his mind; she'd fill in the rest. . . . But why give her that much information, that much satisfaction? Start confiding in someone, and they started feeling close, and that bred expectations, and that made the whole thing a big pain in the ass.

The little mobster gnawed at buttered toast and realized he was getting mad at Katy. Last night he'd been a bastard; he had to justify it somehow, so today he was digging in his heels. He slurped coffee and turned a hard eye on her. He decided she wasn't that pretty. Her eyes were undramatic and when she pouted her mouth looked sharp. She was moody, sometimes she was lukewarm in the sack, and when vacation was over he'd probably break up with her. Enough already. Be a sport, pay a couple months' rent on the studio in Murray Hill, and have it over with.

Thinking that, he felt restless in advance. He pushed his plate away, said, "Come on, let's take a drive or somethin'."

"Fine," said Katy, even more eager than he to be out of that hotel room.

As if it were her fault, he added, "I mean, Christ, we been here days and haven't seen a thing."

She almost answered that, then realized there was no point. Silently, she blotted her mouth on her napkin and moved off someplace private to get dressed.

19

Carlo Ganucci was surprised how readily Tony Eggs had agreed to sit down with Nicky Scotto. He thought he'd say a flat-out no, or at least demand to be persuaded.

Sitdowns were a nuisance. It was always someone bitching, and in the end you didn't give them what they wanted, and they went away madder than they were before; or you granted what they asked for, which almost always meant that someone else got mad and started looking for a meet.

So when, the evening before, the *consigliere* had passed along Nicky's request to get together, he'd done so in the offhand manner of a man expecting a terse and bothered refusal. But Tony Eggs had not seemed bothered. In fact he'd almost smiled. Dry lips twitched briefly back from yellow and insecurely rooted teeth, and his eyes took on a gratified gleam. "Good," he'd said.

"Good?"

"Good. Tell 'im ten tomorrow morning."

Now it was the appointed time, and Nicky Scotto, plucking at his cashmere turtleneck and smoothing the lapels of his slate-blue mohair suit, had just walked into the social club on Prince Street.

He was trying to look casual and confident. He waved to a couple of goombahs playing poker in a corner, kidded with the lackey behind the coffee counter. But when his espresso was handed to him, he couldn't quite keep the cup from chattering against the saucer. He squeezed it hard to hold it still, before moving to the inviolable table at the rear, where the two old men were sitting.

He waited for a nod from Tony Eggs, then almost daintily hitched up his trousers and joined them. Raising his demitasse, he said, "Tony. Carlo. Thank you for your time. *Salud.*"

He swallowed some coffee, struggled to put the cup down cleanly. A silent second passed, and he quickly understood that no one was going to help him keep the conversation going. Carlo Ganucci looked sleepy and feeble, the thin skin sallow and papery around his eyes. Tony Eggs appeared as inclined toward chitchat as a tree. Nicky cleared his throat, made a theatrical gesture of blowing into his hands, and said, "Fuckin' freezin' for November, huh?"

Neither old man answered that. Tony Eggs pulled his tongue down from the roof of his mouth. It made a clicking sound that seemed very loud.

Nicky tried again. "Okay, why I'm here, the reason, it's about the market."

Nobody responded. Carlo looked down at his crumbling yellow fingernails.

"I'm really happy to be runnin' it again," said Nicky. "Wanted to thank you for the opportunity."

"Who said it's an opportunity?" Tony Eggs Salento rumbled forth at last.

This flustered Nicky. He reached for his espresso cup, put it down again, tried a couple times to get a sentence started. Outside, horns honked and cabbies cursed each other.

Tony Eggs, suddenly loquacious, went on. "Hey, Nicky, how much that suit cost?"

"Eighteen hundred." He tried to keep the pride out of his voice, almost managed. He loved that suit. It wasn't just the money he'd been able to pay for it. It was that the guy who made it was in great demand, and wouldn't tailor clothing for just any-body.

The old boss pursed his lips. His own suit cost two-fifty off a downtown rack, and he'd had it twenty years. "Do me a favor," he told his young lieutenant. "Take the jacket off and stomp it."

"Excuse me?"

"If you'd like this meeting to continue, put the jacket onna goddamn floor and walk all over it."

Nicky licked his lips, glanced from underneath his brows at one old man and then the other. Maybe this was some kind of a test, or better yet a joke. But he saw no whimsy in their eyes. He waited an instant longer for a reprieve that would not come, then stood up, hesitated, and finally slipped out of his jacket and dropped it to the floor. For a moment he regarded it with heart-break and nostalgia, as though it were a dying pet. The old linoleum was dusty and cracked, with tarry fissures that would claw at a gray silk lining. And who could say what unspeakable residue of fish slime or dogshit might be clinging to his shoes?

His legs trying their damnedest to hold him back, he side-stepped onto the swath of custom-tailored mohair. He made a weak, little grinding motion then stepped off again.

"More," said Tony Eggs.

"More?"

Gingerly he stepped again onto his jacket; then, with a per-verse and mounting energy, a cresting wave of debasement and inchoate rage, he stomped the precious garment. He marched on it, he ran in place; he improvised a cha-cha, launched into a sort of demented Mashed Potato. His chest grew warm, his face flushed. He ground his heel into a sleeve, heard a seam rip open under the unsprung fury of his war dance. A drop of sweat broke free from a sideburn and trickled down his cheek, and he kept jumping on his jacket for several seconds after Tony said to him, "Okay, Nicky. Now siddown."

He sat. He was breathing heavily. He looked down at his ravaged jacket, and he almost wanted to cry. Cry, or tear it thread from thread, till no two pieces of it hung together, till it was as utterly destroyed as though it had never been made.

Softly, relentlessly, Tony Eggs Salento said, "Enough fun and games. Now we talk. . . . I know why you came here, Nicky. You came here 'cause you want the market back. But here's the problem: How can you expect to get it back when you still don't understand why you lost it inna first place?"

Nicky looked down at his hands, very pink against the green felt of the table. Carlo Ganucci gave a weak and sudden burp, the burp of a man whose innards weren't working right.

"Why'd ya lose the market, Nicky?" Tony Eggs went on. "Not because ya didn't run it good. Because ya got above yourself. *Capice?*"

Nicky tried to lift his eyes, but couldn't. His jaw worked and he felt it deep inside his ears.

"Ya got to where ya thought that Nicky Scotto was more important than the job. The suits, the nightclubs—they gave you a hard-on, they got you laid. Fine. But, Nicky, listena me. I'm sevenny years old and I ain't been inna can in forty-five years. Why? 'Cause I wear cheap suits and I stay home at night, and I don't rub the feds' faces inna shit I'm gettin' away with. Ya see?"

The lieutenant raised his face at last. Around his mouth and eyes, defiance and humiliation were contending, as on the face of every child who's been scolded.

"So, very simple," Tony Eggs resumed, "here is why you lost the market. You lost the market because you acted like a dumb trash show-off punk who was bound to fuck up big time and get himself nailed. . . . Now, have I made you feel like a piece a shit?"

There was no answer to that, so Nicky Scotto just looked around the room. Had the poker players heard all this, the lackey behind the counter?

"'Cause here's the funny part," said Tony Eggs. "I like you, Nicky. You're hungry. Ya work hard. Ya got potential. So now I'm in, like, a difficult position."

Nicky moved his lips. Getting his voice to work again was like starting up a long-parked car whose battery had run down. "What's difficult about it?" he managed.

The boss pulled on his long thin face. "I think you've learned a lesson. All things bein' equal, you deserve a second chance. But inna meantime, Big Al's got the market, and up until a couple days ago I was very happy wit' the job he was doin'."

Hope scratched at Nicky like loose threads in his underwear. He looked down at his violated jacket, felt a sudden spartan contempt for it. Who needed fancy suits? "And now?" he said.

Tony Eggs scratched his neck. He leaned his head forward to do so, and his throat went stringy in his collar. "Al made a couple judgments that sorta shook my confidence. Took vacation. Picked the wrong guy ta leave in charge while he was gone. It's not enough to fire him about. But—"

"But what?" said Nicky.

Tony Eggs leaned far back in his chair. So did Carlo Ganucci. The two old men took deep, sighing breaths, then, in unison, leaned forward once again.

"Nicky," said the boss, "I'm a pretty simple guy. I've always believed that the best man for the job is the man who wants the job the most."

Scotto pressed his ribs against the table, grabbed the edges of it with his meaty hands. "So what can I do—?"

Tony Eggs cut him off with a shrug. "I'm not you, Nicky. I don't know what you should do. Think about it. You'll come up wit' somethin'."

The boss looked away, and Nicky felt suddenly drained, belatedly realized that the old man's unblinking stare had been on him for a long, long time. He brought his hands in front of him, sat through a few seconds of silence before he understood that the sitdown was over. Without another word he rose to go. The rubber cups on his chair legs made ugly squeaks against the old linoleum.

"Your jacket," Tony Eggs reminded him as he started moving toward the door.

Nicky left it lying where it was.

"Cold outside," said Carlo Ganucci.

Nicky didn't turn around. With only his thin cashmere sweater for protection, he broke out into the unseasonable chill of the November morning, his mind already chewing on the question of what he had to do to get the market back.

20

Alan Tuschman, fleeing everything and nothing, ran farther than he should have.

He ran till his saliva was all used up, till he could feel the separate, grinding pieces that comprised his knees, till small fillets of muscle began to quiver in his buttocks. By now he was way up near the airport. Absently he watched planes take off and land, thought about the passengers briefly trading one life for another, carrying in their luggage the people they might be if nobody they knew was watching. The sun grew higher, shadows seemed to evaporate on hot pavements. The breeze dropped and the ocean took on the fuzzy sheen of brushed aluminum. Fifi's tongue hung down almost to the sidewalk, swung like a damp pink pendulum as she unflaggingly ran.

Just beyond the airport, the island curved, and there was a wide place in the promenade where people sometimes parked their cars, to fish, or windsurf, or just to look out at the Straits. Nearing that curve, sweat in his eyes and fog in his brain, Al saw something that at first glance made him smile. It was a new gray Lincoln, spotless but for the inevitable goo of squashed bugs on the windshield, and it had a New York license plate that said BIG AL.

Hmm, thought Alan Tuschman. Small world.

In the next heartbeat, though, something darker and indefinably discomfitting pressed in on him. He felt somehow crowded in his own skin. As if the basic fact of his uniqueness were being questioned. As though the borders of the little space he took up in the world were being suddenly contested.

He didn't have long to think about it. After half a dozen more strides, he saw the tall woman he'd spoken with on the way to the beach. She was sitting on the seawall, wearing pink shorts and a lime-green top, looking out across the ocean. The big, drooling rottweiler that he'd first seen on Duval Street was lolling around her ankles.

Al stopped running. He didn't exactly decide to stop. He just pulled up short, sucked in a breath, and yelled out, "Hi there!"

The woman turned toward his voice. It seemed to Al that she started to smile then caught herself. Her eyes flicked toward the Lincoln then back again. Blandly, uncomfortably, she said, "Oh, hi."

Fifi ran over and started yipping at the rottweiler, crouching on her chicken-wing back legs and sticking out her flat and tiny face. Ripper quailed, retreated behind Katy's slender calves.

Al Tuschman, proud of his dog, said, "Don't worry. She won't hurt him."

Katy almost smiled before erasing it again, gave Fifi a quick pat on the head. Her face tightened and her hand pulled back as the Lincoln's driver's-side door clicked open.

Al Marracotta got out. He hadn't previously seen the point of getting out to look at water that you could see just as easy through the windshield, but now he did. He was on the far side of the car, and could barely peek over its roof. He secretly came up on tiptoe to appraise this sweating palooka who was talking to his girlfriend. The guy looked strong. Moisture glistened in his whorls of thick black chest hair, veins stood out in his neck and arms. But strong was strong, and tough was tough, and Al Marracotta had long ago learned that the two generally had squat to do with each other. He snarled at the interloper and turned to Katy. "You know this guy?"

"We met at the beach." She sounded weary, maybe frightened, saying it.

"Two minutes you're outa my sight, you're pickin' up guys at the beach?"

Katy said nothing, looked down at the tangle of dogs at her feet.

Al Tuschman, trying to be helpful, agreeable, said, "Hey, we said hello. We hardly talked." Then he gestured toward the Lincoln's stern. "You know, my nickname's Big Al too."

Al Marracotta didn't like that. He was not a man inclined to share. Not girlfriends, not nicknames, not anything. He pushed forward his chin and said, "What of it?"

Disarmed by the readiness of the other man's hostility, Al Tuschman gave an awkward and retreating laugh. "Nothing. Just a funny coincidence, that's all."

Al Marracotta sneered and looked away. "Real fuckin' funny." To Katy, he said, "Come on, flirt, we're outa here."

She took a deep breath then rose from the seawall. She didn't look at Alan Tuschman, but he noticed once again how gracefully her long body folded and unfolded. Still, once she'd risen, there was a stiffness and a hesitation in her step, and anyone could see that she didn't want to get into that car. The cowardly rottweiler stayed behind her legs the whole way to the door, its veiny testicles bouncing as it leaped into the backseat.

Big Al Marracotta burned rubber as he pulled away. Big Al Tuschman sat down to rest where Katy had been sitting, used his balled-up shirt to dry his chest, and tried not to think about the long, stiff-jointed walk back to his hotel.

"Come on, Donnie, what else could he of meant?"

They were sitting in the fish market office. It was cold and it smelled of clamshells and the blue tang of slowly melting ice. Donnie Falcone kept his big funereal topcoat on; its lapels flapped as he gestured. "Coulda meant a lotta things," he said. "Up the take. Expand the territory. Increase the tribute. Ya know, do somethin' t'impress 'im. He didn't tell ya start a war."

Nicky Scotto drummed his fingers on his metal desk. Ambition was keeping him warm; he was still wearing the cashmere turtleneck alone. "What war?" he said. "I'm talkin' 'bout takin' out one guy."

"Lunatic!" said Donnie, pulling on his long and pliant face. "Listen ta yourself! You ain't takin' out nobody. Fuhget about it."

Nicky leaned back in his chair. It was a crappy chair, the cheap springs creaked as he leaned back, but, boy, did it feel comfortable. His face went dreamy, piggy black eyes losing focus.

Donnie leaned far across the scratched-up desk, grabbing for his friend's attention like he was reaching for a grip on someone halfway out a window. "Nicky, listena me. This wanting the market back. It's like a whaddyacallit, an obsession already. It's makin' you crazy."

"Crazy?" Nicky said placidly. "No. It's business, Donnie. Tony needs ta see how much I want the job. This is what he said."

Donnie closed his eyes a second, seemed to be praying for more patience. It didn't come. He sprang up from his chair, did a pirouette on the scuffed and damp floor, and pointed an accusing finger at his friend. "Goddamit! This is what I tol' you from the start!"

"*What* is what you tol' me from the start?"

"This crazy bullshit wit' the clams, the puking. It was never about that. Right from the start you were lookin' for a way to get the market back."

Nicky Scotto didn't bother to deny it. He folded his hands and smiled. He looked around the office. Minute by minute it was feeling more like his again. Pretty soon he could throw away the pictures of Big Al's wife and kids. Throw them in a Dumpster with the fish guts and the slime.

"For the love a Christ," his friend implored, "don't go any further wit' this, Nicky. The man has friends. Allies. You don't know the shit you're steppin' into."

Nicky Scotto pursed his lips, cocked an ear toward the shouts and laughs that now and then filtered in from the market, sounds full of vigor and comradeship and profit.

Then he said, "Hey, Donnie, ya know where I can get some cheap but decent suits? Right off the rack like?"

21

When the call came from New York, Squid Berman was at the aquarium, doing research.

He studied up on barracuda, with their steam-shovel jaws and beveled pins for teeth; on manta rays, whose three-foot tails were barbed like those of ancient devils; on giant octopi, whose suction-cup legs could reduce a man to a polka-dotted cushion of suppurating hickeys. He spent an entertaining hour and took away a couple good ideas.

He got back to the motel to find Chop all excited, rubbing the top of his head and not stopping till his hand had stroked his stump of neck and was reaching toward his shoulders.

"Talked ta Nicky," the car specialist reported.

"Didja tell 'im about the lobsters?" Berman asked with pride. "Didja tell 'im about—?"

"He wants ta change the job."

"Change the job? But I just been thinking—"

"He wants we clip the guy."

Squid's face fell and he sat down on the bed. His bony hands fretted in his narrow lap and his knees would not stay still. "Clip the guy? Ah fuck. I don't wanna clip the guy."

Chop was pacing the length of the dresser. His face was changing too, getting into character for the new assignment. Skin tightened at the edges of his eyes, his lips flattened out and pulled in against his teeth. "Squid," he said, "don't tell me you're goin' tenderhearted on me."

"It isn't that," said Berman. "Guy dies, doesn't die, who gives a shit? It's just that . . ." His tongue probed around inside his cheeks, he gave a series of spasmodic little shrugs.

"Just what?"

Squid threw his hands up in the air. "Just that this has been, like, a really one-of-a-kind job so far, and now the motherfucker's makin' it bourgeois."

"Boozh-wah?"

"Ya know. Ordinary. Obvious. I hate that shit."

Chop said, "We get an extra fifty grand. It's gonna be a piece a cake."

Disgusted, Squid turned his back, looked at a dead fly snagged and hollowed out in a spiderweb at a corner of the room.

Chop continued anyway. Without seeming to notice he was doing it, he tugged at his wrist like he was pulling on a glove. "We grab the piece a shit outside his hotel. Take 'im up the Keys, ice 'im, dump 'im inna mangroves. Boom, it's over. T'ree hours later we're home, checkin' out titties on South Beach. Beautiful."

Petulantly, still looking away, Squid said, "I'm not doin' it."

Chop pivoted around the bed, wedged his way into the other man's field of vision. "Whaddya mean, you're not doin' it? Come on, now, don't embarrass me. I tol' Nicky no problem, we'd do it."

Berman sulked and salivated. He swallowed hard, his hands fluttered like contending birds. He shook his head.

Chop Parilla pawed the carpet, breathed hard through his mouth. In desperation he said, "I never knew Sid Berman to go half-ass on a job."

This got to Squid, hit him where he lived. He blinked, he squirmed, he moved his tongue to a mouth corner and left it there awhile. Finally he said, "Okay, okay, we'll take him out. On one condition."

Chop's eyes rolled up toward his low and deeply furrowed forehead. "What's the condition?"

Squid gave a determined sideways tilt to his head. "We finish the job the way we started it."

"And fuck is that supposed to mean?"

"We take 'im out by seafood."

Chop roughly spanked his thighs as he sprang out of his crouch. "Fuckin' seafood? Squid, Jesus Christ! Why ya gotta make everything so difficult?"

Calmer now, more settled in his mind, Squid folded his bandy arms across his chest. It wasn't about difficulty. It was about unity, integrity. Did you begin a statue with a hammer and chisel and suddenly switch to a chain saw? No, you were true to the tools you started with. That was a basic rule of craft. Fundamental.

Chop hadn't dropped his protest. Fists balled, knees bent in a simian slouch, he was working off frustration in great bounds around the narrow, mildewed room. "Ya take guys out wit' guns," he said. "Ya take guys out wit' knives. Baseball bats. Piana wire. What kinda horseshit is ya take a guy out wit' seafood?"

Knowing that he'd won, Squid spoke very softly. "Death by seafood, Chop," he said. "Either that, or you get yourself a different partner."

Alan Tuschman leaned forward at his tiny table at an outdoor restaurant that overlooked the harbor, and bit deep and lustily into his grouper sandwich.

The thin crust of the Cuban roll caved in beneath the clamping of his teeth; mayo squished against his gums; the crunch of onion lit a small fire on his tongue; and the fish's charbroiled surface blended the tastes of ocean and woods. He savored the bite a good long moment, then washed it down with beer.

He couldn't remember when he'd tasted food so vividly, and vaguely wondered why it seemed so new and marvelous. Perhaps his recent sufferings, coupled with the humid vacancy of his days, made him more appreciative of simple things, the mundane pleasures too often shouted down by busyness, routine. Maybe it was just that his long run had quieted his mind and opened up his body, lulled him back to basics.

In any case, he thoroughly enjoyed his lunch and was in calmly buoyant spirits as, led by Fifi, he strolled back to his hotel. Everything was oddly perfect on that stroll. A brilliant sun warmed him, but seemed to duck behind a scrap of cloud whenever he grew too hot. Locals with groceries in their bike baskets smiled at him as if he'd suddenly come to belong. Papery bougainvillea petals came unstuck in soft breezes and fluttered down russet and fuchsia in his path, and he decided that today was the day he'd get naked at the pool.

He strolled through the gate of Paradise, and the desk clerk called to him.

Al's posture drooped, his euphoria imploded. By now it was Pavlovian. What next? The desk clerk had bad news only, and delivered it always with a smarmy and malicious smile. On legs suddenly grown heavy, Al walked into the office.

The clerk looked at him from between the ruby studs above his eyebrow and the purplish bags beneath his eyes. His mouth was sardonic, his tone as irritating as ever, but shockingly, his news today was good. "There's someone waiting for you at the pool," he said. "A woman."

Al took in the information as though his ears were in his pants. "A woman," he punchily echoed. "Waiting for me."

"You're the tall guy named Al."

"This is true." He swallowed. He knew who it was, of course. His near-lover, the woman with the wonderful thick hair. The woman whose unclothed torso he'd briefly held against his own. She'd come to realize he wasn't kinky after all, that the lobsters

123

in the sheets were some grotesque but blameless accident. She'd returned in the sober light of day to finish what they'd started. It would be even sweeter for the long delay.

Alan Tuschman pulled down smartly on his shirtfront, wished he hadn't had the onion on his sandwich. He turned with almost military crispness and walked out toward the pool.

He scanned the helter-skelter ranks of lounges for that mass of springy hair, the fleshy shoulders and heavy breasts that he remembered.

Then he spotted Katy, the woman with the nasty boyfriend. She was laid out long and thin and ill at ease, save for Al the only person in the place with clothes on.

22

"Hi," she said as he sat down on a lounge beside her. She said it sheepishly, but packed into the single syllable, as well, was a suggestion of bent humor and a head-shaking acceptance of the fact that things seldom went as planned.

Al fumbled through a greeting in return.

"Surprised to see me," she said. It was not a question. She patted Fifi's knobby head. The dog licked her hand.

"How'd you know where—?"

"You told me," she reminded him. "On the road to the beach."

"Ah."

She glanced furtively around the courtyard at the European threesome, the fuzzy lesbians, the basted gay men with their bronzed and dimpled buns. "Kind of an amusing place."

"Kind of is," said Al. He had no idea why she was there, but could not help suspecting some sick game with himself as beard. His gaze wandered over to the courtyard gate. He half expected to see the sneering jealous boyfriend come barging through it, shaking his fists and sticking out his feisty chin and making an appalling scene.

Katy followed his eyes, understood his thoughts. The playfulness fell out of her voice, and suddenly she sounded very young and very lost. "I just walked out on him," she said. "I didn't know where else to go. I'm sorry."

Al looked at her more closely then. The sun was in his eyes, and it wasn't until he shaded them with his hand that he saw the red place on her jawbone, just below the ear.

She saw him looking at it, and was horrified and ashamed. She hadn't known there was a mark. Her composure let go and she cried for half a second. A tiny whimper escaped. A tear swelled at the corner of her eye, then vanished, as though by sheer act of will she could suck it back.

"Are you okay?" Al Tuschman asked her.

She nodded that she was, and looked away. It was all so stupid, she was thinking. So pointless. The second they'd sped off from the promenade, Big Al had started cursing at her, calling her names. She was a tramp, a slut, an ingrate. She'd crossed her arms and rolled her eyes and slunk against her door. He drove a little ways up the Keys, then stopped and had a couple drinks while she sipped lemonade. For a while he calmed down; then, as they were getting back to town he started in again. Ugly words, ugly accusations. Finally she stood up for herself. She'd done nothing wrong. All she'd done was talk to someone for three minutes, and if he couldn't handle that, then he was really pathetic.

That's when he hit her. They were stopped at a red light, heavy traffic. He yanked a hand off the steering wheel and slapped her. It was a weak and awkward smack. It didn't hurt, and what made it yet sadder was that even Katy could see that he was trying to hold himself back. But he hadn't managed; he'd hit her. She stared at him a second. He stared back with what might have been remorse. But it was too late. She got out of the Lincoln and on milky knees she stormed away. She'd heard horns honking but didn't look back.

Now, at poolside, she took a deep breath and started sitting up. "Look," she said, "we don't even know each other. I shouldn't be bothering you like this."

"Are you bothering me?" Al Tuschman said. Mainly he was asking himself. "Hey, I'm on vacation. I'm bored out of my mind. Let's talk."

She hovered halfway out of her lounge a moment, studied

Alan Tuschman's face. There was kindness, she felt, in the spacing of the features. Big eyes, wide apart. A full and candid mouth. Fleshy olive cheeks with here and there a small and unembarrassed crater. She liked his face, yet found herself searching for the things that she was more accustomed to—suspicion, guile, temper. When she couldn't find them, she grew briefly confused. Her practiced toughness let go a little bit, and her back eased down again onto the chaise. "Oh, God," she said. "This is a helluva vacation."

Al pursed his lips, folded his hands. "Look," he said, "maybe you'll give things a little while to calm down—"

"Then what?" she interrupted. "Go crawling back? Look, I'm done with him about twenty seconds before he's done with me. And he's the wrong guy anyway. It was a stupid thing to be involved in in the first place."

"Why?" asked Al.

She gave a mirthless laugh. "Too many reasons to go into. Why feel even worse?"

"Okay," he said. "So what'll you do?"

She twisted up her mouth and shrugged. "Get a flight back home, I guess."

"What about your things, your luggage?"

Her face went briefly sour as she thought about the thongs, the garters, the underwire bras Big Al had bought her. "There's nothing there I care about," she said.

"You have a ticket?"

Katy shook her head. "We drove. The car. Remember?"

At this Al gave a rueful snort. "I drove too. I had a car back then. Same license plate. Isn't that a pisser?"

"Same license plate?" said Katy.

"I mean, Jersey, not New York, but, yeah, same plate."

Katy's mouth stretched into a cockeyed smile. "Christ, I wish you had a different name."

Al had no response for that, so he said, "You really sure you wanna leave?"

She didn't answer quite as fast as she meant to. But she sighed and said, "Yeah, I'm going. I'll try to find a friend up in the city, see if she can wire down some money."

"Wire money?" said Al Tuschman. It seemed like such a quaint idea, he smiled.

Katy took offense, her eyes unblinking beneath the spiky hair. "Look," she said, "I'm twenty-nine. Sometimes I work as a waitress. Cocktails, mostly. Lately I made the idiot mistake of letting a rich boyfriend pay my way. I happen not to have a credit card. That shock you?"

Blindsided by her sudden vehemence, Al Tuschman leaned back a little way. Why was she daring him to look down on her? "Hey," he said, "I'm not judging you."

She dropped her eyes, her hands fidgeted on her tummy. "Ah, shit. I'm judging myself. Nothing to do with you. I'm sorry."

Al said, "Three minutes, that's like the fourteenth time you've apologized."

There was a silence broken only by the ceaseless tittering of the Europeans and the soft splash of a naked man stepping gingerly into the pool. After a moment Al heard himself say, "Listen, if it's really what you wanna do, I'll lend you the money for a ticket home."

Katy looked at him, still fidgeting. With wonderment and not without mistrust, she said, "Why? Why would you do that for me?"

Al blew a little air between his lips, softly rubbed his hands together. "Why?" he said, and for a moment he wasn't the least bit sure himself. Then he leaned down, and in a conspiratorial whisper he continued. "I'll tell you why. 'Cause you and me, we're the only people in this town who will admit that vacation's going lousy." He reached a hand across the narrow space between their lounges. "Come on. Let's see about getting you a flight."

Chop Parilla should have known better, but he still imagined that maybe he could talk Sid Berman into doing the job his way. Over a late lunch at a dim and dusty place called the Half Moon Tavern, he said, "Jesus, Squid, this job could get done so much faster wit', say, a thirty-eight."

"Right," said Berman, eating french fries the long way. "And the Sistine fuckin' Chapel coulda got done so much faster wit' a roller. Zere somethin' that you're drivin' at?"

"I'd like to get back home sometime," said Chop.

Squid Berman frowned. Such thinking was beneath him. You didn't think of home when you were on a job. You didn't think of anything except the job. That was concentration. That was purity.

Chop gnawed the paltry meat off a chicken wing. "Sistine Chapel? Zat in Little Havana?"

To avoid laughing in his partner's coarse, uncultured face, Berman looked away. As he did so, in one of those serendipitous opportunities that only the concentrated mind is quick enough to seize, something caught his eye.

It was a stuffed fish nailed onto the cheap, fake paneling of the wall. The fish's back was an electric blue, its belly a metallic silver. From its gorgeously arched spine protruded a large webbed fin as graceful as a Japanese fan; extending from the tapering head was a nose that stretched and stretched, Pinocchio-like, into a two-foot spike.

Transfixed, Squid stared at the creature a long moment, then gestured for the waiter. "That fish," he said. "Zat a . . . whaddyacallit?"

"Sailfish," said the waiter.

"It's beautiful," said Squid.

The waiter nodded in wistful agreement. He was a burly guy who liked to fish. He wished that he was fishing now. "People catch 'em just beyond the reef," he said. "Usually release 'em nowadays. People don't make real trophies anymore."

"How'd they used to do 'em?" asked Squid.

"The real ones? They'd peel back the skin, sever the backbone, pop the eyes, scoop the brains out with a little pick—"

"Hey," said Chop, "I'm eatin' heah."

"Sorry," said the waiter. "The new ones, they're just paint and plastic over Styrofoam."

"But that one's real?" asked Squid. It was important to him that it was.

"Pretty sure," the waiter said. "Been there years and years."

Casually, Squid said, "How sharp's the nose?"

"You mean its sense of smell?"

"No. I mean, the nose, how sharp, ya know, for sticking things."

The waiter let out a respectful sound. "Like a razor. That's how he feeds. Gets into a school of jack or yellowtail and just starts slashing. Sometimes hacks 'em up, sometimes runs a fish right through."

Moisture was pooling beneath Squid's tongue. He swallowed hard, said to Chop, "Hey, Joe, wouldn't it be great to tell the folks back home we caught one a those?"

Parilla, still working on his plate of wings, his celery and blue cheese dressing, was slow on the uptake, didn't answer.

Squid said to the waiter, "How much ya want for it?"

The waiter gave a nervous laugh. "It isn't mine. It isn't for sale."

"Okay, okay, but how much is it worth?"

The waiter shrugged. "You see 'em now and then, antique stores, estate sales, three, four hundred."

"Take two thousand?"

The waiter paused to see if he was kidding.

"Cash. Right now," Sid Berman damply said. "Look, we gotta drive back t'Ohio right after lunch."

The waiter said, "You're serious. I'll ask the manager."

While he was gone, Chop said, "Two grand, Squid? You're fuckin' crazy."

Squid was looking at the seafood with the razor nose. "Worth every penny," he said. "The absolutely perfect ending don't come cheap."

They left with the stuffed fish tucked under Squid's proud arm like something he'd won at a carnival.

23

For Big Al Marracotta, things went from bad to worse. He'd reached that stage of being mad where he had no clue who he was really mad at.

Back in his hotel room, alone, he nipped into what was left of last night's scotch and decided that everyone was betraying him, everyone was letting him down. His goombahs up in the city. One asshole gets himself indicted. Does anybody think of telling Al, giving him some notice? No, he's gotta be put through the embarrassment, the humiliation, of having it thrown in his face by the bosses. And what do they do? Do they talk to him like a man, a respected colleague? No, they cut him right out of the loop, treat him like a punk who needs a lesson, and put his worst enemy in charge. Nicky Scotto. Preening wiseass conceited cocky shithead!

And why does all this happen? Why? Because he's trying to have a short vacation with a woman who turns out to be an ungrateful flirty bitch. Couple of hours on her own, she's throwing herself at some big hairy guy with muscles. And does she have one shred of sympathy or understanding for what he's up against, the pressure that he's under? Does she cut him any slack at all? No. He has one tiny second of losing his temper, and she has the gall to walk.

Well, she'd be back—he had no doubt of that. All her stuff was here; he was still her ticket home. She'd walk off her hurt feelings, size up her situation, and return.

But what if she returned and found Al moping and drinking in their empty room? How would it look? It would look like he was a little bit lost without her, like he had nothing better to do than brood and pace and wait to see if they could turn things around and maybe try again.

It wouldn't do to have her see that, think that. Wouldn't do at all.

So Big Al Marracotta, clutching his glass in one hand, started undressing with the other. He'd get into his cabana suit and go down to the pool. Let Katy know he wasn't about to piss away the day just because she got huffy. Let her see that he was perfectly content to tan alone, sneaking peeks at the breasts and asses of other men's girlfriends, sipping coladas at the swim-up bar without the hassle of a moody, flirty woman cluttering up his mind.

"Nothing till nine-thirty," said the desk clerk, muffling the phone against his chest. He said it with a smile, happy in the knowledge that it caused inconvenience to the suburban salesman and his unregistered, unpaid-for visitor.

"I'll take it," Katy said, bearing down to hold on to her resolve. Leaving was never easy, and leaving something awful was in some ways harder than leaving something almost good.

"So what now?" Al asked her, when the booking had been made. "Wanna hang out here?"

Secretly, the desk clerk winced. Ruby studs moved above his eyebrow.

Katy bit her lip, considered. "What I'd really like to do is go back to the beach. See that green water. Wanna come along?"

This sounded good to Al. After these few days wholly on his own, it was a relief to have someone else suggest a plan. But he could not help glancing down at his blistered feet. "How 'bout we call a cab."

Katy suddenly brightened. Her jaw relaxed, her eyes got wide, she stopped looking like somebody's mistress and resembled instead a kid with a day off from school. "Let's rent bikes!" she said. "That's what people do here. Rent bikes and ride around with maps."

Al cleared his throat to stall for time. He hadn't ridden a bicycle in many years.

Wanting to be rid of them so he could settle back into his semi-doze, the desk clerk said, "There are a couple here that you could use."

So they got on clunky one-speed cruisers and rode off to the beach.

Al put Fifi in his basket. She clamped her tiny claws around the wire mesh as her master jerked the handlebars, causing palms and mopeds and other bicyclists to sweep past in a sunshot blur. Katy seemed unhindered by her high-heeled sandals; without apparent effort she stood up on the pedals and held her slender butt above the seat. They rode through the faux-Bahamian development and down the sandy road between the navy fences until they reached the shore.

Afternoon was well advanced by then. The Australian pines threw long and feathery shadows. Sunburned people with beach chairs held in the crooks of their arms were heading for the parking lot. On the water, catamarans were returning from the reef; the yellow sun seemed at moments to balance on their giant masts. Al and Katy sat down at a spot where the sloping sand was at an angle like a lounge.

Katy curled up, knees to chest, and stared out at the water as though she didn't expect to see anything so beautiful for a long, long time, as if trying to memorize the shifting patterns of emerald green with gold-white flashes. At some point she glanced at Alan Tuschman's striped Bermudas. "Jeez," she said, "I didn't even give you time to change. You could've swam."

"Not me," said Al. "Swam here yesterday. Got chased by a shark."

"A shark?"

"Were, like, thirty other people swimming. Thing zeroed in on me like it had radar."

Katy shook her head. "Car heist. Shark attack. Now you're stuck baby-sitting me. You always so unlucky?"

"You always so down on yourself?" he countered.

It was mostly just a reflex quip, but Katy took the question seriously. She'd kicked off her sandals; now she sighed and buried her toes in sand. "No," she said. "I don't think always. Just the last thirteen, fourteen years or so."

Al did not know what to say to that. He lay back on his hands, felt hot sun underneath his chin.

As if she were talking to herself, Katy said, "Before that I think I was a pretty happy kid. Felt safe. Felt confident. Then I sort of messed it up."

Alan Tuschman briefly weighed the words, then said, "Got pregnant?"

Katy swiveled toward him, sand making a crunching sound beneath her. "How'd you know?"

"I did the math and took a wild guess."

Katy stared down at her knees.

Al said, "Come on, everyone gets pregnant at that age."

"Not exactly everyone."

"Get pregnant, crash a car—everybody makes the same mistakes."

"Maybe," Katy said. "But not everybody's from a really Catholic family in a really Catholic neighborhood."

"Ah," said Al. "You had the kid?"

Katy nodded. "Dropped out of school. Hid out. A sinner with the nuns."

There was a pause. Offshore, a schooner tacked, its sails flapping like wet laundry until they filled.

Katy looked away and said, "I don't talk about this stuff."

"Hey, we're on vacation."

She didn't quite see what difference that made. "Your life is still your life."

"Okay. But you're allowed a little breather from it now and then."

Katy pouted. She watched Fifi busily digging a hole in the sand, wondered if the dog had some deep purpose in doing so. She surprised herself by going on. "You give away a baby, it's supposed to haunt you, right? Well, call me unmaternal, it isn't that for me. I mean, sure, it's weird to think I have a kid out there somewhere. But he, she—they're better off adopted. That's the simple truth. What gets me, though . . . I just lost my momentum. Never really got on track again. Forgot how to be a regular person around regular people. Understand?"

Al half nodded. He wanted to say something but nothing would come.

It didn't matter. Katy wasn't stopping now. "You know what it's like? It's like when people choose up sides in the playground. But now it's like the teams are the good people and the bad people. And once you make a big mistake, and your father calls you terrible things and your family is ashamed of you, you get put on the bad team. And then the people on the bad team are your friends, whether or not you really like them. They're your people. The good people—you sort of stop understanding them, stop knowing how to talk to them, stop knowing how to meet them even. So you're stuck. It doesn't change. You see?"

Al came up a little ways on sandy elbows. "Except it can change. Any day."

She tried to smile, waved her arms like she was swatting hope away. Again she looked off at the water. The colors kept changing as the sun slipped lower. Finally she said, "It's nice to talk to you." She twisted up her mouth. "I just wish you had a different name. Nickname, even. Didn't you ever have a different nickname?"

Al hesitated, then confessed. "Had one all through childhood. Hated it."

"What was it?"

He shook his head.

"Come on," she urged. "We're on vacation."

He reached forward, brushed some sand from above his dog's eyes. "Tusch."

"Tusch?"

"Last name's Tuschman. And as a kid I had a big behind."

"Tusch," she said again. "Mind if I call you that instead of, you know, that other name?"

Al grimaced though he didn't really mind.

"Come on," she said, "it's only for a few more hours."

He grabbed his dog and wrestled her a little bit. "Okay. What the hell," he said. "Only for a few more hours."

24

Big Al Marracotta was quietly flabbergasted when Katy had
not returned by sunset. Very gradually, in blips of irritation and
waves of masked regret, he lost his certainty that she was coming
back at all.

He'd been drinking at a measured pace all afternoon, never
quite getting drunk, but proceeding on a slow slide from anger
and frustration to befuddlement and self-pity. At moments he
even felt a grudging respect for his vanished girlfriend, for her
moxie in standing up to him and skipping.

When thoughts like that began occurring to him, he'd wade
over to the swim-up bar and have another cocktail.

The day dragged on. Eventually the sun dipped behind the
building; an oblong of shadow crept across the pool. People
started leaving. They left in couples; they had other things to do;
and Big Al hated them for it. Curtains were drawn across the
sliding glass doors of the lanai rooms. The shutters were closed
on the towel kiosk. With maybe half a dozen sun-fried people
still glued to their lounges, Big Al got up to leave. He was
damned if he was going to be the last one there, lying by himself
like some kind of loser.

He went back upstairs to the room. In spite of himself, pretending that he wasn't doing it, he snooped around to see if Katy
had perhaps been by. Everything was as before. Her suitcase on

its stand next to the armoire; her makeup kit on the bathroom counter, unzipped and gaping open. The two big bags of goodies from the porno store. They mocked him now: all those toys and no one to play with.

He sat down on the bed, reached deep for another dose of anger to chase away the gloom. "Fuck her," he said aloud, though with faltering conviction. He had three more lousy days down here before returning to the shitstorm in New York, and one way or another he was going to make them memorable.

He picked up the phone, called room service, and ordered himself a steak and a bottle of red wine.

Half an hour later, the waiter's knocking on the door woke him from a leaden sleep.

Katy and Al Tuschman watched sunset at the beach. They saw the sun squeeze out of round just before it touched the water; saw its reflection rise to meet it, transforming it for a time into a fat and melting candle; saw it slip at last beneath the surface like a vast quarter sliding down a slot.

Watching it together both was and was not wonderful. Sunsets were supposed to be romantic. You were supposed to watch them with your arm around someone. At the final instant, you kissed as a token of shared passage from bright day to tender evening, and then you strolled off in the twilight hand in hand.

Al and Katy, mere acquaintances in a nutty situation, did none of that. They sat with their knees and elbows close but not touching. As near as they came to contact was in taking turns petting the dog. They stared off at the sky until the sparse, underlit clouds had gone from flaming pink to a powdery lavender; then by silent agreement they stood, unceremoniously slapping sand off their bottoms. Al resisted looking at his watch. In the wistful awkwardness of the moment, he wasn't even sure if he wanted the time until Katy's departure to go faster or more slowly than was natural.

They walked to their bikes. Finally Al said, "Feel like a drink? Something t'eat?"

Katy, not used to being consulted, just shrugged at first, then said, "Sure."

They pedaled off between the navy fences, through the fake development; then, on Thomas Street, before they'd reached the busy part of town, they heard music coming from behind a wooden fence that was painted blue and pink and green. A hand-scrawled sign said the place was called Coco's. In place of valet parking, it offered a row of bike racks that were full of locals' clunkers.

"Chance it?" asked Al Tuschman.

Katy nodded, widened her eyes. They crammed their fat-tire bikes in among the others and went around the fence.

They walked through a short passageway and were immediately outdoors again—in a side yard paved in nothing but stomped earth. Well-spaced tables leaned in ruts, and no two tables matched. A hammock was strung between a rubber tree and a mahogany; an old man and a child seemed to be asleep in it. Chickens roamed around; Fifi sniffed their tracks. The music was Caribbean, took its slippery rhythms from the scratch and recoil of blowing palms, the surge and fizz of lapping waves.

Al and Katy moved to the far end of the place, found a vacant table with a rooster on it. Al shooed the bird away; it cackled out a protest, then half flew, half hopped, first to a chair back, then the ground.

"This is excellent," said Katy, sitting down.

Al was happy she was happy, pleased with himself for stumbling on a place she liked. He had to remind himself this was not a date.

The waitress came over and they ordered margaritas.

Clinking salty glasses, Katy gestured up toward swaying fronds against the jewel-box velvet of the sky, over at the dim bandstand where a Bahamian trio, cool beyond words, played like they could play forever, and said, "Cheers. Now *this* is what

I pictured. Now I feel like I'm on vacation." She sipped her drink and added, "Better late than never, huh?"

The comment made Al Tuschman unpleasantly aware of the watch on his wrist. "Hungry?"

She pursed her lips. "I could eat."

They ordered jerk chicken and popcorn shrimp.

Pretending to scratch a bug bite, Al sneaked a look at the time. It was ten of eight, and he too was only now beginning to feel like he was truly on vacation. Unless, that is, vacation truly felt like being lonely, and paranoid, and discombobulated.

"So Tusch," said Katy, "can I ask you something? Traveling alone—it's a fantasy of mine, I envy it. The freedom. You love it?"

Al pulled on an ear. "Has its moments," he said. "But the novelty's sort of over. I spend a lot of time alone."

She studied him, the strong shoulders and big kind face and curly hair. "How come?"

He shrugged. "I work a lot. Where I live, the 'burbs, it's sixteen-year-old girls in Camaros or soccer moms in minivans. I live long enough, I'll catch the next wave of divorcées."

"Ever married yourself?"

"Long time ago. Too young. Wrong person."

It was as good a time as any to signal for another round of drinks.

They clinked glasses once again, knocking loose damp salt. A breeze moved through the yard, carrying smells of spent flowers and clove and cinnamon from the kitchen. Katy took a small sip of her cocktail, then looked up and down and left and right, and said out of the blue, "Wanna dance?"

Al had still been thinking vaguely of his ill-considered past. The question took him by surprise. He pulled his brows together, let slip a nervous laugh, then glanced quickly, furtively around the yard. People were eating. People were drinking. Nobody was dancing. "I don't think this is a dancing place," he said.

"Come on," she said. "It's dirt. There's chickens. Who cares?"

"I don't know how to dance to this stuff."

But Katy was already getting up, her long body smoothly unfolding. "Please?" she said, holding out her hand. "I wanna be able to remember that I danced by moonlight in Key West. Come on—two minutes of your life."

With grave misgivings, Al Tuschman dabbed his big lips on his napkin, rose on creaky ankles.

Katy stood before him, ballroom style. He took her hand, which was very cool from cradling her drink. As lightly as he could, he held her waist. Warmth came through her shirt, he felt the long muscles that let her bend and rise so neatly. He silently counted several beats, then they started dancing. The dance they did was a little like a stiff-kneed samba, a little like the first foxtrot kids ever learn, sweaty-handed in the junior high school gym.

They'd danced for maybe thirty seconds, made it three quarters of the way around their small table, when the waitress showed up with their plates in either hand, trailing plumes of fragrant steam.

They dropped their hands and sat back down. A few people briefly applauded.

Al's face was flushed. His knees tingled and he was very aware of the pulse in his neck. None of this had to do with holding Katy in his arms; of that he was quite sure. She had a plane to catch in an hour and a quarter. She was the mistress of a jealous bully; she imagined she was finished with him, but chances are they would drift unwholesomely together once again. Besides, she wasn't even Al Tuschman's type—that spiky hair, the suspect lashes matted with mascara. No—this accidental excitement he was feeling . . . okay, this thrill—it didn't have to do with her. All it was, was nerves from standing up to dance with people watching. Neither more nor less than that.

He sipped his margarita and looked across the table. Katy was smiling broadly above her plate of shrimp. Her eyes were bright, and sinews stood out in her throat. "That was great," she said. "That was the nicest thing I've done down here. Thanks."

To his amazement and chagrin, Al heard himself say, "Wanna do it more?"

Katy had just picked up her fork. Now she was a little bit confused. She looked from Al to her shrimp and back again.

Himself confused, Al said, "I don't mean right this second." He seized his knife, cut into his chicken, and smiled weakly.

They had some bites of food.

"How's the time?" asked Katy. She said it as neutrally as it could be said, but still there was something like death in the words.

"Sucks," said Al. "How's the shrimp?"

"Umm," she said. Her mouth was full. She gestured for him to try some.

He did. He chewed awhile. Then he put his fork down. He looked at Katy, who was not his type and who, at the very least, was on an instant messy rebound. But they'd watched the sun go down together. They'd danced. He'd eaten off her plate. Knowing that he shouldn't say it, he said, "That plane. You really wanna go?"

She looked away and wiped her mouth. "Oh, Jesus. Please don't ask me that."

He sipped his drink. It had lost its chill and tasted very salty. The tireless musicians played without a lapse. He said, "Simple question. What's so terrible I'm asking?"

Katy said nothing. Her fork jabbed toward her shrimp again, and then it stopped midair.

Al found himself staring at her fingers. He could see that they were bearing down, blanched around the nails. He wondered if he was tipsier than he'd realized. Fumbling, he said, "Look . . . hey, listen . . . I don't know exactly how to say this. I'm not asking you to sleep with me."

Katy only gaped and blinked at that, touched, relieved, befuddled, and just a little bit insulted all at once.

"You wanna stay," he rambled, "we could see the town. Dance. There's a sofa in my room."

Katy dropped her fork, picked up her drink. "A sofa?" She looked past Al at the shrubbery, the arching palms, the orange mist around the streetlamps on this rare and humid night. Incredulous, she said, "You're asking me to be your roommate?"

25

Big Al and his rage woke up together from their nap.

Sitting on the edge of his vacant bed to eat his room-service steak, he thought angry thoughts that made him chew so hard he could feel it in the sockets of his teeth. An infuriating sense of wasted time assailed him. Time wasted on a moody broad who dragged him away from running his business and then turned out to be a flaky brat. Katy's betrayal—what else could he call it?—made him hanker to humiliate her, but it was tough to take revenge against someone who wasn't there. It called for ingenuity.

He ate his steak, drank his wine, and thought it over.

After a while, he dropped his utensils, mopped his mouth, and pushed away the rolling table, pushed it so vigorously as to tip the tiny bud vase with its single drooping orchid.

Leaning to his right, he opened the drawer of his night table and grabbed the knife he kept always within reach. It was long and slender with a brushed edge and a razor point, good for filleting and concealment. The plastic handle was flat and unobtrusive. The narrow blade slid smartly into a supple leather sheath; when he wore it on his person it barely made a bulge in his sock.

He admired the weapon a moment, then leaped the short distance between his small feet and the floor. Theatrically, he paused before moving with the measured steps of a toreador toward Katy's suitcase, still propped up on its stand. Knife in hand, he contemplated her lingerie, then leaned into a slow and lewd assault upon it.

He lifted up a lacy bra, severed the well-formed cups one from the other. He raised a translucent red negligee, vented it at chest and tummy. He skewered panties, halved thongs into the shapes of slingshots. He wrestled with stockings, tatters of nylon falling around him like dark snow. In his gradually accelerating fury, unsprung clasps and ribbons of spandex were tossed around the room.

Titillated by his deranged exertions, Big Al broke into a rutting sweat. He destroyed a final garter belt, murdered a last chemise, then threw himself into an armchair and surveyed with pleasure the black and pastel mess he'd made. Let her come back, he thought, and find *that*.

In the next heartbeat he edited the thought; in fact, erased it. He wasn't thinking about her coming back. He didn't want her to come back. He was over it already. He was moving on.

He'd be going out tonight. Hitting the bars. Pick up a sex-starved tourist or, failing that, a hooker. Get back on track, vacationwise. And, just in case his former girlfriend Katy happened to swing by to retrieve her things, let her find him with someone else. Let her see how easily replaced she was, how little she'd really mattered.

Katy and Al Tuschman finished up their dinner, then lingered over coffee to hear the island music and watch the chickens scratching in the dirt.

By the time they left the courtyard, it was well after nine. Heading for Duval Street, they slowly pedaled their borrowed bikes through air the temperature of skin. Katy now and then heard airplanes flying in and flying out, wondered which one she was supposed to be on. She was surprised at herself for staying; more surprised to have been invited. Now and then she stole a look at Al, wobbling along beside her with his dog in his basket. Straightforward, decent, he was just the sort of man she'd forgotten how to understand. Grateful for his gallantry, she told herself that when they parked the bikes and walked, it would be nice to take his arm. But she doubted she would really do it because she doubted that he wanted her to. That's how much she didn't understand him.

Duval Street was crowded and it gleamed with the ghoulish colors of humming neon. Drunks weaved among tourists trying to be drunk. Southern girls strutted by in tight lace shirts, their piled hair fighting off the dampness.

Al and Katy locked their bikes to a tree. Al bent down to tie his shih tzu to a parking meter. The dog looked at him with resignation and maybe just a hint of blame. They picked a bar more or less at random.

The place had music but no dancing. After a while Katy tapped Al on the back of his hand. He was looking at the bandstand, he hadn't expected to be touched, and he jumped a little bit. "Still wanna dance?" she shouted.

He did, but the truth was that his nerve had been eroding. Dancing at Coco's was one thing—it had just happened. Now he was *planning* to dance. This was different. "First let's have another drink," he shouted back.

Around eleven they were on the sidewalk once again. Retrieved the yawning dog. Left the bikes and strolled up the still-mobbed street. Katy thought to take Al's arm but didn't. After a couple of blocks they saw, reflected on parked cars and café umbrellas, the edgy, shattered light of a disco ball. They traced the flecks of glare to a second-floor club above an outdoor restaurant. Katy looked at Al. Al swallowed hard, wrapped Fifi's leash around a bike rack.

They went upstairs and danced. Danced like Al hadn't danced in many years, and like he never thought his grinding knees and gnarly ankles would let him dance again.

They left around one-thirty. A red moon was low in the west.

Fifi was tangled in her leash and sulking. They reclaimed their bikes and shakily headed home toward Paradise, much too tired and too secretly nervous at being roommates to notice the Jaguar parked across from the hotel in the ragged shadow of the buttonwoods.

Big Al Marracotta's evening had not been going all that well.

He'd been in several bars, and he was fairly drunk before he'd started. But he'd made a plan and he was sticking to it. For the sake of both economy and sport, he'd decided to give it until midnight to find some sex he wouldn't have to pay for. Your basic pickup. Sex with a lonely visitor who needed her cigarette lit, who was waiting for her package tour to be made complete.

But with this stratagem he'd gotten nowhere. Women kept turning their backs on him. Big Al wasn't used to this. The places he went to in New York—they were Mob places, and he was recognized, if not by name, at least by type. The women there were looking for that type. This made Al mistakenly imagine that he was attractive. But these tourist women—from Iowa, from Ontario—what did they know from Mafia? Too ignorant to be impressed with what he did, they saw him only for what he was: a short gruff pushy guy with shiny shoes.

After midnight he started looking for a hooker. To his surprise, this turned out to be not so easy either. Again, it was a question of style. Al's eyes were peeled for a good old-fashioned New York whore: the slinky one-zip dress, the blowjob lipstick, the stockings with their dark tops showing just a little. Al couldn't seem to find that type, though he looked in several likely joints, and had a few more drinks in the process. Stumbling now on a sidewalk no longer horizontal, he wandered toward the oceanfront, looking for a floozy by the seawall. Nothing doing.

Once more he staggered up Duval Street. A fleeting spasm of wisdom came to him in the guise of nausea, told him he was probably too smashed to function anyway, and he may as well go back to his hotel. But just then, half a block away, he spotted a woman who came very close to his ideal. She was tall. Her skirt was short, her stockings obvious. In silhouette her chest made a long grade to the summit. She was standing outside a bar that Al had missed, finishing up a cigarette. She met his eye; he was sure she did. She dropped the butt on the sidewalk, snuffed it out with a twist of high-heeled shoe that refreshed Big Al's libido, and sashayed back inside.

He followed her in, moved through close-packed tables, and found her at the bar. As was right and fitting, she was unsurprised to see him. Not without some difficulty, he climbed onto a barstool next to her. "Buy you a drink?"

"I love that opening," she said.

Al didn't take the sarcasm personally. Sass was part of the routine. He liked it. He gestured toward the bartender. They ordered drinks and he sized her up. Good wig but arousingly fake, blond above dark brows. Thick, cakey bands of eyeliner continuing past the edges of her eyes. Powdered cleavage delving into tempting shadow.

The drinks came. Al said, "Ya don't mind, let's get down to business."

"Can we have a toast at least?" the hooker said. Rather forcefully, she clinked his glass. "Bottoms up."

They drank. Al said, "I want the whole night and I don't want no to anything. How much?"

The hooker let her cold glass rest against her lip a moment. "Five hundred."

"That's big-city prices," Al observed.

"So? You wanna get fucked or you wanna ride the subway?"

Al looked down at the hooker's backside. "Riding the subway doesn't sound like such a bad idea."

"Five hundred. Free transfer."

"Deal," said Al. "Let's go." Gingerly, he started climbing down.

The hooker didn't budge. "Can't a girl even finish her drink?"

Grudgingly, Big Al climbed up again. The sudden change of direction made him just a little dizzy. He sipped his drink, and somewhere between the sip and the swallow he got the first inkling that something was not exactly right. He couldn't put his finger on it. He looked at the hooker. There was something a little too playful at the corners of her mouth. He glanced all around the bar. He liked tall women but this looked like a hoops squad. Redheads whose necks were on the thick side, brunettes with voices huskier than average. And there was something in the air, something barely smellable beneath the layers of flowery perfume, an elusive whiff of mannish sweat.

Big Al dropped his slurring voice. "You sure you're a woman?"

The hooker said, "Honey, I'm all the woman you can handle."

She said it a little louder than it needed to be said, and it dawned on Al that she wanted other people to hear it, that other people had been listening all along. Through a fog of alcohol he dimly realized that this was not the normal sass, that he was being mocked. His lips pulled taut across his teeth and his hairline started itching. "Don't fuck with me," he said.

The hooker gave an unafraid, coy shrug that really pissed him off.

With his chin he gestured toward her crotch. "I find a dick down there, I swear ta Christ I'll cut it off."

"*Now* you tell me, sweetie. Cost me a Miata to have a fancy surgeon do that very thing."

Big Al Marracotta blinked, and in the blink he was visited by a terrifying image of a hairy ersatz vulva between two hairy thighs. What was it made of? Pig intestine? Scrotum skin? Where did it lead? He said to the hooker, "You fucking faggot."

"Yeah, ain't it grand?" she said, and threw the rest of her drink in his face.

It took Big Al a moment to react. Then, eyes burning, cheeks dripping, he reached down blindly toward the knife he carried in his sock. But before his fingers could find the handle, the hooker grabbed him by the shirtfront and shoved him backward, stool and all. To Al, it felt like he was strapped securely in his seat but the airplane had disintegrated. His head snapped forward then back, his knees had somehow got above his face, he saw the ceiling skating past like a nightmare of galloping sky. He tucked and felt his stomach slide up toward his throat and waited for the sickening collision with the ground.

Two six-foot drag queens caught him just before he hit the floor. Putting dignity aside, he rolled off the stool onto his hands and knees, then scrambled to his feet. His legs trembled and his head was pounding and his innards churned. He longed to punch someone but didn't dare. A large and perfumed group had gathered all around him. Their heaving and emphatic bosoms left him barely room enough to wobble toward the door.

2 6

Al Tuschman hadn't brought pajamas. Katy Sansone had no clothes except the ones she was wearing. They tried not to acknowledge a certain awkwardness as they prepared for bed.

Brushing her teeth with an index finger, Katy examined the outdoor shower and said through toothpaste, "Hey, Tusch, y'ever go to sleepaway camp?"

He was washing his face, reaching for a towel. "Coupla summers. Sports camp, mostly."

"Me, I never did. Always wanted to. Crickets. Marshmallows. Canoes. Ya have canoes?"

Al looked at her. Her eyes were sleepy and her mouth had softened with fatigue. There was an intimacy in seeing someone so frankly tired. They kept talking because they couldn't stand to have the intimacy of silence added to it.

"Canoes," he said. "A raft you could swim to in the middle of the lake. Steps were slimy. Squished between your toes."

He sidled out of the bathroom. In the armoire by the picture of the greenish women with the greenish breasts, he found an extra pillow and a light blanket. He took them over to the sofa in the alcove. Fifi, exhausted and confused, followed him and sniffed at the upholstery. Al turned off the light. Skulking in shadow, he stripped to his jockey shorts and lay down. The sofa was not quite as long as he was, but if he curled his legs it wasn't bad. The dog jumped up and settled in against his feet.

He heard the toilet flush. A wedge of light came through the bathroom door then was extinguished. Katy padded toward the bed; Al could tell her shoes were off. He didn't want to hear it, but he heard the zipper of her shorts. He heard the soft tick of buttons as she laid her blouse over the back of a chair. The bed squeaked a little when she sat down on it, and he could not help wondering if the sheets felt cool or warm against the backs of her long legs. He heard her swivel and lie down. He was relieved to think that by now the cotton blanket was pulled up beneath her chin.

After a moment, she said, "Tusch?"

"Yeah?"

"I think it's really great you're letting me stay here. I think it's really great we danced."

Trying to sound more sleepy than he felt, Al said, "I'm glad you're here."

"Really?"

"Really. Go to sleep."

She was silent for a moment. A soft breeze lifted the curtains from the windowsills.

"Tusch?"

"Yeah?"

"Hear the crickets?"

"I think those are tree frogs."

"Hey, I'm from Queens. G'night."

The sheets rustled once and then Katy seemed to be asleep. Al lay there for a while in his gallant curl. Then he reached down and dragged the dog underneath the blanket till it was nestled in between his arms and chest, and drifted off himself.

Outside in the Jag, Chop Parilla said, "So, Squid, we don't get fancy, right?"

Sid Berman didn't answer, didn't even look Chop's way. He was gathering his concentration, and besides, killing people made him irritable. He didn't like it at all. This was a matter not of sentiment but taste. Other crimes evolved, unfolded. They had a flow to them, a music. But murder was a blank brick wall that stopped the band, destroyed the flow, forced an ending that, by necessity, was always too abrupt. This depressed him.

Edgy, Chop Parilla went on. "You're in, spear 'im, you're out again, I drive away, we're finished. Right?"

"Right," said Berman grudgingly.

It was getting on toward 3:00 A.M. The moon had dimmed to a mauve smudge and set. The streets were quiet except for the electric hum of the streetlamps and a very occasional howl or cackle from a passing drunk. The air had cooled just enough for a patina of condensation to form on the windshields of parked cars.

"What about the broad?" said Chop.

"What about 'er?"

"I don't like it there's someone with him."

"Picked up a chippy. Getting laid before he dies. I think that's kinda nice."

"Nice we got a witness?"

"Chop," said Squid, "imagine this. You've just fucked a guy. Next thing you know he's got a fish stuck through his heart. You gonna notice much besides the fish?"

Chop frowned, drummed fingers on the steering wheel. "I just wish he was alone."

Squid was getting exasperated. "You're the one so anxious to get finished. Ya want we do 'im tonight or ya want we don't?"

Chop just squeezed his lips together.

But all at once Squid was ready, and with the readiness came an awful thrill he could no longer deny. He felt it behind his knees and underneath his tongue.

Swallowing deep, he opened the glove compartment, reached for his powdered rubber gloves, and pulled them on. From underneath his seat, he produced a cylinder of pepper spray, stuck it in the waistband of his pants. "Come on," he said, "it's time."

Chop petted the dashboard then started the Jag, eased it over to the hotel entrance, and sat there softly idling.

Squid pulled a cut-off stocking down over his face. The nylon squashed his nose and tugged at the corners of his eyes, exposed the red rims of his eyelids. He slipped out of the car, reached into the backseat, and retrieved the stuffed fish with the two-foot spike of a nose. He bounced the pad of his index finger against the tip of it. "Fucker's sharp," he said to Chop.

Chop said nothing, just sat there scanning the street with his passenger door wide open.

Squid slipped through the gate of the hotel, darted into the shadow of an oleander, and took a moment to survey the courtyard. Soft blue light hovered as though it were a solid thing above the pool. Empty lounges were arranged in friendly groupings. Wisps of mist escaped from the edges of the hot tub cover.

He looked toward the office. The light was on, the door was open, and he had no choice but to pass quite near it. He took a deep breath, held it. Hunkering low, the fish under his arm, he scooted by the doorway. Out of the corner of his eye he saw the sleeping desk clerk, elbows on the counter, cheeks resting in his palms.

Squid jogged around the still-damp apron of the pool until he reached the gravel path overgrown with giant philodendrons. Small stones crunched beneath his feet, but nothing stirred as he slipped around to the side of Big Al's bungalow and stood in the darkness near the thatch enclosure of the shower. Through the mesh that muffled his nose and mouth, he sniffed the air, freighted with chlorine and salt and iodine. He practiced his grip on the fish. With his right hand around the narrow place just before the tail, he could use his left to guide the thrust. The fish weighed six, eight pounds and would make an admirable harpoon.

He got the pepper spray ready to immobilize the dog.

Then he crawled beneath the thatch onto the wet slats of the shower. He scrabbled to his feet and tried the bathroom door.

Unlocked as always. He let himself in. Smelled soap and tooth-paste and deodorant. Gave his eyes a moment to adjust to the deeper darkness inside the bungalow, then sidled toward the doorway to the bedroom.

Squinting, straining, he studied the bed as though there were some mystic pattern in the rise and fall of the ripples in the cotton blanket. He knew there were two bodies there. He knew that any second the dog would start to yelp and time would shrink to a twitch and he'd have to take his shot. But meanwhile he could see no more than one inchoate lump between the sheets, one heap suggesting tangled limbs and loins.

Readying the fish, he edged closer, his knees nearly touching the foot of the bed, close enough to hear the whoosh of breath. And from this new perspective, the geometry of the bedclothes told him there was just one person on that mattress. Was it possible? It made sense that the chippy would do her business and then slip out. So much the better. But how had she got past them, watching in the Jag?

No time to think about it now.

He inched up along the bedside, following the cocoon that swathed Big Al from heel to head, passing knees, thighs, waist, measuring the distance to the victim's rib cage, to the heart and lungs that would be pierced. He started lifting the fish. Its lac-quered skin had gotten sticky from the heat of his gloved fingers.

He raised the tail above his head. He balanced the abdomen against his other hand so that the death-spike pointed toward Big Al's torso at an angle like a falling bomb. He caught a sharp breath through the nylon that deformed his face, hitched his arms a notch higher, then locked his bandy muscles, fixed his gaze on the lump of flesh about to die, and brought the stuffed fish hurtling down with all his might.

At that instant Katy Sansone twitched the sheet back from her face.

Squid Berman saw the spiky hair, the forehead that was not Big Al's, and was horrified.

The harpoon was heavy, was descending with a dread momentum. This was a debacle. There was nothing artful about killing the wrong person, skewering a chippy. But the spike was coming down and he didn't have the strength to stop it. All in a heartbeat he was wrestling against the very motion that he'd started, his limbs contending wildly against themselves. He clamped down with his arms, tried to suck back gravity with the muscles of his chest, and managed just barely to deflect the grim trajectory of the spike.

It sliced through the blanket and grazed Katy Sansone's flank before sticking eyes-deep in the mattress, impaled as though it had fallen from the sky.

Squid Berman, his balance thrown off in the grotesque and desperate effort to change the course of wrongful murder, fell flat on top of Katy, pushed off again and started running even as she screamed.

Her scream, at last, woke up the dog, which had been insulated from sound and foreign odors by her master's blanket and his breathing and the safe smell of his chest. But now, hair on end, with no thought whatsoever for herself, the valiant shih tzu sprang down from the sofa and lit out on ticking, sliding paws toward the intruder. She caught up with him as he was escaping through the bathroom door. He paused just long enough to shoot pepper at her nose and eyes, then crawled beneath the shower and was gone. Fifi yelped and ran in circles.

Al Tuschman bolted up as well, as quickly as his cramped legs would allow, and ran the short length of the alcove. Groping for the switch, he turned the light on and discovered, through the rude and sudden glare, a bizarre and inexplicable tableau: a painted sailfish having done a face-plant through his mattress, and Katy quivering like an outsized butterfly freshly pinned in wax.

"Jesus. You okay?" he asked.

She couldn't answer right away. She was trembling and she badly needed to slip out from under the pole-axed blanket, to persuade herself she wasn't really trapped there.

The dog, in torment, found Al's feet, whimpered piteously against his ankles.

He picked her up and stroked her head, and watched the pale and quaking Katy wriggle toward the edge of the sheet.

To no one in particular he said, "God Almighty. And I really thought my luck was changing."

THREE

27

Al Tuschman stood inside the thatch enclosure and held his dog high up beneath a tepid shower. Fifi didn't like the splash and dribble of the water but it was better than the burn of pepper. She trusted that her master was doing the right thing.

Katy Sansone was leaning against the counter by the sink. With a pale green washcloth she dabbed at the thin line of drying blood that stained her right side, just above the waist.

It was three-thirty in the morning. Adrenaline had rendered them wide awake and almost sober. Calamity was intimate but not immediately sexy; they felt hardly any discomfort now, standing in their underwear.

Turning off the shower, wrapping the wet dog in a bath towel, Al said, "Didja see anybody? Anything?"

Katy shook her head, kept dabbing at the blood. The thin red line would disappear and then re-form, a little fainter every time. "Someone fell on top of me. That's all I felt. Didn't even feel the cut. Didn't see a thing."

Rubbing the dog in the towel, Al said, "Maybe the clerk."

They retreated to their separate corners, retrieved their clothes, and dressed. The stuffed fish was still poised in its improbable headstand on the bed, its spined fin spread proudly open like a winning hand of cards. They left it there as evidence.

Outside, the layer of blue light still sat atop the pool. Giant leaves secretly savored the hours of dripping dew. Al carried Fifi as he and Katy crunched over the gravel to the office.

They found the desk clerk dozing with his elbows on the desk. A tiny muted television threw an anemic glare on one side of his face. With a considerate softness, Al said, "Excuse me . . ."

If the clerk heard him at all, he heard him in a dream. A mouth corner tightened, ruby studs moved on his eyebrow.

Louder, Al said, "Excuse me!"

The clerk blinked himself awake.

"Did you just see someone sneak in and out of here?" Al asked him.

"Hm?"

Al put his hands flat on the counter, leaned across them. "Look. Someone just broke in here with a giant fish and tried to kill her. I'm asking if you saw anyone."

Sleepily the clerk said, "Giant fish?"

Al said, "You are really worthless."

People are sensitive when they first wake up. The desk clerk flushed and for an instant seemed about to cry. "You don't have to get nasty, Mr. Tuschman. I've worked eight straight shifts."

"I know, I know," said Al, feeling guilty now. "Rents are high. How 'bout you call the cops for us, at least."

The clerk stifled a yawn then reached stiffly toward the phone. His hand was lifting the receiver when Katy softly said, "No."

Al looked at her in her pink shorts and lime-green blouse and high-heeled sandals. "No?"

Katy's near-demise had focused her attention, and she'd been thinking hard. She'd been thinking about nicknames. About license plates. About how that other Al was treated in the seafood restaurants they used to go to in the city. "Tusch," she said, "I think we better talk."

"Mafia?" said Alan Tuschman. The word felt odd in his mouth, felt like a stranger had borrowed his voice to say it.

Katy blew steam from the surface of her coffee. "I mean," she said, "you never know for sure. But, hey."

She broke off with a shrug and Al looked out the window, checked on Fifi, tied up to a parking meter. They were sitting in an all-night diner on Duval. The bars had just closed and there was something bleakly, forsakenly transitional about the scene outside. It could almost have been quitting time in a mill town somewhere. People wandered, glazed, unsatisfied, wondering what was left for them to do with the dregs of time until they slept. Cop cars cruised by slowly, waiting for the sluggish, drunken fights to start.

Katy went on. "This much I know—he was having business troubles in New York. That's what all of a sudden put him in such a rotten mood. Whoever he works for, they put his worst enemy in charge. That bent him really outa shape."

Al played with his spoon and thought it over. "I just don't see what this poor bastard's business troubles have to do with you almost getting murdered."

Katy sipped her coffee. Out in the unnatural twilight of the sidewalk, two guys started cursing at each other. Softly, she said, "Tusch—or should I say Big Al?—who was supposed to be in that bed?"

Al blinked. He plucked at his shirtfront, twisted his neck from one side to the other. He ran his hands over his torso where the spike would have gone in. "Now wait a second . . ."

Katy waited several seconds, but Al could not continue right away.

Finally, with the brittle logic of someone trying to convince himself, he went on. "Look. He's from New York, I'm from Jersey. He's in seafood, I sell furniture. He's like five foot two, I'm six foot three. Someone mixed us up? . . . Nah, it's too ridiculous."

"Okay, it's ridiculous," said Katy. She paused as a waitress went by with a cinnamon roll. The cinnamon smelled great. "Mind I get a Danish?"

"Get a Danish."

She ordered it and then resumed. "So, Tusch, okay, it's ridiculous. But lemme ask you something. Do you have friends or enemies who are the kind of people who would put rotten calamari in someone's car?"

"No."

"He does."

The Danish arrived. She cut it into wedges and started eating one.

"Lemme ask you something else. Among your circle of acquaintances, are there guys who specialize in finding weird new ways to murder people in their beds?"

Al pulled on his face. It had been a long night and the skin felt very loose. Absently, he picked up and chomped a piece of Danish, swallowed it along with the conclusion he could no longer fend off. "It's one big fat mistake?" he murmured. "The whole thing's been one big fat mistake?"

Katy shrugged and sipped her coffee.

Al sipped his, then suddenly brought forth a quick and honking chuckle. He tried to put some sportsmanship in it but that didn't work. "I don't know whether to laugh or be really pissed."

She looked at him over the rim of her cup. "Be pissed. It might come in handy."

She said it as an ally. He knew she did, but still, the comment worried him. She saw the worry in his face.

"Look," she went on, "I know a little bit about these people. They're bullies. Real tough till you stand up to them."

"Stand up to them?" said Al. "They're killers. Me, I haven't had a fight since junior high."

"Come on. You're big. You're strong."

"I'm chicken."

He tried to say it lightly, blithely, but at 4:00 A.M. things have a way of coming out truer than they are really meant to. Katy's face told Al that his joke had failed but his revelation had succeeded. He prepared to flush with embarrassment. But he looked at Katy's unmocking eyes, and the embarrassment didn't come. He felt relief instead. He heard himself keep talking.

"I've always been chicken. Playing sports. The pressure, the contact, you could get wracked up any second. Always scared. Never admitted it. Can't admit it if you're big. Some people see right through it, though. Like my boss. Ya know what he told me just as I was leaving to come down here? Told me, 'Al, you're big, you're strong, but deep down you're a softie.' Killed me with that."

Katy said, "I think it's nice."

"Nice," said Al dismissively. "Nice for selling dinettes. Less nice for dealing with the Mafia."

Katy started picking up another piece of Danish, put it down again, and placed her hand on top of Al's. Her hand was a little sticky but he liked it. "Tusch," she said, "everyone's afraid. Doesn't matter you're afraid, matters what you do."

It mattered to him. He looked at her and frowned. Outside, a patrol car had turned its beacon on; cold blue light raked across the diner window. Fifi had started barking.

"You'll do what needs doing," she told him. "I know you will."

He doubted it. He said, "How's your side? It hurt?"

"No big deal," she said. "Hey—how 'bout we find someplace to watch the sun come up?"

28

On Long Island, dawn was on a dimmer, the sun thwarted like an unlucky performer who couldn't find the break in the curtain. Light barely trickled through a chilly haze the color of weak tea. It was an hour before there was brightness enough to quell the streetlamps and throw the first, faint shadows from basketball hoops and minivans crouched in asphalt driveways.

In his four-bedroom split-level, Nicky Scotto woke up nervous. He tried to convince himself that it was a happy nervous, the nervousness that came with triumph. Big Al Marracotta should be dead by now. If everything had gone well, that is. His own control of the fish market should be secure—assuming he'd rightly interpreted Tony Eggs' sphinxlike advice.

But what if he hadn't?

Too late, the rashness and the riskiness of his strategy was getting through to Nicky. He'd unilaterally called a hit on a powerful and well-connected man. Cagey old Tony had stopped well short of saying anything that would make him party to the call; he could totally disclaim it with a shrug, a lifted eyebrow. What if something went wrong? What if it was only his ambition that made Nicky imagine that he'd got the go-ahead?

He tried not to think about it. He showered and shaved and dressed for work.

But at the fish market office, his antsiness only increased. Big Al's things were still around. The edges of his family portraits stuck out from underneath the phone books. His calendar had a dentist's appointment marked down on it. This gave Nicky the creeps, brought home to him the enormity of what he'd set in motion.

Besides, he could not get comfortable in his cheap new suit. The rough wool chafed him behind the knees. The stiff sleeves bound him at the elbows. His lapels would not lie flat, and he could not banish the thought that when he saw guys whose lapels stuck out like that, he thought of them as pissants.

The morning went very slowly. He kept waiting to be summoned to the pay phone across the yard, to get the news that his nemesis had in fact been iced. He tugged on his lapels. The call didn't come.

Finally, around ten-thirty, he broke down and decided to get in touch with Florida.

He left the office, went outside, trudged through oily puddles and around the loading dock, and lifted the freezing-cold receiver to his ear. Inhaling diesel, exhaling steam, he dialed. The phone rang a long time and then a sleepy Chop said, "Yeah?"

"So what's the story?"

"Nicky?"

"No, Santa Claus. Didja do 'im yet?"

Chop struggled up onto an elbow, used his other hand to rub his eyes. "Well, not exactly."

"Fuck is not exactly? Ya did 'im or ya didn't."

"We tried," Chop said. "He wasn't in his bed. Some broad was there."

Nicky could not help being curious. "Tall broad?"

"How you know?"

"Lotta attitude? Kathy, Kitty, somethin' like that?"

"Squid went in wit' a stocking on his head," said Chop. "I don't think they chatted."

Nicky did a little dance to warm his feet. "Okay, okay. So when ya gonna try again?"

Dryly, Chop said, "I guess when Squid wakes up."

There was a pause. Nicky shivered and tried to figure why his cheap new suit made him sweat indoors but didn't keep him the least bit warm outside. Must be a fucking blend.

"Nicky," Chop went on at last, "this isn't turning out to be as easy as you think it is."

"Come on. The guy's on his own, ya know where he is—"

"Squid won't use a gun or a knife."

"So let 'im use a wire, an ice pick—"

"He won't use anything but seafood."

"Say wha'?"

"Seafood. He started the job wit' seafood, he says he won't finish any other way. Last night's try was wit' a sailfish."

"Sailfish?"

"Stuffed. Ya know, the nose."

"For Christ's fucking sake," said Nicky.

"You wanted a genius," said Chop. "You got one."

Nicky chewed his lip, wrapped himself in the cold, metal housing of the phone wire. "Chop, I ain't got time for this. Tell Squid—"

"I've told him," Chop interrupted. "The fucking guy's impossible. I don't know what he's gonna do. Get a octopus ta strangle 'im? Give 'im a heart attack wit' men-a-war?"

Nicky finally realized that, on top of his frustration, he was getting very scared. He'd hired lunatics and they were blowing it. His plot would be discovered and he'd be sure as hell rubbed out. Every hour that passed increased the chances it would go that way. In a pinched, congested voice, he said, "I want him done today. Today."

Chop said calmly, "Nicky, I'm bein' as straight wit' you as I can be. All I can promise you is seafood. I can't promise you today, I can't promise you tomorra—"

Nicky Scotto slammed down the phone, slammed it down with such gusto that he felt the lining in the right shoulder of his cheap new suit begin to tear.

In the narrow bed across from Chop's, Squid Berman was still pretending to be asleep. But he couldn't quite hide that he was smiling. He was winning. He was happy. He was doing things his way and not letting anybody spoil it.

Big Al Marracotta had had worse outings, but they'd generally entailed someone ending up in a car compactor or a garbage dump. For an occasion not involving death, the misery of this last night would be hard to top.

Humiliated in the drag bar, he'd staggered up Duval Street, back toward his hotel. But his nerves were shaken, and he needed one more drink. He had it, then resumed his journey. His legs were tired, however; the walk seemed long, and he decided to break it up by stopping for another cocktail. By 4:00 A.M. he was within two blocks of the Conch House. Cruelly, the lights came up in the last place that would serve him, and he threw himself into the meandering stream of diehards on the sidewalk. Surrounded by taller men, unseeing and unseen, he'd stumbled right past the glaring window of an all-night diner. A stupid little dog had singled him out to bark at.

Back in his room at last, he took some aspirin and immediately threw up. Rising from the bowl, he'd wandered to the bedroom and walked around in dizzy circles, looking down at the tattered shreds of Katy's underthings. Then he'd passed out, small and alone and smelling foul, on the huge bed meant for frolicking.

He awoke now to a shard of late-morning sun slicing through the drapes and a monumental hangover. His eyeballs had dried out, his cheeks stuck to his gums. His kidneys felt like they had sugar crystals deep inside them. He put a pillow on his head but could not get back to sleep. Finally he called room service, ordered every purported cure that he could think of. Tomato juice. Oysters. Soft-boiled eggs.

In the agony of waiting for his breakfast, he tried but failed to fend off a terrible admission: vacation, all in all, was going lousy.

For a rare and blurry introspective second, he wished he could pinpoint and repair the moment it had all gone wrong, but he knew that he could not. He'd lost his girlfriend and he felt like hell. He was bored stiff with lying in the sun. Business problems were preying on his guts and he saw no way to turn the thing around.

The embarrassing truth was that he might as well go home. Back to wife and work and aggravation, back to the stinking weather and the smell of fish.

He just had to find a way to explain it to himself, and to others, so that it wouldn't look like he had caved, so that leaving early wouldn't feel like a defeat. Once he'd figured that one out, he was ready to get on the road.

29

Katy and Al Tuschman had finished their coffee, then retrieved the dog and gone to the pier at County Beach to watch the sun come up.

They'd sat on rough boards damp with night, their feet dangling above an ocean so still that it reflected pale blue stars amid the gold-green streaks of phosphorescence. For a moment Katy's head had rested on Al's shoulder. He didn't know if she had meant to put it there or if she'd briefly nodded out. He'd thought to touch her hair, but didn't. He'd stroked the dog instead.

Just after six, the eastern sky had turned a rusty yellow and swallowed up the constellations. Narrow, scattered slabs of cloud went lavender, and the water changed from black to a strange and depthless burgundy. When the sun cracked the horizon, it was instantly too bright to look at. The air grew hot in seconds and the tropic day came on so suddenly that there was no way to be ready for it. Caked sand sparkled; shadows stretched away from palms, opaque and confident, like they'd been there all along.

Taken by surprise, Al had shaded his itching eyes and was overtaken by a yawn. "What now?" he said.

Katy shrugged and yawned in turn. Pelicans flew by. Fifi stood and stretched over her front paws.

Thinking aloud, Al went on, "We go back to the hotel, we're sitting ducks."

Katy had squinted against the glare that skipped across the ocean like a spray of pebbles. "Maybe that's not the worst idea."

"Maybe not the best."

"Face them," she went on. "Explain things, get it over with."

Al thought about the fish stuck in the bed. "If you get time to explain."

Katy yawned again. It was a deep, sinuous yawn that made her feel the cut on her side. "Probably they won't do anything daytime."

Big, strong Al Tuschman considered that, then said, "What's the argument against bolting? Fleeing? Running away?"

For that Katy had no answer she could put in words. She just looked at Al with intimately tired eyes, and he understood, though he couldn't say it either. The only argument against fleeing was that if they bolted now they would lose each other. He'd get a flight to Newark, she to LaGuardia, and since they were very different from each other and weren't lovers, that would be the end of it. That's what happened when vacation was over and real life reasserted its habits and limits and demands. After sunset and sunrise and sharing a room, after dancing, and talking in their underwear, they'd go back to being the selves that they were used to, and it would seem preposterous, impossible that they would hang around together. That was the only argument against bolting right this minute.

Al bit his lip, looked down at the twinkling ocean. Not totally persuaded, he said, "I guess they won't try anything in daylight."

They stood and stretched. Fifi shook herself, dried her damp fur in the hot morning sun. They strolled slowly back to Paradise, where they soon fell sound asleep, side by side, on shaded lounges near the pool.

A block and a half from the fish market, beneath a torn green awning on a bent and rusty frame, there was an Irish bar. It had a chrome steam table filled with cylinders of soggy vegetables, and a plastic slab where a man in a spattered apron carved hunks of fatty meat. The place smelled of cabbage and stale beer and in the lull before lunch hour it was a perfect place to talk.

In a booth way at the back, Nicky Scotto was leaning forward above a Heineken and saying, "I gotta go to Flahda. Right away."

"Don't do it," said Donnie Falcone, solemn in his big black overcoat.

"It's the only way," said Nicky. Desperation made him lean still farther.

Donnie leaned in too. Their noses were close. They could smell each other's aftershave. "Think. You can't be seen in Flahda. It's suicide. What about the guys you—"

"They're fucking up," said Nicky. "Unbelievably, they're fucking up. I gotta do the fuckin' job myself."

"You told me they were pros," said Donnie. "I don't see what's the—"

"Problem?" Nicky interrupted. Furiously he swigged some beer, wriggled against the booth to try and stop the itching from his cheap and crappy suit. "Here's the fuckin' problem." He told Donnie about his hired men's determination to finish the job with seafood.

"Jesus Christ," said Donnie, and he shook his head of beautiful black hair. "Where'd you find these guys?"

"Chop's solid," Nicky said. "Does cars in Hialeah. I've worked wit' 'im through Miami. But the other guy—Squid. He's good people but he's crazy."

Donnie rubbed his cardboard coaster; little tubes of paper rolled beneath his thumb. "Nicky, listena me. You cannot let yourself be linked—"

The other man locked his jaw to keep his voice from getting loud. "I'm runnin' outa time! How much longer's he gonna be down there? Two days? Three?"

"Nicky, please. Stay out of it. Let it run its course."

"They fuck it up," the man in the bad suit rambled, "and then what? Big Al gets outa Flahda. Comes back and takes over the market. Now he's surrounded wit' goombahs—"

"And you're no worse off than you were before," Donnie pointed out.

"Except I am," said Nicky. "'Cause I got my heart set on it. 'Cause in my mind it's done already."

"Nicky, please. I'm begging you—"

"I'm goin', Donnie. I got to. First plane I can get on."

Donnie pursed his lips and slowly pushed himself upright in the booth. He scratched an eyebrow and said, "Nicky, I got a question for you. From the very start a this whole fuckin' mess, every single thing I tell you not to do, you do it. Why you bother askin' my advice?"

Surprised by the question, Nicky blinked. He thought the reason should be obvious. Absently, he tugged at his gapping lapels. "'Cause you're my friend," he said.

30

After his late breakfast, Big Al Marracotta ate more aspirin, then pulled on his cabana set and went down to the pool. He simply didn't know what else to do.

But the midday sun ratcheted up the dull ache in his head until it was an unbearable throbbing, so he retreated into the shade and looked at women, shamelessly stared as they coaxed their bathing suits down over the pale crescents at the base of their buttocks, as they rearranged their bosoms after diving.

After a while he waded to the swim-up bar, had a Virgin Mary, and then another. He sucked the lemons, chewed the ice. Very gradually, the spices and the celery joined forces with the aspirin and made him feel a little better. He dunked his head in the pool, and the cool water seemed to siphon pain away. He ate an order of conch fritters. They expanded in his stomach and made him feel almost okay.

In its grim but loosening grip, the hangover now seemed less like an overwhelming fact than an arduous but necessary passage. On the far side of that passage lay something like peace of mind, in the form of several benign, face-saving fibs he could tell himself about vacation.

Sipping yet another Virgin Mary, he was beginning to believe it had all worked out for the best. He'd had a bunch of first-rate sex, then got rid of Katy without tears or complications. He was due to ditch her anyway; it was a good thing it happened now, so

he could have his blowout then get back to New York. Face it—
he was needed there. He counted. He was an important guy, and
nobody's patsy. He'd proven that by taking vacation when he
damn well wanted to. But now he'd be big about it, responsible,
and go home early. Impress the hell out of Tony Eggs with how
fast and neatly he could get the market back in order.

Resolved, almost happy, he waded out of the pool, reclaimed
his cabana jacket. He air-dried for a minute, then went up to his
room.

Upstairs, he sat down on the bed and tried not to realize he
was nervous. He studied the telephone, silently rehearsed. The
words, the tone of voice—it had to be exactly right. He breathed
deep and dialed Tony Eggs' social club.

An underling answered. The underling was allowed to pass
along the call only as far as Carlo Ganucci.

The old *consigliere* got on the line and said hello.

"Carlo!" said Big Al, bearing down to put some Florida sunshine in his voice. "How are ya?"

Ganucci's eyeballs had turned yellow and he was down to a
hundred fifteen pounds. He wasn't sure what was killing him
but he knew that he was dying. He said, "Fine. How're you?"

"Tan. Rested. Fabulous," said Big Al. "Tony there?"

Carlo tried to do his job. "Zere a message I can give 'im?"

"Please," said Al. "I'd really like to talk to 'im myself."

There was a pause. Ganucci figured that Tony probably didn't
want to be bothered with this call, but resisting, arguing, took
more strength than he could spare. He padded off to get the boss.

The line was vacant for what seemed to Al a very long time.
He strove to keep his concentration. Be upbeat, he told himself.
Cheerful. Strong.

Finally Tony Eggs picked up the phone. He didn't say hello.
He said, "So how's the weather down in Flahda?"

The sarcasm put a ding in Big Al's confidence. But he had a
game plan and he stuck to it. "Beautiful," he said. "Incredible.
But listen—"

"What ya got left down there?" Tony interrupted. "Two days? T'ree?"

"This is why I'm callin'," said Big Al. "I mean, it's great down here—the sun, the palm trees. But, hey, I got responsibilities. You got, like, a situation up there. I'm a guy does the right thing. So I'm comin' back early. Leavin' today."

Tony didn't answer right away. Big Al knew why. He was impressed. Grateful. Maybe even touched. Didn't know exactly what to say. Al basked in the silence, knowing that things had worked out for the best and he was scoring a lot of points.

At last Tony said, "Don't bother."

Big Al squirmed against the rumpled sheets. "Excuse me?"

"Don't bother. Take your time. Enjoy yourself."

Al squeezed out half a laugh that sounded sick. "Hey, that's nice a you, but my mind's made up. Where things stand wit' the market—"

"The market isn't your concern no more."

"What?" He jumped down from the bed, wrapped himself in phone cord.

Tony Eggs was very calm. "It isn't yours no more. I gave it back ta Nicky."

Numbly, Big Al echoed, "Gave it back to Nicky? Just like that?"

Tony said nothing.

"After the fuckin' job I did for you?"

"You did okay, Al," Tony Eggs conceded. "But your time there, it was, like, a tryout."

"A tryout? A fucking tryout? No one ever said anything about it bein' a tryout."

Tony put a shrug in his voice. "Well, that's what it was."

"Sonofabitch!"

"And inna meantime, Nicky convinced me just how bad he wanted it. Me, I like a guy who's hungry."

Big Al took tiny steps that led him in a circle. "I can't believe I'm hearin' 'iss."

"Believe it, Al," said Tony. "No hard feelins, huh?"

Marracotta tried and failed to keep a note of pleading out of his voice. "Don't do this ta me, Tony!"

"Enjoy the resta your vacation."

Big Al heard the phone click in his ear. He held the receiver at arm's length and stared at it a moment. His first impulse was to bash it against the wall, but he was suddenly too drained to do it. He replaced it gently in its cradle, sat down softly on the high edge of the bed.

In the social club on Prince Street, Tony Eggs Salento turned to his favorite nephew, Donnie Falcone.

Donnie said, "Thought fast on that one, *zìo.*"

Sorrowfully and mordantly the old boss shook his head. "Those guys are both such fuckin' losers."

In the courtyard at Paradise, Al and Katy had slept for hours as the other couples and the European threesome woke up and breakfasted, as the sun rose higher and tested their parasol of leaves and fronds.

They slept until the crisscrossed straps of their lounges had impressed their pattern on legs and arms and faces, and they now awoke among naked people basted with sunblock, breathing air perfumed with coconut and chlorine.

Katy yawned and stretched and rubbed the corners of her mouth. "Delicious sleep," she slurred. "Needed it. Delicious."

Cottony and not quite awake, carrying over some refrain from a vanished dream, Al Tuschman blinked at her and mumbled words that were mashed by the weight of his cheek against the lounge. "Mishin tibby hoppy."

"Hmm?"

With effort he rose up on a crampy elbow. Fifi squirted out from underneath his lounge and tried to lick his chin. He said, "People kept saying it to me when I first got here. 'Mission to be happy.' 'Happiness our mission.' Sounded stupid then."

up to her elbows, the lapels were wrapped modestly around her throat. Her hair was wet and combed straight back and she hadn't bothered to put on makeup. She sat down on her lounge so that her knees were level with Al's chest.

He had to say something, so he said, "Nice shower?"

She didn't answer that. She said, "Tusch, I think it's time. Don't you?"

He knew what she was saying but he needed to be absolutely sure he knew. He'd started down the gallant path, and they probably should have fled by now, and as the hours passed he knew he should be getting more afraid; but he couldn't say or do a thing until he was absolutely certain what this tall young woman in his bathrobe was saying to him. So he just stared at her a moment.

She reached out and touched his hair again. "Time," she said again. "For us. Don't'cha think?"

Katy came up on an elbow too, and rearranged her blouse. "And now?"

He yawned and pulled his eyebrows close together. "Person doesn't just change," he said. "Score the basket. Close the sale. Ya know, those are missions."

"But you didn't answer the question," Katy pointed out.

"Yeah, I know I didn't," he admitted. Absently, he tugged his lower lip. The air felt great. Someone dunked in the pool and the water made a beautiful sound. Lizards clung to croton branches and billowed out their ruby throats. Al Tuschman gave an embarrassed little laugh. "Ya know," he said, "I think I sort of half believe it."

Katy reached across the space between their lounges and touched his hair. She didn't mean to do it; it just happened. His hair was dense and springy and a little moist from the heat of sleep. She quickly pulled her hand away and spoke immediately, as though to erase the fact that the touch had happened. "Mind I take a shower?"

He nodded and lay down flat again, thinking about her fingers in his hair, trying to forget that someone out there had in mind to make a dumb mistake and murder him. She went to the bungalow. The housekeeper apparently had been too shocked or baffled to make the bed. The stuffed fish, its blue and silver fin unfurled, still had its nose deeply buried in the mattress. Katy pulled it out. The nose offered a fair bit of resistance and made a creaking, scratching sound as it was withdrawn. The puncture in the sheet was neat and round.

She put the trophy on the dresser, then straightened out the tortured blanket and folded it neatly at the foot of the bed. At first she didn't know why she was bothering to do those things just then.

She stepped into the thatch enclosure and had a long warm shower.

When she went outside again, she was wearing a bathrobe that Al did not immediately recognize as his. The sleeves were rolled

31

Nicky Scotto's plane was just then landing in Miami, settling onto a tire-scarred runway that shimmered in the heat of afternoon.

In his sticky suit he hurried through the terminal, past pyramids of plastic oranges and mobs of South Americans checking in with televisions and Pampers boxes, and caught the jumper flight to Key West. It was a short flight but the attendant went through twice with drinks. People traveling in tank tops wolfed beers and margaritas out of cans, getting ready to be loud and silly.

Nicky thumbed a magazine, then looked out the window as the small plane started its descent. Where the flats began, the water of the Gulf thinned out from indigo to milky green; tide-scoured channels branched and meandered among the splotchy russet and maroon of coral heads. Colonies of mangrove sprouted inexplicably; gradually they thickened into islands, scraps of forest with their feet in swamps. Beautiful, thought Nicky. Lots of places to dump a body.

He caught a taxi at the airport and went straight to Chop's motel.

In the still-searing sun of four o'clock, he climbed a flight of outdoor stairs then knocked on the hollow, rotting door of the hired killers' room. The door was opened by a heavily sweating guy in a sleeveless T-shirt. Veins stood out in his neck and arms.

Nicky said, "You must be Squid."

"That's right," said the bandy man. He didn't offer his hand and he didn't smile.

Nicky tried a compliment. "Always heard good things about your work."

"When I get to do it," Squid said dryly. "Come in, ya want. I'm doin' calisthenics."

Nicky stepped over the threshold, closed the door behind him. Ignoring the guest, Squid dropped to the ratty carpet, started doing push-ups, the kind where you clap between each one.

"Where's Chop?" asked Nicky, sitting on a damp and musky unmade bed.

"He's doin' somethin'," grunted the man on the floor.

"He's workin' for me," said Nicky. "What's he doin'?"

"I don't really know," said Squid. He rolled onto his back and started doing sit-ups.

"I fuckin' told him when I'd be here," Nicky said.

Squid didn't bother answering that, and Nicky's irritation ripened quickly in the steamy climate. His two great hit men. One didn't have the decency to be there to greet him, and the other was an exercise freak who was giving him attitude. Where was the respect? Adding to his annoyance, the room was broiling hot and stank of mildew. He took off his jacket. His thin gray turtleneck was wet under the arms and along the spine. "This dump ain't got AC?"

Squid was curled up like a bug, hands behind his head, his left elbow reaching for his right knee. "While I'm sweated up?" he said. "You crazy?"

Nicky rose, started walking toward the bathroom to throw cold water on his face. Halfway there, his very fragile patience disappeared. "Am *I* crazy?" he said. "You wanna take a guy out wit' a stuffed fish hangin' on a wall, and you ask me if *I'm* crazy?"

Squid kept on with his crunches. With a quiet but implacable resentment, he said, "All I know is, ya hire guys to do a job, y'oughta let 'em do the job."

Nicky stood right over Squid. "Look, you seem to be forgetting whose job this is. For what I'm payin' you—"

Squid did not like looking at Nicky's crotch and up his nose. He sat and swiveled on his haunches. "You think this is about the money?"

Scotto was stumped by the question. What else could it be about?

"Fuck the money!" Squid went on, sitting lotus-style on the floor. "This is about symmetry. Completion."

Nicky blinked at him, scratched his ear, resumed his journey toward the bathroom.

"Fuck the money!" Squid repeated to his back. "The money for this hit, which now you're making about as elegant as a Kotex, fuhget about it. All I want's my per diem."

Nicky turned around. "Your per fucking what?"

The door opened. Light rolled into the room like a giant wedge of yellow cheese. Chop stepped in behind it and Nicky jumped right down his throat. "Where you fucking been?"

Unfazed, Chop said, "Picking out a spot. Ya know, for later. You guys been gettin' ta know each other?"

Big Al Marracotta had sat for a long time on the high edge of his hotel bed, sat there stunned, like a man amid the charred and tangled wreckage of what used to be his house. Too fast for sanity to track, everything was gone. Work; power; status; sex life— vanished. Just another aging middle-level wise guy once again. He stared at the wall and tried to get used to the idea.

Eventually he rose on numb legs and showered. He barely felt the water on his skin or the brisk rub of the towel.

Hiding in a hotel bathrobe, he walked in absent circles around his suite, tried out different armchairs. He noticed vaguely that the light outside was changing, turning golden. Soon it would be sunset. The big event of every day. Some event! Then again, at least it could not be taken away. In a morbid mood of anti-celebration, he decided he would leave his room to drink champagne as the sun was going down.

He got dressed. Stepped into sharkskin pants and, by force of habit, tucked his slender knife inside his sock before putting on his shoes. He combed his half-inch helmet of salt-and-pepper hair and headed for the rooftop bar.

Big Al was not a sentimental guy, had always moved too fast for nostalgia to catch up with him. Riding the elevator, smelling the sea, whose tang penetrated even to the airshaft, he didn't realize he was acting out an unamusing parody of his first evening in Key West. Reliving the sunset of just a few short days ago, when he'd been a big shot and a lover. Going back to the beginning, as though he could start vacation over and get it right this time.

Katy and Al Tuschman lay beneath the punctured blanket on the punctured bed and talked about their plans.

"Maybe South Beach for a coupla days," said Al. "Rent a car and drive right up."

Katy stroked his chest. She liked the way the whorls of hair wrapped themselves around her fingers. "You sure you wanna be with me that long?"

He ran a hand over the smooth rise of her hip. "Come on," he said. "Don't start that stuff. Coupla days in South Beach. Finish with a real vacation. Whaddya say?"

A breeze moved the thin curtains of the room. It was cooler than the breeze had been before and it lacked the brickish smell of high afternoon. The day was ending and the crazy, mistaken dangers of night were coming on.

"I say whatever we're gonna do, we better get started doing it."

She kissed him once then moved to get up from the bed. Al held her close a moment more, reveled in her length. Her toes tickled his insteps, their loins nested without contortion, her tanned cheek fit like a violin in the hollow of his neck.

He marveled once again at how smoothly she unfolded, as she rose to walk off toward the shower.

32

Across the street, in the lengthening shadow of the button-wood hedge, Squid was sulking in the backseat of the Jag. Chop sat observant and serene behind the steering wheel. Next to him, Nicky Scotto, jumpy and perspiring, kept plucking at his trousers, and gave off the funky acetone smell of a nervous man whose clothes were wrong for the tropics. He was very aware of the weight of the pistol Chop had given him; it pulled down on an inside pocket of his jacket and made him lean that way. He stared at the wooden gate of Paradise and said to no one in particular, "Ya sure he's coming out?"

"Fuck knows?" said Squid, enjoying the other man's discomfort. "Guy gets hungry, thirsty, he's comin' out."

Nicky prayed in secret that it would be soon. He could feel in his bowels that his nerve was wearing thin. He'd killed before, but never a made man. An equal. Someone with friends who solemnly believed in getting even.

Chop picked up where Squid left off. "Or if he has ta walk his little dog."

Nicky was plucking at his sticky pants and watching the shadows slowly stretch across the street. "Little dog?" he said. "He's got a big dog."

Chop Parilla felt just the faintest of misgivings but held his face together and said nothing, only looked across the street and drummed lightly on the steering wheel.

186

In the backseat, Squid Berman was taking a bleak pleasure from seeing more and more that the guy who wouldn't let him complete his masterpiece was a total idiot. Not bothering to mask his contempt, he said, "Have it your way, Nicky. Guy's got a big, gigantic dog."

"We're leaving," said Al Tuschman to the desk clerk with the ruby studs above his eye and the purple bags beneath them.

The drowsy fellow seemed indifferent yet confused. He glanced at the departing guest's suitcase, and at the woman who had not been with him when he'd arrived, and at the register before him on the counter. "You're booked for two more nights."

Al said, "I know that. We're going."

The clerk tried his best to look concerned. "Was everything all right?"

"No," said Al. "There's a gash in the mattress."

"A gash?"

"You might wanna think about security. Where can we rent a car right now?"

"Right now?" Time being featureless for him, he had to glance down at his watch. "Only place, the airport."

Putting his room key on the counter, Al said, "Would you call us a taxi, please."

He and Katy headed for the office door. Al held his suitcase and Katy held Fifi. The clerk watched them go, and could not help seeing some vague personal failure in their retreating backs. Through his exhaustion he rallied for one last burst of rote and insincere professionalism. "Please come back and see us!" he chirped.

Al looked across his shoulder. "Yeah, right."

But when he crossed the office threshold and stood for the last time in the courtyard with its pool and hot tub, its lounges where people rubbed and cooed and chattered, a strange thing happened: he suddenly felt a fondness for the place. In spite of everything, in spite of what, minute by minute, had felt like loneliness and awkwardness and misery, it now seemed to Al that he'd had a pretty good time there. He was tan and freshly showered. He'd caught up on his rest and had a tall new lover at his side. In some cockeyed, screwball way, vacation had turned out pretty well.

He took a last deep breath of chlorine and spent flowers, a last look at the closely tended palms with a yellow sunset glow behind them. He leaned close to Katy and kissed her on the neck, and then they headed for the wooden gate.

Across the street and thirty yards away, Chop Parilla watched as Al Tuschman dropped his suitcase and Katy bent down smoothly to put the leashed dog on the ground. He squeezed the wheel of the idling Jag and pointed with his big square chin. "There he is!" he hissed.

Nicky Scotto felt the urgency deep down in his guts. He narrowed his eyes and craned his neck. He squinted down, he stretched and strained, but finally he had to say, "There *who* is?"

In the backseat, Squid Berman chewed his tongue and thought, Is this guy a moron or what?

"Big Al!" said Chop.

Nicky tightened down his abdomen and rubbed his eyes and felt the gun against his ribs. He grabbed the dashboard and leaned far forward. "Where?"

Christ, thought Squid, the motherfucker's blind!

"Right there!" Chop said. "Wit' the tall broad and the dog!"

Nicky stared, and stared, and saw a stranger. A long and sweaty moment passed. Then he said, "Come on, don't fuck around."

For a heartbeat no one moved. Then Chop shifted very slightly in the driver's seat and slid his gaze to the rearview mirror, silently but desperately conferring with his partner.

Nicky tracked his eyes, saw the look on his face—hangdog,

crestfallen. In a nauseating instant, he understood. He said, "You fuckin' assholes! You think that's Big Al?"

"That *is* Big Al!" insisted Squid.

"You're telling me who Big Al is? I don't know that fuckin' guy from Adam!"

"The license plate—" said Chop.

"Fuck the license plate! Geniuses! Ya got the wrong guy all this time!"

Neither Chop nor Squid had anything to say to that. Chop just looked down at his knuckles. Squid thought ruefully about his brilliant work. Some masterpiece—wrong from the start.

"I tol' you," Nicky hammered on. "Little guy, big dog." He gestured toward the threesome quietly waiting for their taxi on the dusky sidewalk. "Zat look like a big dog ta you? Zat look like—"

He stopped himself mid-rant. Something had clamped on to his attention. A spiky head of raven hair above a pert, small-featured face above a healthy chest above a long thin pair of legs. He said, "Wait a second. Who's the broad?"

"You know everything," Sid Berman said. "You tell us."

"Come on, come on. Who is she?"

Chop shrugged. "Some broad that he picked up. Wasn't with 'im at the start."

Nicky looked harder. Long neck, slightly pointed chin. He'd seen her in New York. He was sure of it. At various bars and seafood joints. Sassy. Pouty. With a way of looking bored. He said, "Shit, I think that's Big Al's girlfriend."

Everybody was confused. Squid could not help saying, "Big Al's girlfriend. But not Big Al."

"Shut up," said Nicky. He plucked at his pants and tried to stitch his torn-up thoughts together. After a moment he said, "We're grabbing them."

Chop began, "But you just said—"

"Shut up. Go."

He put the idling Jag in gear.

33

Al and Katy had been talking about the great time they would have in South Beach. Long walks by the ocean. Cocktails in the crazy lobbies of old lime-green hotels. Finger food in suave cafés as beautiful people glided past on Rollerblades.

When the Jaguar stopped in front of them, Al tried to make a little joke. "Pretty fancy cab."

Katy smiled but did not have time to laugh. She looked up to see a suit moving toward her, caught a sickening glimpse of a big hand wrapped around a gun that gleamed a dull blue in the deepening dusk.

Squid spilled from the backseat right after Nicky. He bounded over to Al Tuschman and poked the muzzle of a pistol between his ribs.

Fifi barked. Nicky kicked her in the snout. He grabbed one of Katy's wrists and wrenched it behind her back and let her feel the gun against her spine. "Inna car," he whispered. "Not a fuckin' sound."

He used her long arm as a lever and pushed her to the Jag. She dragged the dog behind her; no one seemed to care.

Squid prodded Al Tuschman, who moved like he had just woken up. His suitcase, ghostly, stayed there on the sidewalk.

It happened too fast for real fear to grab on until they were seated in the car. That's when the milky feeling swelled up from the stomach, the cold burn moved down the legs. Al and Katy and the shih tzu were huddled in the back with Squid. Nicky swiveled toward them, his pistol poking lewdly through the slot between the bucket seats.

Chop drove away. Drove calmly, slowly. A sightseer's pace through peaceful, unsuspecting streets, past clapboard houses whose emerald and coral and turquoise shutters hoarded up the fading light.

Nicky said to Katy, "I know you." The simple statement was a horrid accusation. "Kitty. Kathy. You fuck Big Al. Am I right?"

Katy said nothing. By now she vaguely recognized her captor. One more thug from the thuggish places she used to let herself be taken. She could not recall his name. Frankie, Funzie, Petey, Sal—what did it matter? They were all preening, back-slapping show-offs; she could seldom even tell who were friends and who were enemies.

After a moment Nicky wagged the gun toward Al. "So who's this other asshole?"

Katy stayed silent. So did Al. Squid reached across and slammed the butt of his gun into the tall man's solar plexus. Fifi tried to nip his hand. "Answer the fucking question."

Al had a hard time getting his breath to hook up with his vocal cords. Weakly, he managed, "Name's Al Tuschman."

Squid's eyes pinwheeled. *Big* Al Tuschman, any chance?"

"Wit' a license plate that says so?" put in Chop.

"Yeah," admitted the furniture salesman.

"I tol' ya!" Chop insisted.

"Shut up," said Nicky Scotto. "Let it go, already." To Katy he said, "But ya didn't come here wit' this asshole, did ya? Ya came here wit' the real Big Al."

Katy said nothing. Chop wound slowly through the streets. Cats skulked along the curbs. Brightening streetlamps put orange starbursts on the windshield.

"So where the fuck is he?" Nicky said.

Katy kept quiet. She was not a traitor. For the last few days she'd worked hard at killing her old life, shedding the hurt parts that had inhabited that life; she didn't need to kill old boyfriends too.

Nicky Scotto sucked his teeth, said with confidence, "You're gonna tell us."

She didn't.

Nicky plucked his clothing and tried a different tack. "This new asshole—you like 'im? I mean, I get the feeling you and him are hangin' out together now."

Katy said nothing. Al soothed his quivering dog.

"Listen, Kitty—"

"Katy."

"Katy," Nicky said. "Lemme put this very simple. Someone named Big Al is gonna die tonight. It can be the other one, who frankly is a useless scumbag, or it can be this guy you seem to like. I'm givin' you the chance to decide. Take a minute. Think it over."

He produced a toothpick from a jacket pocket, chomped it. Chop drove. He loved to drive; he could drive all night.

Katy looked at Al. It was too dark to really see his eyes. She saw his pitted cheek, one corner of his mouth. She liked his face but she couldn't bring herself to speak.

Nicky got impatient. He said to Squid, "Show the lady we're sincere."

Squid licked his lips and reached his hot, damp arm around her back; the hollow of his armpit cupped her flank. The gun was in his hand and he pressed the muzzle into the soft place behind Al Tuschman's ear. Contextless, obscene, it dented the flesh, traced out the seam between the skull and jaw. She felt Al tighten, felt his breathing stall. Squid cocked the hammer. The click seemed very loud.

Her shoulders sagged. She said, "Okay, okay."

The gun stayed where it was.

"Last I know, he's at the Conch House."

Squid withdrew his arm. Nicky almost smiled. The toothpick danced between his teeth. He looked at Chop.

Chop said, "That sucks."

"Whatsa matter?"

"Can't grab 'im there," the driver said. "Big fancy busy place. Tons a people. Guards."

Nicky plucked at his itching trousers. Chop serenely made left turns, right turns. Al touched Katy's knee with a hand that wasn't steady.

After a silence, Squid's voice had the harsh, damp rasp of a kazoo. "So she brings 'im to us."

Nicky looked at him.

"Come on," he said. "Two days ago they were an item. Big tall sexy babe like this, she lures 'im down."

Katy closed her eyes, forced herself to inhale.

Nicky considered. "We do 'im there?"

"Too closed in," said Squid. "Grab 'im's all we do."

Chop turned in the direction of Duval Street.

Squid swallowed, then kept talking like Al and Katy weren't there. "We give 'er an hour. She doesn't bring 'im down, the new Romeo is dead. We're no worse off than now."

Al Tuschman held his dog against his stomach. The quiet residential streets turned garish as they neared Duval. Neon flashed; the humid air took on blue and orange grains. Chop wove among mopeds and bicycles and pedicabs until he found the Conch House's garage.

He pulled in between a low ceiling and an oily concrete floor under evil, maddening fluorescent lights. He passed up some open spaces, crawled along until he saw a dark gray Lincoln with a New York plate that said BIG AL.

"Sonofabitch," he muttered. He parked across an aisle and a couple of slots away. He lowered the windows and switched off the engine. The air stank of exhaust.

With the motor off it was ungodly still. Nicky pushed back his sleeve and checked his watch. He spoke to Katy but pointed his gun at Al. "Ya got an hour, sweetheart. Smile pretty."

She kissed Al Tuschman on the cheek and climbed out of the car.

34

Katy was still wearing her pink shorts and lime-green top and high-heeled sandals, and the concrete floor felt very hard against her feet.

She walked stiffly to the elevator and tried to clear her head. She knew some things she wished she didn't know. She knew that thugs were liars, that there was not the slightest guarantee that she and Tusch would go free if she produced Big Al. She knew, as well, that she could probably escape, alone. Men like this—the truth was that, for all the jealousy and posing, women didn't matter to them; their deepest passions—hate, revenge, a pathetic need to be respected—were reserved for one another. With lack of regard came an insulting form of safety; she knew that she could simply disappear. And she knew she wouldn't do it.

She rode up to the top guest floor, approached the suite she'd shared with Big Al Marracotta. She tried to practice what she would say to him, but no words would come; there was nothing to rehearse. He would want to touch her, of course, reassert his claim. She shivered at the thought. She paused a moment at the door, then knocked.

There was no answer. She knocked again. Hearing silence in return, she bit her lip and pictured him at the rooftop bar. Pictured him with such intensity as to put him there, because, if he wasn't, there was no way she'd find him in an hour. She went back to the elevator.

It was crowded on the rooftop. Smoke swirled. A piano player labored bravely against the giggling and the clank of ice and the whirring of the blenders. Katy, a woman alone in pink shorts and heels, pushed through the clustered bodies at the bar; a hand brushed against her buttocks. She broke through to the rank of small tables that edged the room, that owned the pricey windows. Waitresses careened with endless trays of fritters. Couples drank from salted glasses. And there, at a dim table in the corner, a sweating silver bucket poised in front of him, sat Big Al Marracotta by himself.

Katy, unseen, studied him a moment before she approached. He looked not just small but diminished, shrunken, like something revisited from childhood. His helmet of hair seemed unnatural, puppetlike. There was a hint of the primitive and stupid in the sensual looseness of his mouth. She braced herself and moved toward him.

He looked up from his glass and saw her when she was several steps away. The distance gave him time to select a pose. He was beaten down, defeated, and if he let it show he might know the sweetness of being comforted. But no way would he let it show. He stretched his neck inside his collar, stuck out his stubby chin.

"'Lo, Al," Katy said.

He turned his head way up to look at her. "You're back." He was surprised and yet it sounded smug.

"Ask me to sit down?"

He gestured toward a chair. "Where ya been?"

Sitting, she said, "Needed some time alone. You shouldn't have hit me, Al."

He might have said he was sorry. He *was* sorry. He said, "Didja come here to start another argument?"

She glanced at the champagne bottle. Big Al gestured for a waitress to bring another glass.

"I came," she said, "to see if maybe we should try again." She crossed her long legs. The edge of the tablecloth touched her skin just above the knee.

Al felt a twinge in his pants. He looked away like he was giving the proposition careful thought. He'd told himself he was through with Katy, especially when it seemed that she was through with him. Besides, without the market, who knew if he could even afford her anymore? But in the meantime she was tall, she was young, she was here.

The waitress brought a glass and poured for both of them. To Katy's relief, that drained the bottle.

She let Big Al play hard to get. She put her hand on his wrist. "I have an idea," she said. "Let's go someplace new, forget about what happened here, start fresh. A couple days in South Beach, maybe. Whaddya say?"

Big Al pursed his lips. He was struggling up from dismal depths, and the only way he knew to climb was to step on someone else. He said, "So ya realized when ya had it good."

Katy tried hard not to wince, used her glass to hide her face. "Yeah, Al. I realized."

He tipped his flute up to his sloppy lips, tapped out a final drop, pretended that he'd come to a decision. "Okay," he said. "Let's go downstairs."

She pictured the giant bed, smelled again the rank sheets and sour pillows. She turned coy to mask a sudden panic. "Okay," she said, "but just to pack."

"Right. Whatever. Sure."

"I mean it, Al. I don't wanna be here anymore."

He gestured for his tab and signed it. They rose and moved through the crowd toward the elevator. People looked at them— the slick and cocksure guy with the tall and chesty babe—and Big Al Marracotta felt almost back on top again.

Downstairs in the stifling and hellishly lit garage, Nicky Scotto plucked his sleeve and checked his watch. "Three quarters of an hour gone," he said. "The bitch ain't comin' back."

In the rear seat of the Jag, Squid Berman swiveled toward Al Tuschman. "Guess you didn't impress her much."

Al said nothing, petted his dog. He was very afraid but as time wore on and adrenaline subsided, his fear lost its jagged edge and became a smooth, round weight that was simply there, a background noise. Tentatively resigned, he found himself thinking almost calmly of morbid, dreadful things. What would become of Fifi if he got killed? Would she end up in some adoption agency full of horny, uncouth mutts in cages floored with filthy shredded newsprint? What about Moe Kleiman? Corny, generous old Moe—would he somehow blame himself?

And while he was on guilt, he felt terribly guilty about Katy. She'd drawn the tougher card by far. While he just sat here quietly communing with his cowardice, she was out there, acting, scheming in the face of her fear. Let the thugs say what they wanted; Al didn't for an instant doubt that she was trying her best to ransom him. That's who she was—a person who would try her best. But what if she just couldn't pull it off? What would a maniac like Big Al do if he realized she was trying to betray him? That was a question that made the background noise of Al Tuschman's fear rise again to a hideous jangle.

Minutes passed. Making chitchat, Nicky Scotto said to Chop, "So we ain't got Al but we got a place?"

Chop's eyes flicked to the rearview mirror before he answered. "Perfect place," he said. "Scoped it out this afternoon."

There was a silence.

Squid said to Nicky, "Ain't you hot, that suit on?"

Nicky didn't answer that, just plucked at the hated fabric and checked his watch again. "Ten minutes," he said. "Bitch ain't comin' back."

35

Big Al Marracotta's hands were groping toward Katy's breasts before the door had even closed behind them.

She seized his wrists, labored mightily to keep some playfulness in her voice. "Later," she said. "We're packing. We're going. Right?"

"What's the hurry?" said Big Al. He freed his hands and grabbed her hips and made lewd wiggles with his tongue.

Katy realized something in that instant. Realized that not only did he repulse her now, he'd repulsed her from the start, and that had been part of the appeal. Crazy, but no more.

She spun away, moved toward the stand that held her suitcase. Her breath caught when she saw the violence Big Al had wrought against her things, the slashed and sundered bras and panties and stockings. "Jesus," she said. "I guess you were pretty mad at me."

For one second he looked sheepish, then seemed stupidly proud of himself and of his rage. "Yeah," he said. "Pretty mad. Blind mad. Mad enough for anything."

Fright climbed up her throat with a taste of salt and iron. She managed something like a smile, said, "Guess you'll have to buy me some new things up in South Beach."

He liked that, as she knew he would. Made him feel like a sport. He licked his lips as he pictured her modeling a fresh batch of cheesy lingerie. He glanced over at the bags of sex toys. "Got some goodies to bring along."

She tried her best to look intrigued. "Sooner we get on the road . . ."

He leered at her, and ran a hand across his crotch, and moved off to the bathroom.

Katy lunged to the armoire, started stuffing clothes into Big Al's luggage. Cabana sets, black shirts, expensive shoes. Desperation made her wildly efficient. She went to the phone and called down to the kennel. Even moved the bags of sex toys toward the door. By the time Al Marracotta had peed and put himself away and combed his helmet of salt-and-pepper hair, all that was left to do was to gather up cosmetics. She swept tubes and bottles from the counter and announced that they were ready.

"The dog?" he said.

"They're getting him."

Not one to carry his own bags or retrieve his own car, Big Al Marracotta said, "Didja call a bellman? A valet?"

"They're all backed up," she lied. "Like half an hour. Come on, I'll carry stuff."

She bent to lift his suitcase. He put his hand on her flexing ass. "Why so anxious, babe?"

She bit her lip and forced her hips to move against his hand. "Come on, Al. Different place, different bed. Come on."

She moved off toward the door. He followed. It seemed to take forever for the elevator to arrive.

Nicky Scotto checked his watch then pointed his gun at Alan Tuschman's chest. "Ah, shit," he said. "Looks like we gotta kill ya."

Al stroked his dog and tried not to tremble. He thought he'd show himself that much, at least—get through this without quaking or crying or wetting his pants.

"Nothin' personal," Nicky went on. "Y'unnerstand, we don't follow through, people lose respect."

Chop made a somewhat sympathetic sound. "All over a stupid license plate. A stupid nickname."

"Wit' all the other nicknames you mighta had," put in Squid. "Knucklehead. Limpdick . . ."

Fifty yards away, the chrome doors of the elevator opened.

The rottweiler came out first. Penned in much too long, it strained at its leash, strained so hard it choked itself and wheezed.

The waiting killers heard the wheezing and the tick of paws against the oily cement floor. They looked up through the sickly bluish light, and in a moment they saw Katy, listing slightly on her high-heeled shoes as she balanced a fat suitcase, and Al Marracotta, rearing back against the weight of the leash, a pair of shopping bags sagging in his other hand.

A vindicated Nicky Scotto whispered, "Ya see? Ya see! Little guy. Big dog. Let's go."

Low and silent, he slipped out of the Jag, Squid Berman right behind. Squatting down between two cars, they readied their pieces as the footsteps drew closer. They held their breath and fixed their gazes on the vanity plate at the rear end of the Lincoln.

Big Al finally stood next to it. He put the shopping bags down on the cement and fished in his pocket for a key. He fumbled with the key, then had some trouble fitting it to the lock. He rubbed his eyes and started over. Everything seemed to be taking an unnaturally long time. At last the trunk swung open. He bent to put in the bags.

That's when Squid and Nicky came springing toward his rumpled, helpless back.

"Get your fuckin' hands up, Al!" said Scotto.

Katy dropped the suitcase, stepped aside fast.

By reflex, not yet knowing who it was that had the drop on him, the little mobster did as he was told. The leash fell from his hand. The restless but simple rottweiler, paralyzed by sudden freedom, sat down on the floor and let its tongue hang out. Squid Berman bounded close to Al, frisked him from his armpits to his groin.

"Now turn around," said Nicky.

Big Al pivoted, and when he saw his colleague from New York, he was a little afraid and quite pissed off, but mostly he was just confused. His confusion, like morning clouds, burned off one layer at a time, and the first thing he understood was that Katy, with her teasing talk of fresh beds, fresh lingerie, had set him up. He looked at her. "You fucking cunt."

She felt bad for him in spite of everything. Felt bad for his wife and kids, who probably thought he was an okay guy. She couldn't meet his eyes.

But Big Al couldn't figure out what Nicky Scotto wanted from him. Their little contest was over. He'd lost; Nicky had won. He said to his enemy, "Why the fuck—?"

A long moment's mayhem stifled his question.

Fifi had grown quiveringly alert in her master's lap. She smelled danger and the rottweiler. In whatever canine way she understood the battle, she was determined to do her part. She dug her paws into Al Tuschman's crotch and, before he could restrain her, she propelled herself out the Jaguar's open window.

Paws skidding on the slippery cement, she charged at Ripper, furiously yipping all the while. The chickenhearted rottweiler half stood up, retreating slowly, quailing. Then it made an epic blunder and turned its back. Beneath the russet bull's-eye of its ass, its showy testicles dangled and swayed, the right one lower than the left. Fifi made a mighty leap and grabbed them in her teeth.

The big dog howled and yelped and spun in tight and anguished circles. The little dog hung on, fur flying backward, legs and tail streaming out behind as though distended by the motion of some insane amusement-park ride. Ripper's scrotum stretched like pizza dough; Fifi flapped like laundry in a gale. Finally she loosed her grip, went scuttling across the floor. Ripper, whimpering and bloodied, ran limping for the exit.

Big Al Marracotta, hands still in the air, said, "Jesus Christ! My dog!"

"You don't need 'im anymore," said Nicky Scotto. "We're goin' for a ride."

Al tried to keep the terror out of his voice. "Nicky, come on. You got the market—"

"You're giving it ta me?" said the man with the gun. "That's very nice."

"Come on, don't kid around. I talked ta Tony. I know what's what."

Now it was Nicky who was a little bit confused. He labored not to let it show.

"It's yours," Big Al went on. "Fair enough. I ain't happy, but congratulations."

There was a pause. The lights buzzed. Drunken street noise filtered in. Katy sidled farther away from her former boyfriend.

Nicky said, "Tony tol' ya this?"

"Yesterday. Said the market goes back ta Nicky. Said my time was like a tryout. I'm pissed but that's life."

Scotto pursed his lips, scratched his eyebrow, pulled his ear. For an instant he lowered his gun. Then he said, "Nice try, Al. Had me goin' for a second. But don'tcha think Tony woulda called me first?"

Weakly, Big Al Marracotta said, "He didn't?"

"You got balls," said Nicky. "I give ya that."

Using his pistol to point the way, he gestured toward the Jag. Big Al didn't budge. Squid moved close and shoved him along.

Chop pulled the lever that released the trunk. It yawned open slowly, like the mouth of a whale. Nicky said, "Hop in."

Big Al said, "Please. You're makin' a mistake. Call Tony—"

Squid raised his gun butt, gave him one brisk hack where the spine ended and the skull began, and caught him neatly by the armpits as he sagged. He muscled him into the trunk and slammed the lid on top of him.

Nicky turned his gun toward Katy and ordered her into the car.

She stood where she was. Trying to sound firm, trying to convince him with her righteous certainty, she said, "You got your guy. We can go now, right?"

"Sorry, sister. Job ain't finished yet."

"But you said—"

Squid was moving toward her across the oily floor. He grabbed her almost gently by the elbow.

Nicky interrupted her. "What I said is that I don't like witnesses. Get inna fucking car."

Ushered by Squid, dizzy on her high shoes, she slid into the backseat once again, allowed herself a shudder and a groan as she nestled next to Tusch. Fifi bounded onto his lap, licked their joined hands.

"That's quite a dog you got," said Squid.

Chop drove off slowly through the scattered drops of blood that the rottweiler had left behind.

36

Halfway to Stock Island, Big Al Marracotta woke up in the trunk.

It was pitch dark in there, with just a small supply of viscous air that smelled of grease and rubber. The tires were loud as their treads sucked at the pavement, and he bounced with every seam in the road. Potholes sent him flying against the underside of the lid. He curled up and cradled his head and wondered if it was absolutely certain that he was being taken to die.

In the passenger compartment, things were not much cheerier. For a while no one spoke. Al and Katy leaned against each other, their flanks growing very warm where they touched. The heroic shih tzu perched proudly on her master's lap as a few hideous miles of U.S. 1 slipped past in what was now full night. There was the glare of fast-food joints and desperate strip malls, crappy motels shilled by giant signs that throbbed like boils. Nicky Scotto plucked at his pants and wondered if, with Big Al gone and the fish market solidly his, he might ease back into wearing decent suits.

Chop approached the little bridge at Cow Key Channel. Squid pointed to a hollow on the far side of the road. "That's where we picked up your stupid license plate," he told Al Tuschman. "Tailed you all the way to your hotel. You didn't notice nothin'."

No, the furniture salesman admitted to himself, he hadn't. But why would he have? He wasn't a criminal, didn't have violent enemies, didn't have to live life looking back across his shoulder. He'd arrived in Key West, just a few short days ago, as one more average schmo with average hopes for his vacation. Get a tan, maybe meet a woman. Step, however briefly, however meekly, outside the self he was by habit, and go home with life enriched by a memory or two. Modest expectations; sane expectations. Why would he have noticed, or believed, that two maniacs suddenly were out to get him?

They drove past tattoo parlors, liquor stores.

In the trunk, Big Al Marracotta bounced and rolled, and tried to avoid admitting he was terrified by getting more and more pissed off. Disagreements happened; guys got iced. He accepted this, except when it was happening to him. Now it all seemed senseless and unjust. Why was he getting killed? Because that putz Benny Franco got himself indicted? Because Tony Eggs didn't make a phone call?

Or was it even crazier and more infuriating than that? Was he getting killed because he took vacation? This was the price of a goddamn week away from work? Or was it that he took vacation with a no-good, ingrate tramp who sold him out?

Baffled and furious, he bounced, he tumbled, and gradually he realized that he was running out of air. He had to pull hard from the bottom of his lungs to inhale; he smelled his own stale breath going into him again. In the blackness of the trunk, he felt a sudden excruciating loneliness, previewed the unspeakable remove of being dead, and the helpless and humiliating sorrow of it only made him madder. He swore to himself a solemn pledge: if he was going down because of all this unfair craziness, these betrayals and these blunders, he wasn't going down alone.

Curled up, panting, he reached toward his ankle. He felt for the slender knife that Squid's hurried frisking hadn't found. One knife against three guns—there was no chance he could save himself. Yet there was a certain spiteful comfort in knowing there was still somebody weaker he could hurt. Pulling the weapon smoothly from its leather sheath, he tucked it up his sleeve between the bounces of the car. He pulled hard at the rank and thinning air, and took a final nasty pleasure from figuring how he might slash and tear the woman who had turned on him.

Chop turned off the highway at MacDonald Avenue, then wound through streets of deepening dreariness.

Dim and secret bars gave way to crowded plots of rusting trailers lifted up on cinder blocks; the trailers yielded to a precinct of windowless garages housing auto-body and machine shops. Where the asphalt ended and the road became humped gravel dotted with deep foul puddles that would never dry, there were random shacks with kinked and crumpled metal roofs, their grassless yards littered with splotched banana leaves and decomposing fronds. Streetlamps grew sparse; they wavered in uncertain, percolating ground that was only inches higher than the ocean. There was a smell in the air of sea corrupted, a salty stink like that of anchovies kept too long in the tin.

Chop serenely drove; the Jaguar clattered over stones. Dead ahead, inexplicably standing sentinel in the middle of the street, there was what appeared to be an ancient tollbooth. It leaned on rotting stakes; boards were missing from its wooden flanks; there was no glass in its windows.

On closer inspection, it proved to be the box office for a long-abandoned drive-in theater.

Beyond the tiny building, bathed in wan and opalescent moonlight, stretched the ghostly parking field. Low concentric mounds built up of shells and bits of coral lifted vanished cars to perfect viewpoints. The posts that had held the scratchy speakers poked up crooked from the contours. The screen itself—its paint long seared away by sun and salt, its plywood face splintery and scarred—loomed patiently, waiting for the inevitable wind that would send it crashing down.

Chop rode the mounds like waves, finally broke the silence. "Good place, huh?" he said to Nicky.

"Beautiful."

Gasping in the trunk, Big Al Marracotta bounced and rolled with every hump.

The driver headed for what once had been the snack bar, a fragrant place of Milk Duds and malteds and soggy burgers wrapped in foil. Boarded and imploding now, it was only something to hide behind. Chop pulled up near it and switched the engine off.

37

They climbed out of the car.

Nicky plucked at his damp and hated suit. Squid twisted his torso, stretched his bandy muscles. Chop halfheartedly produced a gun, but seemed to wish he was still behind the wheel.

Fifi jogged in little circles, then paused to sniff the seam where the snack bar met the ground, detected memories, perhaps, of ancient popcorn, archaic franks. Katy rose up tall on her high-heeled sandals. The night air was still warm against her legs; she concentrated on the feeling. Al Tuschman stood close to her and looked up at the rotting, tilting movie screen backed by a spray of starlight. Drive-ins had been big in Jersey. He remembered going in pajamas as a little kid. Life seemed very safe then.

Nicky and Squid trained their pistols on the Jaguar's trunk. Chop flipped a lever and the lid yawned open.

Moonlight wedged in, and Big Al Marracotta squinted at the sudden brightness, sucked greedily at the rush of salty air. Nicky said to him, "Get up."

It wasn't that easy. His legs had cramped, his blood grown grainy and stagnant. He rocked and strained, flopped like a fish on the beach. Eventually he was sitting on the trunk's sharp lip, his small feet not reaching to the ground. He looked straight at Nicky's gun and said, "You really don't have to do this."

"Hey," said Nicky, "you've seen my cards. Gotta finish out the hand."

Big Al bit his lip, looked around. Absently, he said, "Fuckin' drive-in? Ain't seen one a these in years."

No one joined the conversation.

Big Al stared over at Katy, measured the distance between them. Twelve, fifteen feet. She was standing next to the big guy with the curly hair. Not touching, but very close. He said to her, "So you're wit' this asshole now?"

Katy didn't answer that.

Big Al said, "Boom—just like that. After all I done for you."

Katy said nothing.

Big Al shook his head. And lightly shook his arm, so that the tip of his knife rested against the heel of his hand just at the edge of his cuff. "Well," he said, "win some, lose some. No hard feelings."

He looked down a moment then said to Nicky, "Bitch cost me a lot. Still, good girlfriend, lotta ways. Mind I kiss her goo'bye?"

Nicky seemed bleakly amused by the show of gallows sentiment. It was all the same to him. They were both dead people anyway. He just shrugged by way of answer.

Big Al eased down from the trunk. His weird hair gleamed like plastic in the moonlight. Shells and knobs of coral crunched beneath his shoes. Slowly and deliberately, he turned his back on the men with guns and shuffled toward his former girlfriend. For a moment that boy-devil grin was on his face, then his lips got hard and flat. Katy leaned backward on her shoes but couldn't get her feet to move.

He approached without hurry. The ground crackled beneath him. He turned his wrist just slightly so that it faced away from Nicky and Chop and Squid. When he was a single stride from Katy, he twitched his hand and the knife blade slid down across his palm and he caught the hot handle in his fingers.

Alan Tuschman saw the blade glint in the moonlight, saw Big Al Marracotta crouch ever so slightly to turn his next step into a thrusting lunge.

He had no time to think. He had only that fraction of a heartbeat in which the brave man acted while the phony hero postured, and bargained with his nerve, and thereby lost the moment. Al Tuschman didn't hesitate.

Stomping fear, throttling caution, he threw himself in front of Katy, across the path of Big Al Marracotta's jabbing blade. He grabbed at his namesake's flailing arm but didn't catch it cleanly; Marracotta jerked his hand free and stabbed up toward Tuschman's neck. The salesman deflected the thrust, but the knife slashed past his shoulder. He felt it cut his shirt and slice his skin and bit through to the yielding flesh. With the ooze of blood came less pain than an ecstatic charge, a hectic self-forgiveness of past shirkings and doubts and fallings-short.

Wounded and wildly heedless, Al Tuschman bulled straight at the man with the knife. Marracotta thrust again. The tall man seized his pumping arm; the knife flashed and wiggled like a snake. For a long moment the two Als pressed against each other in a dreadful stalemate, then the mobster lost his footing on the loose and chalky gravel, and they both went tumbling to the mounded ground.

Fifi circled and barked and nipped at Marracotta's ankles. Amid the tumult, no one noticed that Squid had slipped away. No one paid attention to the grinding start-up of a different engine.

Al Tuschman scrambled flat on top of Big Al Marracotta, slugged him awkwardly across the chin. The short man kneed him in the groin and rolled him over and strained to lift the arm that held the knife. The salesman kept a hand clamped around the mobster's wrist and struggled to hang on. Marracotta lifted, grunted . . . and Tuschman suddenly let go, bucking and shoving as Marracotta's unsprung arm flew up and wrecked his balance. The little gangster tipped over and crashed onto his side. The impact of his landing shook the knife out of his hand; it skated over shells and coral for half a dozen feet.

Big Al went crawling after it. He was about to grab it when a pair of long bare legs moved in to block his path.

Katy Sansone lifted up a high-heeled sandal and kicked him

in the face. He saw the shoe hurtling toward him and then he felt his nose cave in, spiky shards intruding on his passages. Like a half-crushed bug he tried to keep on crawling, swimming toward the knife, but Al Tuschman had him by the feet, pulled him back across the lacerating shells.

The desperate and preposterous tug-of-war went on for several seconds, then Nicky Scotto sauntered over and, with a wagging pistol, called it off. Dryly, he said, "Amateur wrestling. Tag-team. Very entertaining."

Big Al lifted his neck and rolled his eyes way up like in a painting of a saint, saw Nicky's gun poised not far above his head. He tried to speak but blood and mucus had pooled in his throat and for the moment he could only gurgle. He kicked his legs and made a reflexive attempt at standing.

Nicky cocked the hammer of his pistol. "Don't bother getting up," he said. "You'll only fall back down again."

That's when the truck came tearing around the back side of the snack bar.

It whined and roared, its tires spitting gravel out behind as it rocked on the uneven ground. Glowing softly in the moonlight, the writing on the trailer said LOWER KEYS SEAFOOD COMPANY—EAT FISH LIVE LONGER. Through a glaring silver starburst on the windshield, Squid could just barely be seen, manically grinning, spasmodically swallowing. He drove straight at Big Al.

"Jesus Christ," said Nicky, as everybody scattered.

Al Marracotta, his back to the screaming vehicle, crawled and reared and scrabbled to his knees but was flattened by the fender and pounded like a cutlet by the left front tire. It crushed his ribs; the doubled rear wheels wrung his innards out like sponges, made them into paste. He twitched once like a shocked frog, and after that was still.

The truck's momentum carried it another fifty yards. It came to a skidding halt on the coral rubble and slowly turned around. Squid paused a moment then revved it high in first, slammed it into second.

"The motherfucker's crazy," Nicky said, though it would be another moment before he realized that the seafood truck was coming back for him.

He didn't realize that until the truck had veered so that its hood ornament was pointing squarely at his face. Disbelieving still, he yelled out, "Hey!" And when the truck did not change course, he raised his gun and shot the windshield out.

Squid Berman, hunkered down beneath the dashboard, reveled in the spray of broken glass.

Nicky Scotto fired again, this time murdering the radiator, and then he started running, his stiff, cheap jacket flying out behind. He took off over humps and mounds, past headless speaker posts sprouting bouquets of disconnected wires. Squid dogged him like a cowboy, pivoting and leaning, motor whining like a whinnying horse. Nicky ran along the contour of a mound, seemed for a deranged moment to be racing across the drive-in screen. Finally, legs heavy, breath failing, he turned around to fire once more. The bullet exploded a sideview mirror, but after that, winded and dispirited, the doomed man could hardly do more than jog.

The truck caught up with him but failed to run him over. It somehow lifted him behind the knees and waffled him against the grille, broken but alive. A disembodied hand raised up grotesquely, wagged a moonlit gun above the level of the hood. Squid Berman floored the truck and headed for a speaker post, used Nicky Scotto's body as a ram to knock it down. The pistol went off skyward as his back was snapped and his lifeless body rolled in its horrendous suit down a hump of shells and coral.

38

"I wasn't afraid! I wasn't afraid!" Al Tuschman had said to Katy in the moment before his knees had buckled and he'd crumpled slowly to the ground.

He sat there now, his back against the Jag, his eyes tracking with a dreadful fascination the homicides by seafood truck. Katy sat near him, dabbing his cut shoulder with a hankie. Fifi smelled her master's precious blood; full of worry and compassion, she wouldn't stop licking his hand.

Chop nonchalantly kept his gun pointed at the captives as he watched his partner run people down.

Then Squid drove back across the humps and mounds and screeched to a stop half a dozen feet away. The truck's windshield consisted now of several snaggled shards quaking in the frame. Antifreeze was dribbling from below and the engine was already smoking. The driver jumped down from the cab, arms twitching, tongue busy at the corners of his mouth.

"Nice work," Chop said to him.

Modest and not completely satisfied, Squid said only, "Aawh."

He did a little pirouette, then pulled his pistol from the waistband of his pants, and for a few moments he paced intently back and forth in front of Al and Katy. Moonlight rained down and a smell of damp rubber rose up from Big Al Marracotta's corpse. Whenever Squid changed the direction of his pacing, his feet broke some seashells and they made a crispy sound.

Finally he paused, leaned low before his captives, and barked right into their faces, "I fucking hate to make mistakes!"

He sprang into motion once again, and added, "It's like noisy, cockeyed, out of tune. Depressing. Ya see what I'm saying?"

Cautiously, Al and Katy nodded.

"Coulda been a masterpiece, this job," the bandy man continued. "Had everything. Theme. Shape. Room ta improvise. Instead I hadda backtrack and erase. And now I got these extra pieces."

"Extra pieces?" said Al Tuschman.

"You, numbnuts."

A puff of breeze made the tilting movie screen groan on its moldy pilings. Squid kept on pacing and Fifi kept swiveling her head to track him. After a time he stopped again, crouched down, and put the muzzle of the gun very close to Alan Tuschman's forehead. He said, "Lemme ask you a fairly important question. Tell me what you did tonight."

A little cross-eyed, Al said, "Huh?"

"You deaf?"

Katy said, "We checked out of our hotel. Rented a car. Drove up to South Beach."

"Meet anyone? See anything unusual along the way?"

"Nobody," said Katy. "Nothing."

"Nothing at all," Al Tuschman blithely said.

"Then how'dya cut your shoulder?"

"Umm . . ."

"Lover's quarrel," Katy said. "Nobody's business."

Squid considered that a moment, then he started pacing once again. In his pacing was the torment of the artist before a canvas that simply would not come together. Sighing, he said at last, "Look, it bothers me ta have ta kill ya. But come on. After what you saw? Nicky woulda took you out. Big Al woulda took you out."

"And look where it got them," said Katy.

"Not the point," said Squid.

214

He did his anguished laps. Chop, impatient, started slapping his gun against his other palm. Al Tuschman's mouth went very dry.

After a moment Katy said, "But we're the ones who did it."

Squid said, "What?"

"Mind if I get up?"

She unfolded very smoothly, brushed coral dust from the backs of her legs. Slowly and deliberately, she moved toward the truck. With Squid right behind her, she climbed into the driver's seat, firmly wrapped her hands around the steering wheel. Then, through the vacant windshield, she called out, "Tusch—pick up the knife."

The salesman rose on shaky legs, found Big Al Marracotta's blade against the pale, rough stones, squeezed the handle in his palm.

Katy said to Squid. "Nice clear fingerprints." She pointed to Al's bloody shoulder. "Signs of a struggle. Stormy history with the deceased. Love triangle gone wrong."

Squid did a crunching pirouette and thought it over. Then he jerked a thumb in the direction of the other corpse. "And Nicky?"

"Showed up in the wrong place at the wrong time."

Squid scrunched up his mouth. "Sloppy."

"Hey," said Katy, "jobs sometimes have extra pieces, right? Besides, it's still easier to believe than what really happened."

"That's a point," the bandy man conceded.

"I ran these guys over," she said. "To save Tusch, who was fighting with the knife. Are we going to the cops?"

Squid pawed the ground, swallowed deeply, pulled his ear. Finally he looked at Chop.

Chop rubbed his stumpy neck, said, "I got nothin' against these people, long as they don't get stupid."

Squid licked extra wetness from the corners of his mouth, said to no one in particular, "Would blow the symmetry, we waste the extra pieces."

"Wouldn't be symmetrical at all," said Alan Tuschman. "Would be like both end tables on the same side of the couch."

Squid told him to shut up.

Feigning confidence, Katy got down from the truck. She tried not to let it show that she was trembling as she offered Squid her back.

But he'd made up his mind. He didn't shoot her. He made a moist noise protesting all the world's rough edges, all the bumps and snags that mocked perfection. Then he put the pistol in the waistband of his pants and started walking toward the Jag.

Chop seemed to remember something then. He opened the passenger door, reached into the glove box, and retrieved a crumpled piece of paper. He handed it to Al.

Al couldn't read it in the moonlight.

"Pick-up order from Sun Motors," Chop explained. "Driver's signature. Proves they came and got your car. They had it, they lost it, they owe you a new one. . . . Myself, I think it looks better in navy."

He went around to the driver's side, climbed in, and started up the engine. Squid settled into the passenger seat and propped a bandy forearm on the window frame. "And get a different license plate," he said.

Al nodded that he would, then moved close to Katy in the moonlight. The shih tzu wiggled among their ankles and wagged its tail. They looked at the car that was about to pull away, and the tableau, in some unlikely manner, suggested a reluctant parting of old friends.

Almost sheepishly, Squid said, "Hey, no hard feelings, huh? Sorry ta fuck up your vacation."

"Ya didn't fuck it up," Al Tuschman volunteered.

"I didn't?" In spite of himself he sounded disappointed.

"Just made it sort of different," the salesman from New Jersey said. He took Katy's hand, took it in the serious way, with all the fingers interlinked. "Made it more a mission, kind of."

EPILOGUE

"Poor Nicky," said Donnie Falcone as he hung up the pay phone in the social club on Prince Street and moved languidly back toward the table he was sharing with his uncle and their dying *consigliere.*

"Stupid Nicky," Tony Eggs corrected.

Donnie came forth with a rueful little laugh, gave his chin a squeeze. "Yeah, not the sharpest knife inna drawer," he said. "Pretty easy ta string 'im along." He sat down and reclaimed his glass of anisette. *"Salud."*

Salud. Health. Carlo Ganucci's eyeballs were bright yellow and the skin of his neck was blue. Tony Eggs had kidney stones and his teeth were loose in their sockets. The two old men joined in the toast.

Shaking his head, Donnie went on. "Right from the start, I knew that all I hadda do was give 'im advice th' opposite a what I really wanted. I tell 'im don't even think about takin' the market back, right away that's all he thinks about."

"He wanted that job bad," Tony Eggs put in, and could not help smiling, showing mottled gums. "Ya shoulda seen the dumb fuck stomp his suit."

"I tell 'im don't even think about goin' ta Flahda," Donnie said, "right away I know damn well he's goin'."

Carlo Ganucci roused himself to say, "But howd'ya know who he was workin' wit' down 'ere?"

Donnie laughed. "I asked him. Casual like. He tells me guy who does cars in Hialeah. Then it's no problem gettin' in touch through our people in Miami."

Tony Eggs tugged at the fraying collar of his plain white shirt. "An' once ya got in touch," he said, "ya knew how ta get the best work from these people. One guy likes ta hijack trucks, ya let 'im grab a truck. Th' other guy has this thing, he wants ta do the job wit' seafood, ya let 'im do it wit' seafood. Ya motivated 'em good."

"Didn't hurt," said Donnie, "that I paid 'em double what Nicky was."

"Aaw, the money's overrated," Tony said. "Point is, you're a natural manager. This is why you're gonna do brilliant wit' the market."

Donnie made an attempt at sounding humble. "I'll try, *zio*. Ya know I'll do my best."

Tony Eggs patted his beloved nephew's cheek. "An' 'iss way," he said, "no one can accuse me playin' favorites. I tried two other guys. My fault they turned out ta be assholes? My fault they took each other out? Am I right, or am I right, Carlo?"

The old *consigliere* smiled faintly at the intrigue. He blinked. It took him a long time to get his crinkled and translucent eyelids to roll back up again.

"But here's one thing I still don't get," Tony Eggs resumed. "I know ya worked a deal wit' our people inna Catskills ta get inta that kitchen . . . but howd'ya poison the clams?"

Donnie leaned in a little closer. "Raw chicken."

"Raw chicken?"

"Took a chicken," Donnie said. "Left it out a coupla days. Got that whaddyacallit, salmonella, going. Took a brush, stuck it up the chicken's ass, dabbed a little funky juice on all the clams. Simple."

The old boss shook his head admiringly, showed his long loose teeth. "Salmonella. Beautiful." His nephew was the right guy for the job. He had no doubt of it. He raised his glass to the fish market's new regime. *"Salud."*

"Salud."
"Salud."

Katy liked the car in powder blue, so powder blue it was. Looked smart with the gray velour upholstery that, Al knew from his swatchbooks, went for twenty-eight, thirty bucks a yard. It was noon when they drove it off the lot in Miami, and they headed straight for the causeway to the Beach, still determined to have a day at least of real vacation.

They parked on Ocean Drive. Stylish cafés on one side of the road, the endless Atlantic on the other. Nothing to do but eat and stroll and gawk at people.

Katy unfolded smoothly, took a gulp of warm salt air. "Finally," she said, "I feel like a regular tourist."

Al Tuschman leashed his dog and locked the car and looked back across his bandaged shoulder. No one seemed to be tailing him, no one fighting for his nickname or contesting the space he took up in the world. "Seems a little tame."

"Tame's okay," said Katy.

He thought about that, and about the life that he'd be going back to. The store, the diners, his garden apartment condo. "Yeah," he said. "I guess it is." He craned his neck at avenue and beach. "Eat or walk?"

"Eat."

They picked a nearby place for its mix of shade and sun, then settled into varnished wicker chairs that faced the sidewalk, ordered drinks and looked absently, distractedly at menus. New lovers. There was everything to say and it was frightening to have a conversation. Chitchat could sound too easily like making plans; plans came too close to being promises. So they silently held hands and people-watched. Models went by with portfolios. Gym-boys sported cut-off shirts that showed their waffled abs.

After a while, Al got reckless. He'd been out of danger half a day and some element of risk was missing from his life. So he said to Katy, "What'll you do when you get back? About your apartment, stuff like that?"

She shrugged, pushed her big sunglasses a little higher on her nose. "Move out, I guess. Find another place, a job."

Al nodded. The nod was neutral, matter-of-fact, but behind it Al was communing with his newfound courage. The brave man didn't posture, didn't bargain. The brave man seized the moment. Blandly, looking half away, he said, "Ever spend much time in Jersey?"

Katy understood that this was not a promise, that no promise was being asked for in return. Still, for new lovers the entire world was wet cement; the lightest stepping left its print. She looked at Tusch but was saved from answering by the waiter's arrival with their lunch.

"Who's got the shore platter?" he asked.

He put it down in front of Al. Half a lobster with a single claw outstretched. Curls of calamari piled up on lettuce. Six clams laid out in a gleaming arc.

Al Tuschman looked at his new lover and just shook his head. "I can't believe I ordered that," he said.

About the Author

LAURENCE SHAMES is the author of six previous Key West novels: *Mangrove Squeeze, Virgin Heat, Tropical Depression, Sunburn, Scavenger Reef,* and *Florida Straits.* He is also the uncredited co-writer of the *New York Times* bestseller *Boss of Bosses.* He lives with his wife, Marilyn, in Key West, Florida.